# UNDERSTANDING
# BUSINESS

 **The BOURNEMOUTH AND POOLE College OF FURTHER EDUCATION**

# Learning
# Resources
# Service

*This item must be returned to the LRC or Department shown above when required. An LRC item must be returned by the last date stamped, or fines will be charged. If not in demand it may be renewed for a further period by post, telephone or personal call.*

# UNDERSTANDING
# BUSINESS

∎

## Alistair Norman

Deputy Head of Business Studies,
Burnley College

## Marie Norman

Senior Lecturer in Business Education,
Bolton Institute

## Peter Shortt

External Liaison Manager,
Bolton College

PITMAN
PUBLISHING

PITMAN PUBLISHING
128 Long Acre, London WC2E 9AN

A Division of Longman Group Limited

© Longman Group UK 1993

First published in Great Britain 1993
Reprinted 1993, 1994

**British Library Cataloguing in Publication Data**
A Catalogue record for this book is available from the British Library

ISBN 0 273 03497 9

Typeset by Mathematical Composition Setters Ltd, Salisbury
Printed in England by Clays Ltd, St Ives plc

# CONTENTS

■

# INTRODUCTION

∎

This book aims to provide you with much of the information you will need to cope successfully with the Core of your course in Business. The Core work is spread right over the course and is based on the information which has been identified by employers as vital to you if you want to get on in business. The book is split into eight main sections and each section deals with an aspect of the Core of the course. The eight main sections of the book are:

- Business organisations
- People in business
- Business systems
- Business environment
- Financial systems
- Business resources
- Marketing
- Business Innovation

These names may not be exactly the same as the ones on your timetable as different centres will teach the course in different ways, but the content is the same. Each unit in the book contains information you will need to help you to understand the work involved in the core of your course and provides regular summaries which will help you to get to grips with the key points in an area quickly.

You will also find some activities to do as you work through the text – these are designed to provide you with some opportunities to apply some of what the book covers. Some of the activities can be done at once, others need some research or further information before you can tackle them; some can be done by you on your own, whereas for others you will need to join with others in a group. While you will still learn from the book if you choose not to work through the activities, you will gain a great deal more if you do at least some of them.

At the end of the book there is a section of assignments which are representative of the sorts of tasks you will have to undertake in order to compile evidence for your portfolio of work. You may choose to work through these on your own or with others.

# 1

# BUSINESS ORGANISATIONS

## Introduction

Throughout this unit the terms business, organisation and business organisation will be used interchangeably. Business organisations surround everyone – the early morning routine recounted below illustrates the importance of business organisations.

*I woke up at 7 am when the alarm clock went off and went downstairs to the kitchen, put on the kettle and went to get the milk from the front door. I made some coffee and watched breakfast TV while drinking it. I made the children's breakfast and then got myself ready for work while the children ate their Weetabix and drank their orange juice. Having got the children ready, I then put the dustbin out at the front of the house to be emptied, put the children in the car, dropped one off at nursery and took the other to school, and then I went to work.*

Consider the number of business organisations which had affected the life of this person between seven and nine o'clock in the morning. First, organisations manufactured all the products used such as the alarm clock, milk, coffee, kettle, Weetabix, orange juice, television, clothes, wash basins, baths/showers, soap, towels and car. Organisations sold the products too. Some service organisations were also necessary – the milk delivery, the nursery and the school. The organisation where the person worked provided goods and services for its customers but also provided jobs, wages and salaries for its employees.

Organisations are very important in our lives and we are surrounded by them – your school or college, the Student's Union, the college refectory, Marks and Spencer plc, the corner shop, British Rail, Woolworths – are just a few that spring to mind. There are millions of significantly different organisations; the organisation which delivered the milk was not the same as the one which sold the coffee, which in turn was different to the nursery, to the school and to the organisation which emptied the dustbins. These organisations differ in that they offer diverse products or services, are owned by a variety of people, are financed in different ways, employ varying numbers of people, and have different reasons for their existence. Organisations are important to individuals and to the economy because they provide both the goods and services and the income required to buy products and services.

Although organisations are different in many ways they all share some common features in that they all have:

● a structure
● systems
● goals
● resources
● culture
● external environment.

This unit will look at:

- some common features of organisations
- how business organisations are classified
- organisational structures
- stakeholders
- organisational goals
- organisational cultures
- the location of business
- business opportunities
- business plans.

## Common features of organisations

Organisations can be very different but a study of organisations will show that they have some features in common and these are discussed in the following sections.

### STRUCTURE

Structure refers to the way a business is organised. Organisations will be structured differently depending on the size, type, product or service offered, and so on. A nursery, for example, may have one manager who is also the owner, three full-time nursery nurses and four part-time employees who help with the children, clean, and look after the toys and equipment. An organisation selling televisions could be very large indeed with a head office and many branches throughout the country, numerous staff involved in sales, finance, personnel, marketing, buying, etc. Both of these organisations have a structure but their structures are organised in different ways.

### SYSTEMS

Systems are ways of working, e.g. administrative procedures, written records, communication systems. The nursery described above has a very informal communication system mainly using face-to-face communication because staff see each other regularly. Sometimes telephone communication is used, for example if staff are ill at short notice and the manager needs to arrange emergency staff cover. The administrative system is also very simple and is operated by the manager who records attendance of children and staff, and keeps records of children attending the nursery, bills and expenditure, wages, etc.

On the other hand the organisation selling the televisions will have many complex systems involving paperwork passing to and from head office, an internal mail system, much use of the telephone and fax to communicate, the holding of regular meetings, and sophisticated financial and other record systems.

Again the two organisations are different, operating very different systems, but a system of some kind is vital to both organisations. Systems are covered in detail in Unit 3, Business systems.

### GOALS

Goals/aims are stated purposes or reasons for existing as a business entity. The nursery may have as its primary aim the providing of a quality child care service at a reasonable cost to the customer. The organisation selling televisions may similarly aim to provide a reasonably-priced quality service to customers wishing to buy electrical goods (since it may sell many products and not simply televisions).

Both organisations have reasons for existing and goals to meet even if some of these reasons are different. Some examples of business aims/goals are:

- to make profit
- to provide a particular service to the community
- to increase market share.

### RESOURCES

Resources are necessary to set up and operate a business. A business needs

- human resources (people),
- financial resources (money),
- physical resources (e.g. equipment, premises).

A small business will require less in the way of human, financial and physical resources than a large organisation, and the mix of resources required to set up and run a business will differ depending on the nature of the business and what it does. For example the nursery needed premises at a suitable location, a few staff, and finance for purchases, wages and to rent or purchase premises. The organisation which sold televisions needed numerous shops, many staff, and a large amount of money for stock.

Some businesses are *labour intensive*, requiring many people to be employed, while others are *capital intensive* requiring large amounts of money and equipment. Similarly, some organisations use a lot of technological equipment while others require more people-based skills.

Resources are covered in three further units – 5 Financial information systems, 6 Physical resources, and 2 People in business and organisations.

## CULTURE

Culture is the style and sets of shared beliefs, habits, patterns of behaviour and traditions developed by the people within the organisation. Culture is sometimes made explicit in the form of an organisation's *Mission* or *Perspective Statement* and can be reinforced, and indeed set, by the perceptions, actions and examples of managers. If, for example, the managers clock watch it is very likely that the staff will too. If the management are seen as uncaring and wasteful of resources then the staff may be too.

## EXTERNAL ENVIRONMENT

External environment is the environment in which the organisation operates. The organisation does not operate in a vacuum; it has customers, competitors, and external controls, e.g. legislation and government regulation. If a nursery was to open across the road from the one in the example above there will be increased competition and this will affect customers, pricing, marketing and perhaps even staff wages. Business organisations need to monitor the external environment to find out changes in customer needs, wants and attitudes which could

affect the business and to identify business opportunities, to find out what competitors there are, what they are doing and assess their impact. A change in the legislation can affect the organisation in many ways, for example the introduction of the need for all people handling food to meet particular statutory standards of health and hygiene will affect an organisation's training programme and procedures. External environment is dealt with in three further units: 7 Marketing, 4 Business Environment and 8 Business Innovation.

---

### ACTIVITY

---

Compare two organisations – your school or college and a local employer.

**1** For each organisation find out:
(a) the goals;
(b) the resources needed;
(c) the structure;
(d) how they are affected by the external environment.

**2** Compare the results of the two organisations:
(a) in which ways are they similar?
(b) in which ways do they differ?

---

## Classifying business organisations

Business organisations can be classified in many different ways:

1 Whether the business is a primary, secondary or tertiary industry.
2 Whether the business is local, national or multinational.
3 Whether the business is in the public or the private sector.
4 By type or legal form.

### PRIMARY, SECONDARY AND TERTIARY INDUSTRIES

Business organisations can be categorised into primary, secondary or tertiary industries depending on what they do. The *primary sector* organisations are concerned with the extraction of raw materials such as coal mining, forestry and agriculture. These materials will be used by organisations in the secondary and/or tertiary industries.

Organisations in the *secondary sector* will make the raw materials into finished goods – manufacturing and construction organisations will be in this sector.

The *tertiary sector* is made up of organisations providing a service, for example banking, retailing, dentistry, dry cleaning.

As an illustration of this, consider the chart below in which apples are grown by a farmer, bought by a manufacturer and made into apple pies, and sold to a retailer who sells them to the customer. The farmer falls into the primary sector, the manufacturer is in the secondary sector and the retailer is in the tertiary sector.

| | |
|---|---|
| Apples grown | *primary* |
| Apples made into pies | *secondary* |
| Apple pies sold to public | *tertiary* |

## LOCAL, NATIONAL AND MULTINATIONAL ORGANISATIONS

Some organisations are said to be local because they are only found locally to the people describing them. Examples of local organisations are independent restaurants and cafes, clothes shops, and the neighbourhood fish and chip shop. Local organisations are formed to meet the specific needs of the population in their immediate vicinity.

National organisations are found throughout the country, fulfilling the same customer needs in many different locations nationwide.

Multinational organisations are enterprises which own and control producing facilities in more than one country. They have a wide range of business interests. IBM, Esso and the Rio Tinto Zinc Corporation Plc are examples of multinationals. The main objectives of multinationals are to expand their operations globally and to gain as large a share of the world market as possible. The parent company controls these global operations through its foreign subsidiaries, which are firms which have been set up in a foreign location by the parent company or acquired through takeover. Multinationals are vulnerable to fluctuations in currency, political changes and protectionist policies by other countries. They are, however, very large and powerful organisations and can often have a strong influence on the way in which Governments act.

Multinationals are also discussed in Unit 4, Business Environment, where you will find a chart of the ten largest multinationals in the world.

---

### ACTIVITY

Obtain the latest annual report and accounts of a multinational of your choice.

Identify
- its main business
- which countries it operates from
- the subsidiary businesses in which it is involved
- any 'social responsibility/sponsorship' activities in which it is involved.

Having looked at the section on multinationals in Unit 4, and seen the value of sales and the number of employees of the largest firms, explain why governments have to take account of their views.

Will a large and rich country be as easily persuaded by a large multinational as a smaller or poorer one? Give reasons for your answer.

---

## PUBLIC OR PRIVATE OWNERSHIP

Organisations can be owned by one or more private individuals within society or they can be owned by the state i.e. by the public at large. State-owned organisations are referred to as *public sector organisations* while privately-owned organisations are known as *private sector organisations*. Table 1.1 shows the types of organisation which are in the public and private sectors.

**Table 1.1 Private and public sector organisations**

| Private sector | Public sector |
| --- | --- |
| sole trader | central government departments |
| partnership | local government |
| co-operative | public corporations |
| franchise | semi-autonomous agencies |
| corporation | |
| multinational | |

## CLASSIFICATION BY TYPE OR LEGAL FORM – PRIVATE SECTOR ORGANISATIONS

Organisations in the private sector can have a variety of different legal forms and structures which affect the way in which they operate, and the liabilities and the powers of the owners and managers of the businesses. The main forms are:

- Sole Trader
- Partnership
- Limited company

Other legal forms of organisation dealt with in this section include the co-operative and the franchise.

### Sole trader

A *sole trader*, also known as an 'independent', is an organisation which has only one owner. The capital for the business has been provided by that individual and he or she benefits from the profits made but also has unlimited liability for any debts incurred by the business. The sole trader has independence and greater flexibility with regard to decision making than large organisations, but growth is slower and raising further capital can be difficult.

There are no legal formalities to complete before commencing trading and no legal requirements governing the layout of accounts. The success of such businesses often rests on the owner's ability to work long hours and if he or she suffers an accident or illness then the business can go under, since its survival often relies solely on one person.

Sole traders are often found in the personal services sector, e.g. hairdressers, mini-cab drivers, small retailers, florists, plumbers, window cleaners and decorators.

Although the majority of businesses are owned by sole traders, there is a high failure rate among one person businesses, especially in the first year of trading. However, many successful big companies began as sole traders; Anita Roddick, for example, set up her own small shop in the 1960s and today the Body Shop can be found in most major towns. Her 'business idea' identified a 'gap in the market' for natural skin products at a time when public concern for the contents of beauty products was growing.

### Partnership

Partnerships are a business type which can either develop out of a sole trader requiring the support of another individual, perhaps with differing skills, or at the outset of a business. The obvious advantages are greater specialisation, the ability to raise more capital, the business can continue to run in the absence of one or more of the partners and the potential of more profitable ideas than may be the case with the sole proprietor.

A partnership is usually set out in a legal document called a *Deed of Partnership* which is witnessed by a solicitor. A partnership is limited to a legal maximum of 20 partners. It is possible to set up in business as a partnership without drawing up a deed of partnership, however, without a formal framework to adhere to the partners are left open to disagreements and such informal partnerships are therefore not advisable.

A Deed of Partnership usually covers the following:

- how much capital each partner will contribute
- how the profits and losses will be shared
- the voting rights of partners
- arrangements for dissolving the partnership
- rules for admitting and expelling partners
- the responsibilities of 'sleeping' partners.

The main disadvantages of a partnership are that each partner is personally liable for *all* the business's debts. In addition the amount of capital that can be raised by a partnership is limited compared with businesses that are organised as companies.

---

### ACTIVITY

---

In groups, draft out the details of what you think it would be important to include in the following partnerships:

**1** A partnership between doctors.

**2** A partnership between four graphic designers.

**3** A partnership between three accountants.

---

## Co-operative

Another business type is the co-operative. You are probably aware of the *consumer co-operatives* operating retail outlets in the High Street which work on the basic principle of sharing profits among their members (by issuing Co-op stamps, etc.). These consumer co-operatives are not as powerful as they were early in the century, particularly in northern England.

Another form of co-operative is the *worker co-operative*. These are businesses which are owned and run by the whole workforce. In a worker co-operative:

- membership is open to all workers.
- each member has one vote
- profits are distributed among the members
- members control the operation of the business.

Worker co-operatives have been formed by the workers of big companies which have closed down 'unprofitable' areas of their businesses. The British motorcycle firm of Norton is an example of a worker co-operative takeover.

Another type of co-operative is the *producers' co-operative* where groups of people club together to produce goods or services, e.g. a baby-sitting circle is a co-operative.

---

### CASE STUDY

---

#### The Natural Therapy Co-operative

*Martin Belt and Marianne Westwood both worked in the personnel department of a large manufacturing company. They were vegetarians and shared a common interest in aromatherapy and reflexology. They were now approaching their early 40s and had begun to question the 'quality' of their lives. They both felt alienated by their current jobs and could see little possibility of renewed job satisfaction or promotion at work.*

*Over coffee one lunchtime they began to discuss the possibility of 'escaping' from the confines of the impersonal organisation for which they worked and going into business together. Marianne and Martin had been taking on clients in their spare time – running Yoga classes, massage and relaxation sessions, etc. Marianne did not have much of a head for figures and finance, but knew she could rely on Martin who had a business and management qualification.*

*As Martin and Marianne shared a large Victorian house, located near the centre of town, they decided to convert this into business premises and home. They discussed the business venture with several of their friends who shared their interests. There were suggestions that the group should also consider running a wholefood shop to complement the services offered. Several of these friends also wanted to support the business and it was eventually decided to set up together as a co-operative. They felt that the co-operative approach would reduce possible arguments, make the members work harder in order to get the business off the ground and provide closer links with their community.*

---

### ACTIVITY

---

Please answer the following questions:

**1** Do you think that a co-operative is a suitable form of business organisation for natural therapy?

**2** What would be the main benefits and disadvantages from this form of organisation?

---

## Franchise

Franchising is a form of organisation and is one of the fastest growing sectors for small businesses. Franchising allows an organisation to expand without having to invest large amounts of capital. The franchisor is the name given to the firm which, for a fee, allows another person to use or sell its product or service and to trade under its name, using its logo and business style. The franchisee is the person who pays the fee and royalty payments on the turnover for the privilege of trading under the franchisor's name. McDonald's, Wimpey, Kall-Kwik printing, Benetton, Body Shop are all examples of franchises.

The advantages for the franchisees are that they have a greater chance of success as they are marketing a product or service which has already been field tested, using a business style which has proved successful. They are also provided with training by the franchisor. They have the benefit of a 'brand name' known to the public which is advertised nationally and the bulk purchasing power of the franchisor. The specialised knowledge and skill of the franchisor's head office is also at the disposal of the franchisee. The franchisor's research and development programme will also benefit the franchisee. It is easier to raise capital as the banks feel that they are taking less risk. Assistance is often forthcoming with site selection, preparation of plans for re-modelling premises, training of staff and purchase of equipment, selection and purchase of stock and getting the business open and running smoothly.

However, there are disadvantages. A franchisee has less independence; the franchisee cannot sell the business without the agreement of the franchisor, for example. The franchisor could fail or the actions of other franchisees could bring the business into disrepute. Buying a franchise is therefore buying a business, but with a difference.

---

### ACTIVITY

#### Assessing a business franchise

In groups identify a 'franchised' product or service. Discuss whether you wish to enter into a franchise agreement with the host organisation on the basis of the answers to the following questions:

1 Are the products/services new?

2 Do they have any advantages over their competitors?

3 Has the franchised business been thoroughly proven in practice?

4 Is it in a growth or declining market?

5 If there is growth, is that growth merely a fashion?

6 How competitive is the price of the product/service?

7 What is the source of supply of the product?

8 Is this source of supply reliable?

9 Are alternative products of comparable quality and price available?

10 Are the products/services based on a trade mark?

11 What is the reputation of the product/service?

12 If it is a successful franchise newly imported from another country, will it have the same appeal in the UK?

You will find information on potential franchise opportunities in many national newspapers and may also be able to get information from the British Franchise Association.

---

## Corporations or limited companies

Limited companies are one of the most common forms of business organisation. New companies are being set up all the time. The main advantages of forming a limited company are:

- shareholders have limited liability
- capital can be raised through issuing shares
- specialists can be employed
- expansion is possible
- economies of scale are possible.

A limited company is a separate body in law from its shareholders and directors. As it is a separate legal entity, a company may act in its own right, create contracts and trade in its own name. The shareholders are not liable for the company's debts above the value of their shareholdings, i.e. if a company becomes bankrupt and has large debts, its shareholders are not responsible for the debts and lose only the money they invested in the company (their shares).

*Private limited companies* must have two or more shareholders. *Public limited companies* have no upper limit to the number of shareholders and their shares are traded on the Stock Exchange.

When setting up a limited company, a number of legal formalities must be observed. A Memorandum of Association and Articles of Association must be presented to the Registrar of Companies in order to receive a Certificate of Incorporation before a private limited company can start trading. The Memorandum of Association sets out:

- the name of the company

- the registered address of the company
- the objectives of the company
- the capital of the company.

The Articles of Association set out the rules which govern the inside operation of the company:

- the rights attached to ownership of different types of shares
- the rules and procedures for issue and transfer of shares
- the organising of company meetings
- the details of how the financial records will be kept and recorded
- the powers and responsibilities of the directors
- how directors will be appointed.

In order for a public limited company to be granted a Trading Certificate, the minimum share capital must be set and the allotted shares must be paid up to at least 25 per cent of their nominal value.

Though a sole trader would gain the advantage of limited liability by setting up a company, it is more costly to set up a private limited company than to start a sole proprietor business. In addition, unlike a public limited company, a private limited company may not advertise for share capital and, therefore, its capital is limited. There are also legal costs involved in registering the business and, as the accounts have to be audited, it is necessary to pay an accountant.

With a public limited company running costs can be high and decision-making processes can be hampered by 'red tape'. The employees of the organisation and the shareholders are not normally in contact with each other, i.e. the ownership and management are divorced. The management of the company will be by a board of directors. Executive directors hold positions within the company and are involved in the day-to-day decision-making process. The board of directors are responsible for appointing senior managers, deciding on how profits will be distributed, establishing major policies, ensuring that all the legal requirements are followed and generally ensuring that the company is a success.

There are a number of forms of business which are less common and which you will need to research if you want to know more about them. The Activity below is intended to provide a framework for you to find out about these less common forms of organisation.

---

### ACTIVITY

Draw up a chart for the following forms of business organisation:

- co-operative
- limited partnership
- private limited company by guarantee
- private unlimited company

to show:

- the ownership of the business
- the liability of the owners for the organisation's debts
- who retains the profits
- the main areas of law which control the setting up of the business
- who makes the decisions as to the running of the business
- how tax is paid on the profits (if relevant).

You should also provide a brief outline of the nature of the business and, if you can find one, an example of a business which operates in this way.

---

## CLASSIFICATION BY TYPE OR LEGAL FORM – PUBLIC SECTOR ORGANISATIONS

The public sector is made up of enterprises which are owned and controlled by the government or local authorities. The argument put forward is that these enterprises provide services for the people of the UK to which they are entitled, for example health care and education. Furthermore it can be argued that some services can only be provided by the government if they are to be carried out properly, e.g. policing, national defence.

The Government still owns a number of industries and businesses on behalf of the nation. However, many former state-run industries were privatized during the 1980s and 90s, e.g. water, electricity, and gas. It can be argued that state-run organisations are less efficient because they do not have any competition and do not face the possibility of going bankrupt, as the government will pay their debts. The government objective in privatising these public corporations is to encourage ordinary people to buy into these companies and therefore participate through share ownership in their operation and success.

Public corporations are set up by Act of Parliament. British Rail is an example of a public corporation which attempts to provide an integrated rail service for the benefit of consumers nationwide and which can achieve this more efficiently through economies of scale. A chairperson is appointed by the government and a board of directors controls the day-to-day running of the corporation.

Central government departments (which are government funded) provide administrative services in specialist fields, like health and the environment, for the whole country. They tend, however, to be large and bureaucratic, responding slowly to change.

Local government departments provide services to the local community; municipal car parks, swimming baths, recreation centres, bus services are examples of the type of services involved. Local authorities contract out some of these services (refuse collection, the cleaning of public lavatories and building maintenance, etc.) to private firms, awarding contracts to the firms which submit the lowest tender. Local councils receive funding from local taxation and central government grants.

---

### ACTIVITY

Prepare a table to identify the way in which the following types of organisation are owned, controlled and financed and how they distribute profits:

- sole trader
- private limited company
- co-operative
- public corporation
- charity
- partnership
- public limited company
- franchise
- municipal services

An example is given below to indicate what is required.

---

**Organisation: sole trader**

| | |
|---|---|
| Ownership: | one owner |
| Control: | the owner will control the business |
| Financed: | the owner will raise finance through personal funds and possibly loans. The sole trader has unlimited liability |
| Distribution of profits: | the owner receives the profits |

---

## Organisational structures

Structure describes the size and relatively fixed formal authority positions, relationships and functions of organisations. Organisations have a structure in order to control activities, to be efficient, and to identify areas of responsibility. As organisations grow a more formal structure develops and areas of activity become clearly defined, e.g. Marketing, Finance, Personnel, Production, Sales. This formal structure can be shown using organisation charts. There are three main structures – hierarchical, matrix and semi-matrix (*see* Fig 1.1).

### HIERARCHICAL

To illustrate a hierarchical structure consider the organisation chart of Sneaker Ltd given in Fig 1.2. This chart provides useful information about Sneaker Ltd:

- type and size of organisation
- job titles
- relationships
- number of levels and span of control

### Type and size of organisation

The chart tells us that this is quite a large organisation in the private sector (although it might be quite small compared with NIKE, the world's biggest trainer company with a 1991 turnover of more than £3000 million). The organisation is a private limited company because 'Ltd', short for 'Limited', is part of its name.

*Size* can be calculated by looking at the

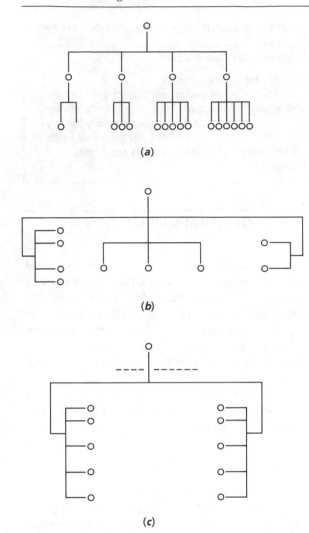

**Fig 1.1 Organisational structures: (a) hierarchical, (b) semi-matrix, (c) matrix**

vertical lines of authority in this way, noting that some of them have more levels than others.

### Job titles

The positions in the Sneaker Ltd organisation chart are described by *job titles*, but some organisational charts describe positions in terms of products: x, y or z. For example, the three plant managers of Sneaker Ltd may be in charge of factories producing specialist sport shoes, fashion trainers and children's trainers respectively. Similarly, the sales area managers could have been designated according to geographical region.

### Relationships

It is sometimes useful to distinguish between *line relationships* which exist between a senior and a subordinate over whom he or she has direct authority and *staff relationships* where an individual may be offering specialist advice or acting as a channel of communication without there being a clear hierarchical relationship between the parties involved.

In Fig 1.2 the continuous vertical lines indicate line relationships as between the group personnel manager and the trainers under his or her control. The group personnel manager also has a *staff relationship* with the sales divisions managers who are at a lower hierarchical level without being under his or her direct authority. The immediate boss of the sales divisions managers is the group marketing manager. He or she may object if the personnel manager 'interfered' with the work of the sales divisions managers, but will understand the need for these subordinate managers to liaise directly with personnel and training staff to help with the recruitment and skills training of the salesforce.

### Levels and span of control

The organisation in Fig 1.2 has a maximum of nine *levels* arranged in *hierarchies*. Hierarchies are different levels of authority presented so that at each level individuals control those below and are controlled by those above. The number of subordinates directly controlled by an individual

number of people at each level and multiplying them by the number of people with whom they have a direct vertical relationship. Thus there are 20 shopfloor workers for each supervisor, three supervisors for each section manager and there are six section managers under the control of one of the three plant managers. You can therefore calculate the number of production workers: 1 production manager × 3 plant managers × 6 section managers × 3 supervisors × 20 shopfloor workers = 1080. Calculating the total workforce of Sneaker Ltd will require you to follow all the

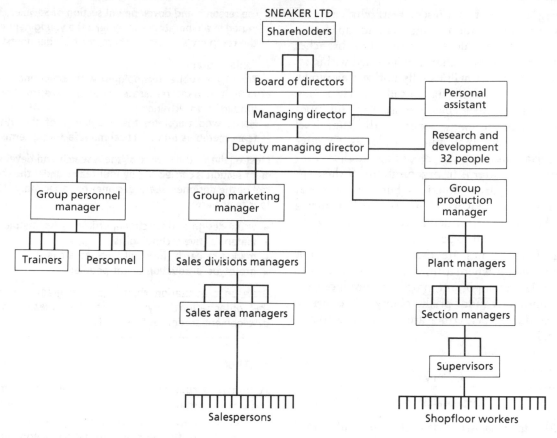

**Fig 1.2 Organisation chart for Sneaker Ltd**

is termed the *span of control*. The more simple the tasks of subordinates, the wider the span of control. Hierarchies are usually narrower at the top. The number of levels in the hierarchy establishes the *height* of an organisation chart. These levels of authority and responsibility are called the *Scalar Chain*. Scalar Chains operate on the general principle that an individual must only receive orders from one superior, though a superior may give orders to several subordinates.

Although organisation charts can tell you a great deal about an organisation they do not tell you everything. For example the Organisation Chart for Sneaker Ltd (Fig 1.2) does not include all the authority relationships, functions and personnel of the organisation. Furthermore any large organisation will have informal or implicit patterns of authority. For example, the managing director's personal assistant is likely to have

considerable informal authority which will be reinforced when acting under the managing director's explicit instructions.

On the hierarchical chart some functions, such as secretarial and other support staff, have not been included and there may be formal divisions of authority among salespersons and production workers which have not been indicated. The chart does not indicate the goals or degree of success of the organisation, or the ways in which it is responding to change. Similarly, the chart does not give any information about the product range, although the company name may indicate that they are involved in the fashion footwear business.

### Organisational pyramids

The relationship between the width and height of

a diagram used to represent hierarchy can vary from one organisation to another and can change as an organisation develops. If all of the branches of an organisational chart are included within an outline shape you will usually notice a hierarchy which can vary from flat to tall (*see* Fig 1.3).

Flat hierarchies characterise organisations where there are many people at the same level and a relatively small number of levels. Creative organisations such as recording studios may follow this pattern. In organisations of this type there are separate functions but it is not clear who is in charge when all are engaged in solving a collective problem demanding different kinds, but not levels, of expertise.

Tall hierarchies are usually found in stable environments where formal status, qualifications and rules are important in order to produce clear accountability and predictability. The armed forces during peacetime are often close to this model.

---

### ACTIVITY

#### Organisation charts

**1** Using the organisation chart of Sneaker Ltd (Fig 1.2)
(a) Calculate the number of people employed in marketing the products of Sneaker Ltd.
(b) Draw a scale diagram – an organisational pyramid – representing the overall hierarchical shape of Sneaker Ltd.

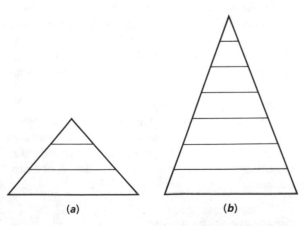

**Fig 1.3 Organisational pyramids: (a) flat hierarchy, (b) tall hierarchy**

**2** The research and development section of Sneaker Ltd is housed in a laboratory run by Jake the young nephew of the company's founder. There are four designers:

- Sonia, a graphic artist
- Timothy, a rubber technologist with computing skills
- Jane, a market researcher with a successful background in advertising
- Harry, who translates the imaginings of the other team members into practical manufacturing terms.

Most of the routine work of the research and development section is carried out by four teams under the control of the designers. Each designer has a secretary. The four teams are:

- visual design and functional efficiency (six people)
- materials (five technologists)
- market research (four full-time researchers)
- prototype production (eight people).

Draw an organisation chart and a diagram showing the organisational pyramid of the research and development section of Sneaker Ltd.

---

### MATRIX

A matrix structure can be described as a grid structure organised around functions, with project managers. Project managers will use services from the various units to accomplish tasks. An example of a matrix organisation can be found in shipbuilding where the organisation is structured into different shops – e.g. machine shop, electrical shop. However, each ship overhaul is a separate project with a manager who uses the resources of the functional shops (or activities) as required. Other examples of organisations using a matrix structure are companies involved in research, construction and aircraft manufacture. Organisations with a matrix structure tend to produce a variety of similar products or services using different functional activities.

### SEMI-MATRIX

In response to a rapidly changing environment, some organisations have introduced a system which combines some staff and some line functions which have been described as semi-matrices. Colleges are one example of this. The organisation chart in Fig 1.4 is for a college with a semi-matrix structure.

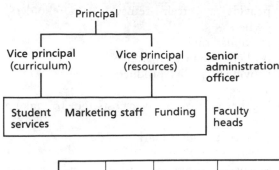

|  | Science | Business studies | Humanities | Engineering |
|---|---|---|---|---|
| GCSE |  |  |  |  |
| A Levels |  |  |  |  |
| TVEI |  |  |  |  |
| Media studies |  |  |  |  |
| Part-time studies |  |  |  |  |

**Fig 1.4  A college semi-matrix structure**

In Fig 1.4 the horizontal and vertical divisions of the organisation chart have different meanings from the linear administrative chart in Fig 1.2 describing Sneaker Ltd. Vice principals are under the authority of the principal and have authority over heads of faculties but the *functions* of the heads of faculty, for funding, marketing etc., may be shared between them or rotated. Heads of faculty also have responsibility for separate curriculum areas, e.g. science and business studies. Staff will be divided into sections on the basis of subject. The complication and intended flexibility arises from the way in which individual staff will also be responsible to, and members of, project teams, for courses such as TVEI and media studies, or responsible for specific groups of students.

The vertical columns indicate the loyalty of an individual member of staff to a subject specialism while the horizontal rows describe the teams. Vertical columns are often *line* relationships, while horizontal teams may be *staff* relationships – but not always! Not all of the boxes formed in this way will have section heads; some section heads will be responsible for subjects and/or courses.

## Stakeholders

*Stakeholders* is the term used to describe all those who have some legitimate relationship with an organisation. The stakeholders must be recognised by the organisation and handled in positive ways, for example see Table 1.2.

Conflict between stakeholders is inevitable as organisations can only generate a finite amount of added value and the allocation of this added value will be determined by the current strategy.

**Table 1.2  The stakeholders in a large financial organisation**

| Stakeholders | Responsibility |
|---|---|
| Shareholders | A fair return on their investment for the risk they take |
| Customers | Information on which to base their decision to buy the product<br>Value for money<br>Service |
| Employees | Fair treatment – no discrimination<br>Fair reward for effort<br>Equal reward for equal effort<br>Responsible attitude to continuity of employment<br>Opportunities for career development and training |
| Unions and staff associations | Provision of information<br>Fair and open procedures to handle negotiations and grievances<br>Bargaining in good faith |
| Suppliers | Open and fair dealings<br>Payment within agreed terms<br>Information about proposals and plans which might affect them |
| Local community | Respect for environmental factors<br>Set an example as a good employer<br>Create and maintain employment, within economic limits |
| State | Observe legal obligations<br>Act as responsible citizen |

Reinvestment might have to take precedence over paying dividends to shareholders or wage increases for the workforce. Potential conflict may also exist between the need to streamline operations in the interests of efficiency and the long-term employment of staff.

## Organisational goals, aims, strategies and targets

Goals and culture are intimately related to each other, but goals are usually more explicit, multiple and liable to change. Goals are directed towards defined targets. These targets will be chosen from production, profitability or efficiency, growth, quality, stability, customer satisfaction, security and satisfaction of organisation members, conquest and defence. Some of these targets are incompatible so choice of goals is a key organisational decision.

Very explicit goals are best termed 'plans' or 'objectives'. The term 'goal' is usually reserved for those intentions of the organisation which are more explicit than culture, but less realisable than objectives. For example, an organisation may have a *culture* that is sensitive to green issues. Its related *goals* would include communicating this value to its customers and suppliers, but it would be impossible to fully communicate this value to all potential customers and certainly impossible to convert all customers to it. However, it would be possible to create systems which would monitor whether or not production materials required the use of rain forest hardwoods. Avoidance of the use of scarce hardwoods would be an *objective*.

Different organisations may focus on different goals. Within an organisation there will be multiple competing goals, but only a few will dominate.

Businesses have aims, objectives and targets to provide them with direction and help them to use their resources efficiently. *Aims* are broad, long-term goals; *objectives* are more specific goals (often medium to long term) and *targets* are very specific, short-term goals. Some examples of aims are to:

● maximise profit

● provide a certain return to shareholders/owners
● maximise sales
● do better than competitors
● provide a quality product/service
● survive
● breakeven, i.e. to cover costs, not to make a loss
● achieve a certain market share.

A business can have several aims and these are often specified in a *mission statement*. Many private sector organisations will seek to maximise profits but also to provide a quality service – unless a quality service is provided, customers will not purchase the product/service and hence profits will decrease. Thus these aims are complementary. In times of recession many private sector firms aim to survive and to breakeven. Sometimes organisations aim to maximise sales, however, this alone does not imply profit because the aim does not take account of costs – sales could be increased but unless the aim is also to control costs the organisation may not even be breaking even. Public sector organisations have in the past had providing a service to the public while breaking even as their primary aims. However, this could lead to inefficiencies and to employees not being cost-conscious. For this reason the Conservative Government of the 80s and 90s pursued a programme of privatisation with the hope of increasing efficiency, reducing costs and providing a more efficient service through increased competition.

Aims are long-term statements of what is to be achieved and organisations need more specific, shorter-term objectives to enable the long-term aims to be realised. At an operational level they also need targets, which are still more specific goals than objectives. This relationship between aims, objectives and targets is exemplified in Fig 1.5, where an aim is broken down into specific objectives and then into targets.

Every part of an organisation could have objectives and targets which contribute to the achievement of the organisation's long-term aims or goals. Each person within the organisation can make a contribution to the aims by having targets set for them – if individual employees

| | |
|---|---|
| **Aim:** | to make *x* profit |
| **Objectives:** | to reduce costs by *y* per cent |
| | to increase product range |
| | to improve customer service |
| | to make *z* level of sales |
| **Targets:** | |
| Purchasing | to find alternative suppliers and negotiate lower purchase prices to reduce cost of supplies by *a*% |
| Administration | to reduce the number of telephone calls made at peak times |
| Sales | to achieve an increase to *b*% in sales |

**Fig 1.5 The relationship between aims, objectives and targets**

achieve their targets, the business is more likely to achieve its aims and objectives. The employees within the business can contribute to the achievement of the organisation's goal through having a good attitude to their work, being trained to do the job properly and working effectively as members of a team. (See Unit 2, People in business and organisations, for team working.)

Because the external environment is not static the organisation has to be aware of changes and to adjust its aims, objectives and targets in order to adapt to them.

### ACTIVITY

**A** Select one organisation in the public sector and one in the private sector. Examine the goals of each and compare them. Explain if the goals differ or if they are the same or similar and suggest reasons for your findings.

**B** In small groups consider the answers to the following questions.

**1** Are there any so-called 'corporate' objectives in the organisation where you work (part-time/full-time)?

**2** Are these published?

**3** Are they informal?

**4** Are these objectives available to everyone?

**5** When were these objectives set?

**6** When were they revised?

**7** Who were they set by?

**8** Have you any influence over the setting of organisational objectives?

**9** What objectives are you pursuing at work?

**10** What purpose?

**11** What reasons?

**12** What goals?

**13** Are your objectives the same as your immediate colleague?

**14** Are they the same as your immediate superior?

**15** Are they the same as your immediate subordinates?

## Organisational culture

*Culture* describes the shared attitudes, beliefs, expectations and actions which determine behaviour patterns within an organisation. Culture develops and shows itself in the way people act and react, and sets the tone of the organisation. *Goals* are desired outcomes of organisational action which focus on defined targets. These targets are not fully achievable.

Strictly, organisations have neither culture nor goals; only people have these. An organisation is 'more than the sum of its parts', i.e. more than a collection of people and technology, and therefore the behaviour of a group cannot be understood entirely by gaining an understanding of the personality and aspirations of each member. A group develops a style, sets of shared beliefs, habits and patterns of behaviour, and traditions. Together these views of the world constitute *organisational culture.* Culture is sometimes made explicit in the form of an organisation's Mission or Perspective Statement.

Rio Tinto Zinc state in their Annual Report and Accounts that they aim:

*to act responsibly as a steward of the resources in our care so that they benefit both the countries in which they are found and the world at large which needs to make use of them.*

At the same time RTZ seeks to create long-term wealth for its own shareholders. It believes that these two objectives go hand in hand; in the long run the one cannot be achieved without the other in a long-term business, such as mining ...

> *It aims to involve the local communities wherever it operates and to promote their well-being.*

Culture is reinforced through collective goals, past achievements and the ways in which new staff who fit in and are 'sympathetic' to the organisation are selected and trained. Culture is resistant to fundamental change.

## TYPES OF ORGANISATIONAL CULTURE

Culture can focus inwards or outwards into the community – examples are given in Table 1.3. *Inward focus* refers to focus on concern about the welfare of employees, their working conditions, the type of work they do and their participation in the decision-making process. On the other hand an *outward focus* refers to concern about aspects relating to the community, either local or national, for example issues such as pollution, safety and social responsibility.

### ACTIVITY

**1** Taking the categories used in Table 1.3 as headings, add to the lists given so that you have a set of possible items under each of the headings for both inward and outward focus.

**2** Are there any organisations you can think of which have mainly an outward or an inward focus?

### Outward focus – a social responsibility

Today many organisations are more conscious of the need to be socially responsible. Social responsibility can be seen to have many benefits in terms of providing jobs and caring for the environment and the community. On the other hand some firms see it as an impediment to profit making and react against social responsibility as being outside the scope of businesses.

### Inward focus

The inward focus of organisational culture can be characterised in terms of management styles with regard to the control of structures and systems. One comparison of working styles begins by asking the questions:

● Has the worker high or low concern for problems of production, profits, deadlines, etc?

● Has the worker high or low concerns for people as subordinates, as individual colleagues and in teams?

From the answers to these questions, five types of worker attitude can be defined which, when reproduced throughout a workforce, indicate the basic types of inward organisational culture (*see* Fig 1.6).

*All mates together* describes an organisation where priority is given to attending to the needs of people. The need for satisfying relationships is especially important and is expressed in a comfortable friendly atmosphere, where work is completed at an easy rate.

**Table 1.3   Organisational culture – inward and outward focuses**

*Outward focus*

| | |
|---|---|
| **Pollution** | reducing noxious emissions to below legal standards, even if competitors are not |
| **Product safety** | being alert to customer vulnerability from packaging, contents |
| **Community** | sponsoring local events and supporting local good works |
| **Politics** | donations to political parties |
| **Defence** | ensuring national security from external threat |

*Inward focus*

| | |
|---|---|
| **Employee welfare** | providing medical care, generous leave, mortgage subsidies, high levels of pay |
| **Working conditions** | safe and pleasant working conditions, social clubs, canteens |
| **Job design** | Job enlargement to increase workers' satisfaction and autonomy |
| **Participation** | workers' co-operatives, quality circles, consensus decisions, share options |

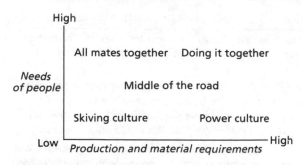

**Fig 1.6 Five types of inward organisational culture**

*Doing it together* – a team with trusting team members who are committed to a common purpose underpins this culture. All are concerned with completion of shared tasks, but realise that this is most likely to happen where there is mutual respect for expertise and contributions.

*Middle of the road*. This term is not meant to insult a culture; it describes a situation where those who manage attempt to balance work tasks with worker morale. Work may be organised in a more fragmented manner than in the team approach (doing it together).

*Power culture* places high emphasis on production and material things. Work is often automated and human interaction is kept to a minimum.

*Skiving*. This culture shows no great concern for social interactions or production tasks. The main priority is to expend the minimum effort without causing the organisation to collapse.

---

### ACTIVITY

#### Inward cultures

**1** The five types of culture described can be individual worker attitudes, but they are used here to describe organisational cultures. From your own experience, describe two organisations or parts of organisations which fit at least *two* of the types.

**2** Where do you fit in as an individual?

---

### GOAL FORMATION

Because goals are more specific than culture and relate more closely to the control of action, their formulation and modification is the result of a more interactive process within the organisation. Goals can be regarded as the outcome of:

● reactions to external forces
● predispositions created by organisational culture
● internal power dynamics.

Internal power dynamics are very complicated and, as their name suggests, constantly shifting. They can include struggles between all categories of people within the organisation. For example, veterans versus new recruits, men versus women, inter-section rivalry and managers versus workers. Within the business category at least eight competing goals can be identified:

1 Production (number and quality of completed tasks)
2 Inventory (a store of completed tasks)
3 Sales (number)
4 Market share (proportion of total possible market)
5 Profit
6 People (satisfaction of members' needs)
7 Size
8 Service

The emphasis which is given to these separate goals and the way in which members of an organisation work towards them are highly influential forces on an organisation's culture.

---

## The location of business

When a person is choosing where to purchase or rent a house or apartment they have to take into account many different factors such as price/cost, size, travel distance from work, personal preference, accessibility (public transport and roads), incentives from the seller (special purchase deals, carpets, curtains), amenities, and perhaps, an element of 'beating the Jones'. When a location is being chosen for a business organisation similar factors need to be considered (*see* Table 1.4).

**Table 1.4   Factors involved in the location of a business**

| | |
|---|---|
| Cost | The cost of property and land is less expensive out of town than in a town centre. The cost of labour is also an important consideration, as is the cost of transport involved in making and receiving deliveries. |
| Accessibility | The quality of the transportation network which is needed in order to allow staff to be able to get to the workplace and for any necessary deliveries to be made must be assessed. Some businesses, such as retail shops, need their customers to have physical access to their premises while for other types of business, for example a mail order firm, this would not be necessary. |
| Resources | The resources required to allow the business to operate need to be available, e.g. electricity and water. Included here is the human resource, i.e. whether sufficient people with the skills needed to work in the business are available. |
| Nature of the business | In some cases the nature of the business itself can dictate location, e.g. products requiring special weather conditions (wind-powered electricity generation). In other cases there could be restrictions on location due to legislation, e.g. relating to pollution (chemical plants, nuclear power generation). Some businesses deal with very specialised products and customers will be prepared to travel to make their purchases whereas other businesses sell products which are more easily obtainable and so require ease of customer access if they are to be successful. |
| Financial incentives | These may be in the form of grants and aid provided by the government or financial incentives provided by the seller. |
| Competition | This can affect location from two aspects. First, a business may choose to locate where there are no competitors in order to have a wider market. Second, a business may choose to locate in an area where their competitors are because customers can be attracted by the fact that there is a choice offered to them, i.e. there is competition. For example, some areas in a town have a lot of restaurants, book shops, theatres or specialist types of shops. |

Traditionally, some factors positively influencing the location of industry have been:

- a supply of skilled labour in the area
- proximity to suppliers
- proximity to raw materials
- access to market/customers
- government grants and assistance
- transportation costs.

However, although these are still important in many ways, the traditional factors are breaking down because people are more mobile and flexible due to improved transportation links, increasing car ownership and the introduction of flexible working systems. In addition, technological changes, which can allow more people to work from home, are becoming increasingly important factors.

Table 1.5 shows some choices an organisation can make when selecting a location, and some constraints which apply to those choices.

**Table 1.5   Some choices and constraints involved in location selection**

| Choices | Constraints |
|---|---|
| Town A or B | Resources |
| Rural or urban | Customers |
| Street C or D | Competition |
| Building E or F | Accessibility |
| Country G or H | Taxes and tariffs |

---

### ACTIVITY

#### Rural or urban?

Weststores Ltd has a chain of department stores, each one being located in a town centre in the main shopping area. The management wish to open two new stores but are considering siting the stores In a more rural, out-of-town location.

(a) List reasons for siting the stores in an out-of-town location.

**(b)** List constraints and/or problems with locating the stores in an out-of-town location.

**(c)** Write your answers in the table below and compare them with those of other students. An example of each has been listed to start you off.

| Reasons for choosing an out-of-town location | Problems/constraints of an out-of-town location |
| --- | --- |
| 1 lower cost of land | 1 will customers travel? |
| 2 | 2 |
| 3 | 3 |
| 4 | 4 |
| 5 | 5 |

## Business opportunities

People who are considering setting up a business for the first time or are expanding a business will be alert to business opportunities. Existing businesses must also identify and take advantage of business opportunities in order to survive. Because customers' needs and competitors' activities are dynamic (i.e. constantly changing), businesses need to find new customers or to identify and satisfy the developing needs of existing and potential customers. To do this it is necessary to monitor the external environment, to be aware of what competitors are doing and to research into customer needs. Gaps in the market can be identified and analysis carried out to decide whether it is feasible to take advantage of the business opportunity or not. There are many different tools available to help businesses in this identification and assessment process. Some example include:

● Marketing research
● Competitive surveys
● SWOT analysis
● Project appraisal
● Skills audit
● Feasibility study

### MARKETING RESEARCH

Marketing research methods are dealt with fairly comprehensively in the Unit 7, Marketing and business performance, where a description of the various methods is given and their uses explained. Marketing research is essential for an organisation because it is a primary information system; it allows the firm to keep in contact with the external environment – what customers think and buy, and what the competition is doing.

### COMPETITIVE SURVEYS

Competitive surveys are conducted by an organisation in order to find out information about competing organisations such as:

● prices
● level of customer service
● level of product knowledge
● image
● products sold
● special offers.

Employees may visit competing firms (if this is possible) and observe and note prices, products, special offers, etc. They may also make telephone calls requesting information about certain products in order to identify the length of time potential customers would be waiting for the telephone to be answered, the level of product knowledge and telephone manner of the staff. A competitive survey gives information about how competitors are responding to change and can generate ideas for possible business opportunities. For example, if a competitor opened a cafe in their store and the cafe was observed to be very busy, it could be that opening a cafe in your business is a good business opportunity worth considering.

### SWOT ANALYSIS

A SWOT analysis is an analysis of a firm or person's Strengths, Weaknesses, Opportunities and Threats in order to identify business opportunities. SWOT analysis can be used by an individual who is considering setting up some kind of business or by an existing business to identify business opportunities and possible actions necessary for continued existence. Figure 1.7 is an example of a personal SWOT analysis to help identify a suitable business idea for a woman

---

**Background information**

Marcella is 21 and unemployed. She is an extrovert who has an interest in fashion and children and likes meeting people. Her mother sometimes held Tupperware parties at home and Marcella enjoyed helping with these as she enjoyed entertaining and helping with the orders. She has lots of friends but many of them are married with small children and babies so she doesn't go out very often. She has a friend, Yanis, whose parents own a warehouse selling babies' and children's clothing at very good prices. Her friends with children are often complaining that they cannot afford to go out very often because of the cost of feeding and clothing children. Marcella can drive and owns a hatchback car. Marcella would like to open a shop but she has very little money. However, Yanis' parents have said that if she wants to sell children's clothes, they will be able to supply her with stock on a sale-or-return basis.

**Marcella's personal SWOT analysis**

*Strengths*
Extrovert
Interest in fashion
Interest in children
Likes meeting people
Can drive
Has a car
Enjoys entertaining
Enjoys helping with party plan
Has lots of friends with children

*Opportunities*
Supply of children's
clothes on a sale-or-return basis
To start a retail business
To sell children's clothes by party plan

*Weaknesses*
Unemployed
Hasn't got much money

*Threats*
Not being able to go out very much
Not developing a career

**Outcome of the personal SWOT**

The outcome of undertaking the personal SWOT led Marcella to consider setting up a business selling babies' and children's clothing by the party plan system. Marcella carried out research to find out if there was a market for such a business by carrying out a survey in the town centre, at her local mother and toddler group and baby clinic. She also telephoned her friends to see what they thought of her business idea. The results were very positive. She was not aware of any competing business of this type, nor were the people who took part in the research survey. Her competitors are mail order firms and retailers, whose prices are higher than the prices at which Marcella can sell her products – low prices made possible by her low costs.

Marcella had to consider costs and other resources but having assessed the business idea she tried it out and it proved to be a very successful venture.

**Fig 1.7 A personal SWOT analysis to identify a suitable business opportunity**

who wants to set up in business. Figure 1.8 is an example of a SWOT analysis of an independent business which has recently been bought by a husband and wife.

---

**ACTIVITY**

Which groups of people would each of the following products and services be aimed at? (Refer to Fig 1.8 if you wish.)

| Product/service | Customer |
|---|---|
| home-made desserts | |
| freshly cooked and carved cold meats | |
| draught beer and cider | |
| a variety of fresh breads | |
| a variety of cheeses | |
| videos for hire | |
| a delivery service | |
| a pinball machine | |

## Background information

Joe and Ella bought a small retail/off licence in a small parade of shops in a large up-market village. (The shopping parade is shown on the map in Fig 1.9.) The newsagent sells a variety of household products such as cleaners, shampoos, deodorants, milk and sliced bread. It opens early in the morning and closes at 6 pm. The fish and chip shop is fairly traditional, opening in the afternoons and evenings. The shop selling vacuum cleaners is rarely open at all. The fruit and vegetable shop sells, in addition to a basic selection of fresh fruit and vegetables, a small variety of cakes, basic types of bread, and some groceries such as tinned vegetables, tinned fruit and puddings. Its opening hours are 9 am to 5 pm.

The shopping parade is located in an area where there is a mixture of elderly people, young married couples, families and single young men and women living with their parents, in apartments or owning their own houses.

Joe and Ella took over their business, immediately changing its name to 'Joel'. The business was very run down and, although it was supposed to be primarily an off-licence, it had very little stock. It also acted as a general store but stock was low here too. Overall, custom was very poor.

Joe is very good at making desserts. Joe and Ella carried out a SWOT analysis to determine what to do with the business.

### Joel's SWOT Analysis

| *Strengths* | *Opportunities* |
| --- | --- |
| Good position | |
| Large catchment area | Large potential market |
| Variety of people | Different market segments to sell to |
| Pub across the road | A lot of potential passing trade |
| Licence | Sell to people coming out of the pub at closing time and expand product range |
| Joe can make desserts | Sell home-made desserts to the elderly and to families |
| *Weaknesses* | *Threats* |
| Currently low trade | Some competition for groceries |

### Outcome of the SWOT analysis

The outcome of the SWOT analysis was that Joe and Ella realised the different type of potential customers who were within their catchment area. An analysis of the differing needs of these groups showed that there were many opportunities to gain trade by offering products and services to fill the needs of the various groups, which were not being met by the other local businesses. Joe and Ella offered the following products and services and made a great success of the business:

- home-made desserts
- freshly cooked and carved cold meats
- draught beer and cider
- a variety of fresh breads
- a variety of cheeses
- videos for hire
- a delivery service
- installed a pinball machine

**Fig 1.8  A small business SWOT analysis – JOEL**

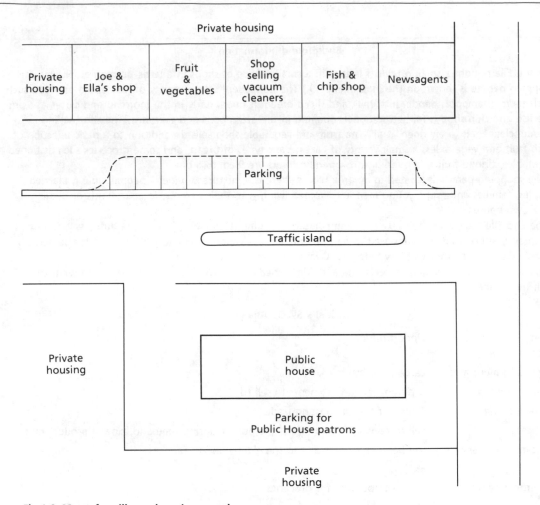

**Fig 1.9 Map of a village shopping parade**

## PROJECT APPRAISAL

Businesses are often presented with many different business opportunities and it may be necessary to choose which alternative offers the most potential, since limited resources place constraints on an organisation's activities. Project appraisal is one method of determining which business opportunity is likely to be the most beneficial to the organisation. There are a number of other techniques available to help managers make such decisions and these are discussed in detail in Unit 5, Financial information systems.

## SKILLS AUDIT

Employees' skills can present businesses with opportunities but can also act as a constraint on the opportunities available to them. A skills' audit may bring to the fore employees' skills which could suggest business opportunities. For example, Dominique and Ken worked in a medium-sized hotel. All staff were able to do a variety of jobs. The hotel had a core of full-time staff and some part-time staff to give flexibility and additional help at peak times. During slack times the staff had little work to do. A skills audit showed that Ken was a qualified hairdresser which identified a business opportunity – a hairdressing service could be offered during off-peak times. Dominique was French and currently taking a teaching certificate. She felt that she would be able to provide training in the French language for leisure and for business people and the hotel facilities were suitable to provide a location for the venture – another business opportunity.

Skills audits can also highlight when business opportunities will not be feasible because the staff do not have the necessary skills to undertake the venture successfully. In such cases, the staff training required to provide the skills could be too lengthy and/or too costly to take advantage of the business opportunity. For further information on skills' audits, see Unit 2, People in Business.

## FEASIBILITY STUDY

A feasibility study is a study carried out to assess the overall viability of a business opportunity. It includes a study of:

- the market and customers
- financial income and expenditure – project appraisal
- resources – physical resources, competence of employees (skills), costs, time available.

Carrying out a feasibility study is a methodical approach to help assess the practical viability of business opportunities and to help decide whether to take up options or not.

---

### ACTIVITY

**1** Identify a business opportunity in your local area.

**2** What resources would be needed for the venture?

---

## Business plans

A business organises and manages resources in order to satisfy customer needs and to make a profit. If businesses are to survive they need to have a planned approach to the organisation and management of resources. This planning can be written down formally in a business plan, which helps to communicate direction and ideas to people both within the business and external to it. The business plan can be analysed by an external body, such as a bank, when an organisation wishes to raise finance. It can also be analysed by departments within an organisation so that they can set goals and targets which are complementary to the business plan. Departments within an organisation can prepare departmental business plans which fit in with the achievement of the overall business plan of the organisation.

People with a new business idea also need to plan ahead and produce a business plan in order to raise finance, to think logically about the business venture and to put their ideas into practice successfully. Many small businesses fail because they have not been properly planned – the market may not have been as large as expected, sufficient research may not have been carried out, not enough capital may have been borrowed, competition may not have been adequately considered.

A business plan for a new business presented to a bank to raise finance should cover the following areas.

1 The business.
2 Ownership and management of the business.
3 The products and services which the business will offer.
4 The market – customers and competitors.
5 The location of the business and identification of premises.
6 Finance – projections and requirements.
7 Marketing activities.
8 Any other relevant information.

The checklist below identifies some questions in each of the above areas which can act as a guide when producing a business plan.

### CHECKLIST FOR PRODUCING A BUSINESS PLAN

#### The business

- What is the business idea?
- What are the aims and objectives of the business?
- What are your personal reasons for wishing to start the business?
- Do you have any relevant skills for starting and running the business?

## Ownership and management of the business

- What legal form will the business take (e.g. sole trader, partnership, private limited company)?
- Who will own the business?
- Who will manage the business?
- What employees are needed?
- What skills do the various people who will take part in the management and operation of the business have?

## The products and services which the business will offer

- What products and services will the business sell/provide?
- What equipment and premises will be needed to provide the product or service?

## The market – customers and competitors

- Who are the customers?
- Who are your competitors?
- What product/services do your competitors offer?
- How will the product or service differ from competitors? What is its unique selling point or position?
- Where are your competitors located?
- What is the size of the overall market?
- What is your market share likely to be?
- What potential is there for expanding your market share?

## The location of the business and identification of premises

- Where will your business be located?
- Why is the location suitable?
- What are the costs of the premises?
- What are your future requirements with regard to premises?

## Finance – projections and requirements

- What costs will be incurred to start the business?

- What income are you likely to receive from sales?
- What level of sales is needed to break even?
- What is your cash flow forecast for the first year of trading?
- What is your first year's budget?
- How much money are the owners putting into the business?
- How much money do you need to borrow?
- What are your working capital requirements?
- What are your long-term borrowing requirements?
- How are you going to repay the money you have borrowed?
- What is being offered as security for the money borrowed?

## Marketing activities

- How are you going to market your product?
- What marketing research have you carried out to support your venture?
- What have been the results of your marketing research activities?

## Any other relevant information (examples)

- Curriculum vitae for managers/owners
- Photographs or drawings of the products
- Data from marketing surveys
- Photographs or plans of the premises
- Draft promotional material
- Sample questionnaires
- Names and positions of any advisers.

The business plan therefore covers all aspects of a business – business objectives, resources needed for the business and how resources will be managed and organised. Information to help you to answer the above questions or general background reading can be found in various units throughout this book; for examples see the table opposite.

## THE CHANGING NATURE OF THE BUSINESS PLAN

A business plan may be a formal procedure which helps managers to plan ahead and to prepare for the future. However, when the business

| Topic | Unit |
|---|---|
| Generating business ideas | 8, Innovation and change<br>7, Marketing and business performance |
| Aims/objectives of the business and legal forms | 1, Business organisation |
| People needed for the job/an analysis of job skills | 2, People in business and organisations |
| Marketing the product<br>Marketing research<br>Customers | 7, Marketing and business performance |
| Location | 1, Business organisations<br>6, Physical resources<br>8, Innovation and change |
| Physical resource requirements | 6, Physical resources |
| Financial planning<br>Breakeven analysis<br>Cash flow forecast<br>Budgeting | 5, Financial information systems |
| Marketing activities<br>Sales promotion<br>Marketing research | 7, Marketing and business performance |

plan is devised figures are calculated as 'best estimates' and forecasts of future happenings, and the reality may be different to what is in the plan. For example, there may be a number of reasons which cause sales to be lower than expected – a new competitor may enter the market or the local or national economy may go into recession. This means that the business plan must be dynamic and flexible, not remain fixed or unchanging. A business needs to respond to its environment and therefore business planning must be an on-going process; it needs to take place regularly and should never be seen as a one-off event.

The business plan is monitored and controlled by comparing the estimates with reality and taking appropriate action if any discrepancies are large enough to cause problems. For example:

● If a business had agreed a certain overdraft facility as a result of their cash flow forecast and in reality find that their customers are taking longer to pay bills, they may need to ask the bank for a higher overdraft limit or to consider factoring. Factoring, in this context, means that the bank will provide an advance on the value of the invoices sent out by the business so that the business can avoid the problem of not having sufficient cash flow to cope with paying wages, purchasing stock and meeting other expenditure.

● Sales may be lower than expected and the business could alter their marketing plan to include changes in the products offered, and to reconsider pricing and promotional strategies.

To summarise, the business plan is a very important planning tool for any existing business as well as for a new business venture. The plan involves the collection of data and estimation of sales, costs, profits, borrowing requirements, etc. The plan is a statement of the business objectives and ideas, descriptions of products and the market, etc., but it also acts as an action plan with timescales and targets against which reality can be reviewed and monitored – and appropriate action taken where necessary. The business plan involves the presenting of the project or business idea and aims, analysing and researching the market and customers, and a plan to show the requirements and management of human, financial and physical resources within a time schedule.

# 2

# PEOPLE IN BUSINESS

## The importance of people

Employees of a business, sometimes referred to as human resources, make the organisation work. In any business, no matter how much technology or money is being used, people are still essential:

- to plan
- to think
- to work equipment
- to manage.

An organisation can only function effectively if the right skills are recruited, developed and used appropriately.

This unit covers a variety of areas concerning people in business – the human resources of a business – and seeks to answer questions such as:

- What kind of jobs do people do in a business?
- How do you find the right staff?
- How do you induct staff and train them to do their job effectively?
- How do you manage and motivate staff, and provide effective leadership?
- How do you plan personal tasks and use time efficiently?
- What causes stress and how can people try to reduce unhealthy levels of stress?
- How do people work most effectively in teams?
- How do you plan, organise and run meetings?
- What are disciplinary and grievance procedures?
- How does the employment relationship end?

The employment relationship is governed by important legislation and this will be dealt with throughout the unit when it is applicable.

## What kind of jobs do people do?

The jobs people do in a business depend on the type, function and size of the organisation. The process of defining the kind of jobs required within an organisation should start with the analysis of the tasks which need to be carried out in order to make the organisation function effectively. These tasks will then be analysed in order to identify the skills needed to perform them. Tasks will then be combined to form jobs or roles for individuals, i.e. jobs are *designed*. The design of the jobs will affect motivation of staff and this should be considered when the jobs are being designed.

Unfortunately it is not always possible to design jobs in this way. Very often what happens is that when someone leaves a job a straight replacement is found to fill the post. This leads to some jobs becoming a lot larger or harder than others as, over time, more work comes into one area of the organisation or there are developments in another area which reduce workload. The effect of this is to make some employees overworked and to underuse other staff. In either case this will have an adverse effect on both the staff and the performance of the organisation. Whenever someone leaves an organisation there is an opportunity to review the job which they did and see if the work can be realistically reallocated in a more efficient way. An appraisal of the jobs which people have should also be a regular feature of the review and planning processes of the business, and should lead to the reallocation of tasks where advantageous. No one should consider their job to be 'set in stone' and unable to be changed as the organisation and the work develop and change.

Skills are often divided into physical and mental characteristics of an employee, for example strength is needed for some jobs, the ability to operate a computer for others and the ability to cope well with complex calculations in another job. Any job will require a mix of many different skills. Some skills, such as the ability to get on with other people, are required in almost every job. Others will be specialist skills which are only required in a very few jobs. You may also look at specifying the experience and the knowledge which the ideal person for the job should have. So, a job advert may ask for '... three years' experience in a marketing environment and the ability to speak and write fluent French' thus specifying the experience and knowledge necessary to do the job. There is often a thin dividing line between a skill and knowledge, for example would you consider the ability to write and speak a foreign language to be a skill or knowledge?

---

### ACTIVITY

#### Skills mix and jobs

1 Think of a business idea.

2 List the main tasks that would need to be done to run the business.

3 Analyse the tasks to identify the skills needed to do them.

| Business idea: | |
|---|---|
| *Tasks* | *Skills* |
| | |
| | |
| | |
| | |

---

In a small organisation, there may only be a few people employed and each person may do a range of jobs. For any business to operate effectively the products/services need to be marketed and sold, supplies need to be obtained, administration needs to be carried out, financial records need to be kept, staff need to be recruited and trained, and wages need to be calculated. In a large organisation these functions will employ a number of specialists, however, if the organisation employs only a few people these jobs still need to be carried out. Normally the manager, who may also be the owner, will deal with the recruiting and promotion, wages and finance, and will supervise and manage operations. An accountant may be employed as and when required to do the final accounts. Other staff employed may also be required to do a full range of different types of duties.

In comparison, a large organisation has specialised people to do different types of tasks. The organisation will be split up into different departments or sections, each one having a different function, e.g. administrative, finance, personnel, marketing, operations or production, public relations, etc. Each function will have staff who do different jobs, therefore, there will be different roles and levels of responsibility within each function. Large organisations will have several levels or layers of responsibility, generally referred to as senior management, middle management, supervisory management and workers/staff.

**Senior managers** – set policies and procedures and develop the organisation's mission statement setting out the aims of the organisation. Examples of senior manager positions are chief executive, directors.

**Middle managers** – implement the policies and procedures and liaise with supervisory managers.

**Supervisory managers** – supervise the day-to-day activities of the workplace and deal with problems with workers.

**Workers** – sometimes referred to as subordinates, employees, or staff of the business. (Technically all people employed by the business are staff or employees. However, the distinction is often made to identify management and supervisory positions from the general workforce.)

**Table 2.1**

| Skill | Examples of jobs/roles |
| --- | --- |
| Manual/operative | jobs involving manual work or operating equipment and machinery e.g. machinist, fitter |
| Administrative | jobs requiring clerical work e.g. clerks, receptionists |
| Service/technical | jobs requiring technical skills e.g. technicians setting up and maintaining equipment |
| Professional | jobs requiring professional training e.g. doctors, solicitors, accountants. This also includes people with specialist expertise e.g. market researchers, computer analysts, personnel managers, though these are not in the traditional 'professional' category. |
| Managerial | jobs requiring management and supervisory skills e.g. sales managers, marketing managers, supervisory roles, assistant managers, personnel directors |

There are many other types of roles held in organisations such as assistant managers, employee/trades union representatives, specialist and professional staff.

- Managers tend to have *assistant managers* who work with them and are able to deputise for them should the need arise. For example, if the manager is unable to attend a meeting, the assistant manager may go in his or her place.
- Employee/trades union representatives are elected to represent the workforce so that they have a stronger voice to protect their interests, particularly over issues such as pay and conditions of service.
- Specialist and professional staff carry out specialised roles which may span the organisation, such as having responsibility for health and safety. Accountants, solicitors and doctors are examples of specialist staff, often also described as professionals.

Within the organisation there will be jobs requiring different skills such as manual skills,

administrative skills, technical skills, professional knowledge and skills, and managerial skills. Examples of these are shown in Table 2.1.

---

#### ACTIVITY

Select two large organisations, one in the private sector and one public sector organisation:

1 Obtain an organisation chart for each organisation.

2 What functions/departments is each organisation divided into?

3 For each function listed on the chart identify job titles and roles which are manual/operative, administrative, service, technical, professional or managerial.

4 Identify which people (if any) hold the positions identified below and find out (i) their job titles and their role in the organisation and (ii) the training, qualifications and experience necessary to do each of the roles:

- chief executive
- director
- manager
- employee/trades union representative
- specialist
- professional
- senior management
- supervisor
- assistant

5 Identify other roles/functions and find out the training, qualifications and experience necessary to perform them.

---

### ROLE CHANGE

Roles and the responsibilities of jobholders within organisations are dynamic because business is dynamic. Some factors which can change role responsibilities are:

**Legislation** – Many legislative changes have had an effect on the jobs people do. The introduction of equal opportunities legislation, for instance, caused a rethinking of the jobs and responsibilities held by women. Health and safety legislation has introduced the need for employees to take on roles such as health and safety officers.

**Customer feedback** – Feedback from customers can help to improve the service and/or products received by customers. This may involve the introduction of new processes which will affect the work done by employees.

**Appraisal** – Appraisal can change job roles through negotiation and evaluation of current work and past work undertaken. This may result in the reallocation of work in order to distribute work more fairly or jobholders may benefit from programmes such as job enlargement or job enrichment, which seek to provide more interest and stimulus in the jobs people do.

**New technology** – The introduction of new technology will involve new processes, new working methods or procedures and require people to acquire new skills and accept new responsibilities. For example, a typist may have learnt to use a wordprocessor and have moved on from there to using other packages, such as desktop publishing and spreadsheets. A move such as this will be a major change from the original job.

**Internal policies dealing with emergencies** – The need for bomb wardens, safety wardens and more control over health and safety may result from the introduction of new company safety policies or regulations such as the Control of Substances Hazardous to Health Regulations.

There are many other factors which may change individuals' job roles over time – such as the need for increased efficiency, new products being introduced as a result of competition, and change in the environment within which the business operates. This area is examined further in Unit 4, Business Environment and Unit 8, Business Innovation.

---

### ACTIVITY

Read the descriptions of the jobs of Carol and Ahmed and give examples of (i) factors which might change their responsibilities and (ii) how their responsibilities may change.

> *Ahmed works in a personnel department where as part of his job he maintains personnel files. He files documents, and ensures files are updated. There are thousands of files and they are kept in filing cabinets.*
>
> *Carol is a waitress in a cafe. Her job involves taking orders, serving customers, and clearing, cleaning and resetting tables.*

---

## JOB DEMANDS

Jobs can place different types of pressures on people and require different levels of skills (physical and mental) and knowledge to perform them. Some jobs involve a high level of decision making, place a great deal of responsibility and accountability on the holder and require an advanced level of skills. Other jobs may be less demanding intellectually but physically very exhausting because of long hours worked or a requirement to be constantly at peak alertness. The differing demands jobs place upon their holders is sometimes reflected in the scales of pay.

---

### ACTIVITY

**1** Analyse the jobs identified below in terms of the level of decision making and accountability, and both physical and mental skills required. (You may interview people doing the various jobs if you wish.)

- Accountant
- Personnel officer
- Teacher
- Refuse collector
- Tax inspector
- Clerical assistant
- Waitress
- Bank manager

In presenting your answers to this task you may want to use a format like the one below:

Job: _____

| Decision making | Accountability |
|---|---|
| | |
| | |

Mental demands          Physical demands

**2** Find out the average rate of pay for the jobs (using statistical information or by analysing jobs advertised in newspapers, jobcentres, journals and any other means).

Mark your answers on the scale provided, and consider the following questions.

## Pay scale

| £000s | Jobs |
|-------|------|
| 30 | |
| 27.5 | |
| 25 | |
| 22.5 | |
| 20 | |
| 17.5 | |
| 15 | |
| 12.5 | |
| 10 | |
| 7.5 | |
| 5 | |

(a) Do you feel that the pay for all of the jobs was fair?
(b) What seem to be the main factors in determining whether a job is well paid or not?
(c) Should pay be determined differently so that some of these people are paid more and others paid less than they are at the moment? On what basis would you make these decisions?

## MANPOWER PLANNING

Having the right number and type of employees and managers will help an organisation to function effectively. Individual managers will have a number of people under their supervision which is known as the *span of control*. This span of control should not be too large for the manager to cope with effectively. What is manageable will depend, in part, on the type of supervision required. For example, it will be harder to supervise the work of a very specialised member of staff working on a complex and individual project than the work of a person carrying out a routine job with clear performance targets. It is also necessary to ensure that there is the right skills mix to allow the work to be carried out to an agreed standard which helps the objectives of the organisation to be achieved. The process of making sure you have enough of the right staff is called *manpower planning*.

Manpower planning also involves ensuring that the organisation has enough suitable labour to provide the required service in the future as well as in the present. Manpower is planned in order to meet short, medium and long term objectives of the organisation. People are expensive to employ and therefore, as with other resources, manpower needs to be planned if organisational objectives are to be met without wasteful overmanning or often equally costly skills shortages.

---

### ACTIVITY

Apart from the cost of wages, what other costs may a business have to bear as a result of employing someone? Select a job you know the salary for and try to put a figure on these extra costs. An example has been filled in on the table below to give you a start:

Job: _____

Basic salary: _____

| Extras | Cost |
|--------|------|
| National Insurance, pension etc. | About 20% on top of salary |
| | |

---

Manpower planning involves answering questions such as:

1 What is the nature of our business?
2 What kind of manpower is needed at all levels?
3 What is our existing manpower?
4 What changes are likely to take place within our existing manpower (e.g. retirements, redundancy)?
5 In what way does our existing manpower differ from what is required?
6 What changes will/may take place in the business?
7 What changes in skills or size of workforce are necessary?
8 What is the existing potential of the staff?
9 What action is needed to respond to changes?

Manpower planning is a quantitative approach. It makes an organisation plan ahead and be better prepared to meet future human resource needs. It also allows an organisation to plan the cost of labour in order to budget more precisely and provides a plan for aiding the balance between retirement, promotion and recruitment of staff. It helps to identify future training needs. Computerisation of personnel records has enabled manpower planning to become more detailed.

Manpower planning is carried out by the personnel or human resources department in liaison with other functions within the organisation and is a way to determine what human resources are required to meet the organisation's aims and objectives as defined by function.

Manpower planning involves analysing manpower information – manpower demand (manpower required) and supply (manpower available) are estimated for the organisation and the discrepancy between the two is then corrected. If, for example, there is likely to be a demand for another 20 skilled production staff, resulting from the success of a new product and 16 people are likely to become available from another project which has finished, there will be a gap of four people to be found. This may be done by recruitment or by retraining other staff in the organisation to fulfil these roles. Other options would include hiring temporary or casual staff, if the demand is not likely to be long term, to avoid the cost of recruiting full-time staff. Manpower planning also has to deal with the less pleasant situation where the organisation may require fewer staff as a result of a fall in demand or the introduction of new technology. This planning for a reduction in the number of staff can be harder for the organisation than planning for more staff. Inevitably such a situation will cause all sorts of rumours and fears and the plan should be clear and sensitively communicated so that people know what is happening and why.

## THE PROCESS OF MANPOWER PLANNING

The process of manpower planning is outlined in Fig 2.1. Not all organisations will go through all of the stages but there should be some level of planning similar to this, even in small organisations. Though it will probably not need to be as formal as the process set out here, it should still happen.

## WHERE DO WE GET INFORMATION FOR MANPOWER PLANNING?

Personnel records can provide the information relating to manpower supply, e.g.:

- age
- sex
- grade of job/job category
- earnings
- qualifications
- department
- recruits
- leavers
- promotions
- transfers

Other information such as age of joining, time in job, length of service and results of appraisals can also be useful. Many organisations now have computerised personnel information systems to analyse manpower data.

## MANPOWER PLANNING AT LOCAL, REGIONAL AND NATIONAL LEVEL

Manpower needs to be planned for not only at an organisational level but also on a local, regional and national basis to ensure that skills which are required to help keep the economy alive exist and will continue to do so. The government produces statistics giving the numbers, sex, ages, qualifications, occupations, locations and movement of populations at national, regional and local levels. Demographic sources include:

- *Social Trends*
- *The Employment Gazette*
- *Annual Abstract of Statistics*
- The Department of the Environment
- Economic bulletins published by the banks
- Office of Population Censuses and Surveys
- The CBI (industrial trends).

These sources of information are useful in helping organisations plan where to locate industry and in identifying skill shortages and analysing training needs in order to ensure adequate provision of training courses. A supply of labour is essential for the economy to function –

| Gather information on the supply of labour and the type of labour likely to be needed by the business in the immediate future, the short-term and the longer term future | Gather information on the supply of labour in the organisation and the skills available to the business from the existing labour force; or soon to be available as the result of training programmes. |
|---|---|

Compare the needs of the organisation and the resources available to it in the:

- immediate future
- short-term future
- longer term.

Forecast the needs of the organisation on the three levels identified above. What numbers of staff will be needed? What skills will they have to have if they are to be effective?

Will there be a requirement to shed any staff? Can this be avoided by retraining or redeploying them?

Plan a strategy to shed or recruit the staff needed and to put into practice any updating of skills or retraining of staff which will be needed to ensure that the right people are available, with the right skills, at the right time. Any temporary gaps may be filled by casual staff or people on fixed term contract rather than permanent employees.

**Fig 2.1 The manpower planning process**

hence human resources have to be monitored and managed on a large scale. One example of how demographic data can be useful was when it demonstrated what came to be known as the 'demographic crisis', where an ageing population and a decline in the number of school leavers left industrialists concerned for their future source of employees. Women were attracted to college courses to reskill and improve their skills so that they were able to return to work after raising a family. The growth in private nurseries for pre-school children has also been a noticeable result.

## STAFFING LEVELS

Like all types of resources the number and types of employees an organisation can actually employ is restricted by what the organisation can afford to pay. Too many staff and the organisation will not be able to operate because labour costs will be too high, too few staff and it will not survive because it will be unable to provide a satisfactory level of service to customers or to produce quality products.

The law of diminishing returns states that when you apply more of a variable factor (in our case labour) to a constant factor (e.g. physical resources) output increases up to a point but then decreases, so that output can actually decrease when extra members of staff are employed. Look at the information in Table 2.2 and then work through the Activity to illustrate this principle.

**Table 2.2**

| Number of employees | Number of rooms cleaned per hour |
|---|---|
| 1 | 4 |
| 2 | 9 |
| 3 | 16 |
| 4 | 19 |
| 5 | 18 |
| 6 | 16 |

Table 2.2 shows the number of rooms in a travel lodge cleaned per hour with different levels of manpower.

---

### ACTIVITY

**1** Calculate the average number of rooms cleaned (output) at each staffing level and complete the table below.

**2** Calculate the marginal output at each level of employment (i.e. the number of extra rooms cleaned by employing an extra person).

**3** Why does the average output increase and then decrease?

**4** What extra information would you need before you could recommend the appropriate level of staffing for this business?

---

| Number of employees | Number of rooms cleaned per hour | Average output | Marginal output |
|---|---|---|---|
| 1 | 4 | 4 | |
| 2 | 9 | 4.5 | |
| 3 | 16 | | |
| 4 | 19 | | |
| 5 | 18 | | |
| 6 | 16 | | |
| 7 | 15 | | |
| 8 | 14 | | |

---

Some organisations can choose between technology and people for some jobs, hence technological advances affect the type of human resources required.

The organisation's goals affect the type of people employed, for example a company which wants to trade with a particular country will require employees with specific language skills. (Many managers now say that people with language skills are an asset because of the Single European Market.) Similarly, if a firm is wishing to diversify into new products it will employ people with the required skills.

---

### ACTIVITY

**1** Find out the objectives of your organisation, section or department. If you are a full-time student you could use your work experience placement or college.

**2** What skills are needed to achieve these objectives?

---

## THE FLEXIBLE EMPLOYEE

Employees who have many skills are very valuable because they are able to do many jobs and can adapt more easily to change. In times of recession employees who are more flexible are less likely to be made redundant than those with narrow skills. In a changing business environment the flexible employee is much sought after and many organisations have undertaken programmes to broaden the skills of their employees so that they are able to take on different job roles. One obstacle to this flexibility has been the attitude of some trade unions – often for good reasons such as safety – that jobs designated for someone with particular skills, such as an electrician, should not be carried out by anyone else. A good multi-skilling programme will, however, take account of this and allow a plumber or fitter who has acquired some electrical skills to undertake simple work but also ensure that for anything more complex they know that they need to call in an expert. One of the criticisms of schemes to broaden the jobs which people do is that they can tend to make people 'jacks of all trades and masters of none'. This is a very real problem if it means that the organisation is not actually making full use of the special skills for which someone was initially recruited.

People may also develop to take on extra roles as a result of programmes such as:

- *Job enrichment* – this is where an attempt is made to introduce more variety into a job in order to motivate and interest an employee who may otherwise become bored. This is quite often done in jobs which are repetitive or there is a high level of routine. By introducing new work, people are provided with a challenge and the opportunity to get rid of areas of their work with which they are bored.
- *Job enlargement* – this is similar to job enrichment but involves making a job larger, i.e. it takes in more similar tasks in addition to the ones which are already part of the job. This may be introduced as a result of a fall in the level of work or because of an employee's increasing skill level. This can quite often be accompanied by regrading or other incentives to take on the larger job. As

with job enrichment, the intention is to provide variety and motivate staff.

- *Job rotation* – this is where jobs are swapped around periodically to allow staff to try different jobs and acquire new skills. In this case there will often be a system where one employee trains another in their job before the rotation is made. Job rotation helps to encourage teamworking and allows people to see some of the problems which other people face in their jobs.

---

## ACTIVITY

For each of the above make a list of what you see as being the main advantages and the main problems. The format below may be useful.

| Technique | Plus points | Problems |
| --- | --- | --- |
| | | |

---

## MAKING USE OF SKILLS

Some organisations do not make the best use of the skills of their employees and many people complain that their jobs are boring and feel that they could do more or different work. If people feel that they are not being given the opportunity to use the full range of their talents and abilities, they may become alienated and indifferent to both their work and employer.

One way to make the best use of the skills of employees is to carry out a skills audit. To do this you can find out information such as the type of work employees have done in the past, their qualifications, hobbies and interests, courses they have been on, etc. You can also gain valuable information about peoples' skills if you also find out their aspirations and the type of work they enjoy – people normally enjoy what they are good at.

An audit like this can help the organisation to be more efficient in many ways. For example, if a vacancy becomes available, perhaps an existing employee can fill it – and internal appointments can provide incentives to staff. Similarly, if a member of staff is absent from work, perhaps another member of staff has the necessary skills to deputise. There are many stories recounted by people where the managers have, after some years, found out that their employees have unused special skills or knowledge. One example of this is a woman (Kate) who worked as a filing clerk – she was very bored and intended to leave as soon as the job market picked up. By accident her manager found out that in a previous job she had worked as a mortgage adviser. As a result, the firm hired someone else to do the filing and Kate helped people to complete their mortgage application forms and explained the various types of mortgages available and the terminology used etc. Kate was stimulated by her new job which capitalised on her previous experience and the organisation was also able to improve business by developing its service to its customers.

Auditing human resources can give an organisation or manager valuable information about the skills of each employee and allow him or her to make the best use of staff. This can lead to increased job satisfaction, which in turn increases staff motivation. An organisation can also save money because they may be training one person in certain skills which another member of staff already has but is not using. A business may also be hiring extra labour to do a job which existing staff may be able to do within their normal job hours. The following case studies give examples where this has happened.

---

## CASE STUDY

*A health, beauty and fitness business paid an outside firm to design and print their advertising literature and publicity material. One day during a coffee break the manager overheard Jane and another employee discussing their college days and heard Jane saying that she did desktop publishing and really enjoyed it. The business already had a computer to compile a database of clients and to keep track of their weight and measurements, so the manager bought a DTP package which Jane could use. Now Jane produces all the advertising and publicity leaflets when she has slack times. Jane enjoys this and has produced all kinds of materials which have enhanced the image of the business.*

*Amanda was a hairdresser in a fairly quiet salon away from the town centre. Business needed to improve and it was becoming necessary to make one hairdresser redundant. Amanda suggested setting up a creche in the salon to attract women with children to use the salon. Her manager said that they could not afford to hire a qualified person to set up and supervise the creche. As Amanda had taken an NNEB course before she trained in hairdressing, she said she would be able to set up the creche and provide supervision when required in order to attract more trade.*

Auditing human resources allows you to find out capabilities of staff and other information in a *planned* way. This contributes to the manpower planning exercises which are necessary to ensure that there are suitable levels and types of manpower to run the business.

The type of information collected by an audit depends on the use to which it is going to be put. General information such as that contained in the following list can be of use:

- age categories
- sex
- qualifications
- job role
- training
- experience
- previous jobs (within and outside the organisation)
- what the person sees as his/her skills
- what other people see as his/her skills

However, more specific information can also be of use to an organisation. Consider the health, beauty and fitness business in the case study above; the manager could have found out if any of the staff had desktop publishing skills rather than relying on finding out by accident. Much of the required information may already be available within the organisation – on application forms and personnel and training records. To collect further information, interviews and/or questionnaires can be used. Questionnaires can be restrictive because the space allocation may be inadequate but more so because people will only answer the questions asked and much valuable information may not be collected as a result.

One factor to bear in mind when collecting information of a personal nature is that it has to be carried out with the co-operation of staff. Some people may resent being asked certain questions and may resist, other people may not think they have many skills or qualifications and this could lead to embarrassment. When carrying out audits therefore:

- always ensure you have management support and approval
- gain the co-operation of employees
- explain the purpose of the audit to employees
- do not pressurise any employee to answer questions which they resist
- always respect people's personal lives and privacy
- ensure and respect confidentiality.

---

### ACTIVITY

With the permission of your supervisor or tutor, carry out an audit of the human resources used in the department or section in your workplace or college. Use the same department you used in the earlier activity where you were asked to find out about the department or section's goals.

**1** For each employee find out:

(a) age category
(b) sex
(c) qualifications
(d) job role
(e) training
(f) experience
(g) previous jobs (within and outside the organisation)
(h) what the individual sees as his/her skills
(i) what other people see as his/her skills
(j) any other relevant information.

**2** Collate the information.

**3** Do the skills available to the organisation meet its needs?

**4** What can you deduce from the information analysed?

---

## Finding the right staff

Having carried out an analysis of human resources required by the organisation and compared this to the human resources which the organisation currently has, a mismatch may have been discovered leaving a gap to be filled. This should be identified in the manpower plan. Depending on the nature of the gap it may be filled by:

- better use of the available manpower
- recruitment of new staff
- induction
- training
- using independent contractors.

As has already been discussed, by finding out the skills of your staff you are able to make better use of them. However, the way in which jobs are designed can also make better use of human resources. Recruitment of new staff gives the opportunity to bring new skills into the organisation but it is important to recruit people with *relevant* skills. In order to settle new employees into the organisation and the job, they need to have an induction into the firm and job. Training can be used to fill knowledge/skill gaps and can be carried out in many enjoyable and cost-effective ways.

Outside contractors can be used to fill a one-off requirement which does not warrant a full-time employee or which is a very specialised or expensive skill to employ. For example, small firms do not employ full-time accountants or solicitors; they hire an independent accountant to work for them as and when they need financial advice or help. Organisations may also wish to pull expertise into the firm to meet specific problems which may never occur again, e.g. management consultants to help reorganise a business. Advertising agencies are similarly used on an 'as required' basis, as are many other services that organisations do not wish to be involved in, such as:

- window cleaning
- building or renovation work
- maintenance work.

All these services are necessary for the smooth running of the business but would be too expensive to provide 'in-house'. In addition, they would demand valuable managerial and staff time if they were to be organised within the business. By using specialist contractors, an organisation receives a good service with a minimum of extra work.

## RECRUITMENT AND SELECTION

The recruitment and selection of suitable staff is crucial to the health and strength of the organisation. It is through recruitment and selection that the human resources required to meet the organisation's objectives are found. Employing someone who does not have the skills you need can be an expensive mistake – it may cause other staff to be disheartened and stressed and will also cost the organisation more in training.

This overall process is examined in the following activity. It begins with a clear analysis of the job that is to be filled. You need to decide whether the organisation's needs are better served by full-time or part-time staff and whether temporary or permanent staff should be employed. Sometimes there is only enough work to hire a part-time temporary employee to help the organisation over a short-term busy period, or the work may be seasonal and you will then require a full-time temporary employee for the busy season. On the other hand, some organisations choose to recruit many part-time staff rather than fewer full-time staff because it allows them more flexibility. However, this policy has disadvantages too.

### ACTIVITY

Consider the advantages and disadvantages of employing each of the four categories of staff listed below and complete the table.

| Category | Advantages | Disadvantages |
|---|---|---|
| Full-time permanent | 1 | 1 |
| | 2 | 2 |
| | 3 | 3 |
| Full-time temporary | 1 | 1 |
| | 2 | 2 |
| | 3 | 3 |
| Part-time permanent | 1 | 1 |
| | 2 | 2 |
| | 3 | 3 |
| Part-time temporary | 1 | 1 |
| | 2 | 2 |
| | 3 | 3 |

---

## JOB DESCRIPTION

| | |
|---|---|
| **Job title:** | Financial Assistant |
| **Responsible to:** | Head of Financial Affairs (Postholder: Ms A Carter) |
| **Responsible for:** | Two administrative assistants in the section |
| **Main tasks:** | To assist the Head of Financial Affairs with the compilation of bids for funding for specific projects. To gather information relating to company projects and compile it into a format for presentation to the Financial Management Group. To brief the Head of Financial Affairs and other staff on the background to project proposals. To work with staff in other sections to revise and rework bids in the light of decisions of the Financial Management Group. |
| **Pay and conditions:** | As set out in the Contract of Employment Statement and in the conditions for staff appointed on Grade C1. |
| **Date of compilation:** | 14 March 19XX |

**Fig 2.2 A job description**

When you have decided which category of staff you need, you need to provide a clear outline of the job (this is known as a *job description*) and the potential for further progression within the organisation. This will then allow you to provide clear recruitment criteria with a description of the person you are looking for, identifying the skills, qualities, qualifications needed to do the job (this is known as a *person specification*). Examples of job descriptions and person specifications are given in Figs 2.2 and 2.3.

### PAY

The wage or salary awarded to a job needs careful consideration. Employees obviously want fair pay while the company needs to make a profit, which it will not achieve if pay is too high. However, the level of pay may determine the quality of people who apply for your vacancy, though this is not always the case – some excellent employees get paid less than they deserve. Some factors which need to be considered when determining pay are:

- level of skill required
- qualifications required
- hours and conditions of work
- fairness
- equal pay legislation
- the availability of labour
- the nature of the job
- the grade
- the 'going rate'.

---

# PERSON SPECIFICATION

Applicants for the post should meet the following essential criteria:

* Aged 25-45
* Two years' experience in a public sector finance environment
* Ability to operate Smart II computer software
* Qualified to AAT Intermediate level or equivalent
* Able to demonstrate drive and enthusiasm
* Willing to work away from home on occasions.

In addition, it would be desirable for applicants to meet the following criteria:

* Ability to speak one modern European language at a basic level
* Ability to operate WordPerfect wordprocessing software
* An interest in, and commitment to, the work of the charity
* Experience of working independently
* Experience of supervising staff

---

**Fig 2.3 A person specification**

Pay normally reflects the skills and qualifications required for the job, balanced against the availability of labour. A job that requires a high degree of technical skills which are rare will attract higher pay than one which requires a low level of skills which many people have. However, this is also balanced with the nature of the job, and hours and conditions of service – many low skilled jobs are highly paid because employees have poor working conditions, the work is heavy or the hours worked are 'unsociable'.

Pay has to be *seen to be fair* (this is known as *equity theory*). This means that the pay for the job must be considered fair in relation to its demands, in relation to other jobs within the organisation and when compared to the similar jobs in other organisations. Hence, organisations and job seekers find out the 'going rate' for

certain jobs. The Equal Pay Act provides that a woman should get paid the same as a man where she is engaged in:

1 like work to a man;
2 work rated as equal to work done by a man;
3 work of equal value to that done by a man.

---

### ACTIVITY

1 State the main provisions of the Equal Pay Act.

2 Does 'equal pay for equal work' mean that jobs have to be identical for equal wages to be received?

3 Employers are required to pay men and women approximately the same wages for substantially equal work. What does 'substantially equal work' refer to?

**4** In certain circumstances different pay can be awarded to individuals performing identical jobs. Give examples of such circumstances.

**5** Read the following cases and for each case state whether you think it is fair for the employer to pay Jonathan more than Jane.

(a) Jane works as a supervisor in a factory. Jonathan works in the same factory doing the same supervisory post. Jonathan is paid more than Jane.

(b) Jane works as a cook in the managers' canteen of a large firm. Jonathan works as a chef in the employees' canteen. Jonathan is paid more than Jane.

(c) Jonathan has worked as a teacher in a large school for five years. Jane got a job in the same school two years after Jonathan. Jonathan is receiving a higher salary than Jane.

(d) Jonathan and Jane are both accountants in a large organisation. They carried out their training at the same time and received the same grades in examinations. They were both paid the same before and after training, however, Jonathan has a company car and Jane does not.

## COMMUNICATING THE VACANCY

The vacancy is communicated to the public through job centres, newspapers, journals, notice boards and word of mouth. Some firms use specialist employment agencies to recruit staff. Failure to use suitable methods or media to communicate the vacancy will mean that you are unlikely to attract people with the skills you need. For example, organisations advertise certain jobs in relevant journals – personnel and training jobs are advertised in *Personnel Officer* and other relevant journals because people interested in this area of work read these specialised journals, and teaching posts are advertised in *The Times Educational Supplement* for similar reasons. Many executive type jobs are advertised in *PER*, a publication available from job centres, rather than on the notice boards at the job centre itself. You may communicate the vacancy internally (within the organisation itself) and/or externally.

Advertisments should give essential brief information about the job, the organisation, the type of person required, how to obtain further information and how to apply for the post. They will normally be written in an organisation's 'house style' and an organisation may have very specific rules about how the advertisement should look (*see* Fig 2.4).

Cost is a major factor in advertising a job and the medium chosen. Two lines in a local paper will be a lot cheaper than a series of advertisements in the high circulation national newspapers and the decision as to where to advertise will be based on the needs of the organisation and the likelihood of finding the person or people required locally. For example, a top level job requiring specialist skills would probably need to be advertised nationally while a lower level job, requiring more commonly-available skills may be successfully advertised locally.

When advertising a post ensure that the advertisement does not breach the Sex Discrimination Act or the Race Relations Act. These Acts make it unlawful to discriminate on the grounds of race or sex when recruiting staff. Many employers have equal opportunities policies and state on their adverts that they are 'an equal opportunities

---

**Lifesave**
*A Charity working for Health Care for all.*

Lifesave
Charnley House
Liverpool Road
Skelmersdale
Lancashire

**FINANCIAL ASSISTANT**

This nationally known charity requires a Financial Assistant to help our regional groups to put together bids for funding from our central funds. We are looking for someone with experience of work in the public sector who is prepared to travel and spend some time away from home. Limited foreign travel may be involved.

We offer a salary commencing at £9100 and a pleasant working environment, based in our Skelmersdale offices.

Application forms can be obtained by writing to us at the address above and further details can be obtained from Jan Carter, Head of Financial Affairs.

We are an Equal Opportunities Employer.

**Fig 2.4 A sample job advertisement**

employer'. It is perfectly legal to advertise for a particular sex or race in cases where being male or female or of a particular race is genuinely required to do the job. These situations are known as Genuine Occupational Qualification and include:

1 Where authenticity makes it desirable that a person of a specific race or sex be given a job. For example in the case of a play.
2 The job requires the person to be of a particular sex in order to preserve 'privacy or decency'; for example a toilet attendant.
3 Where the job involves work with a social group whose interests are best served by the appointment of someone from the social group; for example an Asian woman to work with Asian women.
4 Where a job involves work in a country outside the United Kingdom where a person of a particular race or sex would be unable to do the job effectively; for example many Middle Eastern countries have a lot of resistance to dealing with women as managers.
5 In the provision of care, such as in retirement home dealing with residents of one sex.

Apart from breaking the law, discrimination may also limit an organisation's pool of potential recruits by discouraging applications from people who may be excellently suited to the job.

---

### ACTIVITY

Which of the following statements would be illegal if they were used in a job advertisement? Give reasons why.

**1** Barman wanted for busy pub.

**2** Ladies, earn some extra cash!

**3** Lady required as a helping hand to a very old woman.

**4** Waiter/waitress required for Chinese restaurant – must be Chinese.

**5** Female disco dancer required – must be under 21.

---

## SHORTLISTING

At this stage in the recruitment process you match the job requirements with the application forms and/or CVs of the people who apply, selecting the most suitable applicants to invite for interview. If you have many applications it would be too costly and time consuming to interview them all and often some of the applicants are obviously not suitable. This is where your detailed job description and person specification are essential because they give you a clear description of the job, the skills and the ideal person you need for the job.

---

### ACTIVITY

Using the job advert, the examples of job description and person specification given in Figs 2.2 and 2.4, read the following application forms and reference letters and shortlist the best three candidates to invite for interview. Explain the reasons for your choice.

---

# Lifesave

*A National Charity working for Health Care for all*

## Application for Employment

**Post:**  Financial Assistant ( ref 12/bn/jc)

Please complete this form in black ink or in typescript as it will be photocopied.

**Personal details:**

| Name | Address and Telephone | Date of Birth |
|---|---|---|
| J Wilson | 27 Acre Grove Denham, Surrey | 16.08.72 |

Are you registered Disabled?  Y  (N)        If Y  please give registered number:

**Education and Qualifications:**

Please list your education from age 11 and relevant academic qualifications obtained starting with the most recent:

| Institution | Qualifications | Dates Started | Left |
|---|---|---|---|
| Alderhill College | A levels (x2) | 9/90 | 6/91 |
| | Accounts (D) Sociology (C) | | |
| Carr Head High School | 6 GCSE incl Eng, Maths, French | 9/84 | 6/90 |
| | | | |

**Application form from J Wilson**

**Work experience:**

Please list your work experience as you consider it to be relevant giving a brief description of the duties of the posts held.  Please start with the most recent employment.  Attach another sheet if you feel you need more space.

| Post & Employer | Duties of post | Started | Left |
|---|---|---|---|
| Control Information | clerk | 6/91 | 12/92 |
|  |  |  |  |
|  |  |  |  |
|  |  |  |  |

What is your current salary? *N/A*

**Further Information:**

Please include any further information you feel will support your application

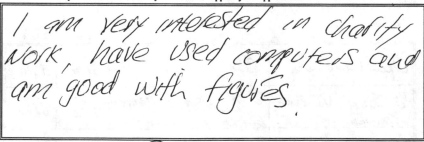

I am very interested in charity work, have used computers and am good with figures.

Do you have a criminal record?  Y  (N)
(If Y please enclose details in a sealed envelope marked 'FAO Personnel Manager only ')

Do you give your consent to the above response being verified if you are appointed?  Y / N

**Declaration:**

I declare that the particulars above are true and correct.  I am not related to any person in a position to influence this application.

Signed: *I. Wardy*      Date: _____

# Lifesave

*A National Charity working for Health Care for all*

## Application for Employment

Post: Financial Assistant ( ref 12/bn/jc)

Please complete this form in black ink or in typescript as it will be photocopied.

Personal details:

| Name | Address and Telephone | Date of Birth |
|------|----------------------|---------------|
| JAMES DENT. | 17, School Lane Oxford. | 14.1.64 |

Are you registered Disabled?  Y / N          If Y please give registered number:

### Education and Qualifications:

Please list your education from age 11 and relevant academic qualifications obtained starting with the most recent:

| Institution | Qualifications | Dates Started | Left |
|-------------|---------------|---------|------|
| Open University | B.A. Accounts. | 6/90 | date. |
| St. John VI Form Oxford. | 3 'A' Levels, Maths B English C, French C | 9/80. | 6/82 |
| Constable Hall School, Oxford | 9 'O' Levels 3@A 2@B 4@C. | 9/75. | 6/80. |
| | | | |
| | | | |

**Application form from James Dent**

### Work experience:

Please list your work experience as you consider it to be relevant giving a brief description of the duties of the posts held.  Please start with the most recent employment.  Attach another sheet if you feel you need more space.

| Post & Employer | Duties of post | Started | Left |
|---|---|---|---|
| Unit- 7 Windows, Oxford. | Financial Contool (Assistant) | 7/92. | 1/93. |
| Dem Ltd. (DIRECTOR) | Self employed business consultant | 6/90. | 6/92 |
| | | | |
| | | | |

What is your current salary?  £ 11,000.

### Further Information:

Please include any further information you feel will support your application

I have present and relevant work experience and now wish to use this to the wider benefit of the community.

Do you have a criminal record?  Y (N)
(If Y please enclose details in a sealed envelope marked 'FAO Personnel Manager only ')

Do you give your consent to the above response being verified if you are appointed? (Y) N

### Declaration:

I declare that the particulars above are true and correct.  I am not related to any person in a position to influence this application.

Signed: J. Dem.   Date: 10.3.

# Lifesave

*A National Charity working for Health Care for all*

## Application for Employment

<u>Post:</u>  Financial Assistant ( ref 12/bn/jc)

Please complete this form in black ink or in typescript as it will be photocopied.

<u>Personal details:</u>

| Name | Address and Telephone | Date of Birth |
|------|----------------------|---------------|
| M. Summers | 118 Omerod Rd Nelson. | 16.09.59 |

Are you registered Disabled?  Y / N          If Y  please give registered number:

<u>Education and Qualifications:</u>

Please list your education from age 11 and relevant academic qualifications obtained starting with the most recent:

| Institution | Qualifications | Dates Started | Left |
|-------------|----------------|---------------|------|
| St. Theodor's Grammar | 8 'O' Levels | 9/70 | 6/75 |
| " | 3 'A' Levels | 9/75 | 6/77 |
| Burnley College | AAT Intermediate + Advanced | 9/80 | 9/84 |
| | | | |
| | | | |

**Application form from M Summers**

**Work experience:**

Please list your work experience as you consider it to be relevant giving a brief description of the duties of the posts held. Please start with the most recent employment. Attach another sheet if you feel you need more space.

| Post & Employer | Duties of post | Started | Left |
|---|---|---|---|
| Pendle Borough Council | Financial Trainee Promoted to Financial Officer | 7/77 | 11/88 |
| Carter Hall Engineering | Credit Control Manager | 12/88 | Date |
| | | | |

What is your current salary? £10,200

**Further Information:**

Please include any further information you feel will support your application

> I am very much involved with charity work locally and, due to domestic circumstances, am free to move to a post which I would find rewarding. I am computer literate and speak fluent German.

Do you have a criminal record? Y /(N)
(If Y please enclose details in a sealed envelope marked 'FAO Personnel Manager only ')

Do you give your consent to the above response being verified if you are appointed? (Y) N

**Declaration:**

I declare that the particulars above are true and correct. I am not related to any person in a position to influence this application.

Signed: M. Summers    Date: 14 March .

# Lifesave

*A National Charity working for Health Care for all*

## Application for Employment

<u>Post:</u>  Financial Assistant ( ref 12/bn/jc)

Please complete this form in black ink or in typescript as it will be photocopied.

<u>Personal details:</u>

| Name | Address and Telephone | Date of Birth |
|---|---|---|
| Hilary Thompson | 16 Charnoss Grove Didsbury, Manchester | 1/5/47 |

Are you registered Disabled?  Y / N          If Y  please give registered number:

<u>Education and Qualifications:</u>

Please list your education from age 11 and relevant academic qualifications obtained starting with the most recent:

| Institution | Qualifications | Dates Started | Left |
|---|---|---|---|
| Baines Secondary | School Matriculation | 9/58 | 6/63 |
|  |  |  |  |
|  |  |  |  |
|  |  |  |  |
|  |  |  |  |

**Application form from Hilary Thompson**

**Work experience:**

Please list your work experience as you consider it to be relevant giving a brief description of the duties of the posts held. Please start with the most recent employment. Attach another sheet if you feel you need more space.

| Post & Employer | Duties of post | Started | Left |
|---|---|---|---|
| Post Office | Counter Assistant | 8/63 | 4/72 |
| | Raising a family | 5/72 | 1/80 |
| Henderson Ltd (builders) | Accounts Clerk | 2/80 | Date |
| | | | |

What is your current salary? £8,000

**Further Information:**

Please include any further information you feel will support your application

I have a lot of accounting experience including operating a computerised system. I have, in the past, been actively involved in charity fund raising.

Do you have a criminal record? Y / N
(If Y please enclose details in a sealed envelope marked 'FAO Personnel Manager only ')

Do you give your consent to the above response being verified if you are appointed? Y / N

**Declaration:**

I declare that the particulars above are true and correct. I am not related to any person in a position to influence this application.

Signed: H. Thompson Date: 14 March .

# Lifesave

*A National Charity working for Health Care for all*

## Application for Employment

**Post:**   Financial Assistant ( ref 12/bn/jc)

Please complete this form in black ink or in typescript as it will be photocopied.

**Personal details:**

| Name | Address and Telephone | Date of Birth |
|---|---|---|
| Michael Gibbs | 36 Longton Cl. Skelmersdale | 1 Apr. 1962 |

Are you registered Disabled? Y / N        If Y please give registered number:

**Education and Qualifications:**

Please list your education from age 11 and relevant academic qualifications obtained starting with the most recent:

| Institution | Qualifications | Dates Started | Left |
|---|---|---|---|
| Skillshop | NVQ Accounting Level 3 | 9/91 | 9/92 |
| Hertford Hill High School, Hertford. | 6 'O' Levels including English + Maths | 9/73 | 6/78 |
| | | | |
| | | | |

**Application form from Michael Gibbs**

## Work experience:

Please list your work experience as you consider it to be relevant giving a brief description of the duties of the posts held. Please start with the most recent employment. Attach another sheet if you feel you need more space.

| Post & Employer | Duties of post | Started | Left |
|---|---|---|---|
| Smith, Hawkins Accountants. | General Financial Assistant | 9/91 | 9/92 |
| Carry-All Hauliers | Loader/ Driver | 6/78 | 6/83 |
| British Rail | Finacial Trainee. | 9/84 | 4/90 |
| | | | |

What is your current salary? ___N/A___

## Further Information:

Please include any further information you feel will support your application

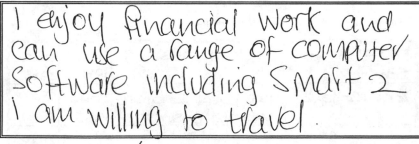

I enjoy financial work and can use a range of computer software including Smart 2 I am willing to travel.

Do you have a criminal record? X / N
(If Y please enclose details in a sealed envelope marked 'FAO Personnel Manager only ')

Do you give your consent to the above response being verified if you are appointed? Y / X

## Declaration:

I declare that the particulars above are true and correct. I am not related to any person in a position to influence this application.

Signed: __Michael Gibbs__     Date: __12 March.__

# Lifesave

*A National Charity working for Health Care for all*

## Application for Employment

**Post:**   Financial Assistant ( ref 12/bn/jc)

Please complete this form in black ink or in typescript as it will be photocopied.

**Personal details:**

| Name | Address and Telephone | Date of Birth |
|------|----------------------|---------------|
| Ayo Chucks | 33 Compley Avenue Hoston, York. | 11.07.49 |

Are you registered Disabled? X / N        If Y  please give registered number:

**Education and Qualifications:**

Please list your education from age 11 and relevant academic qualifications obtained starting with the most recent:

| Institution | Qualifications | Dates Started | Left |
|-------------|---------------|---------|------|
| Hoston High School | 4 'O' Levels | Sept. 1960 | June 1965 |
| York College | A Level English A Level Business Studies | Sept. 1965 | June 1967 |
| Lancashire Polytechnic | BA Business Studies (2:2) | Sept 1971 | June 1974 |
|  |  |  |  |
|  |  |  |  |

**Application form from Ayo Chucks**

**Work experience:**

Please list your work experience as you consider it to be relevant giving a brief description of the duties of the posts held. Please start with the most recent employment. Attach another sheet if you feel you need more space.

| Post & Employer | Duties of post | Started | Left |
|---|---|---|---|
| British Home Stores | Retail Assistant | July 1967 | August 1971 |
| Greater London Council | Financial Trainee (1974 – 1977) | July 1974 | Dec. 1984 |
| | Manager—Control Section (1977–1984) | | |
| Harrop, Johnston + Smith | Senior Accounting Assistant | Jan. 1985 | To Date |

What is your current salary? £8,400

**Further Information:**

Please include any further information you feel will support your application

> I have considerable financial experience including nearly 10 years in the public sector. I currently use both smart II and word perfect. My degree specialism was in public sector accounting. I currently work as a volunteer 'Samaritan.

Do you have a criminal record? Y (N)
(If Y please enclose details in a sealed envelope marked 'FAO Personnel Manager only ')

Do you give your consent to the above response being verified if you are appointed? (Y)/ N

**Declaration:**

I declare that the particulars above are true and correct. I am not related to any person in a position to influence this application.

Signed: A. Chucks     Date: 13 March.

# Skillshop
## *Training for your future*

Lifesave
Skelmersdale
Lancashire


Dear Mrs Lloyd

I have received a request for a reference for Michael Gibbs.

I have known Michael for one year when he attended an Employment Training Programme. Whilst on the programme he obtained a National Vocational Qualification in Accounting and he learned to use the computer. Reports from tutors indicate that he is generally punctual, has good attendance and mixes well with others.

In the past Michael has worked in Finance and, I believe, enjoyed the work very much. I have no hesitation in recommending Michael for the post applied for.

Yours sincerely

Mr Wyatt
Training Manager

Letter of reference for Michael Gibbs

# Control Information Limited
## Control House, West Road, Denham, Surrey

Lifesave
Skelmersdale

Dear Mrs Lloyd

With reference to your request for a reference for
Jonathon Wilson, I hope the following information is useful
to you.

Jonathon worked at our firm for 18 months. During this time
he demonstrated an ability with figures and was very
methodical.

I would urge you to contact me should you require further
information as to the work Jonathon did or the time he
spent with us.

Yours sincerely

Mrs Hirst
Training Manager

**Letter of reference for Jonathon Wilson**

# Unit Seven Windows

*Unit 7 Hall, Green Park*
*Oxford*

Lifesave
Skelmerdale

Dear Mrs Lloyd

You have requested a reference for Jamey Dent, and I have pleasure in providing one.

Jamey worked with us for six months, during which time he destroyed the happy working atmosphere in our office. He was not committed to his work, constantly tried to stir up trouble, and had arguments with many of our staff.

I would not recommend Jamey for the post.

Obviously, this reference is confidential, but should you require more information please do not hesitate to contact me.

Yours sincerely

*M Bell*

Mrs M Bell
Personnel Manager

**Letter of reference for Jamey Dent**

# HARROP, JOHNSTON & SMITH
## Accountants
### 32 The Crescent, Scarborough, North Yorkshire

Lifesave
Charnley House
Skelmersdale
Lancashire


Dear Mrs Lloyd

I received your request for a reference for Ayo Chucks.

Ayo was appointed for his post with us six years ago. He has always shown a high level of interest in his work. During his time with us he attended AAT courses and has been successful in these qualifications. He is punctual with very good attendance. He has an ability to work on his own initiative and solve problems. He works well with other staff and has trained some of our junior staff to use computers in their job.

I highly recommend Ayo for the post as I think he will manage the job very well.

Yours sincerely

Mr N Gills
Accounts Manager

**Letter of reference for Ayo Chucks**

# JOHN WATT ACCOUNTS SERVICE
## 24 Lancaster Gate, Lightholme
## Manchester

Lifesave
Charnley House
Liverpool
SKELMERSDALE
Lancs

Dear Mrs Lloyd

I have today received your letter requesting a reference for Hilary Thompson.

Hilary worked as an Accounts Clerk whilst I was Accounts Manager for Henderson Limited. I found her work to be satisfactory. Unfortunately, this was five years ago and I have not seen her or heard from her since.

I am sorry I cannot be of more help to you.

Yours sincerely

*L. Watt*

Mr Watt
Training Manager

**Letter of reference for Hilary Thompson**

# Carter-Hall
## *Manufacturing Engineers*
## *Unit 27 Lomeshaye Industrial Park, Nelson*

Lifesave
Skelmersdale

Dear Mrs Lloyd

Thank you for your request for a reference for Marion Summers.

Marion has been employed by us for the past four years and during this time she has maintained a keen interest in the job. She is normally punctual and her attendance has been very good indeed. She works well with other staff and uses computers regularly in her current job.

I wish Marion every success and highly recommend her for the post for which she has applied.

Yours sincerely

S Grant

Ms S Grant
Manager

**Letter of reference for Marion Summers**

**Fig 2.5 Tell us a little about yourself . . .**

## PREPARING FOR THE INTERVIEWS

This involves a number of preparations:

1 References have to be taken up – although references can be misleading it is essential to take them up. (Note, however, that references from a current employer are often not taken up until a candidate has been offered the post.)
2 Select a date, time and place to hold the interviews – check that staff who will be on the selection panel are available.
3 Invite your candidates for interview – this is normally done by letter.
4 Decide on how the interview will be conducted and prepare necessary documentation.
5 Ensure all staff who take part in the interviews are properly briefed about the job, the interview procedures, and have read the candidates' application forms/CVs and references.
6 Prepare questions to ask the candidates – ask open-ended questions rather than closed questions. Open questions encourage the candidate to talk and may give them the opportunity to display their abilities. Closed questions invite yes or no answers and therefore do not allow the candidate scope, often

creating a tense atmosphere. Many people like talking about themselves – closed questions do not give them the opportunity to do this and block communication, so avoid these communication killers. Be careful not to ask questions which could imply any kind of discrimination.

Being well prepared means that you can give your full attention to selecting the person who is right for the job and the organisation, while helping to project a good image of the firm.

## THE INTERVIEW

Although it is becoming more common to use other selection methods, the interview is still the most popular method. The skills of the interviewer are therefore crucial in order to bring out the information required and to find the best person for the job. Ensure that you are not disturbed during the interviews by putting a notice on the door of the interview room – interviews in progress, please do not disturb – and arranging for your telephone calls to be redirected to a deputy.

---

**Smith & Sons**
*120 Windley Street, Cambridge*

Ms J Jones
40 Highland Close
Cambridge

Dear Ms Jones

Thank you for attending the interview last week. I am pleased to offer you the post of Accounts Clerk in our Sales Department, at a starting salary of £9000 per year.
Your commencement date would be 1 May 19XX.

As discussed, office hours are 9.00 am to 5.15 pm with one hour for lunch. You will be entitled to three weeks' annual paid holiday.

Please confirm in writing by return that you accept this appointment on these terms, and that you can take up your duties on 1 May.

Yours sincerely

M W Smith
Personnel Manager

---

**Fig 2.6 An example of a letter of appointment**

Put candidates at their ease. Don't waste time by asking obvious questions which are answered on the application form – this also gives the candidate the impression that you have not taken the trouble to read it carefully. Ask questions which are open, clear and precise, and relevant to the post. Ensure you give the candidate enough time to respond fully to your questions. Listen carefully to the candidates' replies.

Interviewing can be stressful for interviewers as well as for interviewees so act as naturally as possible so that you and your candidates feel comfortable.

Make a record of each interview, immediately after it finishes, for future reference. This can serve the dual purpose of protecting you in case a candidate accuses you of illegal discriminatory practice and allowing you to find a suitable employee in the future at short notice and minimum cost.

## SELECT AND INFORM THE SUCCESSFUL CANDIDATE

Select the best candidate for the job and inform him or her in writing (see the example in Fig 2.6). If a current employer's reference has not been taken up, do so at this stage.

Do not select someone who is unsuitable for the job. If none of the candidates are what the organisation is looking for, readvertise the post to invite more applicants, perhaps using a different medium.

## OTHER SELECTION METHODS

The best person for the job can actually appear to be the worst candidate at interview. To help select the right person some firms use a range of other techniques, for example:

- psychological tests
- ability tests
- biodata.

These can give the interviewers more information about the nature and ability of the candidates, and hence the decision does not rest solely on the interview.

### Psychological tests

There are several well-known tests developed by psychologists to help selection and which claim to identify and/or confirm an applicant's competence or suitability for the job. The tests are standardised so that applicants can be compared to each other and to applicants of a similar background. Examples of psychological tests are aptitude tests and personality tests.

*Aptitude tests* are designed to find out whether the applicant has an aptitude for the type of work involved and skills needed or whether the applicant has the potential for developing the skill. The tests are used to predict whether the candidate will be, technically, able to do the job.

*Personality tests* (also known as questionnaires and inventories), are designed to examine a candidate's personality by identifying characteristics such as:

- introversion/extroversion
- confidence
- dependence.

Personality tests are designed to ascertain whether a candidate is temperamentally suited to the demands of a post.

Psychological tests are also referred to as *psychometric tests*.

### Ability tests

To give an indication of how people may perform in the job some firms sample these skills by giving written tests of arithmetic and English or by asking the candidate to solve problems or demonstrate skills which are required by the job. For example, applicants for a post involving wordprocessing may be asked to wordprocess a document.

### Biodata

Biodata is other information about the candidate which is supposed to indicate what sort of person the candidate is rather than simply elicit job-related information. For example, data about the applicant's hobbies and interests may reveal that a candidate does a lot of voluntary work in a home for the elderly which would be relevant if the job being applied for requires patience.

The use of biodata allows the interviewer to look at the interviewee as a whole person and not just in the narrow job sense. A lot of information about the person, as a person, may be obtained.

## WORK EXPERIENCE

Providing work experience to school, college and university students, and YT and ET trainees are good ways to help recruit because you can try out the people before employing them. Many young staff are recruited in this way. From the organisation's perspective, it is safer employing someone you *know* is capable of doing the job and is dependable.

---

### ACTIVITY

With other students, role play interviewers and interviewees using the shortlisting you carried out in the activity above.

(a) Decide who will play the various roles.
(b) Interviewers select appropriate selection methods – interview, job tests, etc.
(c) Prepare necessary materials – questions, documents, etc.
(d) Invite candidates for interviews.
(e) Role play the interviews.
(f) Select the most appropriate candidate, giving reasons for your choice.

---

## REFERENCES

Most job applications require people to provide the names of at least two referees. One of these will normally be the current employer. References tend to be of limited use because people select referees who will not be unpleasant about them if at all possible. Current employers are also careful about saying that someone is a poor employee. This is partly because they could possibly be sued for defamation of character if the person concerned objected to the reference and the referee was unable to prove that the statements in it were true. It is also suspected that an employer may give a poor employee a good reference in order to be rid of them.

Informal networks of contacts exist in some industries, where people will contact each other by telephone in order to get a view of the ability of an employee and some references will invite potential employers to do this. A phrase such as 'if you require any further information please feel free to contact me by telephone between 10 and 12 on Monday 23, when I will be in my office' may mean that there is something the referee would like to say which they are not prepared to put down in writing.

Some reference requests simply ask for an opinion of the candidate without specifying style or content – the referee can write whatever they like; others will supply a form and ask the person giving the reference to rate the person concerned on a number of factors such as:

- attention to detail
- ability to get on with colleagues
- punctuality
- level of wordprocessing speed.

These forms tend to be faster to complete than an open letter and will often contain more useful information. Any request for a reference should be accompanied by the details of the job applied for as this will make it easier for the referee to judge if the person is suitable for the job.

References should be honest and accurate but, unfortunately, many are very neutral and tend merely to be used as a check that the applicant has not failed to disclose anything major, such as having been fired from a previous job.

### ACTIVITY

Read the reference below and say what you think the writer really means.

---

Dear Sir
Re: Mr D _____ , Applicant for the post of Financial Assistant

I received your request for a reference yesterday and am glad to be able to comment on Don's suitability for this post.

Don has worked with me for three years and during this time I have found him to be a most imaginative employee, who has provided innovative ways of dealing with many of the problems he has encountered in his work.

Don gets on well with some of his colleagues and has taken full advantage of the social life on offer in the company over his time with us. His health has improved recently after a severe bout of illness a couple of years ago and he has only been absent from work on three occasions in the last month.

I note from the job description that the post requires an attention to detail and the ability to work unsupervised. I have every confidence that Don would be able to acquire these skills over time.

If you require any further details please feel free to contact me prior to your interviews between 10 and 12 on Monday 23 when I will be in my office (ext 413).

Yours faithfully

C Thomas
Accounts Manager

**EMPLOYMENT PROTECTION (CONSOLIDATION) ACT 1978**
**SECTION ONE**

**STATEMENT OF PARTICULARS OF EMPLOYMENT**

**ISSUED BY:** Mr and Mrs Ridding (Employer)

**NAME OF EMPLOYEE:** Linda Simpson

**DATE OF COMMENCEMENT OF EMPLOYMENT:** 1 February 1993

**DATE OF THIS NOTICE:** 1 February 1993

1.  **JOB DESCRIPTION**
    You have been appointed as a nanny for the employer above mentioned. Your duties will be as specified in the Job Description attached to these particulars of employment but this should not be taken as exclusive or exhaustive. There will be other duties and requirements reasonably associated with your post which you may be required to perform.

2.  **LENGTH OF SERVICE**
    No period of service with a former employer counts as part of your service and the relevant date of commencement of service is as stated above.

3.  **RATE OF PAY**
    You will be paid at the rate of £120 for every working week. No meals or accommodation are included in this payment. This payment will be made weekly in arrears by bank transfer to your bank current account.

4.  **HOURS OF WORK**
    The basic working week will be 40 hours. These basic hours may vary from week to week but will normally be worked over five days in the week between the hours of 8 am and 6 pm. You will not be required to work on Customary or Public Holidays.

5.  **OVERTIME**
    No overtime is payable but extra hours worked can be carried forward as time off in lieu to be added to the basic holidays for the post. Any extra hours worked outside the scope of clause 4 above will be calculated at time and a half for the purposes of working out the relevant time off in lieu.

6.  **ANNUAL HOLIDAYS**
    You are entitled to four weeks paid holiday in each year of employment. The dates should be negotiated with the employer.

7. **PAYMENT DURING SICKNESS**
Such payments will be made in accordance with the current Statutory Sick Pay regulations at the time of the illness.

8. **PENSION SCHEME**
No pension scheme is available and you are advised that it may be in your interest to contact an independent financial adviser in this matter.

9. **HEALTH AND SAFETY**
You have a duty while at work to take reasonable care for the safety of yourself and all others in your place of work who may be affected by your acts or omissions.

10. **TERMINATION**
During the first year of continuous service three weeks' notice of termination must be given by the employer and by the employee. One additional week's notice will be given by the employer and the employee upon completion of each subsequent year of employment up to a maximum of twelve weeks.
The employer reserves the right to pay wages in lieu of notice at their absolute discretion. The above periods of notice may be waived by mutual consent.

11. **DISCIPLINARY RULES**
Dismissal will take place if the standard of work or conduct falls, and after warning remains, below an acceptable level. The following are examples of misconduct, but the list is not intended to be exhaustive:
> Poor timekeeping
> Poor standard of work
> Unauthorised absence.

Summary dismissal without notice will take place if an act of gross misconduct is committed. The following are examples of gross misconduct, but the list is not intended to be exhaustive.
> Theft from the employer
> Forgery or falsification of records
> Any criminal conviction other than Road Traffic Offences
> Misrepresentation
> Physical violence
> Any act which endangers the health or well being of children in your care.

**Fig 2.7 An example of a contract of employment**

## PROVIDE A CONTRACT OF EMPLOYMENT

The Employment Protection Act 1975 provides that an employee who is working more than 16 hours per week should be given a written contract of employment, or a written statement of the particulars of the job, within 13 weeks of starting work. An employee who has worked a minimum of eight hours a week for at least five years is also eligible to receive a contract of employment. The following information should be included:

1 The name and address of the employer.
2 The name and address of the employee.
3 The job title.
4 The date the employment starts.
5 The hours of work.
6 The pay and when payment will be made.
7 Sick pay.
8 Holidays.
9 Pensions.
10 Trade unions.
11 Grievance and disciplinary procedures.
12 Length of notice required by employer and employee.
13 Overtime.

The contract of employment is legally binding. *See* Fig 2.7 for an example of a contract of employment.

---

### ACTIVITY

In groups, draw up a contract of employment based on the one shown in Fig 2.7 for the successful candidate selected in the activity above.

---

## Inducting and training staff

### INDUCTION

Induction is necessary to introduce the employee to his or her peers and supervisor, and to help them to understand what the company is aiming to do. Other vital information such as contract of employment details, map of the organisation, grievance procedures etc. also need to be communicated. Some inductions also provide initial job training. Without a proper induction, new recruits can feel disorientated and out of their depth. High costs of recruitment can be wasted if the 'right' person is lost after a short time in the job as a result of poor induction.

The length of the induction period will depend on the nature of the job and organisation, and, of course, the cost. It is common for induction programmes to contain the following information:

- History of the organisation
- The aims and objectives of the organisation
- Health and safety
- Salaries
- Products and services offered by the firm
- Future plans
- The job of the new recruit
- The department the new recruit will be placed in
- The organisation's structure
- Toilets, refectory and welfare services
- Disciplinary and grievance procedures.

### TRAINING

Training should not be seen as a once and for all activity but as an on-going process. Training is essential to give the employees the opportunity to acquire and develop their skills for their current job but also for their future career development. The dynamism of business means that jobs change too. Training can also highlight people's strengths and weaknesses and can make the employee feel valued and cared for. Training which employees have received can be added to the skills audit. Training can lead to an increase in:

- productivity
- quality of performance
- flexibility in skills of employees
- job satisfaction
- labour retention
- employee morale
- promotion prospects of employees
- safety awareness.

Training needs can be identified based on the deficiencies highlighted in the manpower plan. Needs can also be identified through staff appraisal and through analysis of customer complaints.

Training can be carried out within the organisation itself (in house) or by an outside body. There are many types of training methods which can be used, each of which have advantages and disadvantages, and you probably have

**Table 2.3  Training methods and their uses**

| Method | Uses |
| --- | --- |
| lectures | useful for communicating a bulk of information fairly quickly |
| business games | to give people experience of problem solving and decision making in a fun way |
| case studies | to provide realistic situations for discussion, problem solving and decision making |
| role play | to allow people to experience situations, and learn how people react and why |
| in-tray exercises | useful for learning how to prioritise and use time efficiently |
| interactive video | a system which allows people to benefit from a combination of computer-based information and video pictures in their training. The system will decide what information someone needs and provide it – hence the term 'interactive'. It is a very effective training tool if a lot of people need the same training but it can be very expensive. |
| individual training packages | these can be computerised or printed. They allow individual employees to work through the training at their own pace. |
| coaching | 'sitting next to Nellie' – on-the-job training, with someone showing you what to do, talking you through the stages of the task and supervising you |
| demonstration | useful for showing someone how to operate equipment or to complete documents |

experience of them at your college or in the workplace. Table 2.3 gives some examples of the most common methods, together with examples of when they are most useful.

---

### ACTIVITY

**1** How would you train members of staff to do the following tasks:
**(a)** Serve customers.
**(b)** Deal with customer complaints.
**(c)** Use a computer.
**(d)** Know the fire drill procedure.
**(e)** Use a calculator.
**(f)** Accept a cheque.
**(g)** Accept a credit card payment.
**(h)** Make a Switch transaction.
**(i)** Understand and apply the Sale of Goods Act.
**(j)** Be health and safety conscious.

**2** For each of the following methods identify:
**(a)** circumstances in which it may be used;
**(b)** advantages of the training method;
**(c)** problems which may be encountered in using the training method.

Methods:
- talks
- demonstrations
- role play
- case study
- open learning.

**3** Prepare an induction and training plan for the successful candidate who was selected in the earlier job selection activities (p 66).

**4** Explain how your induction and training plan meets the following organisational objectives:
- To improve customer service.
- To provide a stimulating and caring working environment for staff.

---

The training and development of people has gained in prominence over the past ten years. The recent 'Investors in People' initiative has demonstrated how training is being seen as a key to organisational efficiency and the improvement of quality. Investors in People is an initiative to encourage medium-to-large organisations to train their employees to help develop their skills – in other words to invest money in the people in the business.

No-one can deny that training is an investment – but it is one that costs money and has to be evaluated. It can be difficult to quantify the extra income that is generated in a business as a result of training because some results are not easily quantifiable. Similarly, benefits may not be seen instantly or it may not be possible to pinpoint them to specific training. Certainly some benefits of training are:

- staff feel more confident
- less time is spent correcting errors

- efficiency is increased
- trade is increased
- service to customers is improved
- staff motivation is increased
- staff feel more valuable.

Cost can be a problem. Training costs include not just the direct cost of the training itself but the cost of replacement staff and/or the cost of the work not being done. In addition, replacement staff may not be as efficient as the member of staff who is taking time off for training. It can also be difficult to arrange cost-effective training which suits the specific needs of an individual employee.

Despite the obvious gains to be made from training, it can be tempting for organisations to cut their training budgets in a recession and employees in the training function need to be able to show the cost-effectiveness and benefits of training.

## ACTIVITY

*Billingtons Ltd is feeling the effects of the recession and has decided that it must take action to cut its costs. The directors have decided to make staff in the training department redundant, cutting the training and development budget as a cost-cutting exercise. You work in that department and the training manager has called a meeting of departmental staff in order to prepare a case stating reasons why the training department should not be closed. In addition, she asks that you predict any possible reasons which may be given to explain why the department should close so that she can defend them.*

In small groups play the role of the staff in the training department and prepare your case by completing a table like the one below.

**Roles of the training and development function**

| | |
|---|---|
| 1 | |
| 2 | |
| 3 | |
| 4 | |
| 5 | |

**Advantages of training and development**

| | |
|---|---|
| 1 | |
| 2 | |
| 3 | |
| 4 | |
| 5 | |

**Advantages of having an in-house training and development department**

| | |
|---|---|
| 1 | |
| 2 | |
| 3 | |
| 4 | |
| 5 | |

**Any negative points which could be made**

| | |
|---|---|
| 1 | |
| 2 | |
| 3 | |
| 4 | |
| 5 | |

## Managing, motivating and leading

People who are motivated will work well and will not need to be urged and nagged at in order to perform well. A leader can help to motivate staff or can cause demotivation and indifference within staff. It is the manager's job to provide the right sort of work environment in which employees are motivated rather than demotivated. This is easy to say but can be very difficult to achieve because the culture of the organisation may act against this approach, expecting managers to control by giving orders, shouting loud and punishing failure. In this section we will look at:

- some theories of motivation
- some theories about leadership
- what these theories mean for managers.

### THEORIES OF MOTIVATION

Motivation is when people are 'moved' to do something – they have a motive. Normally, if we say someone is well motivated we mean that they work well and have a good attitude towards their work. Poor motivation in employees can lead to:

- low morale in the workplace
- poor service
- an uncaring attitude
- loss of custom
- loss of profits.

It is, therefore, understandable why employers like to have well-motivated employees. There is, sadly, no magic formula to produce a well-motivated employee but there are several theories of motivation. It is accepted that the design of jobs, selecting the right staff for the job, providing induction, training and appraisal can all help to motivate staff.

There are several theories as to what it is that motivates people. Some of the more well-known theories are those of Taylor, McGregor, Maslow and Hertzberg and these are explained below.

### Taylor

Taylor carried out experiments to see how to get the highest productivity out of workers. He believed that people were only motivated by money and set up the assembly line idea since this was seen as efficient and allowed employees to be paid according to the number of items they produced – *piece work*. Work and method study was introduced to measure and identify the quickest way of doing a task. Taylorism produced very boring jobs and neglected the social environment of the workplace, the benefits of working as teams and of participation.

### McGregor's Theory X and Theory Y

McGregor suggested that there are two types of managers – Theory X managers and Theory Y managers. Each type of manager has different assumptions about people.

Theory X managers assume that employees:

- dislike work
- will avoid work if they are able to
- need to be controlled, directed and threatened in order for them to work well
- like being directed

- want to avoid responsibilities.

Theory Y managers assume that employees:

- can have self direction and self control
- accept and seek responsibility
- are imaginative and creative.

Managers will treat staff differently depending on whether they are Theory X or Theory Y managers. A Theory X manager will direct, control and punish workers to get work out of them while a Theory Y manager will seek participation and involvement from employees.

### Maslow's hierarchy of needs

Maslow devised a hierarchy of needs involving five different types of needs (*see* Fig 2.8). The needs are presented as a hierarchy because Maslow believed that we satisfy lower order needs before higher order needs come into play – for example, we satisfy hunger before social needs. People are motivated by different factors depending on at which stage of the hierarchy they are.

**Fig 2.8 Maslow's Hierarchy of Needs**

In the work situation, consider how each category of needs can be satisfied by completing the activity below.

### ACTIVITY

Identify how each category of need can be satisfied in

the work context. Write your answers in the table below; some ideas have been added to start you off.

| Need | Can be satisfied in the workplace by ... |
|------|------------------------------------------|
| Physiological | (a) money to buy the necessities |
| | (b) breaks from work |
| | (c) |
| Safety and security | (a) health and safety procedures |
| | (b) security of employment |
| | (c) |
| Social | (a) social outings |
| | (b) sports facilities |
| | (c) |
| Self-esteem | (a) promotion |
| | (b) |
| | (c) |
| Self-actualisation | (a) job challenge |
| | (b) |
| | (c) |

Maslow's theory does not always work in practice since some people can be motivated by higher order needs even when their lower order needs have not been satisfied – examples include artists and musicians. However, it generally holds true for the majority of people.

## Hertzberg

Hertzberg's theory states that there are some aspects of work which satisfy people and some which do not – dissatisfiers. Examples of satisfiers and dissatisfiers are given in Table 2.4. The satisfiers motivate employees while the dissatisfiers demotivate and create a negative response. Employers should try to reduce dissatisfiers and increase satisfiers to achieve a well-motivated workforce.

The satisfiers were motivators and the dissatisfiers were known as *hygiene factors* and were concerned with the environment. The hygiene factors did not motivate staff but the absence of them caused dissatisfaction in staff.

---

**ACTIVITY**

**1** Carry out a survey to find out what factors motivate people at work or students on your course and the factors that demotivate them.

**2** What factors motivate/demotivate you?

**3** Do any of the factors resulting from 1 or 2 above relate to any of the theories of motivation outlined above?

---

## THEORIES OF LEADERSHIP

Leadership, an important management role, is necessary for the achievement of the organisation's goals. There are many theories of leadership which try to identify the attributes of a good leader.

---

**ACTIVITY**

Identify a good and a bad leader. What factors make the good leader good and the bad leader bad?

| Good | Bad |
|------|-----|
| 1 | 1 |
| 2 | 2 |
| 3 | 3 |
| 4 | 4 |
| 5 | 5 |
| 6 | 6 |
| 7 | 7 |
| 8 | 8 |
| 9 | 9 |
| 10 | 10 |

---

**Table 2.4   Examples of Hertzberg's satisfiers and dissatisfiers**

| Satisfiers | Dissatisfiers |
|------------|---------------|
| achievement | wages |
| recognition | supervision |
| responsibility | interpersonal relationships |
| advancement | working conditions |
| work satisfaction | policy and administration |

You have probably identified the factors related to the personality of the leader, the behaviour of the leader, and how they can get a group to participate and achieve its objectives. The theories of leadership cover these factors.

## Traits theories

These are theories which relate to the manager's personality – they state that a good leader has certain innate personality characteristics, therefore good leaders are 'born' and someone who is not 'naturally' a leader will never become one.

## Attitude

Managers can have concern for people and/or concern for production. Those who have a high concern for production may neglect their concern for people and vice versa. The people orientated managers, i.e. those who have a high concern for people, will make better leaders.

## Group relations

Group relations theories state that four styles of leadership can be identified:

- authoritative or autocratic
- missionary
- participative
- democratic.

These styles are illustrated in Fig 2.9 along a continuum, with the extreme styles being

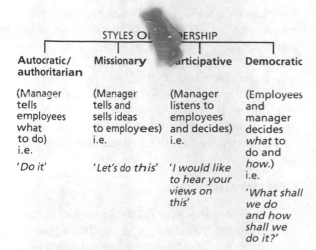

| STYLES OF LEADERSHIP | | | |
|---|---|---|---|
| **Autocratic/ authoritarian** | **Missionary** | **Participative** | **Democratic** |
| (Manager tells employees what to do) i.e. | (Manager tells and sells ideas to employees) i.e. | (Manager listens to employees and decides) i.e. | (Employees and manager decides *what* to do and *how*.) i.e. |
| 'Do it' | 'Let's do this' | 'I would like to hear your views on this' | 'What shall we do and how shall we do it?' |

**Fig 2.9 Styles of leadership**

manager-centred leadership (autocratic) and subordinate-centred leadership (democratic).

## Contingency

The contingency approach would recommend different styles for different situations and people, and propounds the theory that a good leader is one who can select a suitable style and approach which is appropriate for the situation. This means that good leaders are those who can adapt their style to the circumstances in which they find themselves.

---

### ACTIVITY

- What is your leadership style?
- What is the leadership style of managers you know?

---

## WHAT DO THESE THEORIES MEAN FOR MANAGERS?

The theories can give managers an insight into the factors which affect people's motivation and give some useful pointers as to how managers can get the best out of their staff. The following are some examples:

- people are motivated by different things at different times in their personal and career developments
- people like to be involved in making decisions
- leaders can learn how to provide effective leadership
- leaders can adopt different behaviours in different situations
- people like to be involved
- poor working conditions will demotivate staff
- people are motivated by job satisfaction
- people are motivated to satisfy their personal needs
- people have different needs
- people will react to the way in which they are treated by managers.

People like to be consulted and involved. Carry out the following activity to identify areas in which they can be consulted.

---

People tend to be motivated if they are consulted and objectives are negotiated with them. Consultation and negotiation is commonly done through trade unions where they exist – but even where this is the case, negotiation and consultation can also take place at an individual and a group level.

Make a list of what an employer may seek consultation and negotiate about with the following groups of people:

**(a)** The individual employee.
**(b)** Groups of individuals.
**(c)** Unions.

| *individual* | *group* | *union* |
|---|---|---|
| | | |

---

## Planning personal tasks and time efficiently

Time management is the way in which you plan and manage your time. Time is a limited resource and one which we all complain we haven't enough of. The need to use the time resource as efficiently as possible has led to the provision of training to enable staff to manage their time better. Techniques such as prioritising, delegation, co-operation and communication help to improve time management. *Prioritising* means putting tasks into order of importance, with priority being given to the most important or most urgent. *Delegation* is the art of passing some tasks to other people who have the required skills and more available time. *Co-operation* leads to less squabbling and hence less wasted time. Improved *communication* saves time lost through work being duplicated by employees or departments and ensures that individuals are aware of what is required of them.

Individuals have their own personal planning techniques – what are yours? Complete the activity below to identify how you plan and use your time.

Identify how you plan and use your time by completing the following:

*Do you . . .*

- always leave things to the last minute and then panic?            *yes/no*
- prioritise work?            *yes/no*
- do the jobs you like doing first?            *yes/no*
- do the jobs you dislike doing first?            *yes/no*
- write lists of things to do?            *yes/no*

### PRACTICAL TIME MANAGEMENT

The experts recommend the following ways to plan work in order to make the most effective use of your time.

### 1  Set objectives and targets

Clear objectives and targets allow you to focus your attention by giving you specific achievements to aim for. Management by objectives is a method of management which can also improve motivation and communication. Targets can also provide challenges.

### 2  Carry out task analysis

Task analysis is the technique of breaking down a task into its components. This is part of the planning process because it allows you to construct a step-by-step set of smaller tasks which need to be carried out so that nothing is forgotten and there are no broken links in the chain to slow you down. It is also a valuable technique for time management training which will enable employees to organise their time more efficiently.

### 3  Prepare action plans

An action plan lists the tasks to be done and converts them into 'actions'. One needs to plan for action, i.e. set objectives to achieve the necessary tasks – analyse the tasks and plan a timescale.

## 4 Identify critical paths

Most tasks have what are called *critical factors* which if not carried out can curtail progress. The statistical technique known as *critical path analysis* can identify what the critical factors in successful performance of a task or series of tasks are.

## 5 Use planning charts and diagrams

Some people can plan their time better with the aid of planning charts and diagrams. An example of this is a diagram of a critical path. Some people find the production of planning charts and diagrams effective for them because they think more clearly with a visual aid.

## 6 Schedule work effectively

Do the tasks you do not like first, otherwise you will keep putting them off or extend other tasks to avoid doing the unpopular tasks.

## What causes stress and how do people try to reduce stress?

Have you every felt nervous and had butterflies in your stomach? Have you ever had a bad night's sleep because you had something on your mind? Have you ever felt that you couldn't cope? These are effects of stress. Stress affects everyone and people need a certain amount of stress to function effectively. Stress causes adrenalin to be released in the body and the adrenalin keeps us alert – from this point of view a certain amount of stress is good for the body. However, when the level of stress becomes too much for a person to cope with it is unhealthy and causes the body to malfunction. Stress at work may be caused by many things:

- unrealistic deadlines to meet
- problems which we find unable to solve
- disagreements with other staff or a superior
- losing a document
- having too much to do.

Stress can have worrying and damaging effects on people, making them unable to operate. People under high levels of stress have reported feelings of nervousness, vomiting, stomach pains, and feeling that they are on the brink of bursting into tears for no apparent reason.

In order to remain healthy, individuals need to cope with stress and reduce their stress levels if they are becoming unmanageable. Some ways to do this are suggested below.

1 Avoid situations which cause too much stress.
2 Don't take on too much work at once.
3 Learn to say no to unreasonable demands.
4 Plan your time (*see* the above section on planning tasks and using time effectively).
5 Tackle problems as soon as they arise – don't wait until you are unable to cope with them.
6 Allow people to help you.
7 Ask for help if you need it.
8 Do not spend all your time working – relaxation time is vital.
9 Learn to do your job well as this gives you more confidence and reduces errors and complaints.
10 Learn to physically relax tension – there are specific muscular relaxation techniques and concentration techniques which can help people to cope better with stress.
11 Remember that tomorrow is another day; jobs not done today will still be there tomorrow.
12 Be aware of what is causing you stress – when you feel under a lot of stress analyse what is causing it by keeping a note of incidents that have raised your stress level.

If stress becomes a *serious* problem for an individual they will probably need to seek medical help to cope with it. This may also be a good time for the organisation to look at that person's workload and working environment to evaluate whether they have been placing excessive demands on them.

Many organisations have undertaken stress audits to look at what causes stress in their employees and to examine ways in which they could take action to reduce work-related stress. The benefits of doing this are commercial as well as being in the personal interest of their employees:

- Stress causes people to be absent from work and this places more pressure on the other staff, as well as costing the organisation money to replace the member of staff while they are off work.
- If people feel under stress they will not perform their jobs to their full potential and this will damage the performance of the business as a whole.
- People who are under stress will tend to argue more and this will cause a less pleasant working atmosphere. If management do not respond to this situation, it may foster an attitude of 'they don't care about us, so why should we care about them' in the workforce.
- People who are under stress may not handle customers and clients as well as they would normally do and this may have a damaging effect on the image of the organisation.

The levels of stress individuals can cope with vary from person to person and it is not always work which is causing stress in people's lives – they may have financial or health worries which are causing them stress and these are then reflected in their behaviour at work. If this is the case, the organisation will need to look at what support it can offer to help get the person back to peak performance. If the stress is caused by work, there is a good case for looking at the job the person is doing to see whether unreasonable demands are being made on them. If this is the case, steps should be taken to try to alter the job(s) in question so that they are less stressful, enabling the holders of them to perform better.

## Working in teams

Although many individuals are highly creative, teams can be even more creative because of the different ideas, experiences and talents which the various members can bring to a group. *Brainstorming* is a technique used to promote creativity where individuals throw out ideas which stimulate other team members, often resulting in a snowballing of ideas.

## TEAM BUILDING

Much work in organisations is carried out in teams – in fact the employees in a business can be seen as a team. In order to be able to use time efficiently, teams need to operate well. This involves team building – teams do not just 'happen'. Team building involves many factors, for example:

- the selection of the people to be the team members
- decisions about team size
- giving responsibility to others
- accepting responsibility
- accepting ideas from others
- sharing of your own ideas
- accepting that someone else's ideas are more appropriate than yours
- being unselfish
- trusting
- good team leadership with clear direction and stated objectives.

Other practices which can help to build teams are:

1 To allow existing team members to have some say in selecting new members.
2 To select members with a common background. This is why residential activities may be used for team building – you are providing the team members with a shared experience (e.g. Outward Bound management team events). Other types of training can also provide this.

Teams are created by managers to perform certain tasks and team members bring the skills, experiences and personalities needed to do the task in hand.

Within a team people can play different roles – it is suggested that there are seven roles needed for an effective team:

| 1 Chairperson | co-ordinates the activities of the team |
| 2 Shaper | the unofficial chairperson |
| 3 Ideas person | creative person and problem solver |

| 4 | Critic | to highlight problems and monitor progress |
| 5 | Team worker | develops the team |
| 6 | Resource provider | provides contact with the environment |
| 7 | Co-worker | implements the ideas |

This does not suggest that an effective group must have seven people since one person may play more than one role. The make-up of the group will affect the way in which it operates and hence the characters of actual people involved are important. The team is more than a collection of individuals, it is the *interaction* between individuals. A group which is too small can be restricted by shortages of skills, knowledge and talents, whereas a large team takes longer to reach agreement and allows more opportunity for conflict, also restricting progress.

It is not always possible to select team members who are temperamentally compatible but, regardless of whether members like each other or not, the work must still go on. However, people who get on well together are more likely to work well as a team and make more progress than those who do not like each other. All members of a team can help to build the team. Some employers encourage their employees to take part in Outward Bound residential activities in order to help build better teams.

## SPECIALIST AND MULTIDISCIPLINARY TEAMS

Some teams are made up of people of the same specialisation while others are composed of people from a variety of specialisms within the organisation. Whether a specialist team or a multidisciplinary team is formed depends on the purpose the team serves.

When groups are developing it is believed that they experience four stages:

1 Forming
2 Storming
3 Norming
4 Performing

*Forming.* Groups are formed and people get to know one another.

*Storming.* People within the groups will have disagreements as members jockey for position.

*Norming.* Group members set rules for the group and agree on group behaviour norms, that is, accepted behaviour within the group.

*Performing.* When the other three stages have been gone through, the team is ready to perform, to begin to do the tasks set.

This model identifies that there will be disagreements in groups and that group norms will be established. These points are significant because disagreements need to be dealt with effectively and groups must establish their own informal rules as well as formal rules in order to function as a team. People in work often form a part of many different teams – each team will have different group members and each will have different informal group norms.

## Planning, organising and running meetings

People working in teams have meetings in order to carry out tasks such as:

- making decisions
- planning
- analysing tasks to be done
- reporting progress or happenings
- sharing technical expertise
- identifying directions.

Meetings can be informal or formal. Some meetings are statutory, e.g. the Annual General Meeting (AGM), where the chairperson of the company acts as chairperson at the meeting and the company secretary takes the minutes of the meeting. Some meetings are held regularly, others take place once a year and occasionally emergency meetings need to be called to address a particular unforeseen issue (e.g. a takeover bid, a factory fire, a possible business opportunity).

### PLAN AND PREPARE MEETINGS

In order for a meeting to be productive it should have clear aims – what is its purpose and what is to be done during the meeting. To be effective meetings need to have adequate planning, preparation and control. The following checklist may be a useful practical aid in this essential preparation process.

## Checklist for planning and preparing for meetings

1 Consider
   - the aims of the meeting, ensuring that a meeting is the best alternative to fulfil the required aims.
   - the people to be invited – invite only people who can make a useful contribution to the meeting. If too many people attend a meeting it can lose its effectiveness as a working group since individual participation becomes difficult.
   - the time, place, etc.
2 Prepare an agenda. An agenda for a meeting should be agreed, prepared and distributed to all participants well *before* the meeting. The agenda will set out what is to be done at the meeting. You may even ask team members for details of items for the agenda in advance. Figure 2.10 is an example of an agenda.
3 Find out when people are most likely to be able to attend – especially key people.
4 Ensure a suitable room is available and book it in advance.

---

### MANAGEMENT ACTION GROUP

### AGENDA

**for the meeting to be held at 1430 hrs on
Wednesday 16 October 19XX
in the Boardroom**

1    Apologies for absence

2    Minutes of previous meeting

3    Matters arising

4    Hours of work

5    Social Club

6    Any other business

7    Date of next meeting

---

**Fig 2.10 An example of an agenda for a meeting**

5 Inform team members of the meeting and supply them with a copy of the agenda to convey its purpose and the order in which items will be discussed. It is essential for adequate notice of the meeting to be given so that participants can arrange their schedules to enable them to attend. This could be done by memo or by a 'notice of meeting'.

6 Ensure team members have any further relevant documents in advance, allowing them time to read them before the meeting.

7 Ensure team members are informed of any other action to be taken or preparation they need to make before the meeting.

8 To help plan for the smooth running of the meeting, identify who will play the following roles as required: chairperson, secretary, minutes secretary, treasurer. The duties of these roleholders are set out in Table 2.5.

## Disciplinary and grievance procedures

Disagreements and problems always happen – where there are people there are problems. Conflict can arise for all kinds of reasons, e.g. an employee is asked to do something outside their job description which they do not want to do, there may be personality clashes, an employee may be regularly late for work. Organisations have grievance procedures to enable employees to complain about their dissatisfactions at work, while disciplinary procedures allow employers to take action against employees if their actions are unsatisfactory.

### GRIEVANCE PROCEDURES

Grievance procedures allow the employee to raise grievances with the management. Organisations set up grievance procedures in order for employees to air their thoughts and deal with their grievances promptly, so that they will not turn into major disputes. The grievance procedure will normally start by the employee reporting the grievance to their immediate supervisor/manager. A grievance will normally be referred upwards to higher levels of management

**Table 2.5  The duties of roleholders in meetings**

**Chairperson**
- understands purpose of meeting
- agrees draft agenda
- starts the meeting
- introduces items on the agenda
- obtains contributions from participants
- maintains control
- checks minutes after the meeting

**Members**
- read appropriate paper in preparation for the meeting
- attend the meeting
- contribute to decisions
- vote
- take own notes
- read minutes and verify accuracy
- take appropriate action
- report back if necessary

**Secretary/minutes secretary**
(Sometimes the minute secretary is separate from the secretary to divide the workload.)
- drafts documents required for the meeting – agenda, notice
- takes minutes, i.e. records what happened at the meeting. There are two types of minutes – *resolution minutes* and *narrative minutes*. Resolution minutes are a brief record of decisions reached; narrative minutes are a summary of the main discussion points prior to the decisions and record all important information

**Treasurer**
The treasurer looks after the finances

if it cannot be amicably settled at a lower level. The grievance procedure should be known and understood by all employees.

### DISCIPLINARY PROCEDURES

Whereas the grievance procedure is initiated by the employee against the employer, the disciplinary procedure is invoked by the employer against the employee (*see* Fig 2.11).

A disciplinary procedure ensures that an organisation can deal with disciplinary problems fairly by following the rules which are laid down and are clearly understood by everyone. The contract of employment and written statement should either give details of disciplinary rules and procedures or refer the employee to other documents which contain the information. Examples

**Fig 2.11 Disciplinary and grievance procedures**

of when disciplinary action may be taken by the employers include if employees:

- have unacceptable levels of conduct
- maintain poor timekeeping
- have poor performance levels
- breach equal opportunities regulations.

Sometimes the employee's conduct may lead to instant dismissal (dismissal without notice or summary dismissal). This could happen if the employee commits a serious offence such as theft, violence or fraud. Whatever the regulations, the employee should know what offences would result in disciplinary action and those which would be considered as gross misconduct, i.e. offences which are serious enough for the employer to dismiss the employee without notice.

Disciplinary action against an employee normally has four main stages:

1 A formal oral warning.
2 A first written warning.
3 A final written warning.
4 Dismissal.

It is normal practice for an employer to give an employee an informal oral warning before the formal oral warning which begins the disciplinary action and to have an appeals procedure for situations where an employee feels they have been treated unfairly. The employer would be advised to keep records of *all* disciplinary matters.

## How does the employment relationship end?

The employment contract can be ended by the employer or the employee. The employee may decide to leave for a multitude of reasons ranging from personal reasons to a promotion opportunity elsewhere. The employer may end the employment contract through dismissal only if there is sufficient reason for doing so.

Sometimes an employee is dismissed unfairly by an employer – it may be that the manner is unfair and/or the reason for dismissal is unfair. An *unfair manner* is where the method by which the employee is dismissed is unfair or unlawful, e.g. adequate notice has not been given. An *unfair reason* is where the employee is dismissed for a minor offence or for an unlawful reason, i.e. without sufficient reason. Where an employee has been dismissed unfairly he/she can apply to an industrial tribunal. If the employee's claim is upheld, the tribunal could order the employer to pay compensation to the former employee or to reinstate him or her. To avoid dismissing staff unfairly employers should consider the following questions:

- Is there sufficient reason to dismiss the employee?
- Are there any other suitable alternatives to dismissal?
- Have I treated this employee in the same way that other staff are treated?
- Is the reason for dismissal fair?
- Will the manner of dismissal be fair?

One reason for dismissal is redundancy which occurs when the *job* the employee is doing no longer exists. The employer should first consider ways to redeploy the employee, however, if this is not feasible the employer can make the employee redundant. An employee being made redundant is entitled to redundancy pay, and his or her rights are protected by law.

---

### ACTIVITY

Visit an organisation (or use one where you work).

1 Find out their procedures for:

(a) disciplinary actions;
(b) grievance actions;
(c) dismissal;
(d) redundancy.

2 Assume you work in the personnel department of the

organisation you visited and answer the questions asked by each of the people in the case studies below.

## ROBIN
### Job: Purchasing clerk

*My supervisor keeps picking on me for no proper reasons. I have tried to discuss this with her but she won't listen. She just tells me to get on with my work and not to bother her. I feel as if I'm being bullied and there is nothing I can do to defend myself. I want to take this further as I am at the stage when I feel that I want to leave the company, but I am not being pushed around. Is there a grievance procedure and, if so, what is it?*

## JACKIE
### Job: Accounts clerk

*My manager keeps asking me to do extra work which is not in my job description. He says if I don't do it, I'll be down the road. He says anyone can do my job. He expects me to work overtime without extra pay but my contract states that overtime is paid at six pounds per hour. I'm expected to do the work of someone who is off ill as well as my own. I don't mind helping out, but she has now been off for six weeks. Do I have to do all this extra without pay? If I refuse can he just sack me?*

## FRANK
### Job: Customer service

*I have received an oral warning because a customer complained that I was rude to her. I've been told by Mary, who I work with, to watch out because the next offence will mean the sack. Is this true?*

## JIM
### Job: Senior maintenance engineer

*I heard a rumour about redundancies and I am worried that every day will be my last day here. This is on my mind all the time. Am I entitled to advance notice if I am to be made redundant, and will I get any redundancy money? Do I have any other rights or entitlements if I was to be made redundant? I really would hate to be made redundant, as I have been*

*here for 25 years and worked my way up from the bottom. It would be quite difficult for me to find another job at 55.*

## ACTIVITY

### Dear Angie – Can you help?

Angie is the 'agony aunt' on the staff of the local newspaper and has asked you for help in answering the following letters about employment problems. Can you provide her with reasoned answers?

*Dear Angie*
*I work in a large firm as a trainee manager. I am the only female trainee manager in our department and I get paid £10 less than the male trainee managers.*
   *I feel that this is unfair. Is this against the law?*
*Troubled*

*Dear Angie*
*My friend is pregnant and she does not know how much time she is allowed off work, whether she is entitled to pay when she is off, and whether or not she has the right to have her job back after the baby is born.*
   *Can you advise her?*
*Concerned*

*Dear Angie*
*I saw a job advertised in the local paper for a 'Chinese waiter' to work in a traditional Chinese restaurant. I am not Chinese but applied anyway.*
   *Although I am a fully qualified silver service waiter with excellent references I did not even get an interview. When I phoned to ask why I was not short-listed I was told that it was because I'm not Chinese. Surely this is racial discrimination?*
*Angry*

*Dear Angie*
*My friend told me that you can be sacked if you smoke in the office at work. Is this true?*
*Curious*

# BUSINESS SYSTEMS

This unit deals with business systems, or procedures and methods, which help the organisation run smoothly. Business systems are designed to cope with:

- receiving information
- recording and processing information
- communicating information
- storing information securely.

Organisations have systems for communicating within and outside the organisation, for processing information and systems for measuring and improving business performance. Data and information flows into, around, and out of the organisation. Systems and procedures need to be established not only to allow this information to flow and be used by people who need it, but also to try to ensure that all of this happens in an efficient and cost-effective manner. The aims of this unit are to consider ways in which:

- systems differ from one organisation to another
- organisations communicate with people within and external to the organisation
- organisations process and store information
- organisations measure business performance
- organisations improve business performance.

---

## Different organisations require different systems

Each organisation is different – they may produce different products and/or services, they may be different sizes, they may have grown in different ways. Therefore they have their own procedures or systems designed to cope with their own particular demands. For example, a large organisation will have very formal systems with laid down procedures for dealing with everything from a customer complaint to the training of staff. However, compare this with a small butcher's shop – a sole trader – staffed by the owner and a trainee on the Youth Training Scheme.

The small butcher's shop also has systems but its systems will not resemble those of the large organisation. The large organisation has a central filing department; the small butcher's shop has a drawer in a desk, plus some files in a cardboard box. The large organisation has an accounts department with a debtors' section, a creditors' section, an internal audit section and a costings section, staffed by some full-time accountants, an accounts office manager and some trainee accountants. The accounts department is fully equipped with the latest computer hardware and software. The small butcher's shop employs a freelance accountant to prepare the final accounts and has a simple system for dealing with deliveries and paying invoices which is detailed below.

1 The goods are delivered, the owner checks the delivery and signs the delivery note.
2 The delivery note is then placed on a hook in a little office/tea room at the back of the shop.
3 The invoice arrives and is checked against the delivery note.
4 If the delivery note and the invoice tally, they are clipped together.
5 When the final demand arrives the invoice is paid by cheque.
6 The payment is recorded in the cash book.

This system fulfils the same function as that of the large organisation but the system itself differs because of the amount of staff and the volume of work involved. The small butcher's shop has a very simple system because that is all that is required.

The large organisation has an internal mail system to deal with the vast amounts of paperwork being sent around the organisation. It has people to wordprocess letters, and memos are sent to inform people about meetings. The butcher's shop doesn't need an internal mail system; if the owner wishes to give a message to the trainee he just tells her the message – if someone telephones to speak to the trainee and the trainee is on her lunch break, the owner will take a message on a note pad and give it to the trainee when she returns or he will just remember to pass it on verbally if it is a simple message.

Both organisations need to communicate with people outside the organisation. The large business will place orders by completing purchase orders and the butcher's shop has sales representatives visiting it to take orders – the large business has a purchasing department with professional buyers and systems set up for purchasing. The butcher's shop has a visit from the representative who completes the order form personally and asks the butcher to sign it. The large organisation has an internal telephone system and a switchboard, the butcher has one telephone – no internal telephone system is necessary.

## Communicating with people

Ineffective communications can mean that messages can get misinterpreted or not passed on, action may be slow or not taken at all, and a bad image of the organisation can be given to customers. Poor decisions may be taken as a result of incorrect or insufficient information, business opportunities may be lost, deliveries may be made to the wrong locations, and wrong prices quoted to customers. These are just some of the consequences of poor or inefficent communication systems.

Communication systems are needed to ensure staff within an organisation have the necessary information to carry out their jobs. People external to organisations need information too. Carry out the activity below to identify the needs of some people internal and external to the business.

---

**ACTIVITY**

For each party listed below identify:
(a) examples of information needed;
(b) whether they are internal or external to the business.

| Party | Internal/external | Examples of information |
|---|---|---|
| 1  Customers | | |
| 2  Inland Revenue | | |
| 3  Accountant | | |
| 4  Wages clerk | | |
| 5  Computer operator | | |
| 6  Customs and Excise | | |
| 7  Supplier of raw materials | | |
| 8  Stores manager | | |
| 9  Bank | | |
| 10  General public | | |

---

Poor communication can affect staff morale and confidence. Angry customers can cause stress in staff because it is the staff – not machines – who have to sort out the problems and are on the receiving end of the anger of frustrated customers. The case study concerning the lost order below let staff off lightly in that the customer was calm and simply wanted to say 'forget the order'. However, you can easily imagine a more stressful scenario where the customer is very irate and wants to let the company know precisely how she feels. Constantly being on the receiving end in such situations is very demoralising.

## CASE STUDY

### A lost order

**Customer**: *Hello, I am phoning about an order I placed over a month ago.*
**Staff**: *Haven't you received it?*
**Customer**: *No, that's why I'm phoning.*
**Staff**: *What is your name, please?*
**Customer**: *Mrs Harkins*
**Staff**: *When did you place the order Mrs Harkins?*
**Customer**: *About a month ago.*
**Staff**: *Can you tell me what was the order for, please?*
**Customer**: *It was for 5 kettles and 18 teapots.*
**Staff**: *I'm sorry, I can't seem to trace your order, Mrs Harkins.*
**Customer**: *I'm phoning to say forget it anyway. I have had to buy from another supplier as I am losing sales waiting for your delivery....*

Staff need to feel part of the organisation in order to work towards the objectives of the business. Good communications can improve that feeling of involvement and belonging, and foster team spirit and the sense of working together towards a common end.

Communication with staff can be of two types:

- downwards
- upwards.

Managers and supervisors communicate rules, regulations and tasks downwards but upward communication allows staff to provide information to management in order to help them make decisions and improve systems (*see* Fig 3.1). If communication only flows downwards in an organisation the organisation will miss a valuable source of information about the way in which the business operates. The organisation also risks causing resentment and disaffection in the workforce if they feel that their opinions are neither valued nor wanted.

## TYPES OF COMMUNICATION SYSTEM

Communication systems can be classified in several ways.

1 **By audience:**

- internal
- external

2 **By form:**

- face-to-face
- written
- oral
- documentation
- telecommunications
- electronic.

The classifications overlap, for example:

- face-to-face involves oral communication
- written communication may be external communication
- written communication may be external or internal
- Communicating by fax and by telephone can be an example of telecommunications but are also electronic communication
- oral communication could be external or internal communication.

## INTERNAL AND EXTERNAL COMMUNICATION SYSTEMS

Businesses have systems for communicating with staff within the organisation, *internal communication*, and systems for communicating with people outside the organisation, *external communication*. Examples of what might be communicated within and outside the business are given below.

1 **Internal:**
- notice of a meeting
- information at a meeting
- training on the use of a new piece of equipment
- information on costs and sales
- personnel records

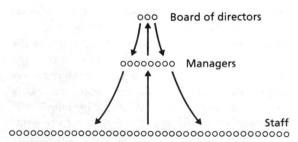

**Fig 3.1 Communication channels – upward and downward**

- holiday rotas
- staff extension numbers

## 2 External:
- to inform the public about the products and services offered by the business
- job advertisements
- invoices sent to customers
- enquiries made to suppliers.

Some information needs to be communicated both externally and internally, for example, employees' national insurance payments, catalogues of products and prices.

To communicate internally organisations use a variety of methods such as: memos, reports, minutes, telephone, face-to-face, documents, directories, catalogues, messages, notices, accident reports, agendas, forms, letters, internal mail (manual and computerised), notice boards, videos and company magazines. For external communications they use: letters, telephones, annual reports, catalogues, advertisements and other methods of sales promotion, Post Office services, fax and face-to-face meetings.

## FACE-TO-FACE COMMUNICATION

Face-to-face communications are used for both internal and external dialogue for example:

### Internal
- a formal meeting of employees to discuss how to implement a new system
- a conversation with a manager to check correct procedures are being used
- an appraisal interview.

### External
- a meeting with a supplier to negotiate price
- giving a sales talk to a customer
- meeting to discuss details of a contract.

Internally, face-to-face communication, can be formal or informal – formal in the sense of meetings with a set agenda or very informally through the 'grapevine' (i.e. through gossip). The grapevine has the advantage of by-passing the formal organisational structure and works on a basis of interpersonal relationships.

Face-to-face communications are used to establish information, discuss progress, solve problems and to socialise in the workplace. The strengths of communicating face-to-face are:

- it is personal
- there is immediate impact
- there is an instant response
- you can see non-verbal signs
- you can often get speedy results
- there is social contact
- you can build up relationships.

Face-to-face communication can be time consuming and inefficient if planning does not take place beforehand, for example, a badly-planned and conducted meeting will waste the valuable time of employees and cause frustration. However, planned and conducted in a professional manner, meetings can prove to be highly productive and satisfying to staff. Sometimes communicating face-to-face can be the most efficient method, both in terms of time and cost. For example, it is more convenient and less costly to ask a question or provide information face-to-face than by any other means if you share an office with the person you wish to communicate with. Complete the activity below by identifying some specific situations when face-to-face discussion would be the most convenient way of communicating.

---

### ACTIVITY

Complete the table below by (a) identifying some specific situations when face-to-face communication would be the best way of communicating and (b) give reasons to support your suggestions. An example has been given to start you off.

| Situation | Reason |
|---|---|
| 1 A supervisor asks a member of staff if they enjoyed the office party yesterday | Personal Sharing the same office |
| 2 | |
| 3 | |
| 4 | |

**ARE YOU**

BORED?   LONELY?

WANT COMPANY?

**THEN WHY NOT HOLD A MEETING??**

R.B.JACKSON

You can talk to people, drink coffee and avoid making decisions.
Sometimes for days ......

**MEETINGS.......**

**THE *PRACTICAL* ALTERNATIVE TO
WORK. YOU KNOW IT MAKES SENSE.**

**Fig 3.2 Meetings ...**

A main weakness of communicating face-to-face is that it can be time consuming. Even asking a simple question of a person can lead to other factors being discussed which may be unimportant and irrelevant to the work situation. Although socialisation at work is important as a motivator, it can also reduce productivity if not controlled. Another problem may be caused by the fact that there is more opportunity for conflict to arise due to disagreements. This can create bad feeling and be destructive, although disagreements may be beneficial if they enable members of staff to see each other's points of view. Non-verbal communications projected may be positive or negative – positive signals can be comforting and encouraging while negative signals can cause discomfort. The power of non-verbal communication cannot be underestimated – your voice may be saying one thing and your body language can be saying something else. Try the activity below to demonstrate this.

---
### ACTIVITY
---

**Tell tale body language**

Look at each of the sketches in Fig 3.3 and read the caption underneath. Does the body language

*That's very interesting...*

*I'm sure we can sort this out...*

*Oh, I am sorry, we'll all miss you...*

*Of course I'm interested*

**Fig 3.3 Body language**

match the message being conveyed in the caption?

## WRITTEN COMMUNICATION

Written communications include: memos, letters, reports, minutes, notices, agendas, advertisements, job descriptions, contracts of employment, catalogues, price lists, and other forms and documents.

Written communications can be used for external or internal purposes. For some examples of external and internal written communications, see Table 3.1.

Written communications should be clear, simple, accurate and to the point. If possible they should be typed or wordprocessed to make them easier to read and give them a business-like appearance. Before you start writing, collect together the information you need – the facts/figures/dates/references etc. Use the standard layout and organisational style if one exists, in order to project the company image. Always ensure a memo, letter or report is well presented and reads correctly before it is sent. Memos, letters and reports should all have a beginning to give the communication a context, a middle giving the message and/or information, and an ending to sum up, make requests or to close the

**Table 3.1  Examples of external and internal written communications**

| External | Internal |
| --- | --- |
| letters of complaint | agenda |
| letters requesting payment | reports |
| letters of enquiry | letters of appointment |
| public notices | notices of meetings |
| advertisements | minutes |
| publicity material | staff bulletins |
| catalogues | catalogues |
| price lists | price lists |
| letters of confirmation | memos |

correspondence. Always check your spelling and read the document before sending it – you may find it useful to let someone else read it since it can be difficult to spot your own mistakes. A computer spell-checker may be useful to identify spelling errors but their use is limited since a spellchecker will only pick up incorrect spellings, not incorrect use of words. Additional programs, known as stylecheckers, will analyse your writing style and correct grammatical errors but there is no substitute for careful, critical reading by an individual.

## WRITING MEMOS

A memo is used to communicate within the organisation (i.e. internal). Memos should be short and to the point without including any unnecessary information. An example of a memo is given in Fig. 3.4 which communicates the following information:

- the name and department of the person the memo is for
- the name and department of the person who is sending the memo
- date
- subject

You will notice that the memo is not signed, although some people will 'top and tail' memos within a section or department by writing in the name of the person to whom it is addressed at the top and signing or initialling at the bottom. Although this is acceptable in a fairly informal situation, it would not be appropriate in a formal memo, say to the Chief Executive.

### ACTIVITY

Your manager Mr Clark, the Purchasing Officer, asks you to write a memo to Mr Brown who is the Administration Officer. The memo is to invite him to a meeting to discuss the purchase of some new software. The meeting is to be held in the boardroom one week today at 10.45am. The meeting is expected to last for one hour. An agenda will be attached to the memo.

1 Write the memo from Mr Clark.

2 Check your memo against the following checklist.

**Checklist**

*Have you...*

| | |
| --- | --- |
| **1** identified the name and department of the person the memo is for? | Yes/No |
| **2** identified the name and department of the person who is sending the memo? | Yes/No |
| **3** put today's date on the memo? | Yes/No |
| **4** identified the subject? | Yes/No |
| **5** signed the memo? | Yes/No |
| **6** used clear, simple language? | Yes/No |
| **7** put all the facts accurately into the memo | Yes/No |
| **8** kept the memo brief and to the point? | Yes/No |
| **9** typed or wordprocessed it? | Yes/No |
| **10** used a suitable layout? | Yes/No |

You should have answered Yes to all of these questions except 5 – there is no need to sign a memo.

## WRITING LETTERS

Like memos, letters should be to the point without including any unnecessary information. Letters are sometimes used to communicate with people inside the organisations, for example, to inform an employee that they have been successful in an interview, or as a formal written warning in the disciplinary procedure. However, letters are generally used to communicate with people external to the organisation. For example they can be used to:

- make enquiries and request information
- confirm appointments, bookings or facts
- complain
- provide information.

```
┌─────────────────────────────────────────────────────────┐
│                                                         │
│                     MEMORANDUM                          │
│                                                         │
│   From:    Jill Fisher                                  │
│            (Training Manager)                           │
│                                                         │
│   To:      Amanda Jones              Date:    15/7/XX   │
│            (Accounts Office Supervisor)                 │
│                                                         │
│                                                         │
│   Subject:  Supervisory training                        │
│                                                         │
│                                                         │
│   The next training session for supervisory staff will │
│   be held on 18 August at 9.30 to 11.00 a.m., and will  │
│   be concerned with leadership skills.                  │
│                                                         │
│   I have reserved a place for you but would be grateful │
│   if you could confirm whether or not you will be       │
│   attending.                                            │
│                                                         │
│   I will need your reply for the end of the month.      │
│                                                         │
│                                                         │
└─────────────────────────────────────────────────────────┘
```

**Fig 3.4 An example of a memo**

Business letters are written on the organisation's headed notepaper and should be written in the organisational style. Letters which are clear, accurate and well presented project a good image of the organisation. Letters should have:

- *Addresses* – of the sender and the receiver
- *Reference* – to enable the letter to be identified
- *Date* – to show when the letter was written
- *Salutation* – to show who the letter is to, e.g. Dear Mr, Dear Mrs, Dear Ms, Dear Sir/Madam, Dear John .

- *Subject* – to show what the letter is referring to at a glance
- *Complimentary close* – to identify who is sending the letter, e.g. Yours faithfully . . . Mr Robinson; Yours sincerely . . . Mark Simms
- *Signature* – of the sender.

If any documents are enclosed with the letter 'Enc' is shown at the bottom of the letter to bring the enclosures to the attention of the recipient. Fig 3.5 is an example of a letter with the above points identified.

2001 FASHION BOUTIQUE

16-18 Wellbank Road
Preston
Lancashire
L62 5PW

— Address of sender

Reference R1/TH ◄——————————————— Reference

Mrs Norma Thomas
12 Willow Trees Ave ◄——————————————— Address of
Preston                                                    receiver
Lancashire

Dear Mrs Thomas, ◄——————————————— Salutation

Collection of Dress ◄——————————————— Subject

I would like to inform you that your dress has been
repaired and is ready for collection.

May I also take this opportunity to enclose our latest
catalogue and two tickets for our fashion show which
will be held on Thursday 24th of this month. We do hope
you can attend as we have many exciting new styles
being displayed.

Yours sincerely ◄——————————————— Complimentary
                                                              close
*Jenny Rafters* ◄——————————————— Signature of
                                                              sender

Jenny Rafters
Manageress

**Fig 3.5  A sample business letter**

## WRITING REPORTS

A report is a document in which a problem or issue is examined in some detail. Information is conveyed, findings are reported, and ideas are suggested and recommendations are made as to the most effective solution or course of action. Reports, like letters and memos, should be accurate, concise and clear. Reports can be formal or informal. Formal reports are written in the third person, which means that the writer does not use 'I'. For example, instead of writing 'I investigated' one would write 'it was investigated' when writing in the third person. Informal report writing allows the use of 'I' – the personal pronoun.

---

### ACTIVITY

Write the following statements in the third person.

**1** 'I was asked to find out about suitable software packages by Ms Crompton.'

**2** 'I found out that there were five suitable packages.'

**3** 'I found the information by reading computer journals and by visiting suppliers.'

**4** 'I think that the one which best fits our needs is model XFT 54.'

**5** 'I discussed the cost of the equipment with my manager.'

---

### Layout of a formal report

It is usual for formal reports to have:

1 A *title page* giving the title, date and writer.
2 A *contents page* to identify where information can be found in the report.
3 An *introduction* setting out the terms of reference, the purpose of the report, who requested the report, who was to prepare the report, the date and any constraints.
4 A section on *procedure*, explaining how the writer went about carrying out the research and tasks.
5 A section on *findings*, giving details of what the writer found out from the research.
6 *Conclusions*, giving a summary of the findings.
7 *Recommendations* of the action to be taken.
8 *Appendices*, giving details of figures, tables and charts.
9 *References* which list any books and other reference materials the authors have used in compiling the report. (*See* Fig 3.6.)

## FORMS AND DOCUMENTS

Forms and documents are a means of written communication, for example, invoices, credit notes, delivery notes, statements, application forms, petty cash vouchers. Forms and documents can be part of both the internal and external communication system, for example:

- *Internal* – invoices tell the organisation how much is owed by individual customers and are used for accounting purposes e.g. records and auditing.
- *External* – invoices are a means of informing customers how much they owe and the terms of payment available.

Some forms and documents are mainly for internal purposes, for example, some personnel record forms, petty cash vouchers, stores requisitions, application forms, time sheets. However, if problems arose which caused external bodies to become involved in the business situation the documents could be made available to the outside body, e.g. if an applicant claimed unlawful discrimination in a job interview, application forms would be available for scrutiny. The main advantages of using well designed forms and documents are that they are:

- in writing
- clearly identified
- clearly set out
- specific to the business requirements
- able to be stored for future reference.

### Documents for recording business transactions

Organisations order, purchase, sell and pay for products and services. These buying and selling transactions can result in the following documentation being sent between the buying and

# Staff Training Needs

**1.0**   **Terms of Reference:**

On the 1st of March the office manager requested the training officer to conduct a survey in order to identify current training needs in the general office.

The report is to be submitted by 19th March.

**2.0**   **Procedure:**

The process below was followed in identifying the required information for the compilation of the report:

2.1   An analysis of the staff's current responsibilities was made by reference to job descriptions on file and supplemented by interview in certain cases.

2.2   The mix of skills required for the jobs currently carried out in the office were identified and confirmed by discussion with supervisors and line management of the staff concerned.

2.3   The current skill mix of staff in the office was ascertained by reference to personnel records and supplemented by interview with staff and supervisors.

2.4   The gaps between the desirable mix of skills in the office and the current mix of skills possessed by the staff in the office was identified from the above analyses.

2.5   The skills gap was discussed with staff and supervisors to confirm that the areas isolated were genuine training needs for the office.

**3.0**   **Findings:**

The findings were as follows:

3.1   Skills gaps exist in the area of customer contact and customer care training with few staff having received any formal training in these areas. Where training has been received this is now dated and the staff would welcome the opportunity to refresh this knowledge. An allied area of training required is in the field of telephone skills.

3.2     Discussions with staff indicated that they felt there to be a need for further training on the organisation's product range in fabrics and the recommendations for care of them as these form many of the queries addressed to the office staff by the public.

**4.0**          **Conclusions:**

The training needs of the staff in the section fall into the categories mentioned above and could mostly be provided via in house training if time is made available to the staff concerned. In the area of telephone skills the employment of specialist trainers should be considered.

**Signed:**    *J. Tattersall.*

**Date:**      *16th March.*

**Fig 3.6 An example of a short formal report**

supplying organisations. (Figure 3.7 illustrates the flow of business documents between the buyer and the seller.)

- *Stock requisitions* – a document detailing stock to be purchased by the purchasing department
- *Letter of enquiry* – a letter from the buyer to the seller requesting information concerning products and prices
- *Quotation* – sent by the seller to the buyer to give details of prices.
- *Purchase order* – a document giving details of an order placed by the buying organisation
- *Advice note* – a document sent to the buyer to advise them of what will be delivered
- *Delivery note* – a document specifying what is being delivered to the buying organisation
- *Invoice* – a document requesting payment
- *Credit note* – a document stating the amount owed by the selling firm to the buying firm (in the event of a short order or returned damaged goods etc.)
- *Debit note* – a document stating additional payment owed by the buying organisation
- *Statement* – a document showing the purchases and payments made and the amount owed

**Other documents**

There are many other documents used by the business to record and communicate information, for example personnel records, travel expense claim forms, insurance forms, VAT returns, petty cash forms, overtime claims, contracts of employment.

Like other methods of communication there are costs involved in communicating using forms

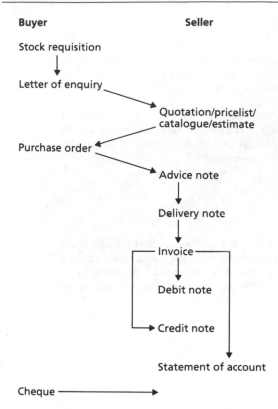

**Buyer**

Stock requisition

Letter of enquiry

**Seller**

Quotation/pricelist/catalogue/estimate

Purchase order

Advice note

Delivery note

Invoice

Debit note

Credit note

Statement of account

Cheque

**Fig 3.7 The flow of business documents between the buyer and the seller**

and documents. Some examples of these costs are design, purchase, printing, completion, checking, and possibly postage costs.

Although the use of documents can be beneficial, in that a record of the information is provided in writing which can be stored and accessed for reference, their completion and processing can be time consuming. Staff may complain about having too much paperwork to deal with and badly designed forms, which may be difficult to complete, add to staff problems.

## TELECOMMUNICATIONS

Some examples of telecommunications are listed below.

● *Telephone* – Communication by telephone can be fast, efficient and effective. It is more personal than using memos but less personal

than talking face-to-face. The telephone is used for internal and external communications and is convenient since you don't need to be in an office to use it.

● *Telephone services* – There are a wide variety of services available to individuals and organisations, such as directory enquiries, freephone, phonecards, credit card and information services.

● *Radio paging* – This can be used for staff who can be difficult to contact or need to be located quickly. Some pagers now have a message facility, enabling a short message to be displayed on a screen on the pager. This often helps save on time spent calling back into the office.

● *Answering machines* – These machines allow callers to leave recorded messages if the person they wish to speak to is unavailable. However, some people do not like leaving messages on answering machines and many feel it is impersonal.

● *Audio-conferencing* – This is a service which links people in different cities by telephone and enables groups of people to be involved rather than the normal two. This facility can save the time and the expense of travelling long distances to join in a group discussion or conference.

● *Confertel* – This is a service which links people by telephone, similar to audio-conferencing but allowing an *international* meeting to take place by telephone.

● *Prestel* – Prestel is a viewdata system which links a computer to information sources by telephone line. Goods and services can be purchased using the system and a variety of information sources accessed.

● *Teletext* – Information services provided by television. Information can be provided for potential customers on many subjects or issues such as roadblocks, travel, news, weather, sport.

● *Fax* – This is a facility which enables a perfect facsimile of a document to be sent and received within seconds. A document is scanned on a transmitter, information is encoded and sent down a telephone line; the message is decoded and printed out by a fax machine at the receiving end. Fax can be easy to use, inexpensive and fast.

● *Telemessages* – This is an electronic letter service. Telemessages may be sent using the telephone, telex or by computer.

## ELECTRONIC SYSTEMS OF COMMUNICATION

**Internal telephone systems** are found in both large and small organisations to aid the communication process. It saves having to go and find someone personally and allows communication between sites. Many large organisations will have extremely sophisticated switchboard systems which will allow them to connect internal conference calls, trace staff around different extensions and automatically send an unanswered call to another extension. Such systems will often also allow firms to monitor call costs and prevent certain types of calls (international calls or calls to commercial information lines) to be barred from certain extension numbers.

**PA (public announcement) systems** are used when a member of staff needs to be located, e.g. they are popular in supermarkets where staff are often very mobile. An announcement is made asking the person who is being addressed to report to a particular place.

**Paging systems** (*see* above section, Telecommunications).

**Radio telephones** are used in vehicles or on large sites so that employees can be contacted and can make contact with other people if the need arises. For example, if they were held up in traffic and were going to be late for a meeting, they could telephone ahead and inform people of the problem.

**Cellular phone systems** can be used to call into the conventional telephone network from a mobile phone. The systems are more expensive to run than a normal telephone but the cost of them is falling and different firms are now offering different levels of service. So, someone who wants a phone for emergencies only could opt to pay a low rental but a high cost per call. A regular user would probably prefer a lower cost per call at the expense of a higher rental. These phones operate wherever you are.

Another type of phone which has recently become available is the Rabbit system which will work anywhere within range of a base station for the system. This means that they are not quite as portable as a cellular phone but the call costs are a lot cheaper and they still give a lot of flexibility to the users of them.

All of these systems are intended to improve business communications and help the personnel of the businesses to stay in touch with each other more easily.

### Electronic mail

Telex is a form of electronic mail. Messages are typed into a telex machine by the sender, and transmitted via the telephone network to a receiving telex machine where they are printed out. Computers can be used to transmit electronic mail, with messages being sent and received through electronic mail boxes. Privately owned fax machines are also becoming increasingly popular examples of electronic mail.

Some advantages of electronic mail are speed, storage, and access to information. Some disadvantages can be security, cost of equipment and services, and the cost of training personnel to use the new technology.

*EPOS* (Electronic Point of Sale) is a valuable communication system. EPOS systems can create efficiency at the point of sale and can store and process valuable information about sales, stock levels, peak times, etc. which can aid management and planning decisions.

---

### ACTIVITY

Read the situations below and:

**1** identify which methods of communication should be used;

**2** explain the reasons for your choice.

Write your answers in the space provided, and discuss and compare your answers with other students.

(a) You want to find the telephone extension of Mr Correy in the finance office and your internal directory has gone astray.
Method(s):
Reason(s):

(b) You need to book a room for a meeting.
Method(s):
Reason(s):

(c) You want a record of what happened at a meeting.
Method(s):
Reason(s):

(d) You are to give a formal warning to a member of staff for being continuously late for work.
Method(s):
Reason(s):

(e) You need to inform employees from various departments about a meeting.
Method(s):
Reason(s):

(f) You need to check if an order has arrived.
Method(s):
Reason(s):

(g) You need to talk to an employee about the poor standard of their work.
Method(s):
Reason(s):

(h) You need to inform a buyer of the cost of their recent order.
Method(s):
Reason(s):

---

## Using communication systems effectively

Whatever methods or systems of communication are used in the organisation they need to be used effectively in order to achieve business objectives.

To illustrate this, consider the following example.

---

### EXAMPLE

*Let us assume that one objective of a business is to have a high level of customer service. A customer telephones to find out some information regarding the price of a product and this is what happens:*

*Salesperson picks up the telephone.*

**Sales staff:** *Hello.*
**Customer:** *Is that Printex Ltd?*
**Sales staff:** *Yes.*
**Customer:** *Can you tell me the price you charge for receipt books, please?*

*The salesperson leans over to find the required information and cuts the customer off. The customer rings back.*

**Sales staff:** *Hello.*
**Customer:** *Is that Printex Ltd?*
**Sales staff:** *Yes.*
**Customer:** *I phoned a few minutes ago and we seemed to have been cut off. I would like to know the price you charge for receipt books.*
**Sales staff:** *Someone has gone off with the price list and I can't remember. Hold the line and I'll go and find out.*

*Customer waits for ages and then puts down the phone and tries another firm.*

---

In this example the communication system was not effective in achieving the business goal of delivering a high level of customer service on several counts:

- the telephone manner of the salesperson was poor
- the customer was cut off
- the customer was kept waiting too long
- the customer was not given the required information.

## USING COMMUNICATION SYSTEMS EFFECTIVELY TO ACHIEVE BUSINESS GOALS

We have illustrated how poor and ineffective use of the communication system will not contribute to the achievement of an organisation's goals. Effective communication involves training staff to use equipment correctly and to communicate effectively, both in writing and orally. Some examples of good practice when using communication systems are given below. There are also spaces for you to add some of your own ideas.

## Telephone

- Answer promptly.
- Have information at hand.
- Prepare before you make a call.
- Be polite.
- Speak clearly.
- Use the appropriate organisational style, e.g. 'Binnotte Ltd, Jonathan speaking, How may I help you?'
- Identify the caller and use their name when speaking to them.

Add some of your
own ideas.

## Fax

- Have a clear master copy.
- Make a photocopy of the master and use the photocopy for the fax transmission.
- Avoid using red and grey.
- Train staff to use the fax machine.

Add some of your
own ideas.

## Face-to-face

- Prepare for meetings in advance.
- Watch body language.
- Be attentive.
- Listen carefully.
- Put forward your views.

Add some of your
own ideas.

## Computers

- Make back-up files.

- Ensure staff are trained in the use of computers and IT.

Add some of your
own ideas.

## Written communications

- Write carefully using clear and direct language.
- Do not make them longer than is necessary.
- Use the organisational style and layout.
- Prepare and send them out in good time.
- Read them carefully before sending them out.

Add some of your
own ideas.

## WHICH SYSTEM TO USE

When deciding which method of communication to use you should consider fitness for purpose, costs, perceptions and security. The systems used in an organisation will depend on the major activity in which the business is involved, i.e. it has to be fit for its purpose. For example:

- A hotel will have systems for bookings, and calculating and taking payments. Manual or computerised systems may be used to carry out these tasks.
- A restaurant will have similar systems to a hotel but the booking systems will be simpler than those needed for hotel bookings.
- A grocery shop will have systems for recording sales but not for making or confirming bookings.
- A travel agent will use Prestel for finding out availability of flights and holidays, a butcher's shop will not need Prestel facilities.
- A college will have systems for enrolling students – a newsagent will not.
- A foreign company selling property in Spain to customers in the UK will communicate with their clients by letter or telephone rather than face-to-face.

The communication system or method used must be suitable in other respects, for example speed may be important in a communication, or a written record of a transaction may be necessary.

## Costs

There are several different types of costs involved in setting up and operating communication systems in an organisation. Some of these costs are:

- *Capital costs*: This is the cost of the equipment or system – the capital investment required.
- *Installation costs*: This is the cost of installing the equipment or system and will include training.
- *Running costs*: This is the cost of operating the equipment or system once it is up and running.

## Perceptions of the user

People have their personal ideas and opinions about different methods of communication. If people perceive the internal mail to be slow or suspect that correspondence may get lost, they will only use it when they have no other choice. Fax is seen as important and is usually dealt with promptly.

## Security

Some methods of communication are more secure than others. For example, a confidential memo to a member of staff should not be sent in the open internal mail without being put in an envelope. Security can be a problem when using computers but operators handling sensitive files may use a password which is needed to gain access to confidential information.

---

# Information processing systems

## INFORMATION SYSTEMS

Organisations deal with a great deal of information every day. Information is essential to enable the organisation to function. Managers make decisions and these decisions are based on information – facts and figures. Information is collected and processed in order to:

- obtain information
- extract relevant information
- distribute to people who need the information
- manipulate data
- present information in different ways
- store information and allow access to it.

Many organisations have both manual and computerised information systems.

## INFORMATION PROCESSING

### What?

Information processing is the activity of ordering and collating the data which has been collected. Some of the operations which can be performed using this data are:

- *Making comparisons* – e.g. between sales of different products, monthly or annual sales figures, production costs, output achieved.
- *Transferring data* – e.g. onto documents such as invoices, statements, into reports, memos or letters.
- *Sorting data* – putting data into categories, e.g. sales achieved by different members of staff, sorting costs into different categories.

### Why?

Information is processed in order to provide it in a form which will be useful to managers who must make decisions based on fact.

### How?

Information can be processed using different methods – computerised methods and manual. Some computerised methods are wordprocessing, databases, spreadsheets, programmes to help decision making e.g. linear programming, critical path analyses, computer-aided design, graphics packages. Some manual methods are making calculations, completing documents manually.

**1** Use a computer to produce the following information in the form of (a) a pie chart and (b) a bar chart.

**2** Explain why these forms of visual presentation can be helpful to some staff in analysing the figures.

|  | Sept | Oct | Nov | Dec | Jan |
|---|---|---|---|---|---|
| Sales (£000 units) | 56 | 26 | 35 | 68 | 180 |

## INFORMATION DISTRIBUTION

### What?

People both within and external to the organisation need information and therefore the information they require needs to be distributed to them.

### Why?

Some examples of why information needs to be distributed to people include to:

- keep them informed of decisions
- give them information about meetings
- update their records
- allow them to make decisions based on the information.

### How?

Some ways in which information can be distributed are by: hand, computer, telephone, face-to-face meeting, fax. Delivery by hand can be time consuming but does not require expensive machinery. Computers can be efficient but costly in terms of capital and installation, running and training costs. Face-to-face and telephone communication is personal but is not recorded on paper.

What information is needed by each of the people listed below? Complete the table.

| Personnel | Information required |
|---|---|
| Wages clerk | 1 |
|  | 2 |
|  | 3 |
| Accountant | 1 |
|  | 2 |
|  | 3 |
| Sales manager | 1 |
|  | 2 |
|  | 3 |
| Salesperson | 1 |
|  | 2 |
|  | 3 |
| Personnel officer | 1 |
|  | 2 |
|  | 3 |
| Training officer | 1 |
|  | 2 |
|  | 3 |
| Office clerk | 1 |
|  | 2 |
|  | 3 |

## INFORMATION STORAGE

### What?

Information is stored in a filing system.

### Why?

Some information will need to be accessed at some time in the future in order to solve problems and help make decisions. A filing system allows information to be stored so it is safe and easy to locate when needed.

### How?

Information may be stored on computer or in manual filing systems or both. Manual systems include equipment such as filing cabinets and files. Documents can be filed in alphabetical, geographical, numerical, chronological or subject order. Using a computer, information can be stored on hard disk in the computer itself, or on separate 'floppy' disks, or both. It is also essential to store the information on a back-up disk.

## ACTIVITY

Give examples of information that would be filed in:

**(a)** alphabetical order;

**(b)** geographical order;

**(c)** numerical order;

**(d)** chronological order;

**(e)** subject order.

## CHOOSING AN INFORMATION PROCESSING SYSTEM

The selection of an information processing system will depend on a number of factors – the amount of work required, the speed at which the work needs to be carried out, the costs, etc. The costs involved include initial capital investment in equipment, running costs, maintenance costs, training and retraining costs.

## THE EFFECTS OF NEW TECHNOLOGY ON INFORMATION PROCESSING

The growth of computerised systems in business has been rapid over the last five years and it is no longer unusual to find even small businesses using computerised systems. Table 3.2 identifies some of the effects of new technology.

**Table 3.2   Some effects of the introduction of new technology**

| | |
|---|---|
| • speed | information can be processed and accessed quickly |
| • accuracy | complex calculations can be made accurately |
| • cost effective | the very rapid growth of new technology illustrates that businesses find it cost effective |
| • stressful | people can find learning to use the equipment stressful. It can also be stressful if information is lost, or cannot be accessed. |
| • harmful to health | VDUs can damage eyes and may harm unborn children |
| • access to information | information can be accessed quickly from many sources |

## ACTIVITY

1 Interview people who use new technology and find out:

**(a)** the type of new technology used;
**(b)** for what purpose it is used; and
**(c)** the effects of its introduction.

2 Record your findings in the table below and compare your answers with those of other students. Add your own personal experiences to your list.

| Types of new technology | Purpose/use | Effect of its introduction |
|---|---|---|
| | | |

# Measuring business performance

Organisations need to monitor and measure performance of the business in order to establish how well the business as a whole, or aspects of it, are progressing. Organisations have systems for measuring and recording the performance of the business which include:

- financial and accounts systems
- targets for production and sales
- reports
- performance reviews
- customer service
- performance appraisal.

## FINANCE AND ACCOUNTS SYSTEMS

These systems are covered in Unit 5, Financial information systems, which deals with the recording and monitoring systems, budgeting and financial ratios which allow business performance to be measured.

It is essential for a business to keep financial records so that performance can be measured, i.e. so that questions such as 'how well is the business doing?' and 'are we meeting our targets?' can be answered.

Financial ratios involve the comparison of one figure with another and the analysis of the ratios tells you how the business is performing. Present performance can be compared with past and projected performance for the future. Analysis of the ratios can highlight areas of the business in which action should be taken. The figures required to calculate the ratios are found in the financial records which are kept by the business. Some of the most common ratios are given below but organisations can develop a number of ratios depending on what they see as useful and relevant to their particular operation.

1 *Gross profit margin*. This is gross profit expressed as a percentage of the organisation's sales. The gross profit margin for a business can be compared with the average for the same type of firm. It can also be compared with previous years' figures.
2 *Net profit margin*. Net profit is expressed as a percentage of the organisation's sales. Calculating the net profit margin will highlight significant increases in overheads.
3 *Stock turnover*. A business needs to have sufficient levels of stocks to operate. High levels of stock can mean that customers' needs can be satisfied immediately, but money is tied up in unsold stocks. If a business's stock turnover increases in comparison to the previous year, it is improving in efficiency.
4 *Breakeven sales*. The breakeven point is an important calculation because it tells you when sales revenue covers costs. Calculating breakeven sales allows comparison with actual or forecasted levels of sales. Monitoring forecasted and actual sales against breakeven sales allows you to be aware of potential problems if, for example, the forecasted or actual sales are too close to the breakeven sales level.
5 *Average credit given*. This allows you to compare how long it is taking to collect debts when a comparison is made from one year to another.
6 *Average credit taken*. This allows you to compare how long the business is taking to pay debts when a comparison is made from one year to another.

## How to calculate the ratios

1 Gross profit margin =
$$\frac{Sales - Cost\ of\ sales}{Sales} \times 100$$

2 Net profit margin =
$$\frac{Sales - Total\ costs}{Sales} \times 100$$

3 Stock turnover =
$$\frac{Stock}{Total\ purchases\ for\ the\ year} \times 365$$

4 Breakeven sales $= \dfrac{overheads}{gross\ profit\ margin}$

5 Average credit given =
$$\frac{Debtors}{Total\ credit\ sales\ for\ the\ year} \times 365$$

6 Average credit taken =
$$\frac{Creditors}{Total\ credit\ purchases\ during\ the\ year} \times 365$$

## SETTING AND MONITORING TARGETS FOR PRODUCTION AND SALES

Many organisations set targets for production and sales staff and the performance of the staff can then be measured by comparing the targets with the actual sales or production figures. The targets set are sometimes negotiated with the employees although in some organisations they are set by management without the involvement of the employees purely on the basis of production or sales figures from previous years. Three types of operating systems can be identified in an organisation – machines, labour and materials. Productivity can be measured for each.

1 **Machines:**
● output per machine-hour
● percentage of time used
● capacity used
● idle time.

2 **Labour:**
● output per man-hour
● idle time.

3 **Materials:**
- quantity converted from raw materials
- wastage
- percentage reworked.

4 **Use of equipment:**
- amount of time equipment is used
- cost per hour used.

5 **Wastage:**
- levels of scrap and wastage
- changes in wastage and scrap levels.

## REPORTS

These can take a variety of forms. Departments within an organisation are often required to produce reports on their performance for management. The report is a means of recording performance and allows actual performance to be measured against set objectives. Companies produce annual reports for shareholders to communicate the measured performance of the company over the period of a year.

---
### ACTIVITY
---

Look at a company's annual report and identify:

(a) How well the company has done in the past year.

(b) How this performance has compared with past years.

## REVIEWING PERFORMANCE

Performance is reviewed by comparing actual performance against the planned performance, identifying the strengths and weaknesses of the business and identifying changes which are likely to affect the business.

## CUSTOMER SERVICE

Business performance can be measured by the extent to which the product or service matches the needs of the customer. Some dimensions of customer service which can be measured are:

- design
- performance
- price

- additional expenses, e.g. installation costs
- delay or waiting time
- duration of product life.

---
### ACTIVITY
---

1 Read the case study below.

2 Map the performance onto the table provided.

*'I was going to a disco. No-one could drive me there, I didn't have transport and it was raining, so I called for a taxi. When the taxi arrived it was an old banger which didn't look very safe. However, since I had waited ages for it to arrive and was already late for my date, I got in. I tried to fasten the seat belt but it didn't work. The driver was very reckless – he had to brake suddenly and I fell against the door and ripped my stockings. Eventually we arrived at the disco. It had taken ages – twice as long to get there as would be normal. When it came to the bill he charged me a fortune, double what I have paid in the past. . . .'*

| Dimension | Rating | | | | |
|---|---|---|---|---|---|
| | High | | | | Low |
| Design | 5 | 4 | 3 | 2 | 1 |
| Performance | 5 | 4 | 3 | 2 | 1 |
| Price | 5 | 4 | 3 | 2 | 1 |
| Additional expenses | 5 | 4 | 3 | 2 | 1 |
| Delay or waiting time | 5 | 4 | 3 | 2 | 1 |
| Duration | 5 | 4 | 3 | 2 | 1 |

Organisations collect information about customer perceptions of the products and services offered through marketing research techniques, *see* Unit 7, Marketing and business performance.

## APPRAISING THE PERFORMANCE OF EMPLOYEES

Performance appraisal involves:

1 Making an assessment or judgement of employee performance.
2 Making an assessment or judgement of employee potential.
3 Making an assessment of the development/ training needs of the employee.
4 Recording the assessment of 1, 2, and 3 above.

The performance of a business depends to a great extent on the performance of the people who work in it. It is the *people* who make the system work and give customers and suppliers their image of the business. So, it is important to make sure that people are able to perform at their best and one of the main ways in which a business can help their staff to perform well is through performance appraisal. The following section will look at performance appraisal in some depth. It will cover the benefits of performance appraisal, its problems, and the systems used.

## What are the benefits of performance appraisal?

Performance appraisal can benefit both the employer and the employee. Let us look at an example to illustrate some of these potential benefits.

---
### EXAMPLE
---

*The following is the transcription of part of an appraisal interview. Gilly is the manager and Oliver the employee.*

*Gilly: Hello Oliver. You have come for your appraisal interview. Do sit down.*
*Oliver: Thank you.*
*Gilly: How are you today? Is your ankle better?*
*Oliver: Yes, thanks. I had the plaster off last week. It's still a bit weak but it's a lot better. At least I can walk on it now.*
*Gilly: I know it's a year since your last appraisal so I'll just remind you of what it's all about. In this interview we will reflect on and discuss what you have done and how well you have done these things over the last year. We will also discuss your future prospects, training and development and I will produce a report of the interview for you to check and sign to show that you are in agreement with it. So shall we start?*
*Oliver: Yes, of course, Gilly.*
*Gilly: Last week I asked you to write down your achievements against the targets which we discussed last year. I asked you to bring this to the interview.*
*Oliver: Yes I have it here. I have met most of my targets – I have learned how to use the wordprocessor and I am now quite fast. I meet the deadlines set, I have learned the filing system and I answer the telephone too.*
*Gilly: That's very good, Oliver. I have had good reports about your work and I know you have worked hard to learn to operate the wordprocessor and the filing*

*system, and your telephone skills have developed tremendously. Are you pleased with these achievements?*
*Oliver: Yes, very much so.*
*Gilly: I know that in general you do your job very well, but are there any areas in which you feel you need more training in order to do better?*
*Oliver: I don't think so.*
*Gilly: Reports about your work are very good, however, I have had a few complaints from other departments that you have been rude to some members of staff.*
*Oliver: I can think of two occasions when I may have come across as short tempered. One was where Mr Lyons phoned to ask for some information from the database. Ross was on lunch and I tried to access the information myself. I got into a real panic and when I returned to the phone Mr Lyons was not happy about waiting so long and not getting the information he wanted. There was no-one in the office to help me. He wasn't happy and said I was useless. I got cross and I wasn't very polite in return.*
*Gilly: I see. Do you know how to use the database now?*
*Oliver: No, although I still get people phoning while Ross is on lunch. But now I just ask them to phone back later.*
*Gilly: I think it would be a good idea for you to learn how to use the database. What do you think?*
*Oliver: I would be able to help with the queries and wouldn't feel so silly. So, yes.*
*Gilly: That's fine then, I will ask Ross if he could give you some training when the office is quiet. What happened on this second occasion when you said you were impolite?*
*Oliver: Mrs Taylor shouted at me for coming in late one day. But I had had a dreadful morning. It was snowing and my train was cancelled. Then when I eventually got to work Mrs Taylor went mad at me, in front of everyone – she couldn't care about how I felt. She is quite often nasty to me. I think she doesn't like me. Anyway I wasn't polite to her in return. Normally I just accept her rudeness but she caught me on a bad morning.*
*Gilly: You said Mrs Taylor is often nasty to you. Do you want to take some action on this through the company's grievance procedure?*
*Oliver: Yes, I think so. She is making my life a bit of a misery really, and I enjoy my work very much.*
*Gilly: Do you think you handled the situations with Mr Lyons and Mrs Taylor in a businesslike manner, Oliver?*
*Oliver: I suppose not.*
*Gilly: What did you do that was unbusinesslike?*
*Oliver: In both cases I got angry and shouted rudely.*
*Gilly: You know this is not acceptable, Oliver. You need to keep calm in situations like this. You may feel*

*threatened and uncomfortable but the answer to the problem is not to fight anger with anger. What would you do if situations like these arise again?*
*Oliver: I will keep calm and explain the situation.*
*Gilly: That's fine then. That will be one of your targets for you to achieve before your next appraisal. Is there anything else we can do to help you with your job?*
*Oliver: No, everything else is fine, but I am hoping to become a supervisor some day. What do I have to do to become one?*
*Gilly: You need some experience and training for supervisory work. Perhaps you could find out if your local college runs courses for supervisors? From this end, perhaps you might like to supervise and help to train the new trainee who will be starting work in this office next month.*
*Oliver: Yes, I would like to do that and I will find out about supervisory courses at College. There is one more point, I am quite good at designing things and some of our clients find it difficult to complete forms S452 and F647. I wonder if you would let me re-design them to make them easier for people to complete?*
*Gilly: We would be grateful if you would. Can we just sum up this interview now and I will complete your report. Your achievements have been.... Your targets are....*

This interview illustrates some of the benefits of performance appraisal. Gilly and Oliver have identified:

- Oliver's achievements at work
- Oliver's strengths and weaknesses
- how to improve Oliver's job performance
- how to use Oliver's strengths for the benefit of the organisation
- problems which affect Oliver, discussed his side of the story and decided how to deal with them
- that Oliver wants to be a supervisor and what action he could take to help him achieve this
- training which Oliver would benefit from
- unacceptable behaviour
- new targets to meet.

All of these benefits will help to increase Oliver's motivation and also strengthen his working relationship with Gilly. Oliver will also feel important to the organisation because his needs are being met and the organisation is taking the

trouble to communicate with him and offer help. He has also received feedback from Gilly on how he is doing.

## What can go wrong with performance appraisal?

Performance appraisal can have negative effects on performance if carried out badly. What would be the effect if Oliver's appraisal interview had been handled badly?

---

### EXAMPLE

*Gilly:   You have come for your appraisal interview. Sit down.*
*Oliver:   Thank you.*
*Gilly:   I know it's a year since your last appraisal so I'll just remind you of what it's all about. In this interview we will reflect on and discuss what you have done and how well you have done these things over the last year. I will produce a report of the interview. I have had complaints from other departments that you have been rude to some members of staff. You know this is not good enough. You can take this as an oral warning.*
*Oliver:   It only happened twice.*
*Gilly:   If it happens again you will get your first written warning....*

---

This interview would have very negative effects on Oliver; he would not be feeling good in any way. Complete the activity below to identify what went wrong with this second appraisal and its possible effects on Oliver's performance.

---

### ACTIVITY

Complete the chart below by identifying what went wrong, how Oliver would feel as a result of the interview, and what effect this may have on Oliver's performance.

*What went wrong?*

1

2

3

*How would Oliver feel now?*

1 _____

2 _____

3 _____

*What may happen to Oliver's future performance?*

1 _____

2 _____

3 _____

## Performance appraisal systems

There are many types of performance appraisal systems designed to measure performance. Some of the more common examples used in organisations are:

- the interview/review appraisal
- rating/ranking methods
- management by objectives (MBO)
- critical incidents.

## Interview/review appraisal

This is the performance appraisal method which was used by Oliver and Gilly in the case study above. It is sometimes known as a progress interview and is used periodically to assess employee performance. If it is used badly it can be very subjective (and therefore ineffective) because it is possible for a manager and an employee to see the same situation differently. Read the following example to illustrate this.

---
### EXAMPLE
---

*This is what the employee and employer are thinking prior to the interview:*

*Employee's thoughts: It has been a difficult year for me. People have been off sick and there have been so many changes to cope with. I'm quite proud to have survived the year and met most targets and deadlines. Of course,*

*I have had to learn about prioritising work. I have had so much to do I have been too tired to go out and have had virtually no social life – but I have enjoyed the challenges at work.*

*Manager's thoughts: Her work standard is slipping – I have not had some information I have requested on time and I have noticed that some other tasks have not been given the priority they deserve. She seems to be complacent and lax about things and often looks tired. I think she must be spending a lot of time at discos.*

The manager and employee had completely different thoughts about the same situation. The manager thought the employee's standard of work was slipping, she was not meeting deadlines and was not giving some areas of work the priority they deserve. He had decided that she must be spending a lot of time at discos because she was tired. The employee felt that she had done very well in a difficult situation and the job had challenged her. You can imagine that if the appraisal interview was handled badly in this case the employee could become very angry.

---
### ACTIVITY
---

1 In pairs, role play an appraisal interview with one person acting out the role of the manager and the other the employee. First role play how *not* to carry out the appraisal, then in a second one, act out how to carry out the interview *properly*.

2 Analyse each role play by answering the following:
(a) What happened?
(b) What effect did this have on (i) the manager (ii) the employee?
(c) What effect might this have on the organisation?

---

Because the appraisal interview alone can be very subjective, further appraisal methods (described below) are often used in conjunction with the interview.

## Rating/ranking methods

**Rating** involves the use of rating scales where the employee is assessed on quality and quantity of work, and personal factors such as motivation, appearance and initiative. The assessment is given a rating on a scale (*see* Table 3.3).

**Table 3.3**

| Dimension | Rating | | | | |
|---|---|---|---|---|---|
| | High | | | | Low |
| motivation | 5 | 4 | 3 | 2 | 1 |
| appearance | 5 | 4 | 3 | 2 | 1 |
| initiative | 5 | 4 | 3 | 2 | 1 |

If you look again at the rating scale in Table 3.3 you will see that it has an odd number of points on the scale. When this happens the manager may be tempted to circle the midpoint, thus avoiding the decision as to whether the employee has a high or low score. Some organisations use rating scales which have an even number of points on the scale to force managers to make a decision as to whether performance or personal factors are satisfactory or unsatisfactory.

**Ranking** involves managers ranking employees from the best to the worst on various dimensions.

## Management by objectives (MBO)

Management by objectives involves the manager discussing and setting targets for the employee to aim to achieve and then the employee's performance is assessed by whether or not the objectives have been met. It is usual practice for the manager and the employee to negotiate these targets. MBO is often used when appraising the performance of employees in management positions.

## Critical incidents

A critical incident is an occurrence (the *incident*) which happens during an employee's working life and which stands out (is important or *critical*). Notes of critical incidents are made throughout the year and provide the basis of information for the appraisal interview. However this method, like the appraisal interview itself, can be problematic. Carry out the activity below to illustrate this.

The employee is Mohammed and the manager is Ayo. Below are the critical incidents recorded by Ayo.

(a) Read Ayo's records.
(b) What conclusion might Ayo have about Mohammed's performance and behaviour as a result of the critical incidents recorded?
(c) Now read the section entitled 'This is Mohammed'.
(d) Identify the problems with using critical incidents as the basis for performance appraisal.

### Ayo's records

| Date | Incident |
|---|---|
| 15/1 | Customer complained that Mohammed was rude. |
| 28/3 | Mohammed couldn't find the files of a very important client. |
| 4/6 | Mohammed was late for work. This was one of the busiest days we have had. |
| 8/8 | Mohammed went home feeling sick. |
| 16/8 | Customer complained that Mohammed was rude. |

### This is Mohammed

'My job involves working in the office doing clerical duties and working on the reception. I like my job very much indeed and most of the time the job goes smoothly. I like the challenge of working on the reception. We often get difficult customers and, to be honest, the rest of the staff can't deal with them. I think it is a bit of a challenge and I seem to have a nice manner with them, calm them down and help to sort out the problem. I've only had a few occasions when I have not been able to calm down an angry customer.

I like to keep the paperwork in order. Some of the staff remove files without using the correct procedures and often put files in the wrong place or documents in the wrong files. I spend any slack time sorting this out and trying to trace missing files. I know it isn't really part of my duties but I don't mind as it saves embarrassing situations like the one I was in at the end of March when I couldn't find the file of a very important client. Ayo, the boss, was really angry. I am rarely off work and I am hardly ever late. . . .'

## IMPROVING PRODUCTIVITY, EFFICIENCY AND CUSTOMER SERVICE THROUGH APPRAISAL

Whatever type of appraisal systems an organisation uses, if operated effectively, it can improve productivity, efficiency and customer service by:

- identifying training needs of staff
- identifying targets
- reviewing progress
- identifying barriers to progress
- identifying improvements to work systems
- identifying employees' needs and goals
- motivating employees
- encouraging communication between managers and employees.

## Improving business performance

Businesses always seek to improve performance; some ways in which they may do this are by:

- maximising efficiency
- making staff multi-skilled
- incentive schemes
- using teamwork
- quality assurance systems
- improving customer service.

## MAXIMISING EFFICIENCY

Business performance can be improved by improving efficiency. One example of efficiency maximisation is to enable people to be more efficient in their jobs by providing training so that they are able to work well and without making many mistakes. Training will enable staff to use equipment correctly, to find information quickly and to make efficient use of their time. Staffing levels can also help to maximise the efficiency of the business (as demonstrated in Unit 2, People in Business). Efficiency can also be maximised through effective use of communication systems.

## MULTI-SKILLING

Some organisations are encouraging their staff to undertake training so that they become 'multi-skilled'. Multi-skilling training programmes give staff the opportunity to train to do jobs other than the ones for which they were initially employed. This not only gives staff more skills, which keeps them employable, but also enables the organisation to improve performance because staff can be used more effectively and flexibly, thus saving time and money.

## INCENTIVE SCHEMES

Incentive schemes take several forms. They can range from staff being paid according to the number of items they produce or sell, to having an employee of the year or salesperson of the year award whereby staff who receive such accolades are rewarded with prizes.

## TEAMWORK

Teamwork can help to improve business performance provided the team operates effectively (see Unit 2 for an examination of team building). Some of these benefits are listed below.

### Commitment

- Belonging to a team can foster commitment to the group and to the tasks being undertaken.
- People will not want to 'let the side down' and can have increased motivation through a sense of belonging and the fact that other people depend on them to carry out their job effectively.
- Through working together, people have shared experiences which can bond people together. This in turn creates commitment to the team.

### Responsibility

- Individuals are responsible to the team which can put pressure on individuals to perform.
- Teams can rely less on supervisors and managers and become responsible for managing their own tasks and solving their own problems.
- People can play various roles and take on responsibilities corresponding to their skills.

## Co-operation

- In a good team, members will co-operate with each other in order to get tasks done.
- The group provides a socially-acceptable environment where motivation and co-operation can flourish.
- The co-operation of people within a team can mean that more can be achieved by the individuals working in a group than if they were working separately.

## Support

- Team members provide support to each other, giving help where it is needed. Members of a team are able to provide both practical assistance and moral support when it is needed.

## Multi-skills

- The more people the more skills – teamwork can provide a pool of skills which the team can draw upon as required. This will enable people to do what they are good at but also to provide training for each other so that they can learn from each other too.

## Innovation

- The mix of skills and the snowballing of ideas can produce innovative ideas.
- Within a group environment, change can be made easier because of the group support provided.
- The risk element can be removed for individuals – risk, like responsibility, rests on the team as a whole.
- Teams can develop a variety of solutions to a problem and change can be more successful as a result. There are more people to identify potential problems and put forward solutions should problems arise during the process of change.

## Quality

- Work produced by a team can be of a higher quality because of the mix of skills which can be brought together.

- All the other benefits mentioned above will increase the quality of work produced.

### ACTIVITY

Consider teams you have worked in which operated well. Identify if the benefits listed below were evident and, if so, give examples of how each of the benefits was exhibited. Record your answers in the table below and compare them with those of other students.

| Benefits | Evident (Yes/No) | Examples |
|---|---|---|
| Commitment | yes | we all worked late one night to finish an order |
| Responsibility | | |
| Co-operation | | |
| Support | | |
| Multi-skills | | |
| Quality | | |

## QUALITY ASSURANCE SYSTEMS

Many organisations have quality assurance systems which can improve business performance because they can improve the quality of products and services, which may increase sales and produce satisfied customers. Quality assurance is covered in Unit 7, Marketing and business performance.

Quality control systems are designed to reduce the number of errors. They involve setting a standard against which to measure performance by, for example, observing and timing tasks over a period of time, obtaining estimates from managers and staff, using time sheets to record activity. The performance of individuals can then be measured against the set standard by inspecting work tasks carried out, sampling, records of work done. Performance can be measured against both the quantity and the quality of work produced by staff. Quality of output can be checked by random sampling, partial checking or by 100 per cent checking. Random checking involves a sample of work being checked from beginning to end, partial checking is checking the most important parts of the work and not all of it, 100 per cent checking involves checking all the work. The system selected for checking will depend on what is being checked, staff available to check, and the cost of carrying out a check. For example legal documents and financial documents are often checked 100 per cent by staff within the firm. Quality can be checked by teams, individuals or by machines. The causes of errors can be identified in order to eliminate them.

## IMPROVING CUSTOMER SERVICE

Good customer service can improve sales and repeat business. This in turn will increase turnover and enhance the reputation of the organisation. Good customer service is a key factor to improving business performance since it helps to gain new customers and keep existing customers loyal.

# BUSINESS ENVIRONMENT

The 1990s have so far been characterised by change – the break up of the Union of Soviet Socialist Republics, the introduction of democracy throughout eastern Europe, the partial re-integration of South Africa into the world economy, the reunification of Germany, further development of the European Community (EC) and the move towards returning Hong Kong back to Chinese sovereignty. Each of these changes, and many more, signify the breaking up of old orders, and the shifting of political and, significantly, economic alliances. Countries are becoming, increasingly, economically inter-dependent and an economic decision made in one country now has important implications for all others. It is against this background that we will examine the business environment of the UK while concentrating on the changes that have taken place, and are predicted to take place, in the national economy.

This unit will assess the impact that some of the above changes have had on the UK economy. In particular we will examine:

- the structure of British industry
- the role of government in the UK economy
- the UK's international role.

## Introduction – making economic decisions

Every day economic decisions are made by businesses, households and governments which, by nature, are similar. Governments and businesses are not in the enviable position of having unlimited resources any more than individuals are and must therefore make choices as to what to do with the resources at their disposal.

Ultimately, however, there are only three key decisions to be made:

- What to produce
- How to produce
- For whom to produce.

### WHAT TO PRODUCE

Since we have insufficient resources to produce everything, we have to make a choice – do we have more of good X or more of good Y? This really is the central problem of any economic system, i.e. the allocation of scarce resources to try to meet a maximum number of wants. Many resources in the world are scarce – raw materials such as hardwoods and metallic ores – and many are predicted to run out in the future, some in the next decade. Many species of both plants and animals are also dying out. Yet, all the while, an increasing world population is making increasing demands upon the world's scarce resources.

---

### ACTIVITY

This short piece of research will enable you to examine the problem of scarce resources.

Draw up a Time Chart for the next 100 years and indicate on the chart the date when a range of plants, animals and resources that you select are predicted to be extinct or used up. (Information to help you complete this exercise may be obtained from Friends of the Earth, the Green Party or any of the other environmental pressure groups.)

---

By making a choice to produce or purchase one thing, other things will have to be forgone – we can't have all the holidays, houses, cars, hospitals, hi-fis, schools, etc. that we want. This problem will not be unusual to you in your own budgeting: choosing a new car may mean going without a summer holiday, having a meal out may mean not buying a new dress. This problem of choice also faces businesses and governments:

- expanding the Army may mean cutting back on hospital building
- building ten miles of motorway may mean cutting the rail electrification programme
- giving aid to Somalia may mean ending student grants.

This cost, measured in terms of what you must give up in order to get something else, is called the *opportunity cost*.

---

### ACTIVITY

Listed below are several recent decisions made by the UK Government. In groups of three, decide what you think the opportunity cost of those decisions may have been and present your findings to the remainder of your group.

- To support UN action against Iraq – the Gulf War.
- To spend £20m on the Manchester Olympic bid.
- To cut direct taxes.
- To produce the new European fighter plane.
- To give a Stamp Duty holiday on house purchases.
- To develop City Technology Colleges.

---

## HOW TO PRODUCE

Once we have decided what to produce we have to decide how to produce it, i.e. the method of production. Do we produce with a lot of labour and few machines (labour intensive) or with little labour and lots of machines and capital equipment (capital intensive)? There are a number of factors which affect this decision:

- the state of industrialisation
- the level of demand for the product
- the level and cost of manpower
- the level and cost of machines
- the policies of both businesses and governments.

There is no 'correct solution' to this question except that which is acceptable to a particular

economy. Once again, however, we can look at the opportunity cost of using one particular method of production by looking at the alternatives those resources could have produced. Rover cars have just opened a new production line in the Midlands that will move productivity in the British car industry nearer to that of the Japanese. This highly automated production line will, however, require less workers. What will be the loss in output within the country and the cost of paying benefit to the redundant workers?

It has been estimated that the cost of keeping one worker unemployed for a year is in the region of £8500. It could, therefore, be argued that as long as the subsidy paid to industry is less than £8500 then industry should be supported by government money in order to maintain employment. The other cost to bear in mind is the effect that the redundancies will have on the local and national economies. The fact that workers are not receiving wages will hit other businesses, local shops and pubs. This multiplier effect obviously worsens the effects of any major redundancies in an area. The local authority could also suffer because when a business closes it ceases to pay the Unified Business Rate so the income the local authority receives from this source will decrease. Similarly, the amount of Income Tax being paid to central government will fall.

---

### ACTIVITY

In groups of three look at the following scenarios and make decisions about the 'best' way to produce. Present your findings to the rest of the group and justify your choice.

(a) You need to produce cigarettes in a low wage economy, where unemployment is high and there is little foreign currency available to purchase capital equipment.

(b) You need to produce cigarettes in a medium wage economy where it is estimated that demand will be low.

(c) You need to produce cigarettes for the UK market.

(d) You wish to produce silicon chips and the production method requires both a large amount of capital equipment and a large cheap labour force. What would you do?

## FOR WHOM TO PRODUCE

If you think that making decisions about what and how to produce are difficult then the decision as to whom to produce for is even more tricky.

In any economy, when the goods and services have been produced a decision must be made as to how the goods and services are to be allocated? The question which follows on from this is: how is the income from production to be allocated? These decisions are largely ethical and political ones, and will vary from country to country and from political system to political system.

---

### ACTIVITY

**1** Construct a table that shows three countries: USA, UK and Russia. Show on the table whether the following decisions are likely to be made by the State or by private individuals who require the goods or service:

- the supply of school places
- the provision of medical care
- the services of an orchestra
- the provision of insurance
- the provision of a telephone network
- the supply of electricity
- the supply of airline flights.

**2** When you have completed your table and discussed your findings with the rest of the group, decide what two main conclusions you can draw from the information.

---

Goods and services can be purchased in one economy and may attract no subsidy or tax benefit while in another economy they may be allocated by the State, according to an agreed political principle. Income from production in the form of wages, salaries and perhaps profits may also be allocated on the basis of how much effort individuals have expended or on how much risk they have taken with capital investment. Alternatively, income may be allocated by a State organisation. These allocation decisions will be looked at more closely in the next section.

---

## Economic systems

All economies are faced with the problem of scarcity and have to tackle the questions of what,

how much and for whom to produce. In any country some sort of economic system must make these decisions, according to a set of economic or political principles. In isolated communities in the Amazon forest economic decisions will have to be made which are similar in nature to those that must be made in China or in the USA. Generally speaking the economic systems that make these decisions can be classified as:

- market economies
- command economies
- mixed economies.

## THE MARKET ECONOMY SYSTEM

This is the system which dominates in western economies and is based on the premise that people are relatively free to buy the goods they want with their incomes. It is also sometimes called the *price system*, as it is the price that allocates resources. To see how it works, we will examine some examples.

The development of compact disc players was one of the major developments in the music industry in the late 1980s. The sale of these hi-tech CD players has generated a massive increase in demand for compact discs and, conversely, a fall in demand for both traditional records (vinyls) and cassettes. Producers of CD-related goods will find that the demand for their products increases and that, in order to maximise their profits, they will be able to charge high prices. At the other end of the scale, sellers and producers of records will see a reduction in demand for their product and they may well have to reduce prices. Ultimately they may have to stop production of records and either go out of business or produce different goods.

The system also applies to agricultural products. In California a disease is threatening to wipe out vineyards which may ultimately reduce the supply of wine and lead to a shortage in shops. Producers and wine merchants will respond by putting up prices. This may lead to producers in other countries deciding to increase production. The initial rise in price may also cause some consumers to switch from wine drinking to beer drinking and if beer producers think that this is a long-term change in demand, they also may decide to increase production. All these decisions have been influenced by either a change in production or a change in demand for a product, which has caused a change in price.

It is this movement in the price of goods and services that rations output, balances supply and demand, and therefore controls the economy. This system is perhaps shown more clearly in a diagram (*see* Fig 4.1).

---

### ACTIVITY

Draw up market decision trees based on the following scenarios:

(a) Acid house parties are regulated by local authorities, leading to a reduction in the number of parties.
(b) More students want university places.
(c) Large scale unemployment in the UK leads to a major fall in the demand for new cars.
(d) High interest rates lead to falling house prices.
(e) A higher birth rate affects the demand for prams.

---

## ADVANTAGES OF THE MARKET SYSTEM

The market system, therefore, consists of firms trying to make the largest possible profit and individuals trying to get the best deal they can from their incomes. This system has many advantages:

● gives freedom of choice
● encourages innovation
● ensures quality
● rewards efficiency.

### Freedom of choice

If people want CDs rather than records, that's what they get; if they want cheap goods rather than quality goods, that's what they get. The choice is firmly in the hands of the consumer.

### Encourages innovation

The system also encourages innovation as firms which develop new products will initially be able

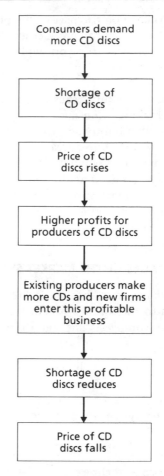

**Fig 4.1 Market system decision tree – CD disks**

to sell at a high price and earn large profits, e.g. the original price of CDs was much higher before a number of firms started competing.

### Ensures quality

The market system should also ensure quality. Most firms now want to build customer loyalty so that the consumer will come back again and again. They can do that by ensuring they produce quality goods – it is easy to sell an inferior good once but much more difficult to get repeat business.

### Rewards efficiency

As price is the decisive factor in the market

system, efficiency on the part of the producer is also rewarded. If you can produce at a lower cost than your competitors, you will be able to increase your profits.

The market system thus relies on consumers and producers making thousands of rational decisions about what to buy and what to produce. It requires no massive bureaucracy to support it; it is very flexible and responds quickly to change. Its supporters argue that the market system is based upon consumer sovereignty and that there is an 'invisible hand' guiding the economy – the hand of the consumer.

## DISADVANTAGES OF THE MARKET SYSTEM

While we have seen that there are significant advantages to the market system there are also certain disadvantages. The main disadvantages are:

- freedom of choice is limited
- lack of market knowledge
- lack of protection for labour
- the market system takes no account of social costs.

### Lack of freedom of choice

Many people link freedom of choice and the market system with democracy. Others would argue that the market system only gives freedom of choice to those with money. Someone living on state benefits, for example, has almost no choice in comparison to a millionaire who will have almost unlimited choice.

### Lack of market knowledge

Choice, of course, is also based upon a thorough knowledge of all the competing options. This knowledge, termed perfect knowledge by economists, rarely exists in practice. When you buy a new car, for example, do you compare all the technical specifications of competing models or do you rely upon recommendations from friends or secondary information from car magazines?

Choice is also limited in another way. Businesses spend millions of pounds on advertising which will be linked to a major marketing and planned production campaign. The marketing of CDs has, in effect, created a market where initially no market existed. Producers carefully target their marketing campaigns, possibly over a long period of time, to influence consumer choice. It would perhaps be wrong for us, therefore, to rely totally on the idea of consumer sovereignty when the markets can be manipulated so effectively by big businesses.

### Lack of protection for labour

Another disadvantage should be obvious from our market system decision tree. If the demand for a product falls, the labour required to produce that product will no longer be required. It is often argued that the market system can lead to high levels of unemployment which may require government intervention.

In recent years the coal industry has shed thousands of jobs because of increased competition from other sources of power generation and from cheaper coal imports, and it has been argued that the government should have intervened to protect the coal industry. Future problems may also arise if the prices of foreign coal and/or other energy sources rise and the UK coal industry is unable to expand to meet an increasing demand. Sometimes government intervention may be required to smooth out changes in price over the long-term – market systems are notorious for responding to short-term rather than long-term requirements.

### Social costs and the market economy

If a business focuses its interest on maximising profit, it may achieve this aim by incurring costs for society in general. For example, there has been much criticism of the Brazilian Government for allowing the widespread depletion of the tropical rain forest. For the individual companies involved, high short-term profits can be made by cutting hardwoods and exporting them to the western world. When these companies' profits are assessed, no account is taken of the revenue that will have to be spent by other governments to counteract the effects of the depletion of the ozone layer that major de-forestation may contribute to. This is referred to as an *externality* and occurs when the activities of a business or individual affect third parties. Another example of an externality is the cost of collecting litter generated by take-away food shops.

Externalities can be both positive and negative. De-forestation and the litter generated by fast food shops are negative externalities. Positive externalities could arise if, for example, a security guard was employed by one business on an industrial estate; the guard's presence would also deter burglars from breaking into adjoining premises, but these neighbouring businesses would not be paying for the benefit received.

---

### ACTIVITY

Draw up a list of activities of local companies that generate externalities. Alongside each item detail how you could pass this cost back to the individual company, i.e. make the polluter pay.

---

One very specific criticism of the market system is that it is not able to supply *public goods*. Public goods have three characteristics:

- non-rivalry in consumption
- non-excludability
- impossibility of rejection.

*Non-rivalness* means that a good being supplied to one individual can be supplied to others at no extra cost – if one person watches television, for example, it does not prevent other people from watching it. The second feature, *non-excludability*, means that you cannot deprive an individual of a public good even if they refuse to pay for it. For example, even if a person refuses to pay local taxes and pays no income tax, they can still make use of public roads and use the services of the police if necessary. This also applies to the third characteristic, the *impossibility of rejection*. Individuals are unable to reject the services of the armed forces – they defend 'the nation', irrespective of personal choice.

As everyone in the community is entitled to and cannot reject a public good then they must each consume an equivalent amount. However, if left to the market public goods would either be paid for very unequally or would not exist at all, so they are best provided centrally by the State.

The distinction between private and public goods is not always clear, particularly in the areas of education and health. These could, perhaps, be classified as semi-public goods. Some people would argue that many more goods and services, like education and health, could be provided through the market system which is an issue we will examine in a later section.

## THE COMMAND ECONOMY

A command economy is one in which decisions about resource allocation and especially production levels are made by a centralised body rather than through the price mechanism. It is called a command economy or planned economy because economic decisions are taken by central authorities who are responsible for planning the whole economy. In this system consumers get, and firms produce, goods and services based on decisions from a central body who take an overview of the economy as a whole. In most systems these comprehensive targets are stated in a series of national five year or ten year plans, from which individual targets are set for specific goods and services, and for each unit of production (i.e. factory, farm, hospital, etc.). A manager in a factory would be directed, therefore, to produce a set number of tractors, or tons of steel, while the managers of huge collective farms would be set targets in terms of tons of potatoes or cubic metres of softwood. In principle the system is simple: the government decides the priorities and sets the targets, and if these are accomplished the plan is successful. In practice, however, targets are subject to negotiation by factory and farm managers in the light of changing circumstances.

### Advantages of a command economy

A planned economy can have substantial benefits. Consider the sporting achievements of former East Germany, a relatively small and poor country which produced so many world class athletes and sports teams. This success arose from the fact that sporting excellence was a valued part of the plan and so resources were used to enable young people with sporting potential to receive high quality training. If the priorities of the people are the same as the planners then resources can be allocated to meet those needs. In the former USSR, priority was given to providing public transport, housing, foodstuffs, education, healthcare and so on.

Command economy systems can also operate very effectively on a relatively short-term basis in times of national emergency. In the UK during the Second World War the government commanded the economy to produce more military goods at the expense of consumer goods and also oversaw the direction of labour to particular occupations (e.g. into coal mining and the so-called 'land army' of farm workers). One result of women being directed to industrial occupations during the First World War was the obtaining of the right to vote for *all* women. This trend of directing women into industrial work was repeated in the Second World War and it is perhaps because women proved that they could undertake many occupations previously thought of as 'men's work' that we see women playing an ever more important and equal role in the economy today.

Unemployment also ceases to be a problem in planned economies. As the planning organisations plan output they also plan labour needs and have to ensure that the right quantity of workers with the right skills are available (i.e. they control supply and demand for labour). Factory managers will also tend to have more workers than are absolutely necessary, to ensure that they always meet their targets.

## Disadvantages of a command economy

Like the market economy, the command economy also has significant disadvantages. If the plans set different priorities to those of the individual then it is clear that individual choice has to be subordinated to that of society in general. Command economies have in general restricted consumer choice and, in many cases,

concentrated on the production of capital goods and armaments rather than on consumer goods. In the former USSR consumer choice was fairly limited, a stylish dress, a modern car, Levi jeans were not consumer items available to the average citizen. They were not produced because the planners had rejected the values of a 'consumerist' society. Many of the goods that were produced were also of a low quality – if people had no real choice then it did not matter about quality as they had to buy the good or go without. Additionally, factories only had to meet quantitative rather than qualitative targets. Quantitative targets would be set in terms of the number of tons of steel to be produced or the total amount of potatoes to be harvested. No quality targets, in terms perhaps of the composition or size tolerance of the steel, were given.

Western press agencies spent many of the cold war years, and more recently, highlighting shortages in the Soviet economy. Each year there would be shortages, especially of agricultural products, as deficiencies in the system were covered up by officials. The planners were also slow to respond to changes in demand as they had to keep largely within the targets set within the relevant five year plan. The co-ordination of all the vast and detailed plans was a tremendous task and it was virtually impossible for the associated bureaucracy to get it right.

The command economy also gives little scope for enterprise or innovation as all decisions come from the state planners and a manager's reward is based on meeting targets. There is no real incentive to develop new products or even to develop more efficient production techniques. The only areas in which innovation and research are encouraged in such a system are the state research organisations, which tend to be linked to the development of military technologies. In many cases it was therefore a case of 'never mind the quality what about the quota'.

## THE MIXED ECONOMY

Modern economies are, in practice, mixed economies containing elements of both systems. Most western economies have a market system with some government intervention in order to deal with failures in the market system. The degree of intervention will depend upon the political make-up of an individual country and how far they see the market system as failing. Over time, as political power in countries changes, the relative strengths of planning and the free market will also change.

To get a television, clothing or food we have to buy from the private sector who exist primarily to make profits. In general, however, if we need education or health care we use resources allocated by the State. In other areas, such as housing, there is a mix of individual private ownership (owner-occupied property) alongside State ownership (council housing which is provided on a planned basis).

In practice all the world's economies are mixed economies, the particular mix varying from one country to the next. The breakup of the Eastern Bloc and the development of independent states has more recently seen the expansion of the market economy into those countries.

The speed of change in eastern Europe has been quite frightening. Even Germany has suffered economically from the merging of west and east. Borrowing by government in Germany to help the reunification process is putting a severe strain on its economy – and that of Europe. Even in the most westernised eastern European economy, Czechoslovakia, the strain is starting to tell and the country is now split into two, a Czech federation and a Slovak federation. In the former USSR there are disputes in many of the new republics and even in Russia itself there is still a significant movement that is seeking to return it to a communist state. Yet in many of the former communist states 'consumerisation' is breaking out. Many of the developments are the result of joint ventures with western multinationals. In the old East Germany for example, the *Treuhandanstalt* oversees the privatisation of the country. Privatisation is generally conducted by tender with much emphasis being placed on management buy-outs. In Poland by the start of 1992 some 850 organisations had been sold off and the government is considering ways of distributing share vouchers to the population. While much of the change has gone smoothly there are still areas of grave concern; it is still impossible to guarantee that none of the states will revert back to communist style command economies.

## The public sector in the UK

The late 1980s and early 1990s have seen a re-emergence of the political debate over nationalisation versus privatisation in the UK. On the left of the political spectrum there are those who believe that more industries and services should be brought under government control, while on the right there are increasing calls for the privatisation of more industries, many of which we have perhaps long considered as being best run by the state. In this section we will concentrate upon nationalised industries but it must be remembered that various state run businesses exist that are not nationalised, such as the British Broadcasting Corporation (BBC) and many other income-generating businesses run by both central and local government. For our purposes we will define nationalised industries as those that are:

- wholly owned by the state
- run by a board appointed by the appropriate Minister of State
- dependent for survival on sales to industry or the public.

This definition would encompass present day nationalised industries like British Rail and British Coal and, in the not too distant past, many more.

This idea of nationalised industries is not new and is certainly not limited to the UK. France, for example, has a significant public sector which includes Renault Cars, the match and tobacco industry and an impressive nationalised rail system. The nationalised industries are also not the preserve of particular political parties. Both early Liberal governments and Conservative governments have been responsible for nationalising such industries as:

- the Central Electricity Generating Board (CEGB)
- British Overseas Airways Corporation (BOAC)
- Rolls-Royce.

The greatest period of nationalisation, however, was that undertaken by the Post-war Labour Government between 1945 and 1951 when coal, steel, railways, road transport, the Bank of England and other smaller industries were nationalised. By the early 1980s the nationalised industries accounted for some 10 per cent of national output, 7 per cent of employment and about 17 per cent of total investment.

## THE CASE FOR NATIONALISATION

The arguments for nationalisation are many and varied (and most can be balanced by an equally sound counter-charge). The case for nationalisation includes the following arguments:

- natural monopolies
- security
- lame duck
- consumer interest
- political
- accident
- finance.

### The natural monopolies argument

Certain industries may be regarded as natural monopolies and that a duplication of such industries would be a waste of resources. Natural monopolies are most closely linked to *public utilities* such as gas, water and electricity, where, it is argued, it would be wasteful to have competing gas or water pipelines running across the country. This view also states that where a natural monopoly exists, it is better to have it under State control rather than in the hands of a private firm which may abuse its monopoly power.

### The security argument

The thrust of this argument is that nationalisation is vital to create or preserve a strategic industry which is deemed essential to national security or independence.

### The lame duck theory

Industries have been taken into state control to enable the contraction of that industry to be managed more efficiently and with the government able to take account of social needs. This was one of the reasons for state control of shipbuilding, Rolls-Royce and British Leyland.

### The consumer interest argument

Because the profit motive is not paramount, nationalised industries may operate more in the interests of the workforce and the consumer. This takes us back to the concept of externalities. The keeping open of rural railway lines or the delivery of post to isolated areas could not be profitably undertaken by the private sector but they both have social value.

### The political argument

The famous Clause 4 of the Labour Party's constitution states:

> To secure for the workers by hand or by brain the full fruits of their industry and the most equitable distribution thereof that may be possible upon the basis of the common ownership of the means of production, distribution and exchange, and the best obtainable system of popular administration and control of each industry or service.

It is for this reason that the post-war years saw a major nationalisation of industry take place under the newly-elected Labour Government. Socialists argue for a high degree of nationalisation in the movement towards an equitable society and believe in national planning, another major tool of socialist economies.

## The accidental nationalisation

The end of the Second World War saw the whole-sale confiscation of German or collaborators' property, much of which ended up in the public sector. In the UK the nationalisation of the railways saw the Government also taking over hotels and travel agencies which had been owned by the private railway companies.

## The financial argument

On the Continent nationalisation has been used to create income for governments by the controlling of particular industries such as alcohol, salt, tobacco and matches. This is particularly the case in France.

---

### ACTIVITY

**1** List the arguments for nationalisation on a sheet of paper and alongside each argument add a counter-argument.

**2** It may be useful to stage a debate with half the group for nationalisation and the other half against.

---

## THE ARGUMENTS AGAINST NATIONALISATION

Like the case for nationalisation, the case against is also fairly inconclusive. The arguments against nationalisation include the following:

- misallocation of resources
- efficiency
- monopoly power
- free market.

## The misallocation of resources argument

Most nationalised industries have relied upon a subsidy from government either when they needed development funds or, more likely, when the industry was in decline. If an organisation needs public funds it can be argued that they are not efficient and that the resources they are using could be more effectively used in other ways. If we take as an example the British ship building industry, which was protected and supported by the government for many years, some economists would argue that it is best to allow this sort of industry to die and to buy ships from more efficient producers overseas. The labour and other resources that are released should then be used to produce goods that we are efficient at producing.

## The efficiency argument

When we discussed market economies we argued that firms could increase profits by reducing costs. In the public sector, with little competition, managers will have no pressure to innovate and may continue producing, perhaps in traditional ways, without looking to improve operational efficiency. Evidence to support these views is fairly inconclusive and there appears to be little difference between cost levels or productivity in the two sectors.

## The abuse of monopoly power argument

One of the reasons for taking firms into public ownership was to reduce the monopoly power of the firm. It can also be said that Governments may abuse the power of a State monopoly by charging high prices or limiting supply. Just because a monopoly is run by the State does not mean that it will be run in the interests of the public.

## The disruption of the free market economy argument

In an economy where the public sector is small it will have only a minimal impact on the market system. As the State sector grows, for example employing up to 10 per cent of the workforce as it did in the UK, it can distort the market economy and in particular the supply and demand, and therefore the wages, of labour. The government has in the past often tried to set pay norms by limiting wage increases in the public sector as an example to the private sector.

## HOW DOES THE UK's PUBLIC SECTOR COMPARE?

Each country will have its own individual mix of the public and private sectors which will have been shaped by political will, economic necessity and accident. Many people have misconceptions about the degree of public sector involvement in the UK in comparison with that in other developed economies. Figure 4.2 shows the public sector provision across a range of industries and a range of countries. Although the picture is constantly changing, some significant conclusions can be drawn.

---

### ACTIVITY

**1** Study the information provided in Fig 4.2. Choose any three countries and account for the differences in the private/public sector mix.

**2** Research the public sector in Japan and Germany and the extent of public sector involvement in the shipbuilding industry. Use your research to complete Fig 4.2.

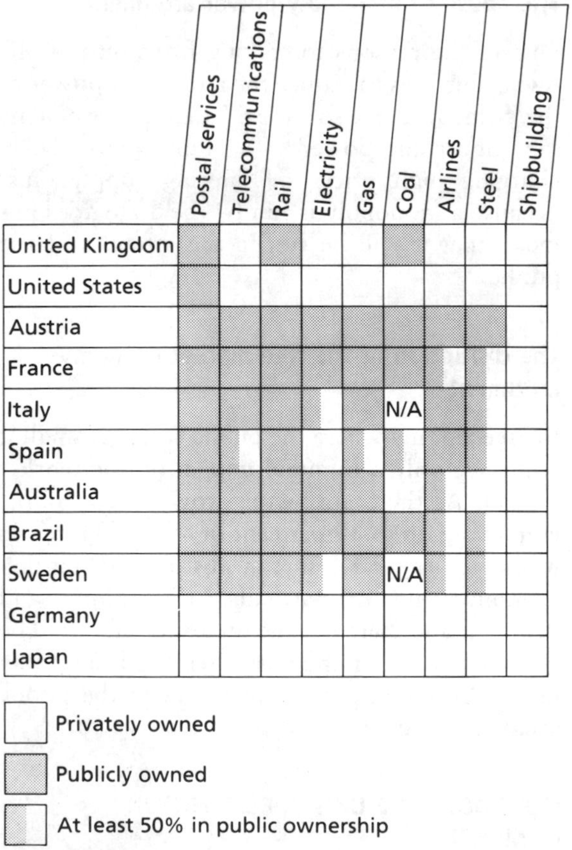

---

What can be said about the public sector in the developed world is that where nationalised firms exist they are usually large scale organisations. In many European countries the largest firm is also often a state-run firm. For example:

- IRI, the Italian metal producer
- Elf Aquitaine, the French oil refining company
- INI, the Spanish mining organisation
- NESTE, the Finnish oil refining firm
- Austrian Industries, the Austrian oil refining firm.

In France, Elf Aquitaine and the nationalised car producer Renault employ between them in the region of 250 000 workers and thus have a considerable impact on the French economy as a whole.

---

## Privatisation in the UK

The situation with regard to the level of public sector involvement in a country's economy is constantly changing. In the UK, if the post-war decade can be regarded as the decade of nationalisation, then the 1980s was certainly the decade of privatisation.

Since 1979 when the Conservatives regained power, over 15 large companies, and many smaller ones, have been privatised (*see* Table 4.1). These have netted the Government something in the region of £30 billion and around one million employees have been transferred from the public sector to the private sector. Privatisation

---

| | Postal services | Telecommunications | Rail | Electricity | Gas | Coal | Airlines | Steel | Shipbuilding |
|---|---|---|---|---|---|---|---|---|---|
| United Kingdom | | | | | | | | | |
| United States | | | | | | | | | |
| Austria | | | | | | | | | |
| France | | | | | | | | | |
| Italy | | | | | | N/A | | | |
| Spain | | | | | | | | | |
| Australia | | | | | | | | | |
| Brazil | | | | | | | | | |
| Sweden | | | | | | N/A | | | |
| Germany | | | | | | | | | |
| Japan | | | | | | | | | |

Privately owned

Publicly owned

At least 50% in public ownership

**Fig 4.2 The public sector – an international comparison**

**Table 4.1   The top ten UK privatisations**

| | (£m) |
|---|---|
| British Telecom | 8685 |
| British Petroleum | 6090 |
| Water Utilities | 5240 |
| Electricity | 5182 |
| British Gas | 5133 |
| British Steel | 2418 |
| British Airports Authority | 1223 |
| Britoil | 1053 |
| Rolls-Royce | 1031 |
| Cable and Wireless | 1021 |
| Total | 37076 |

means that a state-owned industry is sold off to the public, usually by the sale of shares via a major share issue.

## THE RATIONALE FOR PRIVATISATION

Many of the arguments we have already considered against nationalisation can be used to support a privatisation programme. Initially the reason for selling state assets was to make slow, unenterprising state industries more efficient. There can be little doubt that the privatised industries have become more profitable. But this may be at the expense of higher prices rather than increased efficiency. Cable and Wireless, when privatised in 1982, had profits of £90m while six years later they had risen to £295m. The electricity company Norweb increased its profits by 25 per cent in its first year in the private sector.

The theme of wider share ownership emerged with the flotation of British Telecom in 1984. In 1979 less than two million individuals owned shares; by 1990 this had grown to over ten million. It is argued that this is desirable because it gives people a stake in the wealth of the nation. Similarly, workers in privatised firms, who have bought shares on a preferential basis, will have an increased motivation to work hard. Some economists would argue however that the individual rewards from owning a few shares are so minimal that they do not give ordinary people either a stake in their firm or their nation. Despite this the public's appetite for shares appears to be insatiable, with many of the share issues being massively oversubscribed – the Rolls-Royce issue being nearly ten times oversubscribed. It is now reckoned that there are about nine million individual shareholders in the UK and this huge number of potential voters has tended to stifle any Labour Party proposals to re-nationalise industry. Labour Party spokespersons now talk in terms of 'social ownership', a concept which has still to be clearly defined.

It could be argued that one of the major reasons for the spate of privatisations was to boost the Government's revenue and enable it to continue with its long-term policy of reducing personal taxation rates. Thus the Government has often been criticised for 'selling off the family silver'.

Recent evidence from research by the World Bank has shown that, in general, privatisations have led to net gains. Quality has tended to improve, largely because private sector managers have been able to invest while investment by successive governments may have been restricted. Shareholders have also benefited from the profits generated as the privatised concerns were able to increase prices.

## CRITICISMS OF PRIVATISATION

Opponents of privatisation concede that where there is genuine competition, privatisation will spur an organisation to greater efforts. But they point out that many of the larger privatisations such as those of gas, power and water have merely created private monopolies which, they argue, have given the consumer a worse deal. Opponents also argue that privatisation represents the sale of industries owned by everybody, through the state, to those members of the public who are able and willing to buy shares. The government is accused of sacrificing national assets, a concern underlined by the fact that buyers of these shares may also be foreign companies or individuals which may put strategic British industries under the control of overseas owners.

Many people have been persuaded to buy privatisation shares because of the quick profits that have been available, with shares in some of the privatisation issues gaining a premium of up to 50 per cent on the first day of share dealing (*see* Fig 4.3). This situation has led to the accusation that these national assets have been sold off at below market prices, i.e. too cheaply.

### ACTIVITY

**1** Redraw the information in Fig 4.3 using another graph technique. Add to the graph information on the following privatisations: Rolls-Royce, Electricity Distribution, and Powergen. Your horizontal scale should show the privatisations in chronological order. (This could be done using an appropriate spreadsheet package.)

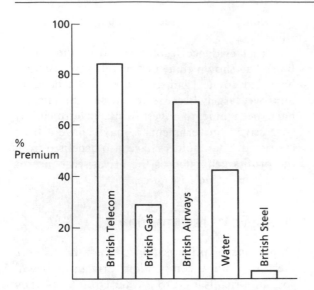

**Fig 4.3 First day premiums on selected privatisation issues**

**2** Has the government got better at fixing share prices over the time scale shown in the graph?

A final criticism of the privatisation programme is that the government has lost income from the profitable businesses it has sold and plans to sell and will eventually be left with only the unprofitable state sector industries that need to be subsidised.

---

**ACTIVITY**

**1** Conduct a survey to test people's reactions to the privatisation of British Telecom. As a group, design a questionnaire that asks people about their perceptions of the quality and price of BT services before and after privatisation. (Unit 7, Marketing and business performance, will give you help in designing questionnaires.)
**2** As a group, give a presentation on your findings.

---

In general it is difficult to say whether privatisations have been successful or not. What is true is that they have challenged many ideas about the public sector. The UK privatisations have become a model for the rest of the world. The UK is now advising much of eastern Europe on the privatisation process and even China has sent a delegation to look at successful British privatisations.

## OTHER ROUTES TO PRIVATISATION

The sale of nationalised industries has been only one arm of the Government's privatisation policy. In the 1990s the main thrust of the Conservative Government will be to increase choice, extend competition and improve the quality of service. This is embodied in John Major's 'Citizen's Charter', the introduction from which appears in Fig 4.4.

---

**ACTIVITY**

Read the Introduction from the Citizen's Charter and answer the following questions:

**1** What is the Government's central principle of essential services?

**2** Where elements of monopoly remain, how can the consumer be protected?

**3** Which factors in the Citizen's Charter will enable the consumer to make their views known?

**4** Are education and health care available to all, irrespective of means?

**5** BT has a virtual monopoly. What regulation protects the consumer? Which company is its only competitor?

---

We now look briefly at alternative ways of privatisation.

### Deregulation

In the past, many nationalised industries had almost complete monopoly power and where they did not they were protected by legislation. The Post Office used to have a monopoly on the delivery of all letter and parcel mail. In 1981 the Government allowed competition for the delivery of parcels costing over £1, which led to a major increase in the number of private carriers and the development of express courier services (e.g. Omega, DHL, etc.). Future policy includes the reduction of the £1 level to one nearer the

---

## INTRODUCTION

All public services are paid for by individual citizens, either directly or through their taxes. They are entitled to expect high-quality services, responsive to their needs, provided efficiently at a reasonable cost. Where the state is engaged in regulating, taxing or administering justice, these functions too must be carried out fairly, effectively and courteously.

This Government continues to uphold the central principle that essential services – such as education and health – must be available to all, irrespective of means. And its consistent aim has been to increase choice, extend competition and thereby improve quality in all services.

In a free market, competing firms must strive to satisfy their customers, or they will not prosper. Where choice and competition are limited, consumers cannot as easily or effectively make their views count. In many public services, therefore, we need to increase both choice and competition where we can; but we also need to develop other ways of ensuring good standards of service.

Many of Britain's key industries and public services have been privatised in the last decade. This has been done in a way which promotes direct competition between providers as far as possible. Where elements of monopoly remain, regulation protects the consumer.

Choice can also be extended within the public sector. When the public sector remains responsible for a function it can introduce competition and pressure for efficiency by contracting with the private sector for its provision.

Finally, choice can be restored by introducing alternative forms of provision, and creating a wider range of options wherever that is cost-effective. This has been a key objective, for example, of reforms in housing and education.

Through the Citizen's Charter the Government is now determined to drive reforms further into the core of the public services, extending the benefits of choice, competition, and commitment to service more widely.

The Citizen's Charter is the most comprehensive programme ever to raise quality, increase choice, secure better value, and extend accountability. We believe that it will set a pattern, not only for Britain, but for other countries of the world.

The Charter programme will be pursued in a number of ways. The approach will vary from service to service in different parts of the United Kingdom. The Citizen's Charter is not a blueprint which imposes a drab and uniform pattern on every service. It is a toolkit of initiatives and ideas to raise standards in the way most appropriate to each service.

The Charter programme will be at the heart of government policy in the 1990s. Quality of service to the public, and the new pride that it will give to the pubic servants who provide it, will be a central theme.

*There are four main themes in the White Paper:*

*QUALITY – A sustained new programme for improving the quality of public services.*

*CHOICE – Choice, wherever possible between competing providers, is the best spur to quality improvement.*

*STANDARDS – The citizen must be told what service standards are and be able to act where service is unacceptable.*

*VALUE – The citizen is also a taxpayer; public services must give value for money within a tax bill the nation can afford.*

**Fig 4.4 The introduction from the Citizen's Charter**

---

price of a first class stamp. Other examples of deregulation include:

- bus and coach transport
- private power stations and gas producers allowed to compete with the newly privatised energy companies
- deregulation of motorway service areas.

---

### ACTIVITY

1 Design a questionnaire to test consumers' perceptions of local bus travel pre- and post-regulation and conduct a survey using it.

2 Using the information obtained from replies to the questionnaire, write a letter to the local press giving your views on deregulation.

---

### The welfare state

Privatisation in the welfare state has taken on a different guise and in most cases has reduced the power of local authorities. One of the first practical moves to implement this policy was the 'right to buy' plan for council house occupiers. This led to an initial take up of the right to buy by some 1 300 000 people, but in the current recession this has dried up to a trickle and many people who purchased their council home have since got into financial difficulties. The government is now taking the policy a stage further by allowing council tenants to move away from local authority control by the setting up of housing associations.

Compulsory Competitive Tendering (CCT) within local authorities means that the local authority must put many services out to tender, inviting bids from both the in-house supplier and the private sector. In areas as diverse as rubbish collection, school meals, vehicle management and the management of leisure centres contracts have been awarded to private providers. Local Management of Schools (LMS) and the setting up of twenty-five City Technical Colleges are another method by which the government is seeking to take a more central role and reduce the power of local authorities.

Each of the newly privatised industries, the remaining public sector bodies and many local authority undertakings are also to be subject to Citizen's Charters.

---

### ACTIVITY

Read the following extract from the Citizen's Charter which looks at its scope.

'The Citizen's Charter applies to all public services. These include government departments and agencies, nationalised industries, local authorities, the NHS, the courts, the police and emergency services. In the private sector it covers the key utilities; it does not encompass wider consumer law.'

1 Why do you think that it does not give improved consumer protection in general to the individual?

2 Which is the only form of transport not subject to a Citizen's Charter? Why do you think that is?

---

One industry that is in the pipeline for privatisation is British Rail, although many would argue that with the sell off of the rolling stock manufacturing division that became British Rail

Engineering Ltd (BREL) and the mass sale of railway hotels it is partly privatised already. The Government still has to decide on the method of privatisation, the choice being whether to sell the whole organisation as a going concern or to split British Rail up into a track authority and a transport authority and allow other private firms to bid for use of the track. British Rail is already subject to Charter targets, most of the regions having to reach targets similar to those shown in Table 4.2.

Despite these initiatives and noticeable improvements in some areas (e.g. the InterCity network), British Rail still suffers from a bad image and all too often runs dirty, slow, inefficient services, especially in comparison with our European counterparts. Excuses for late or cancelled trains also seem to have become a nationwide joke.

---

### ACTIVITY

1 Based on British Rail Charter targets, produce similar targets for your local airport.

2 Is your airport as guilty as British Rail of inventing excuses for late flights?

3 Ask your college if you can negotiate a Students' Charter.

---

Unlike many privatisation initiatives in the past, the latest policies are also striking at the heart of British government. Since 1988, the strangely named Next Steps project has been subjecting government departments to new privatised

Table 4.2   British Rail Charter targets

| | |
|---|---|
| Punctuality | 92 per cent of trains to arrive within five minutes of published times. |
| Reliability | 99 per cent of trains should be run. |
| Cleaning | 100 per cent of trains to be cleaned, inside and out, every day. |
| Telephone enquiries | 95 per cent of calls to be answered within 30 seconds. |
| Check-in times | Waiting limited to three minutes. |

practices. From the issue of driving licences to the administration of the social benefit system, some seventy-five 'executive agencies' are now up and running, and employing some 300 000 officials in them. These agencies are given specific targets to meet which include responding more efficiently to the needs of the consumer. They will also have more freedom to manage and have less interference from central government. Ultimately some of them may follow the route to full privatisation.

# The structure of business and industry in the UK

In the previous Unit we examined in detail the differences between the private and public sectors and looked at how differing economies may be classified. In this Unit we will take a more detailed look at the structure of British business and industry and, at the same time, focus on the theme of change.

## MEASURING BUSINESS AND INDUSTRIAL OUTPUT

If we are to examine industrial output it would be useful to look first at how we can actually measure it. In this section we will answer such questions as how much is produced in the UK; how much people spend and how much people earn.

An important way of measuring the country's economic performance is to measure changes in output. If we are producing more we should all be better off. We could get a rough idea of output in the economy by measuring the number or weight of items produced, but we would then find it difficult to make comparisons; it is for this reason that we express output in terms of a simple common unit, i.e. money.

The value of output produced by all the different production industries and services is known as the gross domestic product (GDP) and is the value of output produced by resources located in this country. If we add to this the interest, profits and dividends produced by British owned resources abroad we have the gross national product (GNP).

The National Income then is an estimate of the output in a country over a given period of time. Information on the National Income is readily available in the UK from government publications such as the *United Kingdom's National Accounts* and the more regular updates in the *Monthly Digest of Statistics*. This information is also to be found in the financial pages of the press and if there are significant changes they will usually rate a mention on the television news. Figure 4.5 shows the National Income for the

| | £million, 1985 prices[1] |
|---|---:|
| Consumer expenditure | 267,988 |
| Government expenditure | 81,755 |
| Gross Domestic Fixed Capital Formation | 71,853[2] |
| Value of physical increase in stocks and work-in-progress | −3,157[3] |
| Total Domestic Expenditure | 418,439 |
| Exports of goods & services | 124,390 |
| Total Final Expenditure | 542,829 |
| *Less* Imports of goods & services | 134,719 |
| Gross Domestic Product at market prices | 408,110[4] |
| *Less* Taxes – Subsidies | 60,013 |
| Gross Domestic Product at Factor Cost | 348,097[5] |

*Notes*
1. National Income figures are based on a standard year. Thus at the moment figures are quoted on a basis of 1985 prices. This allows us, therefore, to accurately chart changes in National Income without having to calculate the effects of increases in prices.
2. This is the total of all capital expenditure by firms in the year.
3. As with any set of accounts, we must also take account of the position at the start of the year and the end of the year. In this case the country has added to total stocks and, therefore, this figure must be deducted.
4. GDP at market prices is the total expenditure in the country in the year.
5. By taking account of taxes and subsidies we can calculate the GDP at factor costs, that is, the value of all expenditure having taken account of the effects of taxes and subsidies.

**Fig 4.5  Gross Domestic Product 1991**

UK in 1991 and the notes following explain the component parts.

Figure 4.5 shows how national income is calculated by summing all expenditure. The national income of a country can also be measured by calculating the level of income or output.

In principle all three methods of calculating the national income will give the same result. This is because the value of output produced is equal to the expenditure needed to purchase it and to the income generated by its production. Figure 4.6 gives a breakdown of the constituent parts of each of the methods used to calculate national income.

---

### ACTIVITY

1 Using Fig 4.6 as a template, show the latest UK National Income figures.

2 Again using the template, show the National Income for any year in the early 1970s.

3 Compare the two diagrams. What are the major changes, if any, in the component parts of UK National Income?

---

## USES OF NATIONAL INCOME STATISTICS

National income statistics and all other statistical returns are not collected simply to keep civil servants in employment; they are needed to enable the government to plan the economy. Most decisions made by the Chancellor of the Exchequer and other ministers are helped by the use of sophisticated computer models of the economy. For example, if the government wants to cut income tax it can see the expected effects of this action by running the information through the Treasury computer.

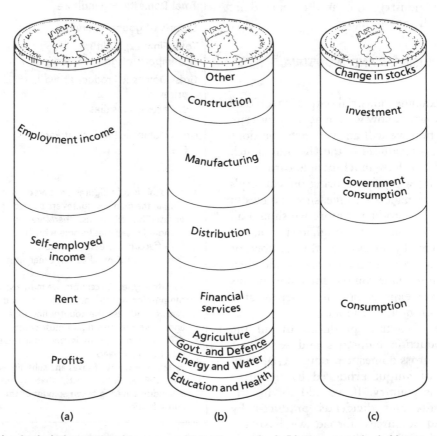

(a)    (b)    (c)

**Fig 4.6 Methods of calculating National Insurance: (a) Income method; (b) Output method; (c) Expenditure method**

National income statistics are used to measure growth in an economy and to measure movements within the economy over time. They are also used as a key indicator of the standard of living and for international standard of living comparisons.

Business people and industrialists make use of national income figures and more especially of the predictions which are made based upon them. By using this information they can assess the likely impact of national income changes on the demand for their product and, therefore, take appropriate action.

## CRITICISMS OF NATIONAL INCOME FIGURES

Although national income figures have their uses and economic planning would be difficult without them, it is also argued that the figures have limitations and are sometimes used for inappropriate purposes.

### NI and paid employment

National income only measures *paid employment* and thus may lead to some distortion in the final results. The work of an unpaid worker, any DIY work that is done or home-grown vegetables produced will not be counted as part of national income. If you look at the situation in many developing nations, this problem becomes more acute as many sustenance activities take place without any exchange of money.

### War and NI

In times of war, output of military equipment will rise considerably and so, therefore, will national income. The output created, however, may not lead to an increase in incomes and the public may feel badly off because they have little to buy since production is being focused on military purposes.

### NI and the standard of living

We would expect that as national income rises our standard of living would rise but, as we have seen above, in times of war resources may just be diverted to military use. The national income figures also fail to take account of the negative effects of production such as pollution, the decimation of tropical rain forests and the depletion of the ozone layer.

### NI and the black economy

The level of the 'black economy', i.e. the output or services that are not declared for tax, varies from country to country and indeed from area to area. In rural areas one farmer will help another bring in the harvest and expect a reward in kind, while in many inner city areas many people work in a cash society where the authorities know little about the level of output or income.

The Inland Revenue has estimated that the black economy accounts for some 7.5 per cent of national income, while others have estimated it at a figure nearer 15 per cent. Other developed countries fare little better in this respect – the black economy in Italy, for instance, has been estimated at somewhere between 12 per cent and 15 per cent of NI. If the level of the black economy in the UK is about 15 per cent of NI, this will have a significant impact on the revenue that the government collects from businesses and individuals.

### Other limitations

When income is measured over time, account obviously has to be taken of inflation. An increase in national income of 10 per cent would mean that income had not changed in real terms if inflation had increased by 10 per cent. Equally a 10 per cent rise in national income may have been achieved due to a 10 per cent increase in population. What is more important than NI or gross national product (GNP) here is *GNP per capita*.

### International comparisons

International comparisons are usually made in terms of a standard currency, most often the US dollar, but the value of the pound against the dollar and other currencies changes almost daily and, therefore, makes international comparisons more difficult. The recent realignment and effective devaluation of sterling makes holidaying in France perhaps 15 per cent more expensive, but in real terms the relative national incomes have not changed.

It is also difficult comparing like with unlike. Countries with warm climates would have different needs to those with a cold climate, developed countries would have different needs to those of developing countries.

The use of national income statistics to aid planning and comparison is, therefore, fraught with difficulties but if care is taken they can be a useful economic tool.

### ACTIVITY

**1** Table 4.3 displays a range of statistical information, including the per capita gross domestic product (GDP) for a range of countries. Show this information in an easily understood graphical format.

**2** Prepare a short report showing which is the 'best' country. You should justify your choice of best country and state what other information you would require to improve your analysis.

## OTHER METHODS OF CLASSIFYING OUTPUT

There has been a marked change in the component parts of national output over the past two decades. Output can be classified as that produced in:

● tertiary industries, i.e.the service sector

● secondary industries, i.e. manufacturing and construction
● primary industries, i.e. agriculture, mining and energy supply.

### ACTIVITY

**1** Draw up a pie chart showing employment in the primary, tertiary and secondary sectors in the UK in 1990 using the information provided in Fig 4.7.

**2** Which sector employs most people?

You will have concluded that the tertiary sector is larger than the primary and secondary sectors, with the tertiary sector now accounting for about 60 per cent of total national output in the UK. The analysis of output can be taken a stage further by looking at output as it relates to Standard Industrial Classifications (SIC) (which divides industries and organisations up into different types) and its international counterpart, the International Standard Industrial Classification (ISIC). By using these classifications we are able to make fairly accurate comparisons of changes in output and employment within the UK and also to examine regional differences.

A good indicator of the level of output in the economy is the number of people employed in specific industries. Figure 4.7, which uses the SIC, shows clearly those industries which have expanded and those that have contracted in terms of employment in the late 1980s.

### ACTIVITY

**1** Draw a bar graph which shows employment by industry and compares 1984 with 1990, based on the data in Fig 4.7.

**2** What conclusions can you draw from your graph?

**3** What other information would you require before you could make an accurate assessment of the state of the individual industries?

Your conclusions will probably show that the only expansion in employment has been in the service sector, while there has been little change in employment in the chemical and office machinery sectors. This conclusion is, however,

**Table 4.3  International statistical comparison, 1988**

|  | UK | Austria | Australia | Belgium | Turkey |
|---|---|---|---|---|---|
| GDP (US$ bill) | 822 | 127 | 247 | 150 | 70 |
| Population (m) | 57 | 8 | 16 | 10 | 54 |
| Cars per 1000 population | 318 | 370 | 497 | 349 | 18 |
| Doctors per 1000 population | 0.5 | 1.7 | 1.6 | 2.8 | 1.5 |
| Infant mortality per 1000 live births | 9.4 | 11.0 | 9.2 | 9.4 | 15.8 |

| | SIC 1980 | United Kingdom | | | | | | |
|---|---|---|---|---|---|---|---|---|
| | | *1984* | *1985* | *1986* | *1987* | *1988* | *1989* | *1990* |
| All industries and services | 0–9 | 21 238 | 21 423 | 21 387 | 21 584 | 22 258 | 22 661 | 22 856 |
| Index of production and construction industries | 1–5 | 7 062 | 6 974 | 6 760 | 6 669 | 6 727 | 6 634 | 6 689 |
| Index of production industries | 1–4 | 6 025 | 5 953 | 5 771 | 5 660 | 5 680 | 5 651 | 5 602 |
| *of which, manufacturing industries* | *2–4* | *5 409* | *5 362* | *5 227* | *5 152* | *5 195* | *5 187* | *5 151* |
| Service industries | 6–9 | 13 836 | 14 108 | 14 297 | 14 594 | 15 218 | 15 627 | 15 868 |
| Agriculture, forestry and fishing | 0 | 340 | 341 | 329 | 321 | 313 | 300 | 298 |
| Agriculture and horticulture | 01 | 321 | 323 | 311 | 303 | 295 | 282 | 279 |
| Energy and water supply | 1 | 616 | 591 | 545 | 508 | 485 | 465 | 451 |
| Coal extraction and solid fuels | 111 | .. | .. | .. | .. | .. | .. | .. |
| Electricity | 161 | .. | .. | .. | .. | .. | .. | .. |
| Gas | 162 | .. | .. | .. | .. | .. | .. | .. |
| Other mineral and ore extraction | 2 | 799 | 779 | 729 | 694 | 689 | 711 | 728 |
| Metal manufacturing and extraction of metal ores and minerals | 21–23 | 231 | 217 | 194 | 177 | 166 | 177 | 194 |
| Non-metallic mineral products | 24 | 221 | 220 | 204 | 194 | 196 | 202 | 204 |
| Chemical industry/man-made fibres | 25/26 | 347 | 342 | 331 | 323 | 328 | 333 | 330 |
| Basic industrial chemicals | 251 | .. | .. | .. | .. | .. | .. | .. |
| Other chemical products and preparations | 255–259/260 | .. | .. | .. | .. | .. | .. | .. |
| Metal goods, engineering and vehicles | 3 | 2 468 | 2 443 | 2 372 | 2 331 | 2 359 | 2 351 | 2 316 |
| Metal goods nes | 31 | 334 | 329 | 320 | 323 | 335 | 335 | 321 |
| Hand tools and finished metal goods including doors and windows | 314–316 | .. | .. | .. | .. | .. | .. | .. |
| Other metal goods | 311–313 | .. | .. | .. | .. | .. | .. | .. |
| Mechanical engineering | 32 | 759 | 764 | 749 | 744 | 764 | 771 | 752 |
| Industrial plant and steelwork | 320 | .. | .. | .. | .. | .. | .. | .. |
| Machinery for agriculture, metal working, textile, food and printing etc industries | 321/322/ 324/326/327 | .. | .. | .. | .. | .. | .. | .. |
| Mining and construction machinery etc. | 325 | .. | .. | .. | .. | .. | .. | .. |
| Other machinery and mechanical equipment incl. ordnance, small arms and ammunition | 323/328/329 | .. | .. | .. | .. | .. | .. | .. |
| Office machinery, data processing equipment | 33 | 84 | 88 | 83 | 82 | 84 | 82 | 81 |
| Electrical and electronic engineering | 34 | 607 | 596 | 573 | 563 | 559 | 561 | 564 |
| Wires, cables, batteries and other electrical equipment | 341/342/343 | .. | .. | .. | .. | .. | .. | .. |
| Telecommunication equipment | 344 | .. | .. | .. | .. | .. | .. | .. |
| Other electronic and electrical equipment | 345–348 | .. | .. | .. | .. | .. | .. | .. |
| Motor vehicles and parts | 35 | 281 | *274 | 266 | 260 | 271 | 264 | 248 |
| Motor vehicles and engines | 351/352 | .. | .. | .. | .. | .. | .. | .. |
| bodies, trailers, caravans, motor vehicle parts | 353 | .. | .. | .. | .. | .. | .. | .. |
| Other transport equipment | 36 | 301 | 288 | 276 | 256 | 244 | 239 | 259 |
| Shipbuilding and repairing | 361 | .. | .. | .. | .. | .. | .. | .. |
| Aerospace and other transport equipment | 362–365 | .. | .. | .. | .. | .. | .. | .. |
| Instrument engineering | 37 | 104 | 105 | 105 | 103 | 102 | 98 | 92 |
| Other manufacturing industries | 4 | 2 141 | 2 140 | 2 126 | 2 128 | 2 146 | 2 125 | 2 106 |
| Food, drink and tobacco | 41/42 | 603 | 596 | 576 | 571 | 561 | 549 | 540 |
| Meat and meat products, organic oils and fats | 411/412 | .. | .. | .. | .. | .. | .. | .. |
| Bread, biscuits and flour confectionery | 419 | .. | .. | .. | .. | .. | .. | .. |

*Source: Department of Employment*

**Fig 4.7  Employees in employment**
*Analysis by industry based on the Standard Industrial Classification 1980*
*At June in each year*

based on the use of only one factor of production – labour. Before we can make an accurate assessment of the state of those industries, we must also look at how efficient that labour is.

Improvements in the productivity of labour arise from improvements in production techniques and in the efficiency of the workforce. For example, despite the fact that the chemical industry shows a modest reduction in numbers employed during the 1980s, in terms of increases in output it was one of the star performers, with production rising by about 27 per cent between 1980 and 1987. This could only have been achieved by a major improvement in productivity. Rises in labour productivity are not exclusive to the chemical industry. It has been estimated that productivity in manufacturing has risen by about 2.5 per cent per annum over the period from 1950 to 1990.

Productivity increases have varied widely from industry to industry, partly of course, because of differences in the scope for the application of new technology. There is obviously more scope for computerisation of the chemical and machine tool industries than there is in many of the service industries such as butchers or solicitors and barristers. Productivity has increased more rapidly in those industries that have been able to replace labour with capital equipment.

It is also informative to make an international comparison of productivity. If we compare the UK with France and Germany, for example, in some industries we lose in the productivity stakes and in others we win. Although international comparisons are difficult, for reasons already indicated, generally the UK has a better productivity record in financial services, construction and chemicals but tends to lag behind in textiles and clothing, metal products and distribution.

## ACCOUNTING FOR DIFFERING PRODUCTIVITY LEVELS

Earlier we stated that improvements in productivity could come about through improvements in labour efficiency or by the use of more capital equipment. In the past the UK would not have fared well in an international comparison of the percentage of capital used in industry. Over the last decade or so, however, the UK has caught up. Most member countries of the EC have capital expenditure figures of between 17 per cent and 19 per cent of total expenditure. While the UK's figure is at the bottom end of the range it has, nevertheless, shown considerable improvement.

If a country is to improve productivity it must also research new products and new processes. It could be said, therefore, that the amount of money spent by an economy on Research and Development (R&D) would be a good indicator of its future potential. In terms of R&D, UK expenditure roughly equates with that of France, is higher than that of Italy, but lags considerably behind that of Germany.

## SIZE OF INDUSTRIAL FIRMS

A further way of analysing UK industry is to make a comparative study of the size of its component parts. One of the main features of industrial development in the past decades has been the growth in the size of firms and an increasing concentration of output in a relatively few large concerns. The days when the majority of goods were produced by many small businesses have long gone. Typically, nowadays, production is in the hands of huge national corporations or multinational giants.

---

### ACTIVITY

**1** Figure 4.8 shows the size of manufacturing units in the UK in 1991. On a suitable graph, display the total figures for the number of units and the number of employees.

**2** What three main conclusions can you draw from your graph?

---

There are two main reasons for the growth in the size of firms:

● economies of scale
● market power.

## ECONOMIES OF SCALE

In general it is probably true to say that larger

| | Total | | | | Analysis by number of employees | | | | |
|---|---|---|---|---|---|---|---|---|---|
| | | 1–9 | 10–19 | 20–49 | 50–99 | 100–199 | 200–499 | 500–999 | 1 000 and over |
| **Number of units** | | | | | | | | | |
| All manufacturing industries | 156 449 | 105 125 | 15 952 | 18 003 | 7 883 | 4 855 | 3 318 | 905 | 408 |
| Extraction and preparation of metalliferous ores and metal manufacturing | 1 581 | 654 | 202 | 277 | 189 | 109 | 104 | 27 | 19 |
| Extraction of minerals not elsewhere specified and manufacture of non-metallic mineral products | 7 336 | 4 653 | 908 | 857 | 451 | 241 | 169 | 47 | 10 |
| Chemical industry and production of man-made fibres | 3 889 | 1 937 | 475 | 538 | 347 | 258 | 210 | 84 | 40 |
| Manufacture of metal goods not elsewhere specified | 15 284 | 9 628 | 1 911 | 2 243 | 808 | 415 | 233 | 37 | 9 |
| Mechanical engineering | 26 258 | 18 285 | 2 711 | 3 146 | 1 015 | 590 | 372 | 102 | 37 |
| Manufacture of office machinery and data processing equipment | 1 297 | 877 | 112 | 144 | 62 | 45 | 29 | 16 | 12 |
| Electrical and electronic engineering | 11 012 | 7 126 | 987 | 1 228 | 651 | 431 | 364 | 153 | 72 |
| Manufacture of motor vehicles and parts thereof | 2 486 | 1 227 | 318 | 363 | 221 | 147 | 123 | 46 | 41 |
| Manufacture of other transport equipment | 2 502 | 1 606 | 232 | 251 | 144 | 95 | 79 | 35 | 60 |
| Instrument engineering | 2 798 | 1 660 | 323 | 411 | 210 | 121 | 58 | 12 | 3 |
| Food, drink and tobacco manufacturing industries | 10 494 | 6 076 | 1 345 | 1 240 | 649 | 517 | 450 | 150 | 67 |
| Textile industry | 5 115 | 3 013 | 469 | 649 | 441 | 306 | 200 | 33 | 4 |
| Manufacture of leather and leather goods | 1 198 | 860 | 134 | 109 | 60 | 25 | 10 | – | – |
| Footwear and clothing industries | 11 346 | 7 932 | 1 017 | 1 166 | 552 | 392 | 258 | 24 | 5 |
| Timber and wooden furniture industries | 15 367 | 11 761 | 1 342 | 1 351 | 532 | 249 | 114 | 18 | – |
| Manufacture of paper and paper products; printing and publishing | 23 540 | 16 965 | 2 285 | 2 502 | 858 | 524 | 310 | 77 | 19 |
| Processing of rubber and plastics | 5 788 | 2 948 | 738 | 1 021 | 527 | 322 | 188 | 34 | 10 |
| Other manufacturing industries | 9 158 | 7 917 | 443 | 507 | 166 | 68 | 47 | 10 | – |
| **Number of employees (thousands)** | | | | | | | | | |
| All manufacturing industries | 4 739.1 | 307.3 | 224.9 | 554.8 | 547.7 | 674.7 | 1 010.2 | 613.1 | 806.3 |
| Extraction and preparation of metalliferous ores and metal manufacturing | 141.8 | 2.3 | 2.8 | 9.0 | 13.5 | 15.4 | 32.1 | 18.1 | 48.5 |
| Extraction of minerals not elsewhere specified and manufacture of non-metallic mineral products | 213.6 | 14.5 | 12.6 | 26.6 | 31.7 | 33.1 | 50.1 | 32.0 | 12.9 |
| Chemical industry and production of man-made fibres | 283.1 | 6.2 | 6.7 | 17.2 | 24.4 | 36.2 | 65.3 | 59.3 | 67.8 |
| Manufacture of metal goods not elsewhere specified | 338.2 | 29.4 | 27.3 | 68.0 | 55.1 | 56.7 | 67.2 | 24.3 | 10.1 |
| Mechanical engineering | 580.2 | 52.8 | 38.9 | 96.4 | 69.5 | 80.5 | 114.2 | 70.2 | 57.7 |
| Manufacture of office machinery and data processing equipment | 59.1 | 2.5 | 1.5 | 4.2 | 4.6 | 6.1 | 9.1 | 10.8 | 20.3 |
| Electrical and electronic engineering | 520.0 | 19.8 | 13.9 | 38.4 | 45.4 | 61.0 | 115.2 | 106.8 | 119.5 |
| Manufacture of motor vehicles and parts thereof | 252.6 | 3.8 | 4.4 | 11.4 | 15.4 | 21.0 | 39.2 | 31.1 | 126.3 |
| Manufacture of other transport equipment | 261.6 | 4.2 | 3.2 | 7.7 | 10.4 | 13.3 | 23.8 | 24.2 | 174.7 |
| Instrument engineering | 85.6 | 4.9 | 4.5 | 12.8 | 14.7 | 16.9 | 18.3 | 9.0 | 4.5 |
| Food, drink and tobacco manufacturing industries | 543.7 | 22.6 | 18.8 | 38.0 | 44.6 | 72.3 | 114.2 | 99.1 | 107.2 |
| Textile industry | 198.5 | 9.1 | 6.5 | 20.8 | 32.0 | 43.1 | 61.0 | 21.4 | 4.5 |
| Manufacture of leather and leather goods | 17.7 | 2.3 | 1.9 | 3.4 | 3.9 | 3.3 | 2.8 | – | – |
| Footwear and clothing industries | 268.0 | 23.8 | 14.1 | 36.5 | 38.4 | 55.2 | 77.1 | 15.8 | 7.0 |
| Timber and wooden furniture industries | 205.0 | 30.2 | 19.0 | 41.0 | 36.4 | 33.5 | 32.5 | 12.4 | – |
| Manufacture of paper and paper products; printing and publishing | 456.8 | 48.3 | 32.2 | 75.9 | 59.7 | 73.3 | 91.3 | 50.4 | 25.7 |
| Processing of rubber and plastics | 230.3 | 9.9 | 10.4 | 32.0 | 36.5 | 44.3 | 56.7 | 21.1 | 19.5 |
| Other manufacturing industries | 83.2 | 20.6 | 6.2 | 15.6 | 11.5 | 9.3 | 13.0 | 7.0 | – |

*Source: Central Statistical Office*

*Notes*
(i)   The analysis follows the Classes of the *Standard Industries Classification 1980*.
(ii)  The employment information is drawn from CSO production inquiries (in particular the Annual Census of Production and the inquiries into manufacturers' sales) and relates generally to 1989.
(iii) Figures may not always add up to total owing to rounding.

**Fig 4.8  Size of manufacturing units 1991**

firms do score over smaller ones. This seems to be a rational conclusion from the dominance of large firms in the UK economy. This is not to say that small firms have been eliminated in Britain. There are some firms which are more effectively organised into small units, still others where the extent of the market is not wide enough to permit the exploitation of scale economies. The 1980s in the UK could be called the 'enterprise decade', with Mrs Thatcher's Government actively promoting the enterprise culture and encouraging the setting up of small businesses.

Specialisation is really limited by the size of the market. In a small market, a worker must be able to turn his or her hand to many different jobs since the demand for any one specialised skill will not be sufficient to keep them continuously occupied. In many small firms it would be fairly typical to see an owner-manager taking on a range of management duties including accounting, marketing, personnel management and production management. Similarly, it will be uneconomic to use expensive items of capital equipment if they have to stand idle for long periods and equally inappropriate to attempt to operate elaborate management structures in a small firm. Production must be on a large scale before full use can be made of either machines or specialists and specialist departments.

It is true of a plant, of a firm and of an industry as a whole, that increased size creates opportunities for specialisation, reorganisation and new types of machinery which make it possible to achieve economies which are impossible where production is on a smaller scale. These opportunities to reduce costs per unit of production are known as economies of scale.

We can distinguish two categories of economies of scale – *internal* and *external economies of scale*. If costs fall as a single firm gets bigger then internal economies of scale exist. These can be divided into five main categories:

**1 Technical economies.** These affect the size of the plant rather than the size of the firm. They cover things like integrated processes in the iron and steel industries, with huge integrated rolling mills. They also cover economies of dimension – a 20 ton lorry does not cost twice as much as a 10 ton lorry. A large firm will be able to use large efficient machines and enjoy the benefits of increased labour specialisation.

**2 Managerial economies.** These create the opportunity to increase specialisation by having lawyers, accountants and marketing staff in-house. Senior management will also be given the chance to delegate and thus concentrate on more demanding strategic roles.

**3 Marketing economies.** This refers to cost cutting in the bulk buying of materials and selling of finished products. Ford Motors, for example, can run their own trains from Dagenham by arrangement with British Rail. Another economy arises where the cost of a product or service is the same, irrespective of the size of the company purchasing it. For example, one advertising hoarding costs the small firm as much to hire as it does the giant multinational.

**4 Financial economies.** These economies come in when a firm has a reputation among lenders and investors. Such a firm will find it easier to raise capital for expansion and will also be able to use the Stock Exchange to raise finance. In addition they may be able to negotiate more favourable interest rates, and other incentives, than smaller firms which are seen as riskier by the investors.

**5 Risk bearing economies.** These enable a big firm to diversify into other markets and products, thus ensuring that all its eggs are not in one basket. Likewise, they can buy from several different suppliers and minimise disruption if a supplier goes bankrupt or has a major strike on its hands.

The other form of scale economy, *external economies of scale*, arise when production costs fall as a result of the group of firms or the industry getting bigger. They are external to the individual firm and can be classified as:

**1 Economies of concentration.** These come about because when a number of firms settle in one area, they derive mutual advantages such as the training of skilled personnel and a skilled and reliable local workforce. A transport infrastructure which supports that particular industry, local markets and specific advisory agencies will also help all the firms in the area.

**2 Economies of information.** In a large industry one sees a number of trade papers, information bureaux, forecasting services, etc. which avoid large costs to individual firms.

---

### ACTIVITY

1 List all the firms that you and other members of your class or your parents work in. Alongside each firm list the internal economies of scale that apply to it and give relevant examples.

2 If there is a concentration of one type of industry in your area, list all the external economies of scale that apply to it.

3 You will have included some small firms on your list. Indicate what advantages they have which allow them to compete.

---

### Factors limiting growth

As the firm grows certain diseconomies of scale may arise and offset the previous economies gained or there may be no economies of scale to be gained. In many service industries where personal attention is needed there may be few or no economies of scale. This would apply equally to the hairdressing trade, plumbing, and painting and decorating.

Even in industries that are generally regarded as large scale, it is still possible to produce economically on a small scale. Once the minimum efficient size of a firm is reached there may only be a few economies to be gained by further growth. You will probably be able to think of local examples of small scale firms producing in the following industries:

- bread
- shoes
- brewing
- textiles.

Communication problems are one of the challenges faced by managers in large firms. A lot of time, and therefore money, is spent in communications in a large firm. The large firm's communication problems may also lead to a breakdown in labour relations. Workers may feel that they are just cogs in a huge wheel and may be more likely to take strike action than those employed in a small firm.

### Small is beautiful

In some industries it can be argued that there are few economies of scale and in the larger organisations there may be significant diseconomies of scale. Many, including Schumacher, have argued in favour of 'technology with a human face'. We all know of the friendly corner shop, the small garage and the little building firm. We probably remember them because we can put a face to their names, something that is impossible in the large corporations. The 1980s have been the 'decade of enterprise', fuelled by a government intent on recreating an enterprise culture. The rationale behind this vision is easy to see.

Small firms tend to be more labour intensive and thus are job-creators. Some 75 per cent and more of new jobs in the UK are being created by small firms. Small firms are also responsible for a more than pro rata number of innovations. Research done in the USA has shown that small firms come up with four times as many innovations per dollar spent on R&D as medium firms and 24 times as many as big firms.

It is also recognised that small firms have better labour relations, lose fewer days in strikes and exercise tighter control over operations.

Smaller firms also benefit the consumer. The more independent firms there are in an industry, the greater the competition and the lower the prices. Almost half of all small firms are in retailing, one of the few genuinely competitive industries in the UK.

### MARKET POWER

All large firms are interested in the extent to which they can control the market and, therefore, the extent to which they can control prices. If you read car magazines you will become aware that the major car producers are more interested in market share than in any other comparative factor.

A good clue as to the dominance of a market can be obtained by looking at the degree of industrial concentration. This can be defined as the degree to which a relatively small number of firms account for a significant proportion of output, labour employed, etc. An industry is 'highly concentrated' if 70 per cent or more of sales are in the hands of five or less firms. 'Low concentration' would be where many small firms constituted the whole industry. Interest in the degree of concentration arises because it is an important determinant of the way firms behave, and of the resulting levels of prices, outputs and profits. We can equate three standard economic models of price theory to the degree of concentration.

**1 Perfect competition** exists where a large number of small firms make up a market, i.e. a low degree of concentration. Since each firm is so small relative to the total market, it has almost no influence on price. A remarkable similarity in price between different firms will be found in this type of industry.

**2 Oligopoly** is where a small number of firms control a large percentage of sales in a particular market, i.e. a high degree of concentration. These firms may adopt policies of collusion, large advertising campaigns and other forms of 'non-price competition' in order to protect their share of the market and restrict new entrants to the market.

**3 Monopoly** exists where one firm dominates the industry and there is, therefore, complete concentration. This type of industry may be typified by the large corporation where there is little or no competition, high prices and possible inefficiencies.

## Concentration

We can now see that if we are talking about highly concentrated industries we are looking at oligopolies and monopolies.

### ACTIVITY

Refer back to the previous activity and add the following information to your chart. For each firm indicate:

(a) Which type of market it is in, e.g. monopoly, perfect competition, etc.

(b) The number of major producers.

(c) The degree of product differentiation.

(d) The degree of concentration.

Your chart should show that there are certain types of industry in the UK that exhibit a high degree of concentration. These would include the car industry, brewing, bread making, banking, washing machine producers, soap powder producers, paint producers, flour producers. If these types of firms exert a significant degree of influence over the price it can be seen that we may pay more than is necessary for many of the goods that we use in daily life. The degree of concentration varies from industry to industry but there is evidence that the level of concentration is increasing. Despite the attempts of the UK Government to increase competition in the brewing industry, the five firm concentration ratio is now about 65 per cent, whereas 20 years ago it was about 50 per cent. This means that only five firms control at least 65 per cent of the brewing industry. Similar figures also obtain for other major industries.

### ACTIVITY

Table 4.4 shows the concentration ratios for a number of major UK industries. Find out the name of the five firms in each case and select one more major industry and find out its concentration ratio.

## Barriers to entry

If you consider the list of industries in the previous two activities you would probably find it easier to list companies in those industries that

**Table 4.4   Five firm concentration ratios**

| Industry | Ratio |
| --- | --- |
| Cars | 98 |
| Washing machines | 96 |
| Refrigerators | 99 |
| Flour | 86 |
| Beer | 62 |
| Bread | 81 |

have gone out of business rather than to list new firms entering the industry. If you are able to find new firms in the industry they will generally be either small and have a niche market or be a subsidiary of an already existing firm in that industry. As firms in a highly concentrated industry are normally large, they will often be reaping massive economies of scale. New firms would find it difficult, therefore, to break into the market because of the massive investment required before they reach an efficient size. Just consider, for instance, the amount of advertising that would be required to launch a new firm on the market. Equally, the investment in plant required by any firm trying to start up in any of the industries shown in Table 4.4 would be immense.

Many large firms also make a range of products within a given industry. Both Little Chef and Happy Eater are owned by Forte. Most of the brands of soap powder are produced by one or other of the two major firms in the industry. Why do you think that they produce new products that compete with their existing products? The reason is simple, if a single firm makes ten varieties of soap powders, then any potential entrant or existing competitor, would be faced by this range of competing products and would, on average, be likely to capture only one tenth of the market. The same can be seen in the car industry where each major manufacturer will have a range of cars and even within a type of car, like a small family car, will have a range of options. This means that their competitors find it more and more difficult to find a niche or gap in the market at which to aim a new product.

---

## ACTIVITY

1 Research the UK washing powder industry and list on a chart the following information about all washing powders/liquids: price, manufacturer, cost per wash (you will have to decide as a group the parameters for this), how each product is differentiated.

2 After completing the chart, count up the number of products produced by each manufacturer and show the maximum and minimum price range.

3 Do you think that the washing powder industry meets the consumer's needs?

---

# The growth of firms

In previous sections we have shown that there has been an increase in the size of firms in the UK and also that more and more of industry is being controlled by fewer and fewer large firms. In this section we will examine both *why* firms grow and *how* they grow.

## WHY FIRMS GROW

Firms grow for a multitude of reasons but it is difficult to pinpoint the specific reason for their growth. If firms gave the true reason for their growth it may help their competitors or may harm their hard-won public image. Nevertheless, we can identify certain reasons for growth:

- economies of scale motive
- monopoly power motive
- defensive motive
- personal power motive

### Economies of scale motive

This is the most frequently quoted reason. Its potential for reducing costs is understood in industry and is also the key to having the ability to pass on cost benefits to the consumer and increase the profitability of the company.

### Monopoly power motive

In practice this is probably more important than businessmen would have us believe. It involves the desire of a firm to increase its size and exert more influence on the market. Many mergers and takeovers are carried out with the object of reducing or eliminating competition. Any public statement to this effect by the company would not enhance its public image and may attract the attention of the Monopolies and Mergers Commission (MMC).

### Defensive motive

Here, a company will increase its size in order to ward off competition from its larger competitors. This is often done by merger and has the advantage of 'instant growth'.

## Personal power motive

Some entrepreneurs derive great satisfaction from being in a position to lead large numbers of men and women and control vast sums of capital. Personal motives are often secondary to the previous motives cited and simply accompany them rather than constitute the sole reason for expansion. They are, however, important. The megalomaniac tendencies of Robert Maxwell should not, for example, be discounted when trying to account for the growth of the Mirror Group of newspapers.

## HOW FIRMS GROW

Firms may grow in one of only two ways:

- internal expansion, when the company itself expands.
- merger/takeover, when growth is achieved by the acquisition of existing companies.

Mergers eventually lead to a network of firms ultimately under the control of one of them. In such cases use may be made of a holding company, whereby the main company owns a controlling interest in one or more other companies which become its subsidiaries. The subsidiaries may, in their turn, own controlling interests in other companies, which are subsidiaries of the subsidiary. In principle there is no limit to how far the process can go. A pyramid of companies can be built up, all ultimately controlled by the holding company.

---

### ACTIVITY

Despite the recession in the early 1990s the number of mergers has not slackened. In the year ending June 1991 the top fifty mergers accounted for some £5 216 000 000. Table 4.5 shows the top 10 mergers by value. As a group, select and research a takeover bid and the relationship between the two companies. Explain the rationale of the takeover.

---

Economists have generally classified mergers in the following ways:

- horizontal integration
- vertical integration

**Table 4.5   Takeovers for year ending June 1991**

| Company | Target company |
| --- | --- |
| Northern Telecom Ltd. | STC PLC. |
| Brierley Investments Ltd | Mount Charlotte Investments PLC |
| Williams Holdings PLC | Yale and Valor PLC |
| Booker PLC | Fitch Lovell PLC |
| Burmah Castrol PLC | Foseco PLC |
| Coats Viyella PLC | Tootal Group PLC |
| Shanks & McEwan PLC | Recham Environment Services PLC |
| Thorn EMI PLC | Thames Television PLC |
| Interpublic Group Ltd | Lowe Group PLC |
| Evered PLC | Bardon Group PLC |

- lateral integration
- conglomeration.

### Horizontal integration

Horizontal integration is the simplest kind of merger. Here firms making the same product join together (*see* Fig 4.9). An example is the merger between AEI and GEC in the electrical engineering industry. In this type of merger competition can be eliminated and spare capacity and unwanted resources got rid of. Although such mergers frequently result in redundancies, it is this sort of merger that makes most economic sense, perhaps for the very reason that it does free up labour and land for other tasks. It may be that politicians or economists should argue for full employment generally rather than adapt a job protectionist position in every individual case. Many of the major mergers in the 1960s and 1970s saw a massive reduction in the UK's industrial base, many of the mergers resulting in wholesale redundancies. Mergers in this period include the amalgamation of over twenty car manufacturers into the present day big three

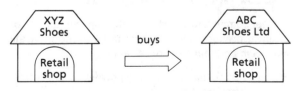

**Fig 4.9 An example of horizontal integration**

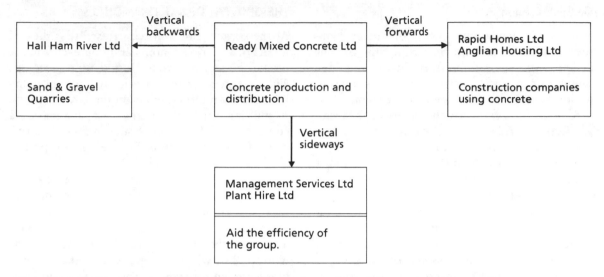

**Fig 4.10 Ready Mixed Concrete Limited – an example of a vertically integrated company**

manufacturers, Ford, Vauxhall and Rover. This was also the era when the high street banks merged, resulting in the so-called 'big five'. It was not until the 1980s, however, that the merger movement began in the insurance sector and it was in the same decade that the major mergers in the retail sector occurred, resulting in the emergence of such retail giants as the Burton Group which encompasses such household names as Dorothy Perkins, Top Shop, Principles, Evans and Debenhams.

## Vertical integration

Vertical integration involves a company buying up firms before or after it in the chain of production – Brooke Bond, for example, own several tea plantations. Another tea firm, Lyons, have indulged in both backward vertical integration, buying coffee factories and tea merchants, and forward vertical integration, with the well-known Lyons Corner House. This form of integration is claimed to add a further degree of certainty in supplies and also of customers, although many firms achieve this by cooperation rather than ownership.

Another type of vertical integration is where there is a sideways merger. A company may take over another not directly associated with its main line of production but which nevertheless support their operations. A manufacturing company, for example, might take over a marketing agency or a packaging company. Figure 4.10 depicts an example of a typical (if there is such a thing) vertically integrated company.

## Lateral integration

Lateral integration refers to the linking together of firms producing unlike products, though there is usually some underlying connection between them (*see* Fig 4.11). For example, a firm making light aircraft may merge with one making small boats; although the products are unlike, there is some similarity in the materials and labour used. Firms whose demand or raw material is seasonal may merge so that the capital, labour and land are used on a continuous basis. The merger of the British Motor Corporation and Leyland Motors is an example of a lateral integration, with one company making cars and the other making lorries and coaches.

**Fig 4.11 An example of lateral integration**

## Conglomeration

Conglomeration occurs when dissimilar firms merge. This has advantages for the firm, making it less vulnerable to market fluctuations, but seems to have no benefit for the consumer. A good example of this type of integration is the P & O Group which now has interests as diverse as ferries, cruise liners, container shipping, construction (in the form of its subsidiary Bovis Construction), catering, and retail centre management – as well as a major portfolio of overseas subsidiaries.

Figure 4.12 shows the diverse nature of the Imperial Tobacco Company which has diversified into many areas, some which are closely related to its core business and others being in different sectors. One reason for this type of diversification in this case is the fear that the government may take action on health grounds to control smoking. Imperial Tobacco is also a subsidiary of the conglomerate Hanson PLC, the tenth highest profit earner in Europe.

---

### ACTIVITY

Draw up a chart for a major public limited company showing all the subsidiaries it owns and indicate on the chart what type of integration their relationship with the parent company represents.

(You will be able to find most of this information in the published accounts of public limited companies which you will also require for other units of this course.)

---

## THE GROWTH OF MULTINATIONALS

At the start of this unit we stressed that the UK is part of a world economy and that events in the rest of the world have to be taken into account. This is especially so if we look at the growing influence of multinationals on the UK economy. A multinational is perhaps best defined as a company with branches or subsidiaries in several countries and those branches are a major part of the company's operations.

Many firms operating in the UK are owned, wholly or partly, by persons or companies located elsewhere. British Petroleum for instance has subsidiaries in over 50 other countries. Table 4.6 shows the top ten corporations in the world, all of which (except for IRI, the nationalised Italian metals corporation) could be regarded as multinationals.

---

### ACTIVITY

1 Redraw Table 4.6 and list the organisations in order of profit per employee.

2 What conclusion can you draw from your figures?

---

One of the most striking features of the above list of multinationals is their size. General Motors will have a turnover that equals the Gross National Product of all but the largest developed nations. What is more difficult to comprehend, perhaps, is that the Chief Executive of General

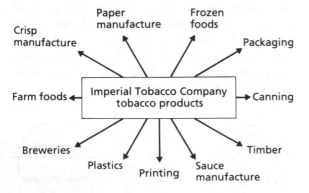

**Fig 4.12 Imperial Tobacco Group – an example of a conglomerate**

**Table 4.6 The top 10 industrial corporations**

| Company | Location | Sales $m | Employees |
|---|---|---|---|
| General Motors | US | 125 126.0 | 761 400 |
| Royal Dutch/Shell | UK/Netherlands | 107 203.5 | 137 000 |
| Exxon | US | 105 885.0 | 104 000 |
| Ford | US | 98 274.7 | 370 400 |
| IBM | US | 69 018.0 | 373 816 |
| Toyota | Japan | 64 517.1 | 96 849 |
| IRI | Italy | 61 433.0 | 419 500 |
| BP | UK | 59 540.5 | 116 750 |
| Mobil | US | 58 770.5 | 67 300 |
| General Electric | US | 58 414.0 | 298 000 |

Motors, for instance, is only interested in profits and earning high returns for the company's shareholders and is not, despite its enormous influence, concerned with the effect its corporate decisions will have on individual countries. In the UK, for example, about 20 per cent of output is produced by foreign-owned firms who owe no allegiance to this country.

In recent years changes in international relations have increased the importance of multi-national firms. Much foreign investment in the UK (for example, Nissan in Sunderland) is to enable companies to exploit world and EC markets without worrying about tariffs, quotas and other barriers to international trade. In 1988 there was much public outcry about the loss of one of Britain's best-loved chocolate manufacturers, Rowntrees, to the Swiss giant Nestlé. Nestlé's rationale for this takeover was to ensure that it had a foothold in the Single European Market, post 1992.

A major advantage of multinationals is their ability to spread technological developments among their subsidiaries and to produce where costs are lowest. The multi-nationals also take advantage of differing tax regimes throughout the world. They ensure that they make as little profit as possible in countries with high levels of taxation by transferring it to countries with low levels of taxation. This is known as 'transfer pricing' and is a practice that countries find difficult to police and almost impossible to legislate against. It is to be hoped that economic alliances such as the EC will in the future be better placed to take appropriate action to curb it.

Multinationals have also been accused of producing in countries where both health and safety regulations, and environmental and pollution controls are at their slackest. A firm based in the USA would, it seems, be quite happy to see workers exploited in South America or cause major ecological disasters in the hardwood rain forests of the world if it is in the short-term interests of their shareholders.

---

### ACTIVITY

In an earlier activity you and your group were asked to list all the firms either you or your parents worked for.

---

Now find out which of those firms have either significant overseas subsidiaries or are part of a major multinational corporation.

---

## Regional differences

So far we have looked at total output in the economy and made a comparison between different sectors of the economy. In this next section we will look at differences between regions of the UK and examine how both central and local government policies affect regional development. First, however, we will examine the relationship between central and local government.

*In the 1980s there has been a move back towards a centrist government and although local authorities still have some control their power is severely limited.*

There has been much debate in the UK during the last twenty years about the relationship between local and central government. This was brought to a head with the move from Rates to the Community Charge, or Poll Tax as it is more generally known (abandoned due to public pressure). While at first sight the Poll Tax appeared to give more control to local government, it did, in fact, increase the power to control by central government.

### THE STRUCTURE OF LOCAL GOVERNMENT

Local authorities are responsible for a wide range of services, from public libraries to social services. The organisation of local government has been the subject of much change in recent years. The power of local government comes from delegated legislation and as government central policies change this eventually affects each local council. In 1963 the London Government Act brought into existence the Greater London Council (GLC). Within the GLC there were 32 Boroughs and the City of London. This system was different from that operating in the rest of the country when the system of counties and districts was created by the 1972 Local

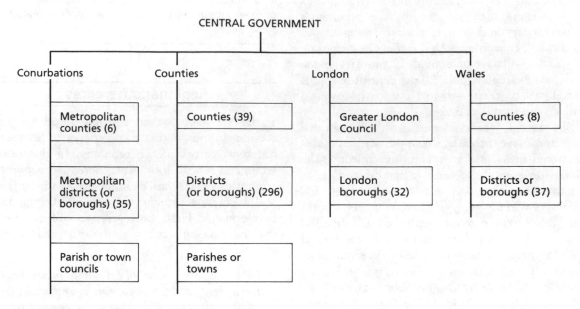

**Fig 4.13 The structure of local government**

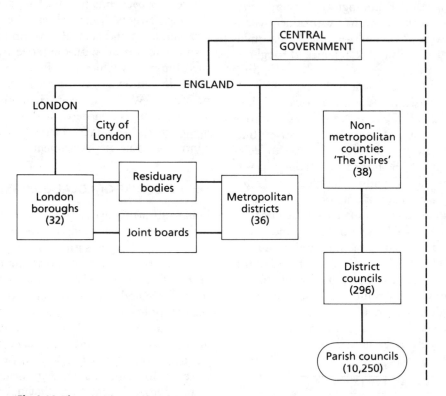

**Fig 4.14 The structure of local government after 1986**

Government Act. The mainly rural areas of the country, the shire counties, were run by county councils which were sub-divided into district councils. The major urban areas of the country were covered by six metropolitan counties – Manchester, Merseyside, Leeds and Bradford, South Yorkshire, Tyneside, and West Midlands – which were divided up into metropolitan districts. This structure is shown in Fig 4.13.

This pattern of local government was modified in 1986 when the GLC and the metropolitan counties were abolished. Some of their functions were devolved to metropolitan districts or the London boroughs while others, such as the police, public transport and the fire service, were to be controlled by newly-created joint boards. These boards were made up of members nominated from the various district and borough councils within the area and, as an interim measure, residuary bodies were set up to wind up the affairs of the different authorities. This structure is shown in Fig 4.14.

---

### ACTIVITY

**1** List the joint boards in your area, show what they are responsible for and who is the chair.

**2** Choose one service offered by a joint board and conduct a mini-survey to assess people's views on the efficiency of the service pre- and post local authority reorganisation.

---

## THE FUNCTIONS OF LOCAL AUTHORITIES

Each local authority will organise its activities to meet the needs of its community as efficiently and effectively as possible. There will be differing priorities over time and within areas which reflect their economic base and, perhaps more importantly, the wishes of the political party in power locally. Figure 4.15 illustrates the structure of Bolton Metropolitan Borough Council which we will use as an example throughout this examination of local government.

## LOCAL AUTHORITY FINANCE

Until 1990 the local element of taxation was provided by the rating system. Rates were a form

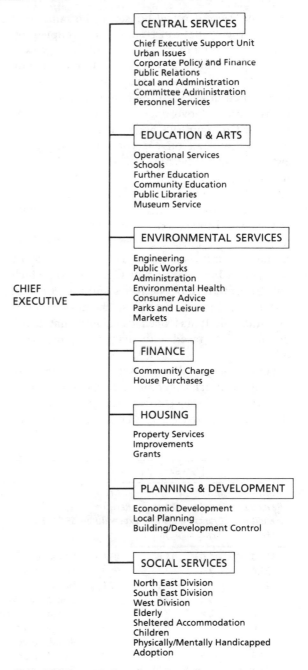

**Fig 4.15 Bolton Metropolitan Council**

of tax on the value of property, both private and commercial, with the occupier of the property paying annual rates of $x$ pence in the pound of an assessed rateable value.

All political parties criticised the rating system, largely because it was seen as unfair. For example, two identical houses in the same road paying the same rates could be occupied by perhaps a family of two adults and three grown-up children while the other could be occupied by a widowed pensioner – the rating system made no distinction between the two households. The Conservative Government replaced the rates with the Community Charge in April 1990. This is a flat rate tax on everyone over the age of eighteen and has become known as the Poll Tax. In theory, the method of determining the total amount of tax to be collected by a local authority is similar to the old rating system, but in reality central government exerts far more control over local authority spending than it ever did before. Because of criticism of the Poll Tax it is to be replaced in 1993 with a new Council Tax, which will be a mixture of the Rates and the Poll Tax systems. It is too early to judge the impact of this new tax but it has been calculated that many people will be faced with significantly increased bills.

Figure 4.16 shows Bolton Metropolitan Borough Council's income and expenditure from all areas. As the Unified Business Rate, the Revenue Support Grant and other specific grants (all being allocated centrally) account for a major part of total income, then control can clearly be seen to be in the hands of central government.

---

**ACTIVITY**

**1** In 1776 Adam Smith, in *The Wealth of Nations*, postulated Four Canons of Taxation. Find out what the four canons are and discuss in groups how closely the Poll Tax meets these canons.

**2** Obtain a copy of your local authority's Income Statement. How does it compare with Bolton's?

---

## TAXING BUSINESS

Although the Poll Tax created a significant amount of civil disturbance, the change in the rating of business properties created an equal, if more muted, furore. The new Unified Business Rate is a national rate set by central government and linked to new, updated, rateable values. Unlike the old system, however, the local authority merely acts as a collection agent for the money which is paid into a central pool and redistributed to each area as an equal amount per

| 1991–92 | | | | | 1992–93 | | | |
|---|---|---|---|---|---|---|---|---|
| Gross Revenue Expenditure £m | Income Specific Grants £m | Other Income £m | Net Revenue Expenditure £m | SERVICE | Gross Revenue Expenditure £m | Income Specific Grants £m | Other Income £m | Net Revenue Expenditure £m |
| 111.0 | 11.0 | 14.4 | 85.6 | Education | 113.6 | 8.3 | 10.9 | 94.4 |
| 26.4 | 2.6 | 2.5 | 21.3 | Social Services | 29.6 | 0.5 | 5.2 | 23.9 |
| 27.5 | 1.0 | 18.9 | 7.6 | Highways | 16.1 | – | 7.3 | 8.8 |
| 6.1 | 1.5 | 2.9 | 1.7 | Planning & Econ. Development | 7.3 | 0.5 | 4.7 | 2.1 |
| 13.0 | 0.8 | 2.7 | 9.5 | Recreation & Tourism | 15.9 | 0.4 | 5.0 | 10.5 |
| 7.0 | – | 3.9 | 3.1 | Environmental Health | 8.2 | – | 4.6 | 3.6 |
| 6.5 | – | 0.5 | 6.0 | Refuse Collection & Disposal | 7.1 | – | 0.8 | 6.3 |
| 13.8 | 10.5 | 0.9 | 2.4 | Other Housing | 13.9 | 9.6 | 1.2 | 3.1 |
| 17.4 | 0.2 | 4.0 | 13.2 | Contingencies & Inflation Provision | 13.9 | – | 1.5 | 12.4 |
| 54.9 | 10.5 | 35.3 | 9.1 | Other Services | 45.5 | 8.6 | 32.7 | 4.2 |
| – | – | – | – | Contributions from Balances | cr 3.9 | – | – | cr 3.9 |
| 0.6 | – | – | 0.6 | Flood Defence Levy | 0.6 | – | – | 0.6 |
| 9.1 | – | – | 9.1 | Passenger Transport Levy | 10.2 | – | – | 10.2 |
| 293.3 | 38.1 | 86.0 | 169.2 | | 278.0 | 27.9 | 73.9 | 176.2 |

**Fig 4.16   Bolton Metropolitan Borough Council – income and expenditure**

council tax payer. In England and Wales the main opposition parties, the Labour Party and Social and Liberal Democrats (SLD), have severely criticised the new system. Both point to figures issued by the Government that show that, overall, nearly one-third of all business premises face rate bills going up by over a half (*see* Table 4.7).

It is predicted that the hardest hit businesses will be small retailers. The Forum of Private Business is predicting that as many as 40 000 small firms could be driven out of business. The Confederation of British Industry (CBI) has also warned that the new system could force businesses to raise prices, adding one point to the Retail Price Index (RPI) over the first two years. The biggest criticism is that the connection between the amount businesses pay and the services they receive will be lost as the funds will be allocated out on a pro-rata basis from the central pool.

---

### ACTIVITY

Again using Adam Smith's canons of taxation, in small groups devise a simple Business Rating System. List each group's contribution and see how clearly they meet the four canons.

---

### LOCAL GOVERNMENT EXPENDITURE

Each local authority will, because of its delegated powers, spend money on a similar range of provisions but, depending upon the locally perceived needs, councils may prioritise differently and thus significant differences in spending patterns may occur. Figure 4.16 shows Bolton Metropolitan Borough Council's expenditure plans for 1991/92 and Fig 4.17 on p 142 shows in detail what the money was actually spent on.

**Table 4.7 Business rate increases in England and Wales**

| Increase | Number of business properties |
| --- | --- |
| More than 100% | 252 000 |
| 50–100% | 246 000 |
| 5–50% | 420 000 |

---

### ACTIVITY

1 Obtain similar figures for your own area.

2 Are there any significant differences?

3 Are there any services that could be better provided centrally and vice versa?

---

## The local authority and the local economy

Whether you are living in the inner city area of Manchester or in an isolated rural Welsh valley, your local authority will have a tremendous impact on the local economy. This will be for two important reasons:

- because of the regulatory powers delegated to it by central government; and
- because of its impact as a major employer and the purchasing power it exerts.

It is upon these two vital areas that we now concentrate.

### THE LOCAL AUTHORITY AND ITS INDIRECT EFFECTS ON THE LOCAL ECONOMY

#### As an employer

By focusing once again on Bolton we can see the impact of a local authority on a fairly typical northern industrial town. Bolton developed as an industrial town in the nineteenth century. Textiles and subsequently engineering and vehicle industries, were the key to the town's prosperity. In the 1960s and 1970s, however, employment in the borough began to fall: from 104 000 in 1977 to an estimated 85 000 in 1986. The primary reason for the decline in employment was the contraction of the key manufacturing sectors in the borough. The decline in employment opportunities in the 1970s was reflected in a rise in unemployment over the period. In 1981 11 per cent of the borough's population was unemployed, compared to 9.7 per cent nationally, rising to 16.9 per cent in March 1986 compared to a national average of 13.6 per cent.

## Some of the Main Services Provided

**Education and Arts   42%**
- 136 schools for approximately 43,300 pupils.
- Approximately 20,000 school meals a day are provided.
- 1 College of Further Education.
- 19 branch libraries in addition to the central library complex.
- 4 museums in addition to the central museum and art gallery.
- Also Youth, Careers and Child Guidance.

**Housing   23%**
- Provision and maintenance of 25,500 Council Houses.
- Promotion of Housing Action Areas encompassing 5,200 properties.
- Also clearance work, housing advice, provision for the homeless, provision of mortgage advances, and rent and rate rebates.

**Leisure Services   4.6%**
- Maintains 628 hectares of parks and open spaces.
- Provides 39 hectares of allotment land.
- 4 swimming baths (including the Water Place).
- 4 sports centres with pools.
- 5 sports centres without pools.
- 7 Community Centres.

**Planning and Engineering Services   8.4%**
- Local planning and development control.

- Provision and management of industrial estates.
- Provision of approximately 5,200 car parking spaces (about 1,250 of which are free), plus additional Saturday only parking of 400 spaces.
- Maintenance of 875 kms. of roads, road safety, and school crossing patrols.
- Collection of 90,000 tonnes of refuse per annum.
- Operation of 7 markets, including the Market Hall.

**Social Services   9.7%**
- 7 children's homes.
- 13 homes for the elderly.
- 1 home, 5 day centres and 5 dispersed housing networks for the mentally ill or handicapped.
- Approximately 5,500 home help cases per year.
- Also aids and adaptations for the physically handicapped, 4 day nurseries, short and long term family placement schemes.

**Other Services   0.5%**
- Public Health Control (including food hygiene, pollution control, pest control, housing fitness and houses in multiple occupation).
- Trading Standards.
- Administration of Justice.
- Registration of Electors.
- Registration of Births, Deaths and Marriages.

**Management and Finance   11.7%**

**Fig 4.17 Bolton Metropolitan Council – where the money went**

---

### ACTIVITY

1 Draw a graph to show unemployment rates in your area and nationally over the last 10 years.

2 What conclusions can you draw from the graphs?

---

The local authority can have a direct impact upon employment through its own levels of employment, but once again the council's hands are tied by central government threats of rate capping. Nevertheless, out of the 85 000 employed in the borough in 1986 a significant proportion were employed by the Local Authority and by the Area Health Authority, the next largest employer. Table 4.8 gives employ-ment in the Bolton area, classified by type of employment.

**Table 4.8   Employment in Bolton 1987, classified by type**

| Sector | Numbers |
| --- | --- |
| Manufacturing | 29 210 |
| Commercial | 29 872 |
| Distribution | 25 342 |
| Other services (incl. construction/building) | 6 086 |
| Total | 89 810 |

---

### ACTIVITY

1 Display the data in Table 4.8 using an appropriate graphical form.

**2** Draw a similar graph for your area.

**3** What contrasts can you draw between your area and Bolton?

### As a buyer

Out of a total budget of nearly £300 million a significant proportion is spent by Bolton Metropolitan Borough Council on goods and services. This obviously has a major impact on the local economy and it is for that reason that several local authorities have undertaken a 'Local Purchasing Initiative' to encourage and support local suppliers. This type of initiative seeks to help the economic regeneration of an area by encouraging local firms to buy from within their area, thus preventing an outflow of funds, and potentially employment, from the area.

---

#### ACTIVITY

What negative features can you see in a Local Purchasing Initiative?

---

### THE LOCAL AUTHORITY AND ITS DIRECT EFFECTS ON THE LOCAL ECONOMY

The importance of the local authority in regenerating the economy of an area cannot be understated. All local authorities now have a department, usually part of the Planning Department, which deals with economic and industrial development. As indicated, Bolton has an above average level of unemployment and it was for this reason that the authority's Economic Development Unit set about identifying the main challenges and developing an economic strategy to address them. When an area suffers high levels of unemployment this will invariably have knock-on effects in a wide range of areas. In Bolton the following key issues were identified:

- low level of growth and development
- poor physical infrastructure
- poor business environment
- low levels of job skills
- low income levels
- social consequences of high unemployment.

---

#### ACTIVITY

**1** Research the key issues defined above in your own area.

**2** On a 10 point scale, how does your area rate on each of the key issues?

---

### DEVELOPING AN ECONOMIC STRATEGY

Some of the challenges that a local economy may face have already been identified. In this section we will look at how policies have developed to enable the development of the local economy.

Since the 1930s Britain has identified areas which have had consistently high levels of unemployment in comparison with the national average. It has developed policies to tackle these challenges under the umbrella of 'regional policy'. These policies have largely taken the form of helping problem areas to develop industry, and therefore create employment. This has been done by providing a range of cash incentives, subsidies and other benefits to companies locating in these areas. There has not been, as in some countries, a significant attempt to move workers from areas of high unemployment to areas of labour shortage. The policies have changed little over the last fifty years, except in degree of emphasis and in the identification of the target regions. The overall benefits of the policies can at best be described as patchy and this failure has led to a much more closely targeted policy aimed mainly at regenerating the inner cities and urban areas.

---

#### ACTIVITY

Draw up a simple chart that shows: Act of Parliament; date; policy; areas supported.

---

Current policy on regenerating urban areas dates from the 1978 Inner Urban Areas Act. The fundamental changes coming from this legislation were that local authorities with areas identified as being in need of regeneration had to bid for funds from central government against specific objectives. The policy was based on partnership between central and local government, and between the public and private sectors. The type of projects that local authorities could bid for were those designed to:

- secure economic regeneration
- improve the environment
- improve facilities and services for those who are, or are at risk of becoming, disadvantaged.

In response to these policies Bolton has undertaken the following initiatives.

## Bolton Business Centre

This was set up as a focus for support for existing firms, new firms and incoming firms. One of its aims is to improve the job skills of the local population, especially the long-term unemployed.

## Infrastructure

The Borough Council recognised that the town was ageing and in danger of losing its popularity as a retail and manufacturing centre. Policies have, therefore, been developed to regenerate the town centre, improve transportation facilities and to reclaim derelict land and develop it for industrial and commercial usage, thereby creating employment opportunities. Despite minor policy changes, these strategies are still being followed through but it is difficult to quantify the success or failure of the initiatives. The local authority can point to the new shopping centres that have been developed, the newly-pedestrianised town centre and improved road system, and the number of new commercial and industrial estates developed, but they are not in a position to say what the impact of these policies has actually been on the local economy.

### ACTIVITY

**1** Produce an A4 poster that indicates to local employers and potential employers the range of support available from the local authority for economic development.

**2** In small groups select one initiative each that has had a positive effect on the economic environment. Make a presentation to the rest of the class which details:

**(a)** the scope of the initiative;
**(b)** the cost;
**(c)** the outcomes.

### ACTIVITY

Undertake an audit of your own firm's impact on the local economy. This should cover, for example, such areas as: total wage bill, uniform business rates paid, employment, etc.

## REGIONAL VARIATIONS IN OUTPUT

Despite the efforts of successive governments and the work of local authorities described above, there are still wide disparities in both the levels and type of regional output. Economic theory suggests that as firms seek to maximise profits they will locate where costs are lowest relative to revenue.

### ACTIVITY

The UK is divided into 10 standard regions: Northern England, Yorkshire and Humberside, Midlands, East Anglia, South East, South West, North West, Wales, Scotland, and Northern Ireland. Individually or in pairs, select one region to research. Find out what industries the region you selected concentrates on and then, with the rest of your colleagues, show this information using appropriate presentational techniques.

Firms, when making location decisions, will be influenced by a range of factors. It should be noted, however, that at the end of the day, there are a number of imponderables that also play a part. Personal choice plays a large part in selecting sites for industry. A report has suggested that the presence of a local golf course could swing a decision in the mind of a manager and many firms start up in the owner's home town. Despite this, certain influences on location can be identified.

## Raw materials

There is still a strong link between some industries and the supply of raw materials. Despite improved transport facilities some industries are still closely tied to raw material supplies.

## Markets

By contrast, industry can be attracted to the other end of the process – the market, where the product is sold. This is particularly true if much weight is gained during processing. For example, brewers and soft drink manufacturers add water to the ingredients brought to them, making the finished product much heavier than the bought-in materials. Again, it is transport costs that seem to be influential.

## Energy

In the distant past energy supply played a large part in locating high energy using industries, for example the textile industry was located near water power. This factor now has little influence though those industries which located in particular areas for this reason tend to remain in them. This is known as industrial momentum or inertia.

## Labour

Labour is much more mobile than the other factors of production but does play a part in location decisions. Firms wanting a particular type of skilled labour are likely to set up where that skill is available. Firms also locate in areas of high unemployment that perhaps offer a cheap, and pliant, workforce. This could have been one of the factors that influenced the location of the Nissan car plant in Sunderland.

## Industrial inertia

When an industry becomes established in an area it is likely that it will carry on in that area, even if the original locational factors no longer apply. Over a period of time the infrastructure surrounding an industry will have developed and that may outweigh other benefits to be gained by relocating.

## Space

Space, and the price of space, is often a key locational factor. You can see many examples of this where industry has moved from town centre sites to cheaper out-of-town industrial estates on ring roads. This also applies to the development of retail sites on the outskirts of towns and the movement of administration units out of the centre of London.

---

### ACTIVITY

In your group, select 10 major industries in the UK and for each one record on a chart the following information: type of industry, names of companies in that industry, location of that industry, and reasons for the location of that industry.

---

Despite many years of government intervention and changing industries, improved transport systems, improved infrastructure and new technologies, there is still a fairly high degree of regional imbalance in the UK. Even in the recession in 1992, unemployment in Northern Ireland was more than double that in south east England and other key indicators mirror that trend. In the end, people will always vote with their feet and no amount of government tinkering with regional policy is likely to persuade vast numbers of people to move to where the work is or industry to move to where the unemployed workers are.

---

### ACTIVITY

Table 4.9 shows the average weekly household expenditure by region in 1991.

**1** Using the data in Table 4.9, say where you would locate a business selling high quality compact disc systems. Justify your decision.

**2** Present the information in Table 4.9 in a better format using an appropriate graphical technique.

---

**Table 4.9   Average weekly household expenditure by region 1991**

| Region | £ per week |
| --- | --- |
| North | 197 |
| Yorkshire & Humberside | 207 |
| North West | 227 |
| East Midlands | 236 |
| West Midlands | 220 |
| East Anglia | 220 |
| Greater London | 267 |
| South East | 265 |
| South West | 241 |
| Wales | 210 |
| Scotland | 209 |
| Northern Ireland | 200 |
| UK | 231 |

## The UK's international trade

In the previous sections we have examined the output of the UK and analysed it both by industrial sector and by region. We have also stressed the growing importance of multinationals and the fact that no country can operate in isolation. In this section we will examine the UK's international trade, examine its trading patterns and partners and look at how free trade is expected to develop in the next decade.

All countries engage in foreign trade in order to enjoy variety of goods and because they cannot produce some things at home as cheaply as they can be obtained from abroad. Countries, like the UK, which cannot produce everything their inhabitants want within the domestic economy are obliged to import goods from abroad, and export goods in exchange.

### HOW MUCH TRADE DOES THE UK DO?

The UK is still one of the world's major trading nations: with just 1.4 per cent of the world's population, we are the fifth most important trading nation. We are not, however, the most 'open' economy in the world, the Dutch, Belgians and other EC countries being more dependent on overseas trade for instance. The importance of the UK's foreign trade in the economic life of the country is shown by the fact that the total value of exports of goods and services is roughly about a third of our national income, but is matched by a roughly similar figure for imports. The UK also accounts for about 10 per cent of world trade.

### WHAT GOODS DOES THE UK TRADE IN?

In some cases we export and import similar goods: for example, British and foreign makes of cars or radios. In other instances we import what we cannot readily produce ourselves, such as pineapples, and export British specialities such as Scotch whisky. Some imported items are exported again (re-exported), with or without being worked on in some way.

Because we have a large population in proportion to our land area (some 233 persons per square kilometre in 1988, compared to 26 for the USA, 161 for Switzerland and 2 for Australia) we cannot produce all the food we eat. Tea, coffee and cocoa we have to import from other countries. We also import wines and spirits, and get our tobacco from warmer climes. In the past we have had to import much of our crude oil but since the advent of North Sea oil we have become a net exporter of oil. Other basic raw materials such as wood and wood pulp, ores and scrap metal, raw cotton and raw wool, form a much larger proportion of our imports than of our exports. On the other hand, 'semi-manufactures' (such as chemicals, textiles and sheet metal) and 'finished manufactures', such as machinery and cars, form a much smaller proportion of our imports than they do of our exports.

Over the past few decades, however, there has been a shift in the pattern of our imports. We now import relatively less food than we did and more manufactures, whether finished goods or semi-finished goods for further processing. Contributory factors are the increasing technology used in UK industry which requires capital goods for investment from all possible sources, the increase in home demand for consumer goods over and above the basic necessities, and the increased efficiency of British farmers. This has been associated with a switch to more trading with our industrialised European partners and less concentration on developing countries. The rising share of manufactured goods in our imports is still of concern and, as over the last 10 years we have seen a major decline in the UK's manufacturing base, any future upturn in the UK economy is likely to lead to manufactured goods being sucked in as UK firms are unable to respond to increased demands.

## Import Penetration Ratios

Even over relatively short periods of time the effect of changing import patterns on the UK can be seen. If we examine the Import Penetration Ratios for a number of products we can see at a glance where the problems lie. Import Penetration Ratios are a simple measure of the percentage of the foreign share of UK markets. A market with a high percentage figure would be one in which there is a high level of imports and one with a low figure would have a low level of imports. The figures shown in Table 4.10 make interesting reading. In just over a ten year period, for example, the amount of foreign cars sold in the UK has risen from just over a third to over 50 per cent. This trend is repeated in other sectors of the economy.

If we select just one sector of the economy, we can see how serious the problem is. In the past the UK may have been the 'manufacturing nation of the world', but not any more. Although the volume of manufacturing output continues a long-term steady rise (with the exception of the current recession), the increase in imported manufactured goods has been astronomical.

Between 1960 and 1983 output in manufacturing rose by 26 per cent while at the same time exports rose by 130 per cent, but imports rose by a colossal 500 per cent.

---

**ACTIVITY**

1 Draw a graph to display the information in Table 4.10.

2 What conclusions can you draw from the graph?

3 For each industry shown, write down both the costs and benefits to the UK and its people of having the Import Penetration Percentages recorded on the graph.

---

The largest share in our exports is taken by finished manufactures, which account for nearly half the total. Examples include engineering products like electrical equipment, engines, vehicles, industrial machinery and armaments.

---

**ACTIVITY**

1 Exports are classified in the following categories: finished manufactures; semi-manufactures; fuel; basic materials; food, beverages and tobacco. Obtain figures for our exports in these classifications (either percentages or raw data) for the latest year and any year at least 10 years ago. Draw a graph to show the information obtained.

2 What two conclusions can you draw from your graph?

---

## Export Sales Ratios

As with import penetration we can also look at the percentage of exports to total sales. Some

---

**Table 4.10  Import penetration in selected UK industries, 1977–1989**

| Industry | 1977 | 1979 | 1981 | 1983 | 1985 | 1987 | 1989 |
|---|---|---|---|---|---|---|---|
| Minerals & mineral products | 12 | 13 | 12 | 13 | 15 | 18 | 17 |
| Chemicals & manmade fibres | 27 | 30 | 31 | 36 | 41 | 43 | 42 |
| Mechanical engineering | 30 | 29 | 32 | 32 | 36 | 38 | 40 |
| Office machinery & data processing equipment | 84 | 92 | 96 | 106 | 100 | 93 | 95 |
| Motor vehicles | 35 | 41 | 42 | 52 | 50 | 48 | 51 |
| Food, drink & tobacco | 17 | 18 | 16 | 17 | 18 | 18 | 18 |
| Clothing & footwear | 25 | 29 | 33 | 33 | 35 | 39 | 40 |

interesting figures stand out: office machinery, 90 per cent; motor vehicles, 35 per cent; chemicals, 45 per cent; mechanical engineering, 45 per cent. We thus find that in those industries where there is a heavy import penetration, exports account for a high proportion of total sales. What has happened in the world economy is that there is very much an interchange of manufactures occurring, based upon the commercial strengths of individual firms making individual products. If we were able to take our classifications down a stage further and show the ratios by product, this point would be further emphasised.

## WITH WHOM DOES THE UK TRADE?

If we went back to the beginning of this century, we would see a very different set of trading partners to the ones we see now. In the early years of the century our major trading partners were the USA and members of the Commonwealth. With the development of trading organisations in Europe, dating back as far as 1958 and the embryo EC in the form of the European Coal and Steel Community (ECSC), our main trading partners are now firmly located in Europe. About 65 per cent of the UK's trade is with just 10 countries. Despite this the UK still trades internationally but the gradual reduction in trade with the Commonwealth is obvious.

Traditionally the UK imported raw materials from the colonies which were utilised to make manufactured goods and re-exported – often back to the colonies. As the Commonwealth countries developed their own industries, it was obvious that the UK had to look for other trading partners. Since joining the EC, the UK has become much more dependent upon European produced food and much less so on food from Australia, New Zealand, etc. Now, as Table 4.11 shows, the UK's trade is firmly embedded in the EC and, as we move toward political and monetary union, this trend will increase.

---

### ACTIVITY

1 Display the data in Table 4.11 in an appropriate graphical form.

**Table 4.11   The UK's top ten trading partners**

| | 1974 | | 1987 | |
| | Imports | Exports | Imports | Exports |
| Country | % | % | % | % |
|---|---|---|---|---|
| Germany | 8.2 | 6.3 | 16.8 | 11.8 |
| USA | 9.8 | 10.9 | 9.7 | 13.8 |
| France | 5.8 | 5.6 | 8.9 | 9.7 |
| Netherlands | 6.9 | 6.1 | 7.6 | 7.3 |
| Italy | 3.1 | 3.1 | 5.5 | 5.2 |
| Belgium/Luxembourg | 3.2 | 4.1 | 4.6 | 4.8 |
| Ireland | 3.5 | 5.0 | 3.7 | 4.8 |
| Japan | 2.5 | 2.0 | 5.8 | 1.8 |
| Sweden | 4.0 | 4.4 | 3.1 | 2.9 |
| Switzerland | 1.8 | 2.1 | 3.5 | 2.3 |
| Total | 48.8 | 49.6 | 69.2 | 64.4 |

2 Indicate two products which we import from each of these countries.

3 Draw two conclusions from your graph.

4 Why do you think that the UK has such an adverse trading balance with Germany and Japan? Why are the gaps widening?

---

## HOW TRADE IS MEASURED

The Balance of Payments of a country is a record of all that country's monetary transactions with other countries during a specific year. It is usually divided into two accounts, the Current Account and the Capital Account. Figure 4.18 summarises the UK Balance of Payments for 1990. As the various items that make up the Balance of Payments are explained, you should make sure you understand those items as they appear in Fig 4.18.

The *Current Account* of the Balance of Payments is the trading account, and it summarises all purchases and sales of goods and services. It is divided into two parts, one showing *visible trade* (exports and imports of physical goods) and the other *invisible trade* (a measure of all services undertaken and paid for). In the early 1980s the UK's Current Balance was positive, that is we sold more goods and services abroad than we imported. From 1986, however, this situation has been reversed and the economy has had a series of current account deficits. In the past it was felt that earnings by invisible trade

| | £million |
|---|---|
| **Current Account** | |
| Visible Trade: | |
| Exports | 102,038 |
| Imports | 120,713 |
| Visible Balance | – 18,675 |
| Invisible Trade: | |
| Credits | 117,350 |
| Debits | 113,055 |
| Invisible Balance | 4,295 |
| **Current Balance** | – 14,380 |
| Transactions in external assets and liabilities: | |
| Investment Overseas by UK residents | – 24,289 |
| Investment in UK by Overseas residents | 24,067 |
| Net currency transactions of UK banks | 8,933 |
| Net currency transactions by other UK residents | 1,606 |
| Official Reserves (addition to) | – 77 |
| Other | 1,840 |
| Net transactions in assets and liabilities | 12,081 |
| Balancing Item | 2,299 |

**Fig 4.18 Balance of payments of the UK, 1990**

would always offset losses on the visible trade side. Again, unfortunately, this is no longer the case, with competition for invisible trade increasing. The list of items that come under the heading of invisible trade includes:

● spending on armed forces overseas
● payments for shipping and aviation services, travel
● the earnings from banking and insurance services
● interest, profits and dividends from overseas investments.

As many countries are now also competing to supply these services, our future earnings are likely to decline. Equally, the massive foreign investment in the UK to develop subsidiaries here in the 1980s will also see increasing profit outflows.

The second part of the Balance of Payments is the *Capital Account*, now more normally listed as 'transactions in external assets and liabilities'. This part of the equation consists quite simply of large movements of money, both into and out of the country, usually for the purposes of investment. It includes flows of short-term capital – the famous *sterling balances*.

It is important to note at this point that there can be a deficit in any part of the Balance of Payments which can be compensated for by a surplus in another part. For example, as previously indicated the UK usually has a deficit on visible trade, or the balance of trade as it is sometimes called, but the surplus on the invisible balance has in the past often been large enough to compensate for it.

Obviously, at the end of the year the Balance of Payments must balance – all a country's imports and spending abroad will have been paid for somehow. What is a problem, however, is if continuing deficits on the current account have to be met by using up a country's reserves of foreign currency or by securing loans from abroad. This is what has happened to the UK in recent years and the Government is attempting to find long-term solutions to the deficits on the current account so that we do not have to borrow so much in the future.

### ACTIVITY

Construct the Balance of Payments for 1991 using the figures given for 1991 in Fig 4.18 and making the following changes: Imports, 116,987; Exports, 92,389; Invisible credits, 108,465; net currency transactions of UK banks, 9,000. All other figures are to remain the same except for drawings, which you should adjust in line with your calculations.

## The importance of international trade

It is still widely accepted by economists that trade is a good thing and that if countries specialise in producing what they are efficient at producing, everyone will benefit. This is not a new theory and goes back nearly 180 years to the economist David Ricardo who first formulated the law of comparative cost. This states quite simply that if countries, or regions, specialise in the production of those goods in which they have a comparative advantage, total world production will increase. This makes possible mutually advantageous trade so that each country ends up able to consume a greater quantity of goods than before. There are no losers in this game of specialisation and, therefore, free trade, which will bring about the maximum specialisation on the basis of comparative advantage, can only raise world production and increase welfare.

How does this theory work? Some countries are in a favourable position in that they can produce goods more cheaply and efficiently than the rest of the world. This does not mean that other countries should produce nothing and buy all their goods from the efficient country, it simply means that they should produce the goods for which they have the least comparative disadvantage. Assume we have two countries, one an industrial economy with a highly-skilled workforce and the other an agricultural economy. If both countries specialise in the production of those goods which they can make most efficiently, the overall output of both manufactured and agricultural goods will be maximised. The two countries then trade with each other and they both gain. This law also applies even if one country has an advantage in producing every good. All that has to be done is to ensure that countries specialise in producing those goods which they are most efficient at producing.

The theory of comparative costs is very simple, yet very powerful. It indicates that trade and specialisation lead to what are known as 'gains from trade' – an increase in total production which should benefit both trading partners. This theory is the basis of the argument that trade between nations should be as free as possible. As with every theory, there are problems in putting it into practice and, because there are other distortions in the world marketplace, it is not always practical.

## REASONS FOR PROTECTION AND BARRIERS TO TRADE

Given the above arguments and the powerful theory of comparative costs, why is it that a whole variety of barriers to trade still exist?

The first reason is that countries have other goals than the maximisation of world output. For example, military/strategic reasons may demand the preservation of a skilled workforce or a large agricultural sector. For example, the French seem to want to cling to subsidising agriculture, the USA subsidises its merchant shipping network. A country dependent on one or two primary products for export earnings may wish to diversify exports to lessen the effect of fluctuations in the prices of these primary products on its ability to import vital machinery and spare parts.

Tariffs are most often justified on the grounds that they protect employment. Such protection is usually considered to be harmful in that it hinders the reallocation of resources out of inefficient industries into expanding efficient ones. However, tariffs may be used only to cushion what may otherwise be a brutal reallocation of resources for the people concerned. In addition, if there are no other jobs to go to and a government is unable to restore full employment through other measures, it is not all that clear to the people directly involved that protection leads to economic efficiency.

---

### ACTIVITY

There was much discussion in late 1992 about the Government's decision to close most of the UK's coal mines and to buy cheaper, imported coal. Obviously, if you take on board the idea of free trade, those inefficient resources used in mining in the UK could be put to better use. The arguments are not, however, clear cut.

Organise a role play in which half the class are miners and their union representatives and the other half are government officials who want to close the mines. Using economic arguments in the debate, try to come to a resolution of the problem.

---

Related to the employment argument is the anti-dumping argument. Dumping occurs where price is raised in the protected home market and part of the proceeds of higher prices are used to subsidise exports so that they can undercut competitors in other countries. British car manufacturers have often accused the major Japanese car producers of this tactic, but this has never been proved. Faced with dumping, a government is clearly justified in protecting its home industry. In fact, however, we often hear allegations of dumping and unfair competition when what is involved is competition on the basis of low wages. However one may feel about the low wages paid in some poor countries, it is hypocritical to cry 'unfair competition' in the face of competition prescribed by the doctrine of comparative costs. Telling poor countries to specialise on the basis of comparative costs and then imposing restrictions on their exports when they do is hardly fair.

Another important justification for tariff protection is the infant industry argument. In many countries tariffs are imposed to protect new or 'infant' industries until they are strong enough to meet foreign competition. The established industries of the industrialised world already enjoy economies of scale and can often exploit a monopoly position in the world market, preventing the development of new competitors. Developing countries may argue that all they are doing is altering their long-term comparative advantage – comparative advantages need not stand still.

Tariffs are, of course, often imposed as a short-term remedy for a Balance of Payments deficit. The problem is, however, that the imposition of a tariff may put off facing up to an underlying weakness in an industry. In addition, it also often provokes retaliation – trading partners raise tariff barriers of their own.

Despite the above arguments, the world is gradually, and sometimes painfully, moving towards the liberalisation of trade. One trend which is perhaps disturbing is that rather than one global economy being created, several super trading blocks are being created.

## ORGANISATIONS WORKING FOR FREE TRADE

Since the end of the Second World War there has been a planned move towards trade liberalisation. This has taken two forms:

- the development of trading blocks like the EC
- multilateral trade liberalisation.

### General Agreement on Tariffs and Trade (GATT)

GATT is the most important institution fostering global reductions in trade barriers. GATT was set up at the end of the Second World War alongside other international organisations for post-war reconstruction. Its remit is to provide a framework for the orderly conduct of trade, as well as a framework within which trade liberalisation can take place.

The mechanism instituted by GATT to promote trade is the *Negotiating Round*. This is a mechanism which periodically brings together the 100 plus *Contracting Parties* (CPs) to agree a package of trade measures. Before the current round of negotiations, there were seven previous rounds which were largely successful in stimulating world trade. The present round, the Uruguay Round, began in 1986 and was supposed to have reached agreement by December 1990, but because of intransigent attitudes of some of the CPs it has not yet concluded its work. The present round, like all others, is focusing on an agreed area in which it wants to stimulate trade and reduce protectionism. The aim would be for countries to agree reciprocal trade concessions. Getting these concessions is sometimes very difficult because of the national vested interests involved. The current hold up in the present round has been caused largely by France's reluctance to agree to major reductions of the subsidies the EC gives to farmers. This obviously helps French farmers gain a competitive advantage, an advantage that has been declared unfair by the USA. Unless compromise can be reached in such situations an international trade war may result – which will be to no-one's benefit.

Further sticking points in the latest negotiations involve the Multi-Fibre Agreement (MFA), which has favoured developed nations in the past at the expense of the developing world. The potential gains to the poorer countries are significant and the remit in this round is to provide a basis for the eventual phasing out of the MFA. As more and more companies take steps to protect their 'intellectual property rights', this issue has also come up for consideration by GATT. In industrialised nations, patents, copyrights and trademarks have been developed to protect the inventor. Outside the developed world, however, these are not really enforceable. Thus, in certain parts of the world you can obtain cheap copies of Reebok trainers, Rolex watches, Benetton tee shirts and so on.

It is vital that the GATT talks succeed in this and future rounds for, as we have seen, free trade ultimately benefits all involved. The problem lies in the short-term attitudes taken by some countries and the enormous influence that some pressure groups, like the French farmers, can exert on their negotiators.

### The European Community

Just as at the end of the Second World War GATT was formed to liberalise trade internationally so too was the European Community (EC) born. The reasons for its inception are similar to those of GATT, plus it was felt that the weakened countries of western Europe needed some form of defensive, economic and political linkage to counteract the power and impact of the USSR and the USA.

---

### ACTIVITY

Produce a 'time map' to show the development of the EC from its inception as the European Coal and Steel Community up to the introduction of the Single European Market in 1992. Your map should include all major changes, including the composition of the EC.

---

As we move further towards political union, Europeans must not forget that first and foremost the EC is a trading block or customs union. It has effectively removed all internal customs duties, to enable businesses to regard the whole of the EC as their domestic market. The EC, while helping trade liberalisation *within* the EC, has set up some formidable trade barriers to goods coming into the EC from outside – the Common External Tariffs (CET). The advantages of this internal trade liberalisation are that it enables greater gains to be made from specialisation and reduced costs, arising from the greater economies of scale to be gained. Once again this is fine from a global perspective, but if you lose your job because your company is relocating at the heart of Europe, perhaps in Belgium, then that is a different matter. If there

was full employment throughout the EC this would not be a significant problem.

Although in theory there is free trade, in practice, by the use of differing levels of VAT and excise duties, barriers still exist. The French, for example, argue that our high levels of excise duty on wine act like a tariff. As we move towards standardised VAT and excise rates this problem will disappear. One of the main causes of problems experienced in liberalising world trade has been the difference in subsidies that are applicable throughout the globe. The USA and Japan give national subsidies of less than 2 per cent of Gross National Product, while in the EC the average is about 5 per cent. The amount of subsidy paid in the EC is also closely linked to the Common Agricultural Policy (CAP) which is currently causing delays on reaching agreements in the GATT talks.

### THE COMMON AGRICULTURAL POLICY (CAP)

One of the main aims of the EC is to achieve common economic policies on issues such as employment, energy, industry, transport and, specifically, agriculture.

The CAP has a number of methods of support, all of which are directed at achieving its aims as set out in Article 39 of the Treaty of Rome:

> ... *to increase agricultural productivity and promote the optimal utilisation of factors especially labour; to ensure thereby a fair standard of living for the agricultural community; to stabilise markets; to ensure certain supplies; and to ensure supplies to consumers at reasonable prices.*

The principal method of support involves maintaining a market price for each commodity within the EC, which is normally higher than the price in the rest of the world and which is normally above the price that would be set if there was no intervention. The EC achieves this in two ways. First, by setting tariffs on imported commodities which brings their price up to the EC agreed market price. This, of course, is one area that GATT is trying to make an impact on to allow free trade. Second, within the EC a system of intervention buying is operated to stop

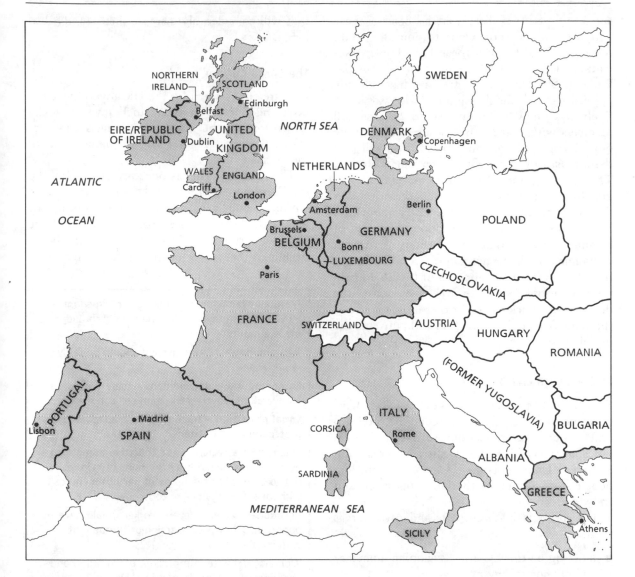

**Fig 4.19 Member States of the European Community**

overproduction flooding the market and having the effect of reducing prices. This acts to put a floor on the market price so that when the market price falls below this level, the EC is obliged to buy what the farmers offer them for sale – at the intervention price. This, as you will probably be aware, has led to the development of 'butter mountains, beef mountains, apple mountains and wine lakes', much of them generated by French over-production. The cost of this intervention, which has a major impact on the EC's budget, is a serious problem. Many attempts at

reform have been made but with little success. The present strategy seems to be to persuade farmers, by subsidy, to 'set-aside' agricultural land and to utilise that land for environmental purposes.

## THE FUTURE OF EUROPEAN UNION

Despite the recent turmoil in Europe's Exchange Rate Mechanism (ERM) and growing uncertainties about the Maastricht Treaty, new candidates are still queuing up to join the EC. This speaks for itself: if there were no benefits those countries would not want to join the club. Members from the European Free Trade Association (EFTA) are keen to join – Austria, Finland, Sweden and Switzerland have already applied for full membership and Norway looks likely to follow. The five could become full members within five years and up until then the new European Economic Area (EEA) will give them most of the benefits of the Single Market. The second group of countries wanting to join are from eastern Europe and these pose a different challenge for the EC. The combination of low income, large populations and lots of farming means that all eastern European economies would be net gainers from EC funds. It is, however, in the interests of the EC to help these countries since, in the long term, the developing markets of eastern Europe and the gains from trading in them will outweigh the initial costs.

## THE MAASTRICHT TREATY

Ever since the formative years of the EC we have been moving ever closer to economic, political and monetary union within Europe. However, when a treaty like the Maastricht Treaty on European Union dots the 'i's and crosses the 't's, people start to analyse the full implications and show concern.

The treaty is in three parts and covers areas such as:

- building on the EC and developing monetary and economic union
- developing 'joint action' for 'foreign and security policy'
- co-operation on justice and home affairs.

All the above proposals still need ratification and it will be some time yet before the full implications of the Maastricht Treaty are clear and the fine print explained. What is true though, for young people especially, is that the advantages of further union will significantly outweigh the disadvantages. An individual's qualifications will be recognised across Europe, they will have the right to live and work where they choose within the EC, plus a whole host of other Euro-benefits that will considerably increase their standard of living.

### The Social Charter

One area of concern for the UK government has been the Social Charter which gives a social dimension to the economic changes that are taking place. *See* Fig 4.20 for the main points of the Social Charter.

The Social Charter is one way of levelling up standards across Europe and ensuring that major national and regional disparities disappear. Although there has been some criticism of the Social Charter it is likely that it would be of benefit to the people of the United Kingdom.

---

**Freedom of movement** – the right of freedom of movement throughout the Community should be made a reality.

**Jobs and pay** – all employment should be fairly remunerated.

**Living and working conditions** – there should be an overall improvement in workers' conditions.

**Social protection** – there should be adequate social protection for all citizens.

**Freedom of association and collective bargaining** – every worker should have the right to belong, or not to belong, to the union of her or his choice without suffering adverse consequences.

**Vocational training** – every worker should have the opportunity to continue training 'throughout working life'.

**Workers' rights to information, consultation and participation** – these should be developed, particularly in multinational companies.

**Health and safety** – every worker should enjoy satisfactory health and safety conditions.

**Children and young people** – should be adequately protected in the area of employment.

**Elderly people** – every retired person should have enough resources to enjoy a decent standard of living.

**People with disabilities** – should get additional assistance to ease their integration into work and society.

---

**Fig 4.20 Main points of the Social Charter**

ACTIVITY

1 Allocate each point of the Social Charter to a small group. Each group should then prepare and give a presentation to the rest of the class, showing what the benefits and costs are of that particular point.

2 After the presentations, debate the Social Charter and come to a resolution on the following motion: 'This house believes that the Social Charter would be of major benefit to the citizens of the United Kingdom'.

## An introduction to law

The final section of this unit on the business environment is concerned with an introduction to the law as it affects business. All businesses are concerned with legal controls which are placed on them by the government and, at various times in this book, there are references to different areas of law.

The aim of this section is to help you to understand some of the basic principles of the law as it affects business. If you have studied law before most of this will be very familiar to you, but it may still be worth revising. The section covers the following areas:

- What is law?
- What sorts of laws affect businesses?
- What is the difference between Civil and Criminal law?
- How do the courts work and how are they organised?
- Who is in the legal profession and what do they do?
- Where does law come from and how is it made?
- What alternatives are there to the courts?

This section is not intended to be a substitute for taking a business law option later on the course but it should provide you with a working knowledge of what the law means to businesses.

### WHAT IS LAW?

It has been said that laws exist just to test the ingenuity of businesses in getting round them.

This tells us something about laws:

- they control businesses in some way
- they are imposed from outside the business
- they are broken from time to time
- they change.

However, this does not really tell us what laws *are*. There are no universally accepted definitions of law, but one that works quite well is 'Laws are rules which can be enforced by the courts if they are broken'. This definition highlights a couple of things about laws:

- they are more than just rules
- they can be enforced if they are broken
- the state gets involved, through the courts, in making sure they are enforced.

ACTIVITY

Which of the following are laws?

1 A sign saying 'Keep off the Grass' in a park.

2 Thou shalt not steal.

3 A notice in a school saying 'Do not run in the building'.

4 The requirement under the Data Protection Act to keep computer information secure.

5 A company regulation that employees must not smoke in the canteen.

Obviously number 4 is part of a law; number 2 is not a law itself, but there is a law which says the same thing (The Theft Act) and the first one could be a local law (known as a by-law).

### WHAT SORTS OF LAW ARE THERE?

Law can be divided up in a number of ways:

- by topic
- by where it comes from
- by whether the State will enforce it or an individual.

### BY TOPIC

There are all sorts of different areas of law which control the operation of businesses – some of the main ones are given in Fig 4.21.

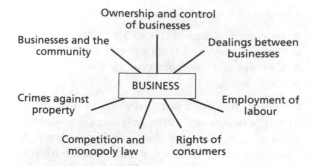

**Fig 4.21 The main areas of law which affect business**

Each of these areas of law will have a number of Acts of Parliament associated with it and there will be rules as to what can and cannot be done in each of the cases. The list above is not a complete list of the areas of law which affect businesses and there are many others which could have been used. A more complete version of this figure (Fig 4.23), giving examples of specific areas of law and whether the state or the individual will be expected to enforce the law, appear in the summary at the end of the unit.

---

### ACTIVITY

**1** Arrange an interview with a local business and try to find out what they see as the main areas of law which affect their business.

**2** Do these areas of law fit into the categories of laws listed above?

**3** Are there any areas you feel have been left out of the list?

---

### BY WHERE IT COMES FROM

There are two main sources of law in this country:

1 Statutes or Acts of Parliament
2 Judge made law or case law, also called Common Law.

### Statutes

Acts of Parliament are passed by both Houses of Parliament but it is the House of Commons which has the key role. In order for proposed legislation (a Bill) to become an Act of Parliament, it must follow a strict sequence of events (*see* Fig 4.22).

**Proposal stage.** Ideas and demands for new laws come from all sorts of areas in the community and from government. Some of the ideas are not adopted, others are of wide interest or use and are adopted as proposals for legislation (Bills). There is only a limited amount of time that Parliament can devote to passing new laws in any Parliamentary session and this places limits on the number of new Acts of Parliament. The main pieces of legislation for a Parliamentary session will be outlined in the Queen's Speech at the opening of Parliament, where the key aims of the Government for that session are stated. Most new legislation will be introduced by the Government as a Government Bill; there are a number of different sources for Government Bills:

● The party manifesto of the party in Government may state that it is an aim of the party to do something. This is usually as a result of the proceedings at the Party Conference where members of the party set the aims for the Party

**Fig 4.22 The sequence of events leading up to the passing of an Act of Parliament**

for the next year and outline the key goals for them to achieve. A lot of the laws which allowed the privatisation of large parts of the public sector over the last decade or so came from this source, for example. It was an aim of the Conservative Party to reduce the public sector and, when they came to power, they introduced laws which would allow them to do this.

- In the case of a 'national emergency' the government may introduce a Bill to respond to an urgent situation – an example of this is the Prevention of Terrorism Act which was passed very quickly as a reaction to terrorist offences.

- Government investigations of one sort or another may highlight the need for a government to take action on some aspect of life in the UK. For example, a lot of the legislation which has affected schools and colleges over the last few years has been the result of investigations by the government into the education system which suggested that the education system needed to be reformed.

- The Law Commission is charged with identifying areas where the law needs to be updated and changed, and advising the Government on the best way to go about doing this. Examples of laws which they have influenced include the Companies Acts which have been constantly updated to make sure that we keep in line with our legislative commitments to the EC, and that our company law is effective both in making sure businesses can operate effectively and in protecting consumers and shareholders from the effects of badly-run or unscrupulous businesses.

Other Bills are the result of suggestions which are put forward by individual MPs of any party (the Private Member's Bills). These suggestions for legislation can come from any number of sources; some of the most common ones are:

- Pressure groups which have lobbied the MP and convinced him or her to support their cause. Many MPs have particular causes or interests with which they are associated and which they will try to put forward for legislation. An example of this would include the various attempts to introduce laws to ban fox hunting – most of these have been introduced by MPs as Private Member's Bills and do not represent the policy of the government of the day.

- An MP may come across a special case in their constituency, or which is brought to them in some other way, which they consider raises a point which is so important that it requires legislation to correct it. Very few Bills of this sort ever make it to the stage of being debated and almost never pass into law.

- MPs may have particular personal interests or 'hobby horses' which they pursue and which they consider to be important. Again, such proposals are not likely to make it to the stage of even being considered as potential legislation.

Private Members' Bills are very few in number and the MPs who have the chance of putting forward a Private Member's Bill are selected by a ballot, so the chances of something becoming law in this way are fairly remote.

Many Government Bills are put into quite a lot of detail at this first stage – even before they go to the House of Commons or the House of Lords. This is usually done by publishing them as:

**White Papers or Green Papers**. These are consultation documents used by the Government to try to find out what the reaction will be to a particular legislative proposal and to attract any suggestions for its improvement before it is formally put forward to become law.

**First reading**. At this stage the general topic and the outline of the proposed area of legislation are introduced. There will be no real debate at this point, but there will be a vote as to whether the proposal should be allowed to go any further, which will be decided on a simple majority.

**Second reading**. More detail is given at this stage and there will be some debate on the general principles of the proposal so that it is clear to all members of the House what is being proposed and roughly how it is intended to work. There will be another vote at this stage which could throw the proposal out – it will need a simple majority to go on to the next stage.

**Committee and report stage**. At this stage the detail is put onto the proposal by a Committee working with a Parliamentary draughtsman (an expert on the wording of laws). The Committee will normally be drawn from all of the parties in Parliament so that there is a fair representation of opinion. The Committee will report back to the House with the changes which it has made to the proposal and the fine detail it has decided. After debate in the House, the proposal can then go back to the Committee for further alterations – this process may be repeated several times.

**Third reading**. This is the main debate on most pieces of legislation. If there are people who think that it should not become law or that it needs to be changed in some major way, this is their chance to argue their point with the almost complete Bill before them. So, at this stage they will have all of the detail which they need to argue the case for or against a particular piece of law. These debates can be quite heated and may last a long time if no decision is taken to put a time limit on the debate. At the end of the debate there will be a vote on the Bill as it now stands (it may have been revised and altered a bit during the debate) and, if it gains a majority, it will go forward for the last stages.

Most Bills will start in the House of Commons and go through this process there. Once this process has been completed in the House of Commons the Bill will go to the House of Lords and a similar procedure will be followed there.

There are some Bills which start in the House of Lords and then go to the House of Commons, but these are relatively rare.

**Royal Assent**. Before any Bill can become law it has to gain the assent of the King or Queen – this is never withheld and is now something of a formality.

Once a Bill has passed through this process it will be known as an Act of Parliament or a Statute (the two terms are interchangeable). There will be a date set when the Act becomes law and this date, known as the commencement date, will be a part of the Act itself. Many Acts become law very quickly after they are passed, others are brought into force in stages and some Acts have parts to them which never become law as they are never actually brought into force. Acts do not die of old age, they remain law until they are actually stated not to be law any longer – this is called 'repeal' and usually occurs when a new Act replaces an older one. The new Act will have a section which states which earlier Acts will be repealed by the new one, or which sections of earlier Acts if the whole Act is not to be replaced.

---

### ACTIVITY

**1** Look in the press and identify a piece of legislation which is going through Parliament at the moment.

(a) Where did it come from? Was it a Private Member's Bill or a Government Bill?

(b) Is it likely to become law soon? – Is it controversial or not?

**2** Look in the press to see if you can find any issues where a group or an individual is calling for action by Parliament in a specific area.

(a) What are they asking for?

(b) What are the chances of this being picked up by an MP or by the Government and becoming law?

**3** Ask a local business if they have had to make any changes to the way they operate their business in the last year as a result of changes in the law.

---

### Judge made law or case law

When a judge hears a case he or she has to make a decision and this decision will be recorded. Often it is judges who have to decide exactly how to interpret a piece of legislation which has come from Parliament, because no matter how carefully the law is drafted, there will always be disagreements as to how it applies in particular cases. There will also be people who try to find loopholes and ways to avoid laws which they do not want to obey. Take a hypothetical example (based on an imaginary Act and fictional cases).

---

### EXAMPLE

*Suppose there is an Act of Parliament, The Fire Safety Act 1995, which states as one of its provisions 'All factories shall ensure that access to all fire equipment and exits is clear and unobstructed at all times'. This may be seen as quite a clear statement of the law. There are,* however, a number of questions which could be raised, for example:

- *Is a shop where T shirts are printed a 'factory' for the purpose of this Act?*
- *Is a loading bay fire exit obstructed if a lorry is parked against it while waiting to unload, with the driver in the lorry but the engine off?*

*Both of these situations could give rise to cases in the courts, where an inspector brings an action against the businesses concerned for breach of the Act and they feel that they have been unfairly treated.*

### R v Smith (1995)

*In an action by the Fire Inspectorate against Printall Ltd for failing to comply with the Act, it was decided that any business where goods are manufactured or processed will count as a factory for the purposes of this Act.*

### R v Jones plc (1995)

*In an action by the Fire Inspectorate against Jones plc for failing to comply with the Act by allowing a lorry to block a fire exit it was decided that a lorry temporarily parked would not break the Act as long as it could be moved immediately in an emergency.*

*Both of these cases can now be used to make the law clearer and will set precedents which other judges can follow – an example of cases making the law clearer.*

There are some areas of English law where there is no Act of Parliament as the basis for the law – these areas consist entirely of case law where judges have made decisions and, over the years, these decisions have built up into a set of clear rules. The best example of this area of law is the law of contract. In these areas of the law a system known as 'precedent' operates, which tries to ensure that the cases which are used are applied consistently so that the law is:

- *certain* – you can predict how a case will be decided if it is the same as an existing one
- *able to evolve* – higher courts can change the decisions which have been made by lower courts
- *consistent* in the way that it is applied
- *flexible* in that new circumstances can be taken into account if they need to be.

The system of precedent works quite simply. If a case is decided by a court at the level of the High Court then any other case which is *identical in principle* to this original case should be decided in the same way if it comes to another High Court hearing. If the case goes to a higher court, such as the Court of Appeal then that court has the right to make a different decision and any court lower down the hierarchy will have to abide by that decision. If the case, or a similar one, then goes to the House of Lords (which is the highest level of court in this country) then they, again, will have the right to change the earlier decisions – and all the lower courts will have to decide similar cases in the same way.

Courts have the right to decide that there is something about a case which makes it different from an earlier precedent and this is called *distinguishing* a case. In such circumstances the courts are free to decide the case in a different way – but only if there is genuinely something different about the case.

---

### EXAMPLE

*To take a simple example, if there is a case brought to the High Court under our fictitious Fire Safety Act 1995 to answer the question 'If a piece of fire equipment is extra to that required by the Act is it still an offence if it is not easily accessible?' the court may decide that it is an offence on the grounds that the equipment is there to be used and staff in the business will be aware of this and expect to be able to use it. If it is not available this will handicap their reactions in the event of a fire if they have to waste time finding out that the equipment is not available to them. The effect of this decision is that any similar cases coming before the High Court in the future should be decided in the same way – unless there are real differences in the case which will allow the judge to decide the case differently.*

---

The case may then be appealed to the Court of Appeal by the business (which feels that it has not been fairly treated by the High Court). This court may decide that the fact that the equipment is extra will mean that there are other means of dealing with the fire available and, as long as access to these is not obstructed, it is not fair to penalise the business for trying to do more than the law actually requires them to do. The effect of this decision will be that if a case of the same kind comes up again at the High Court or Court of Appeal level, it will have to be decided in the same way.

The case may then be appealed again to the House of Lords by the Fire Inspectorate who are unhappy with the Court of Appeal verdict. If the House of Lords reinstate the original decision from the High Court the matter is then closed – any similar cases which come to the courts in the future will have to be dealt with in the same way. The only two ways that such cases can be decided differently are:

- If a similar case goes to the House of Lords they can change their decision in a later case – but this is actually quite rare.
- Parliament may decide that the courts have not interpreted the Act in the way that they would have liked and will pass a new piece of legislation which will make it plain that all fire equipment, whether extra to the basic requirements of the law or not, has to have unobstructed access to it.

## WHO ENFORCES THE LAWS?

Another way of dividing the law up is to look at who is responsible for enforcing it. If the State enforces the law then it is known as *Criminal Law*. If the State leaves it to individuals to enforce the laws, merely providing the court structure within which they can do this, then it is known as *civil law*.

There are a number of key differences between civil and criminal law and it is useful to have a look at them because they have implications for businesses. Most of the law that a business will be affected by will be civil law, in one form or another. But there are a number of areas, health and safety for example, where the criminal law will affect businesses.

The definitions below of the civil and the criminal law are not full definitions as they would be found in a law textbook but they do serve to underline the differences between the two areas:

## Civil law

The intention of the civil law is to provide a way for individual citizens to solve disputes where

one feels that they have suffered a loss as a result of a breach of the law by another. The intention of the civil law is to compensate people for the losses which they have suffered as a result of the breach of the law.

## Criminal law

The intention of the criminal law is for the State to punish those who have broken its rules and to protect society, if necessary, from further breaches of the law by this person or people. The key differences are set out below:

**Civil law:**
- Relies on individuals to bring actions to enforce the law
- Aims to compensate people for what they have lost/suffered.

**Criminal law:**
- Relies on the State to bring the action to enforce the law
- Aims to punish people for the breaches of the law
- Aims to protect society where necessary.

The terms that are used are also quite different, as set out in the table opposite.

The differences here have a number of important implications for businesses:

1 The burden of proof is different: if you are accused of a criminal offence you merely have to show that there is a reasonable doubt that you are guilty, whereas if you are facing a civil action you will have to show that your case is stronger than the other party. This difference comes from the fact that we have a basic maxim in our criminal law '*Innocent until proven guilty*'. This cannot apply in civil law and the court will have to decide a case it hears – the courts don't have the option of declaring a case a draw or saying 'Don't know'.

2 The penalties are different: in civil law the intention is to compensate people for what they have lost – so, if a driver of a car has run into one of your lorries you can assess quite easily the costs involved – the repair, the hire of a replacement vehicle and the loss of driver's time will all

**Table 4.12  Civil and criminal law**

| Terms used | Civil law | Criminal law |
| --- | --- | --- |
| Who brings the case? | The individual concerned – known as the **Plaintiff** | The State – often the police – known as the **Prosecution** |
| What is the name for the action brought? | A civil **suit** – one person **sues** the other | A **prosecution** – the State **prosecutes** the law breaker. |
| What is the person who has the action brought against them called? | The **Defendant** | Should be referred to as the **Defendant** – but sometimes the term **Accused** is used |
| Where will the action be brought? | In the **civil** courts | In the **criminal** courts |
| What penalties will the person bringing the action want? | Money compensation – called **damages** | A **fine** or some **loss of liberty** |
| To what standard does the person bringing the case have to prove it? | On the **balance of probabilities** | **Beyond all reasonable doubt** |
| How will the case be cited? | *SMITH* v *JONES* 1997 | *R* v *JONES* 1997 |

need to be paid for. In criminal law the intention is not to compensate, but to punish. So, if a vehicle has not been taxed, even if this is just an oversight and there is no intention to defraud the State you will probably be fined, maybe quite heavily, for your breach of the law.

3 In civil law you have the choice of whether to bring an action or not; in criminal law the State will decide whether an action is brought. So, if a customer does not pay a bill you have the choice of whether to sue or not. If a customer is caught shoplifting by the police they will decide whether to prosecute, although your views would probably carry a lot of weight.

As mentioned above there are two separate systems of courts in this country; the two systems work in quite similar ways and, if you take the Business Law option on the course you will look at this in more detail. This section attempts to provide a quick guide to the main courts in which you could be involved in cases. It does not give a complete guide to the court system. Most people are quite scared of the courts and there are a number of reasons for this:

● People associate the courts with crimes and with punishments – they only end up in court if they have done something wrong or have not been able to solve a dispute in any other way.

● People are worried about the cost of taking a case to court – even if they have a good case they will be worried that they will have to pay expensive legal bills, and there is always a fear of losing the case.

● People find courts very confusing and very formal – they do not feel easy places to go into and the language and systems used are designed for the legal profession rather than members of the public.

● There can be a very long delay between bringing a case to the attention of the court and the actual hearing, and many people feel that it is just not worth the effort.

### ACTIVITY

Would a business take someone to court in the following circumstances? Read the outline cases below and say whether you think a business would be prepared to take someone to court in each of them. Make a note of the reasons for your answers as well.

**(a)** A customer's child steals a packet of Smarties from a display next to the till in a supermarket. The customer returns the (half empty) packet and makes the child apologise.

**(b)** A customer is caught stealing £32.00 of goods – they only have £19.00 on them but claim they just 'forgot' to pay.

**(c)** A normally very good customer has ignored a bill for £25.00 despite a number of reminders.

**(d)** A building firm has failed to come in to make good some shoddy work and you have had to pay £300 for another firm to put their work right. They will not pay.

What are the differences between the situations where you feel court action is justified and where it is not?

Even given the above, there are a lot of cases which end up in the courts each year for the courts to decide; most of these are disposed of very quickly and will never go beyond the first court they are heard in. A very few cases are appealed to a higher court and, in extreme cases may be appealed a number of times until they reach the House of Lords which is the highest court in the UK. There is also a number of courts outside the country which also have some influence on our law, such as the European Court of Justice, the International Court of Human Rights and the International Court.

## Civil courts

There are two courts where civil cases will start; these are both known as 'courts of first instance' as they are the courts where cases will go in the first instance.

**1 County Court.** This court deals with the less serious civil cases and also has a subdivision known as the Small Claims Court which is designed to provide easy, quick and cheap justice for those who want to bring a case of fairly small value to court. The County Court has legally qualified judges who will decide the case and also assess the penalties which are to be imposed. The Small Claims Court can only hear cases of relatively low value and is conducted in a very informal way. The advantage of this is that it reduces the costs of the case, encourages people to feel that they can cope with bringing the case and does away with the cost of lawyers (if you choose to use a solicitor in the Small Claims Court you will have to pay their bill yourself whether you win or lose). Small Claims Court has been very good for a lot of businesses to bring actions for fairly small amounts that they would not have wanted to bring through the normal court system.

**2 High Court.** This court deals with the more serious cases and has a number of divisions which specialise in different areas of law. As with the County Court it is staffed by legally qualified judges who will hear the case and, having decided it, will also assess the damages which will have to be paid (if any). The costs of such a case can be very high.

## Criminal courts

Again, there are two courts where cases may start – which court will hear which case will depend on how serious it is. Minor offences, known as *summary* offences will go to the Magistrates Court. More serious offences, referred to as *indictable* offences, will go to the Crown Court for trial.

**1 Magistrates Court.** The Magistrates Court deals with over 95 per cent of the criminal cases in this country each year, most of them very minor such as petty theft and driving cases such as speeding. The Magistrates are not legally qualified: they are members of the community who have agreed (for no salary) to act as Magistrates and they are given detailed legal advice by an official of the court (the Clerk to the Justices) who is legally qualified. In the Magistrates Court the job of the Magistrate is to decide on the guilt or innocence of the defendant and to pass sentence on them if they are found guilty. They will get detailed legal advice from the clerk to help them in making this decision. As they are not legally qualified they can only impose fines up to £5000 and prison sentences up to 6 months. If they feel that a case deserves a more severe penalty they will pass it on to the Crown Court where heavier sentences will be delivered.

**2 Crown Court.** The Crown Court will deal with the more serious cases. The court is staffed by a Judge who is legally qualified and there will also be a jury of 12 people to hear a case. In a case it is the judge who will give the jury legal advice, the jury who will decide if the defendant is guilty or innocent, and the judge who will decide on the sentence if the defendant is found guilty.

## Alternatives to the courts

Many businesses now try to make sure that they solve disputes before they get to the courts. The main way of doing this is to say that if there is a dispute between a customer and a business it will be referred to an expert in the area concerned who is independent and is able to consider the case impartially. There are a number of reasons for using this process – known as *arbitration* – rather than letting a case go to court:

- the costs tend to be lower
- there will probably be less publicity
- it can be dealt with quickly
- the awards may be lower
- the business has more of a chance to select who hears the case.

Some firms have been accused of 'fixing' arbitration cases but this will be extremely rare and will not happen where a firm uses a reputable body as an arbitrator in a case. Where the system works well there are a lot of advantages to all concerned in that a dispute can be settled easily, quickly and cheaply to everyone's satisfaction with a minimum of fuss.

## THE LEGAL PROFESSION

The legal profession in this country is split into two groups:

**1 Solicitors**, who are legally trained and deal with all sorts of different matters such as buying houses, proving wills, setting up companies and dealing with small court cases.

**2 Barristers**, who are legally trained but in a different way. Barristers specialise in presenting cases in court, and will often also specialise in one area of law such as tax, or company law.

This distinction is important to you in business as you need to know

- Who to take particular problems to
- What it is likely to cost you to deal with particular situations/problems.

## Solicitors

Solicitors are a bit like a local GP: they will deal with a wide range of problems and will offer advice on many areas. Most businesses will need the services of a solicitor at some point and there can be a number of reasons for this. Some of these are listed below:

- Buying or selling property for the business
- Renting property for the business
- Drafting contracts – of sale or of employment for example
- Suing customers who haven't paid their bills
- Defending anyone who has been sued for any reason
- Advising people on the legality of a deal they are considering
- Helping people to set up a business in a particular way – as a partnership or a limited company for example.

Most solicitors offices will charge by the hour and will be quite happy to give an idea of what their services cost before they start something. Obviously in some situations they will not know what the level of work will be but should state what the charges per hour will be and keep their client up to date on what the costs are at any given point in time. Although you can quite often do the jobs that a solicitor does for you for yourself you will not have the level of skill that they have in, for example, reading contracts and understanding some of the jargon that is used in them. A mistake in this could be very expensive and the cost of a solicitor may then appear to be relatively small.

Solicitors can represent you in the Magistrates Courts but cannot act for you in other courts – for that you will need to employ a barrister.

## Barristers

Barristers are a bit like the surgeons or consultants of the legal world if the solicitor is like the local GP. They have a great deal of knowledge of one specialist area and use it in a specialised way. Barristers are trained to present the cases they are given in court and will do all of the research that is needed to present as strong a case as possible. The barrister will work with your solicitor to prepare and present the best case possible for you. This can be quite an expensive process as you will have two sets of fees to pay as the barrister will always work to a solicitor and will not deal directly with you. If you get involved in a case which goes to the highest level of the legal system you will probably have to involve a senior barrister. There are two levels of barrister

1  **Senior barristers** – known as *Queen's Counsel*
2  **Junior barristers** – known as *Juniors*

If you do have a case which requires the services of a Queen's Counsel (often abbreviated to QC) you will also have to pay for the services of junior to assist the QC.

Barristers' fees are not charged by the hour. Their fees are based on two sets of charges:

●  A '*brief fee*' which is a one-off fee payable for them taking the case. This will be set by the difficulty of the case and the level of research that the barrister will have to be involved in order to get the case into a state where it can be presented in court.
●  A '*refresher*' payable for each day that the case is in court – this is to cover the actual cost of the time the barrister has to spend presenting the case they have already prepared and will, obviously, relate directly to the difficulty of the case as well.

---

### ACTIVITY

Work out the bill for the court case below.

You are involved in a breach of the Health and Safety at Work Act case which goes to the Crown Court. Your solicitor spends some 35 hours of time before the case in correspondence with the Health and Safety Inspectorate. In order to fight the case you take on a barrister who your solicitor spends 6 hours instructing. The case goes on for three days and you win your argument. Your solicitor spends 8 hours in court during this time.

If the solicitor charges £35/hour and the barrister charges a brief fee of £1500 with a refresher of £500 what will the legal costs be?

If you lost the case you would have to pay the legal expenses of the other side and also the court costs; this will probably more than double the figure you have worked out above.

---

If you do get involved in a case which looks set to go to the higher courts this is likely to be a very expensive process and it will probably be in your interests to ensure that the costs of such an action are either covered by an insurance policy or that the company is aware of the level of costs they may have to pay. If you win a case it is quite likely that you will be given an order for costs – that is to say that the person who has lost the case will be liable to pay for your legal costs as well as their own and the costs of the court. This is not automatic, however, and, if the person losing the case does not have the money to pay, the order has relatively little value to you. As most cases are settled in the courts of first instance it is unlikely that you will ever be involved in a case which goes to the highest levels of the legal system.

Many companies have in-house legal personnel who work directly for the company and these people will be paid a fixed salary rather than charging in the way that is outlined above. If your organisation has a lot of legal work it may well be worth considering employing a solicitor or barrister to do this work in house for you.

### SUMMARY

There are a number of different ways of classifying law and all of them have some importance to businesses. In order to look at the different ways of classifying law and put them together to get a picture of how law affects businesses Fig 4.23 below takes the topics we looked at above, and adds

●  a number of examples of specific laws in the areas
●  whether they are statute or case based
●  whether they are primarily civil or criminal

This is not a complete picture of the law as it affects business but it should serve to provide an overview of the area. You will find, in any business, that there are other areas of the law where the business is affected and you may find in a given business that there are some of the areas listed above which do not affect you.

| Area of law | Examples of laws | Statute/ case | Civil/ criminal |
|---|---|---|---|
| Ownership and control | Companies Act, Partnership Act, Trade Unions and Labour relations law, Insolvency rules | Statute | Civil |
| Dealings between businesses | Contract Law, Unfair Contract Terms, exclusion clauses, Sale of Goods Act | Case | Civil |
| Competition & Monopoly | Monopolies and Mergers Commission, European competition law, restrictive trade practices rules | Statute | Civil and criminal |
| Business and the community | Planning controls, Environmental Protection Act, pollution controls, hygiene laws, law of nuisance | Statute | Civil and criminal |
| Labour law | Contracts of employment, Employment protection rules, maternity leave, Health and Safety at Work Act, discrimination laws | Statute | Civil |
| Protection of consumers | Weights and Measures rules, Sale of Goods, Consumer Credit laws, Trade Descriptions Acts | Statute Case | Civil Criminal |
| Property law | Theft Act, Trespass rules, criminal damage, breaches of the peace | Statute | Criminal |

**Fig 4.23  A summary of how legislation affects businesses**

If you feel that you need or want a more detailed look at the law as it affects business you should consider taking an Option or Additional unit with a legal bias to them; these will provide you with more detail and an understanding of specific areas of law as they affect businesses.

# 5

# FINANCIAL SYSTEMS

This unit of the book examines the area of financial resources for business. As already stated, any business needs a mix of three key resources to operate:

- financial
- human
- physical.

Different businesses will need these in different proportions depending on the way that they operate. Whatever the business is, and whatever the level of financial resources it uses, there are a number of important factors to bear in mind:

- It will need to decide where to get money from
- It will need to keep track of money and control it while it is in the business
- It will need to keep track of where the money goes from the business.

This unit aims to help you to examine exactly how this is done. If you want further detail in this area you should look at taking appropriate options or additional units later in the programme.

In any organisation, no matter how big or how small, several key questions have to be asked to assess the efficiency of the business:

- How well have we done?
- What do we do next?
- Which strategy do we select to achieve our goal?

In answering these questions a manager will require information from areas across the business such as:

- sales
- marketing
- production

- personnel
- finance and accounting.

It is this last area, finance and accounting, that we will look at in this unit.

## Finance and accounting

In most firms accounting and finance are in a single division, even though they are relatively distinct functions (*see* Fig 5.1).

*Finance* involves the efficient management of a firm's financial assets with the purpose of maximising the return on them. The *accounting function* involves the management of financial records – receipts, payments, wages, etc. For example, the annual stock check and the recording of all stock coming into and out of the business is an accounting function, as is the daily listing of cheques received and the banking of them. The decision to invest in one project rather than another will, however, be a financial one. Similarly, a decision about which institution to borrow money from is a function of finance. The purpose of accounting is to 'account' for the flow of funds in the firm. The work undertaken by the accounting function will be dealt with in the

| *Finance* | *Accounting* |
|---|---|
| ● Manage financial assets | ● Manage financial records |
| ● Maximise returns | ● Track flow of funds |
| | ● Produce financial statements |

**Fig 5.1 The finance and accounting functions**

accounting unit of your course, though because of the close relationship between accounting and finance there will be some overlap in the core.

## HOW WELL HAVE WE DONE?

Throughout this unit we'll be looking at the development of a small business, 'Bank Top

**Bank Top Nurseries: Trading and Profit and Loss Account for year ended 31.12.XX**

|  | £ | £ |
|---|---|---|
| **Sales** |  | 100 000 |
| *Less cost of goods sold:* |  |  |
| opening stock | 5 000 |  |
| purchases | 65 000 |  |
| less closing stock | 10 000 | 60 000 |
| **Gross profit** |  | 40 000 |
| *Less expenses:* |  |  |
| lighting and heating | 2 000 |  |
| wages | 15 000 |  |
| vehicle expenses | 2 000 |  |
| general expenses | 1 000 | 20 000 |
| **Net profit** |  | 20 000 |

**Balance Sheet as at 31.12.XX**

|  | £ | £ |
|---|---|---|
| **Capital: At start** |  | 65 000 |
| *Add net profit* |  | 20 000 |
|  |  | 85 000 |
| *Less drawings* |  | 12 000 |
|  |  | 73 000 |
| **Represented by**: |  |  |
| *Fixed assets:* |  |  |
| nursery and outbuildings | 50 000 |  |
| vehicles | 8 000 |  |
| plant and equipment | 4 000 | 62 000 |
| *Current assets:* |  |  |
| stock | 10 000 |  |
| debtors | 1 500 |  |
| bank | 3 000 |  |
| cash | 500 |  |
|  | 15 000 |  |
| *Less current liabilities:* |  |  |
| creditors | 4 000 |  |
| **Net working capital** |  | 11 000 |
|  |  | 73 000 |

**Fig 5.2**

Nurseries', to illustrate the scope of finance in assisting business decision making. As we indicated at the start of this unit all businesses will have to have financial information systems and so ideas developed for use in a new small business will also have implications for a large firm and for you as an individual.

In the 1980s Geoff Ring worked as a metallurgist for Manchester Steel in the centre of industrial Manchester. During the recession of the early 1980s Geoff, like many of his colleagues, was made redundant. Geoff took a positive view and with the help of his local college's 'enterprise unit', together with start-up funding from the European Coal and Steel Commission, he set up in business as a landscape architect. He has been very successful and the business has expanded. In 1990 he decided to have a total review of the business and develop a strategy for the next ten years. He asked his accountant to prepare a full set of accounts for the year end. (Fig 5.2).

In this module we will look in detail at the accounts and see how they can be used in assessing the effectiveness of the business.

## The Trading and Profit and Loss Account

Working out the profit on any business venture is a relatively simple matter as shown in the following equation:

$$\text{Profit} = \text{sales} - \text{cost of sales}$$

In essence this is the information shown in the Trading and Profit and Loss Account. For example, if a firm bought goods for £100 000 and resold them for £150 000 the profit would be:

$$\text{Profit} = £150\,000 - £100\,000 = £50\,000$$

### GROSS PROFIT

To simplify matters the Gross Profit and the Net Profit are calculated separately. *Gross Profit* is the excess of sales after subtracting the cost of goods sold. This can be shown as:

$$\text{Gross Profit} = \text{Sales} - \text{Cost of sales}$$

Geoff has made a Gross Profit of £40 000, but in isolation this tells him little unless we compare it with his level of sales. It would be wrong to compare Geoff's profit of £40 000 with the million pound profits made by large firms unless we take account of the level of sales. We can get a better picture of his profitability by calculating the Gross Profit Percentage.

## GROSS PROFIT PERCENTAGE

This is the Gross Profit expressed as a percentage of the sales as shown in the following formula:

$$\text{Gross profit percentage} = \frac{\text{Gross profit}}{\text{sales}} \times \frac{100}{1}$$

for example

$$\text{GP \%} = \left[\frac{£50\ 000}{£200\ 000}\right] \times \left[\frac{100}{1}\right] = 25\%$$

For Geoff therefore the Gross Profit Percentage can be calculated:

Gross profit percentage =

$$\frac{£40\ 000}{£100\ 000} \times \frac{100}{1} = 40\%$$

This still doesn't indicate how well he has done, so other calculations need to be done before we can get a complete picture, as we will see later. The figure for a successful business should stay roughly the same from year to year or show a slight rise and should be roughly the same as the competition. For Geoff, 40 per cent is a reasonable figure as much of his work will be labour intensive.

---

### ACTIVITY

In the present recession Geoff's raw material costs are increasing but he is unable to pass the increased costs onto his customers. What effect will this have on his Gross Profit Percentage?

---

This figure is also used as a check by the Inland Revenue to see whether your figures are close to their guidelines and you are not on the 'fiddle'. Typical figures for a range of businesses are given in Fig 5.3.

**Profit Margin Survey**

| Classification | Average Gross Profit | |
| --- | --- | --- |
| | on cost % | on sales % |
| antique dealer | 51 | 34 |
| baker | 54 | 35 |
| builders merchant | 27 | 21 |
| fish and chip shop | 72 | 42 |
| grocer | 16 | 14 |
| plumber | 203 | 67 |
| off licence | 33 | 25 |
| public house | 45 | 31 |
| restaurant | 100 | 50 |

**Fig 5.3**

---

### ACTIVITY

The Gross Profit Percentage figures shown in Fig 5.3 vary from 20 per cent for plumbers to only 16 per cent for grocers. Why do you think that they vary so much?

---

### ACTIVITY

**1** Individually you should collect Final Accounts from at least three Public Limited Companies in different areas of work, for example, retailing, banking, leisure, industry. (They will be useful throughout this unit.) NB. If you are able to, you may use the Final Accounts of your employer.

**2** Calculate the Gross Profit Percentage for each of the companies.

**3** As a group, draw up a chart showing company name, type of business, Gross Profit Percentage.

**4** What conclusions can you draw?

NB A good source of company accounts is the *Observer* newspaper which provides a free service.

---

## NET PROFIT

*Net Profit* is the excess of sales after subtracting the cost of sales minus all expenses incurred in selling those goods or providing those services. *Expenses* are all those running costs of the business which are necessarily incurred to enable the firm to make a profit and include such items as wages, rates, lighting, heating, telephone bills and travel expenses. This can be expressed in a simple formula:

Net profit = Gross profit − expenses

For example

NP = £80 000 − £20 000 = £60,000

For Geoff's business we can see that:

Net profit = £40 000 − £20 000 = £20 000.

---

### ACTIVITY

Calculate the Net Profit given the following information:

Sales £250 000; Cost of Sales £165 000, wages £18 000; heating and lighting £6000; administration £16 000; travel expenses £1500.

---

### How have we done?

The Net Profit for the above activity is £43 500. Again, this figure in isolation means little, so it is necessary to calculate the Net Profit Percentage.

### NET PROFIT PERCENTAGE

This is the Net Profit expressed as a percentage of sales as shown in the following formula:

$$\text{Net profit percentage} = \frac{\text{Net Profit}}{\text{Sales}} \times \frac{100}{1}$$

which can be expressed in the case of Geoff's business as:

$$\text{Net profit percentage} = \frac{£20\,000}{£100\,000} \times \frac{100}{1} = 20\%.$$

This is a reasonable profit level but once again it should be compared with that of his competitors and analysed over a period of time. If there are any marked discrepancies he should take appropriate action. Geoff, for example, may have had to pay his employees higher wages. This will increase his costs and, therefore, reduce his Net Profit Percentage. Similarly, he might find that a major competitor is making a much higher net profit percentage. This may be because the company is larger and can therefore spread the load of essential expenses like advertising across a much higher level of output.

---

### ACTIVITY

**1** Calculate the Net Profit Percentage for the companies you have chosen.

**2** Add your results to your group's company chart (see the Activity on p 168) and add another column which shows the difference between the Gross Profit and Net Profit Percentages.

**3** Why are there differences between the various companies?

**4** Geoff finds that he has to advertise more and more to keep the same level of sales. What effect will this have on his Net Profit Percentage?

---

### How have we done?

Geoff is pleased with his company's figures to date but he is aware that as interest rates are high he could be making a considerable amount of money simply by investing his capital in a building society and living off the interest.

Geoff can assess the effectiveness of his investment in the business by calculating the Return on Capital Employed.

### RETURN ON CAPITAL EMPLOYED

This is the amount of profit the business has made expressed as a percentage of the capital invested in it. This can be calculated using the formula:

Rate of Capital Employed =

$$\frac{\text{Net Profit}}{\text{Owner's Capital}} \times \frac{100}{1}$$

For Geoff therefore we can see that:

Rate of Capital Employed =

$$\frac{£20\,000}{£65\,000} \times \frac{100}{1} = 30.3\%$$

Geoff is now reassured in that he could not hope to obtain a 30 per cent return on a safe investment.

### ACTIVITY

Answer the following question:

Would Geoff be better off if he worked for someone else earning £15 000 p.a. and invested his capital in a building society?

You will need to collect information from building societies and banks on the different saving and investment schemes available. This information will also be required later in the unit.

Geoff is now happy that he is making enough profit to enjoy a reasonable lifestyle but he is still slightly concerned that he hasn't got much cash available to finance further growth. To help to assess this area of his business he needs to look at the Balance Sheet.

# The Balance Sheet

Whereas the Profit and Loss Account showed the profit for the year the *Balance Sheet* shows the state of the business at one point in time. The Balance Sheet at its simplest lists the assets and liabilities of the business.

## BUSINESS ASSETS

The assets of the business can be divided up between fixed and current assets.

**Fixed assets** are those assets which are used in the business and are not primarily for resale. For example, premises, vehicles, plant and equipment, office equipment.

**Current assets** are short term assets which flow into and out of the business on a regular basis, for example, cash, stock, money owed by debtors.

## LIABILITIES

**Capital** is the owner's investment in the business and therefore is a liability. It is what the business owes the owner.

**Current liabilities** are the bills and other liabilities of the business which are due for repayment within twelve months.

### ACTIVITY

**1** From the following list identify the fixed and current assets, current liabilities and capital: motor vehicles; creditors for goods; stock of goods; debtors; loan from the bank; petty cash; machinery; owner's original investment; office machinery.

**2** In what circumstances could vehicles, premises and office machinery be both fixed and current assets?

## How have we done?

To answer Geoff's question on his scope for growth, or indeed for survival, we must look at his Working Capital.

**Working capital** is the excess of current assets after subtracting current liabilities and is the amount of money available for use in the business.

This can be expressed as:

Working Capital =

current assets − current liabilities

In Geoff's case we can see that:

Working Capital =

£15 000 − £4000 = £11 000. Is it enough?

**The working capital ratio** compares the business's current assets to its current liabilities in the formulae:

current assets : current liabilities

Which in Geoff's case becomes:

£15 000 : £4000    A ratio of 3.75 : 1

The ratio should always be at least 1 : 1 but it should not become too high as this would mean that assets are not being used efficiently. It is however difficult to generalise and it may be that in Geoff's case he needs to maintain a high level of stock.

1 The table below shows information from the accounts of a number of Limited Companies. In each case you are to calculate the Working Capital Ratio and after reading the next section the Liquidity Ratio.

2 What can you say about the ratios that you have calculated?

| Extracts from company balance sheets | | | | |
| --- | --- | --- | --- | --- |
| Company | Current Assets (£m) | Current Liabilities (£m) | Stock (£m) | Debtors (£m) |
| Eastern Electricity | 412 | 297 | 23 | 370 |
| London International | 233 | 168 | 68 | 128 |
| John Menzies | 190 | 185 | 82 | 100 |
| GEC | 3935 | 2050 | 1223 | 1507 |

The ratios that you have calculated vary from just over 1 to nearly 2, but this ratio assumes that we can always turn our assets into money. Since this may not always be the case, other tests of liquidity are required.

A more realistic comparison can be arrived at by calculating the *liquidity ratio*. This calculates the relationship between those assets which are liquid, that is, easily converted into cash, and current liabilities which may be called in for repayment at any moment. For this reason this ratio does not include stock, as for example, in the middle of winter it may be difficult for Geoff to sell or use stock. This is expressed in the formulae:

liquidity ratio =
current assets – stock : current liabilities.

For Geoff this would be:

£15 000 – £10 000 : £400 = 1.25 : 1

1 Using the Final Accounts of your Public Limited Companies calculate the following:

return on capital employed; working capital ratio; liquidity ratio.

2 As a group, add these figures to your existing chart.

3 Using all the ratios that you now have available, which is the 'best' company?

4 Try and list the criteria you have used in choosing the 'best' company.

Geoff now knows that he has a profitable business and is in a stable situation where he can pay off all his debts. He is now becoming much more financially aware and would like to look in detail at the way he costs and prices his landscape projects, especially as he has been offered a large contract from a building firm to landscape 20 gardens in a new development.

At the moment he calculates a price by working out how long the project will take, costing out the materials and adding on a percentage for profit. What Geoff is not taking into account are the costs he incurs just by keeping the business operating. There are expenses like advertising, vehicle costs and rates which he must pay regardless of the amount of business he has. To be able to calculate more accurately Geoff needs to look at the relative importance of his fixed and variable costs.

## FIXED AND VARIABLE COSTS

As in any organisation, Geoff has a range of costs which he must pay regardless of his level of landscaping work. He has to pay rates, interest on loans, administration costs and so on. These are *fixed costs* and he will have to pay these even if in any one week he has no work. Some costs, however, vary in direct proportion to the amount of work or output. These would be items like bedding plants, topsoil and so on, which may be classified as materials and labour. It can usually be said that labour too varies with output since many staff, although paid a fixed wage, are frequently paid overtime or bonuses. These, therefore, are *variable costs* which vary in direct proportion to output.

Although the project he has been offered is large, he now needs to assess whether or not it will be profitable to take the order at a price of only £950 per plot. At present he is charging about £1500 per plot. Geoff extracts the following figures:

| Quarterly costs for 10 standard landscaping projects | |
|---|---:|
| (i)   Direct materials at £80 per project | £800 |
| (ii)  Direct labour at £400 per project | £4000 |
| (iii) Direct costs ((i) + (ii)) | £4800 |
| (iv)  Nursery overhead | £5000 |
| (v)   Total cost (Direct cost + Overhead) | £9800 |
| (vi)  Unit cost | £980 |

Geoff's profit would therefore be:

$$£15\ 000 - £9800 = £5200$$

What would be the situation if he took on the new order?

| Quarterly costs for 20 standard landscaping projects | |
|---|---:|
| (i)   Direct materials at £80 per project | £1600 |
| (ii)  Direct labour at £400 per project | £8000 |
| (iii) Direct cost ((i) + (ii)) | £9600 |
| (iv)  Nursery overhead | £5000 |
| (v)   Total cost | £14600 |
| (vi)  Unit cost | £730 |

His profit would now be:

Sales = 10 at £1500 + 10 at £980 = £24 500
Profit = £24 500 − £14 600 = £9900

Some of the terms used above may be unfamiliar to you. *Direct materials* and *direct labour* are expenses that can be traced to a particular job. For example, how much top soil, peat and bedding plants does he need for a particular job? Materials and labour, therefore, taken together, give me the *direct cost* for a job. He will also incur *overheads* which must be paid regardless of the number of jobs undertaken. For example the cost of heating the nursery and the unified business rate on the business premises. By accepting the contract, therefore, Geoff has increased his profit from £5200 to £9900 even though he has done the job for £950 which is below his original unit cost of £980. How can he, therefore have increased his profit?

The original unit costs included the fixed nursery overheads. Once this cost has been met,

each extra project he undertakes only adds the extra variable cost to the total cost which is £480 per project. This extra cost of undertaking one more project is known as the *marginal cost* which can be defined as: 'the cost of producing one extra unit of output'. So long as Geoff meets his marginal costs of £480 he will add to his profit. (Marginal Costing will be dealt with more fully in the Unit 7: Marketing and Business Performance).

## Geoff's next project

Over the years Geoff has bought a significant amount of equipment, but to enable him to undertake larger projects he is looking to buy a mini-excavator. He knows it will cost a lot of money and wonders whether it is worth the major investment. What techniques can we apply to enable Geoff to make his decision?

## Project appraisal

Geoff is in a similar position to many businesses. He has several different options from which to choose:

● should he buy a new excavator or not?
● which excavator should he buy?

To help him make this decision Geoff should use a project appraisal technique but, in the end, the decision is his.

### DISCOUNTED CASH FLOW

One method of appraising the viability of projects is the Discounted Cash Flow (DCF) technique. Geoff has a choice between two excavators, the Excalibur at £40 000 and the Scimitar at £56 000. The Excalibur is a smaller cheaper version of the Scimitar and Geoff will be able to use it immediately on his present contracts. To make effective use of the Scimitar, however, he will have to negotiate larger scale contracts. Both machines will last 5 years and Geoff has predicted the extra business the machines will generate and therefore the net cash inflows over the five year period (*see* Fig 5.4). The *net cash inflow* is the amount of money the machine will earn less any running costs.

**Excavator project appraisal**

| | Excalibur | | Scimitar | |
| --- | --- | --- | --- | --- |
| Year | Cash outflow | Cash inflow | Cash outflow | Cash inflow |
| 0 | 40 000 | | 56 000 | |
| 1 | | 24 000 | | 20 000 |
| 2 | | 16 000 | | 20 000 |
| 3 | | 10 000 | | 18 000 |
| 4 | | 8 000 | | 18 000 |
| 5 | | 4 000 | | 10 000 |
| | | 62 000 | | 92 000 |

**Fig 5.4**

From this information it is clear that both purchases are profitable:

Excalibur Net Inflow = £62 000 − £40 000
= £22 000

Scimitar Net Inflow = £92 000 − £56 000
= £36 000

Geoff could decide to choose the Scimitar. Whatever he decides he will either have to borrow money to finance the project or use money from the business that could otherwise have been invested to give a return. What he will have to do therefore is 'discount' the future cash inflows to calculate the *net present value* (NPV).

Obviously £100 received in the short term is of more value than £100 received in 5 years' time. The *discounted cash flow* technique which uses the net present value of a project over the course of its life will give us a more accurate assessment of the project's viability.

## WORKING OUT THE DISCOUNT

You are expecting to receive £10 at the end of the year from an investment and interest rates are running at 10 per cent. What is the current equivalent value of that £10?

This can be calculated by using the following formulae:

Present value =

$$\text{Amount} \times \frac{100}{100 + \text{rate of interest}}$$

This gives us:

$$\text{Present Value} = £10 \times \frac{100}{110} = £9.10$$

In the same way we could calculate this for periods of time up to infinity and for varying interest rates.

---

### ACTIVITY

Calculate the present value of the following sums received that have been invested for one year at the interest rates shown:

(i) £1500 at 15%
(ii) £28 000 at 17.5%
(iii) £380 000 at 2.5%
(iv) £5 500 000 at 20%

---

Fortunately tables are available to show the present value of £1 at various rates of interest over given periods of time. An extract is given below in Fig 5.5(a).

We can therefore now calculate the NPV for both pieces of equipment.

The Scimitar produces only a slightly higher Net Present Value and it will therefore be difficult for Geoff to decide. He may in fact buy the Excalibur because it is a smaller machine and

| | Present value of £1 | |
| --- | --- | --- |
| Year | 5% | 10% |
| 1 | 0.952 | 0.909 |
| 2 | 0.907 | 0.826 |
| 3 | 0.860 | 0.751 |
| 4 | 0.823 | 0.683 |
| 5 | 0.780 | 0.621 |

**Fig 5.5(a)**

### Excalibur

| Year | Cash flow | Discount factor | Discounted cash flow |
|---|---|---|---|
| 0 | | | (40 000) |
| 1 | 24 000 × 0.909 | = | 21 816 |
| 2 | 16 000 × 0.826 | = | 13 216 |
| 3 | 10 000 × 0.751 | = | 7 510 |
| 4 | 8 000 × 0.683 | = | 5 464 |
| 5 | 4 000 × 0.621 | = | 2 484 |
| | | NPV | 10 490 |

### Scimitar

| Year | Cash flow | Discount factor | Discounted cash flow |
|---|---|---|---|
| 0 | | | (56 000) |
| 1 | 20 000 × 0.909 | = | 18 180 |
| 2 | 20 000 × 0.826 | = | 16 520 |
| 3 | 18 000 × 0.751 | = | 13 518 |
| 4 | 18 000 × 0.683 | = | 12 294 |
| 5 | 10 000 × 0.621 | = | 6 210 |
| | | NPV | 10 722 |

**Fig 5.5(b)**

will give him better access to sites. In both cases he still obtains a significant Net Present Value and therefore either purchase will benefit the business.

---

### ACTIVITY

Using the information above, calculate the Net Present Value for both pieces of equipment but use a 5 per cent interest rate over a 5 year period. Fig 5.5(b) gives you the Discount Factors to be used.

---

Geoff decides to buy the Scimitar excavator and makes a considerable profit over the next year while fulfilling his contract to landscape the new houses. At the end of this period he is worried that once again he must obtain new business. He has, however, no real idea of how much business he requires in any one year before he starts to make a profit.

What techniques can be used to help Geoff decide on the minimum number of landscape contracts he must undertake in the year before he starts to make a profit?

## BREAK EVEN ANALYSIS

The *break even point* is the level of output that is required to just start making a profit. By using a simple technique, Geoff will be able to calculate the minimum amount of business he must obtain in the year.

*Break even analysis* can be obtained by two methods: by calculation and by graphical analysis.

### Break even by calculation

From information that Geoff has previously provided we can calculate the break even point (BEP) by using the formulae:

$$BEP = \frac{\text{total fixed costs}}{\text{sales price per plot} - \text{variable cost}}$$

$$= \frac{£500}{£1500 - £480} = \frac{£5000}{£1020} = 5 \text{ (approx)}$$

Geoff must therefore undertake 5 full cost projects in a year before he breaks even and starts to show a profit. In simple terms, for every project, the excess of the price (£1500) after subtracting the variable cost (£480) gives a contribution (£1020) towards fixed costs. He therefore needs 5 contributions of £1020 to meet his fixed costs of £5000 and break even. In practice though he will need a lot more projects to give himself a reasonable profit.

---

### ACTIVITY

You are to work out the Break Even Point for the following two examples, in each case clearly showing the 'contribution':

(i)  Total Fixed Costs = £35 000
     Variable Costs    = £3000
     Sales Price       = £8000

(ii) Factory rent £3000; materials £300; labour £200; administration £1000; advertising £200; sales price £1200.

---

## BREAK EVEN BY GRAPH

The break even point can be charted by showing output on the horizontal axis and all costs and revenues on the vertical axis. From the graph it can be seen that the fixed cost is a straight horizontal line, it never varies with output, and that variable costs start from that point. The point at which the sales curve and the total cost curve meet is the break even point (*see* Fig 5.6).

### How to draw a break even chart

1 Select suitable horizontal and vertical axes. Remember that the fixed costs may take up a significant part of the vertical axis.
2 Draw in the fixed cost line. It will be a horizontal line as it does not vary with output.
3 Draw in the total cost line. Remember that at zero levels of production fixed costs are still incurred so that the total cost line will start from the initial level of fixed costs.
4 Draw in the sales curve. As each plot is sold for the same price you need only to plot two points and then join up the intersections.
5 The point where the sales curve and the total cost curve meet is the Break Even Point.

---

#### ACTIVITY

Redraw Geoff's break even chart assuming that his fixed costs are now £6000; variable costs are £500 and the sales price is £1800. What is his break even point?

---

We have assumed that the fixed costs, as their name implies, are fixed. As a business expands, however, as in Geoff's case, the fixed costs may rise as output increases. In Geoff's case the purchase of a new excavator will allow him to increase output and in the future, as business expands, he may purchase another item of capital equipment. The fixed cost line on the graph will therefore show a series of steps (*see* Fig 5.7).

---

#### ACTIVITY

**1** Using Geoff's figures draw up your own graph. Remember that the new excavator will add £1000 to his fixed costs and that it will only be purchased when sales reach 10 units.

**2** From the graph read off the level of profit at output levels 3, 7 and 12.

**3** Redraw the graph using a new sales price of £1750 and variable costs of £500. What is the new break even point?

**4** Check your answer by the calculation method.

---

## A good year for Bank Top Nurseries!

Geoff buys his new excavator and a new van which are partly financed by a loan. The money

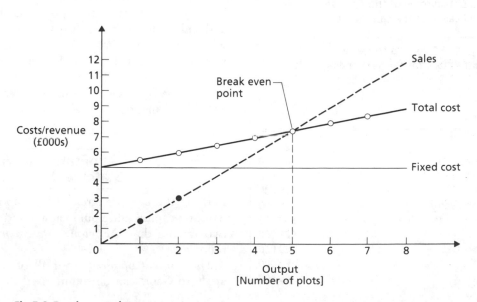

**Fig 5.6 Break even chart**

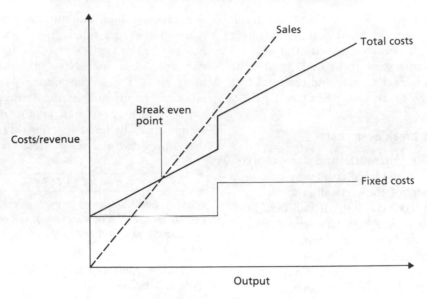

**Fig 5.7 A stepped break even chart**

rolls in from his large new contract. At the end of the year he requires a Trading and Profit and Loss Account and Balance Sheet before he takes his books to his accountant.

---

### ACTIVITY

Produce a Trading and Profit and Loss Account and Balance Sheet for Geoff's company based on the following information extracted from his books. You will have to obtain some of the figures from last year's accounts and calculate the cash figure.

| Bank Top Nurseries Account details for the year ending 31.12.XX | |
|---|---|
| Sales | £180 000 |
| Purchases | £90 000 |
| Closing stock | £15 000 |
| Lighting/heating | £2 500 |
| Wages | £20 000 |
| Vehicle expenses | £3 000 |
| General expenses | £2 500 |
| Drawings | £15 000 |
| Scimitar excavator | £56 000 |
| Van | £10 000 |
| Loan | £23 000 |
| Creditors | £8 000 |
| Debtors | £2 000 |
| Bank | £9 500 |
| Cash | ? |

After looking at the accounts Geoff is somewhat concerned that although his net profits have trebled to £67 000 this is not reflected in his bank balance. He now has a higher creditors' figure and a loan that must be repaid.

### WHERE HAVE ALL THE PROFITS GONE?

The Profit and Loss Account and the Balance Sheet (Fig 5.8) show the amount of profit made in the year and the relative positions at the start and end of the year. Geoff really needs to know where the business has generated funds from and what it has spent them on. This he can find out from a statement called the Source and Application of Funds which is usually referred to as the Funds Statements.

---

## Source and Application of Funds Statement

---

Early in the unit we stressed the importance of working capital and liquid capital and it is these two factors that the *Funds Statement* concentrates on.

The *Sources of Funds*, not all of which may apply to Geoff can be summarised as:

● Net Profit

**Bank Top Nurseries**
**Trading, Profit and Loss and Balance Sheet**
**for year ending 31.12.XX**

|  | £ | £ |
|---|---:|---:|
| **Sales** | | 180 000 |
| *Less cost of sales*: | | |
| opening stock | 10 000 | |
| purchases | 90 000 | |
| | 100 000 | |
| less closing stock | 15 000 | 85 000 |
| **Gross Profit** | | 95 000 |
| *Less expenses*: | | |
| lighting | 2 500 | |
| wages | 20 000 | |
| vehicle expenses | 3 000 | |
| general expenses | 2 500 | 28 000 |
| **Net Profit** | | 67 000 |
| **Capital**: | | |
| at start | 73 000 | |
| add net profit | 67 000 | |
| | 140 000 | |
| *less drawings* | 15 000 | 125 000 |
| **Represented by**: | | |
| *Fixed assets*: | | |
| nursery and outbuildings | 50 000 | |
| vehicles | 18 000 | |
| plant and equipment | 60 000 | 128 000 |
| *Current assets*: | | |
| stock | 15 000 | |
| debtors | 2 000 | |
| bank | 9 500 | |
| cash | 1 500 | 28 000 |
| *Less current liabilities*: | | |
| creditors | 8 000 | |
| loan | 23 000 | 31 000 |
| **Net working capital** | | (3 000) |
| | | 125 000 |

**Fig 5.8**

- Extra capital contributed. For example, to finance the purchase of the excavator Geoff puts another £5000 into the business.
- Loans. For example, he may borrow £10 000 from the bank.
- Sale of fixed assets. For example, the sale of the firm's van.

These will all increase the funds available to the business. The funds may be spent or applied in a variety of ways:

- Repayment of loans.
- Purchase of fixed assets e.g. Geoff buys the excavator.
- Taxes.
- Payment of dividend or drawings. For example, a public limited company may pay its shareholders a dividend or in Geoff's case he may take regular amounts of money out of the business.

Geoff draws up his funds statement as shown in Fig 5.9. From this statement we can reassure Geoff. It is easy to see that a considerable amount of the funds generated have been 'applied' to the purchase of fixed assets. Despite this he has been able to increase his working capital by £9000 and his liquid capital by £7500.

**ACTIVITY**

Geoff's friend who owns a similar business is impressed by the information that a Funds Statement provides and asks you to produce a statement from the information on p 178.

**Bank Top Nurseries**
**Statement of Source and Application of Funds**
**for the year ended 31.12.XX**

| Source of funds: | | |
|---|---:|---:|
| Profit | £67 000 | |
| Loan | £23 000 | |
| | | £90 000 |
| Application of funds: | | |
| Purchase of fixed assets | £66 000 | |
| Drawings | £15 000 | |
| | | £81 000 |
| | | £9 000 |
| Movement in working capital: | | |
| Increase in stock | £5 000 | |
| Increase in debtors | £500 | |
| Increase in creditors | (£4 000) | |
| | | £1 500 |
| Movement in liquid funds: | | |
| Increase in cash | £1 000 | |
| Increase in bank | £6 500 | |
| | | £7 500 |
| | | £9 000 |

**Fig 5.9**

You are also asked to make brief notes for her so that she can understand the results.

| Nichols Nurseries<br>Financial information at 31.12.XX | |
| --- | --- |
| Opening stock | £7 000 |
| Closing stock | £12 000 |
| Increase in debtors | £3 000 |
| Opening creditors | £8 000 |
| Closing creditors | £15 000 |
| Net profit | £30 000 |
| Purchase of van | £11 000 |
| Drawings | £12 000 |
| Cash at start | £6 000 |
| Cash at close | £8 000 |
| Bank at start | (£2 000) OD |
| Bank at close | £2 000 |

## The future of Bank Top Nurseries

At the end of 199 – Geoff decides to review his position. He has a sound expanding business which is clearly split into two interdependent divisions, the nursery and the landscape division. It is clear that the landscape side is leading the expansion and Geoff has invested in this area over the last year. Geoff is now convinced that the nursery side could be expanded. He knows that people with leisure time and disposable income enjoy visiting a nursery given the right facilities. Luckily his nursery is on a prime site on a main road and he effectively has a monopoly position. A piece of land next to the nursery is now available for sale. Its purchase would allow Geoff to expand and offer a wide range of garden products, open a tea room and, importantly, offer facilities for children such as a children's playground or a domestic zoo. He makes an appointment to see the 'Small Business Adviser' at his bank who is quite supportive but recommends that Geoff puts all his ideas together in the form of a Business Plan.

## The Business Plan

A Business Plan is a document which draws together all business considerations to enable a decision to be made about the viability of a project. Each business plan will be different but should include the following:

### PLAN OUTLINE

This should give brief details including information on financial requirements and the key figures from any financial projections.

### THE OWNER

The financier will want to know that you are successful. If, like Geoff, you can show a good track record you are much more likely to attract funding.

### PERSONNEL

You should show that you have the key staff required to enable the development of your plan or, if not, you will have looked at the implications of recruiting staff with the skills needed, or produced a manpower development plan. (This will be looked at in detail in the Unit 2 People in business.)

### THE BUSINESS, THE PRODUCT AND THE MARKET

Geoff should provide details of his business to date and show that there is room in the market for expansion. He should give a brief history of the business and present financial information that will show there has been growth. He should explain the new services that he is to provide and, where possible, support this with evidence of market research to back up his plan. (Much of this is related to market research which will be dealt with in Unit 7 Marketing).

### FINANCIAL REQUIREMENTS AND PROJECTIONS

Geoff will also need to detail how much he wants to borrow and what security he can offer. Geoff may be asked by the bank to use his house as security for the loan. The bank then knows that if he fails to repay the loan, the house can be sold to pay off the debt. Banks have recently, however, been criticised for forcing families to sell their homes to repay debts and are now taking a more enlightened view. In many cases the banks have persuaded individuals to take on loans that they could not possibly afford to repay.

Geoff should also include:

- a twelve month projected Profit and Loss
- a twelve month projected Balance Sheet
- Cash Flow Forecast.

The Cash Flow Forecast will highlight Geoff's projected income and expenditure and is essential if he is to convince the financier that he has the ability to repay the loan.

## The Cash Flow Forecast

The Cash Flow Forecast shows the expected income and expenditure of a business over a specified period of time. In many cases they are produced when preparing a business plan but are also useful as a general forecasting tool. Geoff prepares his cash flow forecast with relevant notes as shown in Fig 5.10.

### ACTIVITY

From the information given below, draw up a cash flow forecast. NB. You can often obtain blank cash flow forecast forms and 'Start Your Own Business' packs from your local bank.

#### 'Trudy's Pantry'

*Trudy has recently been made redundant from her job as catering manager at a large factory. She decides to set up a small sandwich bar 'Trudy's Pantry' near the local college. She provides the following information from which you are to draw up her cash flow forecast:*

#### Projected income

- *Capital of £4000 in the bank.*
- *Cash Sales of £400 per month, rising by £100 monthly during the first year.*

#### Projected expenditure
- *Initial Stock of £1000 paid in advance.*

| | Jan | Feb | Mar | Apr | May | Jun | Jul | Aug | Sept | Oct | Nov | Dec |
|---|---|---|---|---|---|---|---|---|---|---|---|---|
| **Income** | | | | | | | | | | | | |
| Sales: Landscaping | 12 000 | 13 000 | 13 000 | 13 000 | 13 000 | 13 000 | 14 000 | 14 000 | 14 000 | 13 000 | 11 000 | 10 000 |
| : Nursery | 2 000 | 3 000 | 3 000 | 6 000 | 6 000 | 7 000 | 7 000 | 6 000 | 5 000 | 2 000 | 2 000 | 1 000 |
| Total Income | 14 000 | 16 000 | 16 000 | 19 000 | 19 000 | 20 000 | 21 000 | 20 000 | 19 000 | 15 000 | 13 000 | 11 000 |
| **Expenditure** | | | | | | | | | | | | |
| Stock | 8 000 | 12 000 | 12 000 | 11 000 | 8 000 | 7 000 | 7 000 | 6 000 | 6 000 | 6 000 | 6 000 | 5 000 |
| Rates | | | 400 | | | 400 | | | 400 | | | 400 |
| Insurance | | | | 1 100 | | | | | | | | |
| Heating & lighting | | | | 2 000 | | | | 500 | | | | 1 000 |
| Wages | 2 000 | 2 500 | 2 500 | 3 000 | 4 000 | 4 000 | 4 000 | 3 000 | 2 500 | 2 500 | 2 000 | 2 000 |
| Advertising | 500 | 200 | 1 500 | 1 000 | 200 | 200 | 200 | 200 | 200 | 200 | 200 | 200 |
| Vehicle expenses | | | 1 000 | | | 1 000 | | | 1 000 | | | 1 000 |
| Administration | 50 | 50 | 50 | 50 | 50 | 50 | 50 | 50 | 50 | 50 | 50 | 50 |
| Loan repayments | 1 000 | 1 000 | 1 000 | 1 000 | 1 000 | 1 000 | 1 000 | 1 000 | 1 000 | 1 000 | 1 000 | 1 000 |
| **Total Expenditure** | 11 550 | 15 750 | 18 950 | 19 150 | 13 250 | 13 650 | 12 250 | 10 750 | 11 150 | 9 750 | 9 250 | 10 650 |
| Opening cash balances | 11 000 | 13 450 | 13 700 | 10 750 | 10 600 | 16 350 | 22 700 | 31 450 | 40 700 | 48 550 | 53 800 | 57 550 |
| Add total income | 14 000 | 16 000 | 16 000 | 19 000 | 19 000 | 20 000 | 21 000 | 20 000 | 19 000 | 15 000 | 13 000 | 11 000 |
| Less total expenditure | 11 550 | 15 750 | 18 950 | 19 150 | 13 250 | 13 650 | 12 250 | 10 750 | 11 150 | 9 750 | 9 250 | 10 650 |
| Closing cash balances | 13 450 | 13 700 | 10 750 | 10 600 | 16 350 | 22 700 | 31 450 | 40 700 | 48 550 | 53 800 | 57 550 | 57 900 |

**Fig 5.10 Bank Top Nurseries cash flow forecast Jan–Dec 19XX**

- Future Stock, at the rate of £250 per month for the first three months then rising to £300, initially for cash and after three months on 30 days credit.
- Fixtures and fittings of £2000, paid before opening.
- Monthly payments of: rent £200; rates £30; insurance £25; other services £50; advertising and printing £25; with an extra £200 in the first month.

*Work out how much Trudy can afford to pay herself and include that in the cash flow forecast.*

# Budgeting

By preparing a *Business Plan* a firm will have entered the realms of budgeting. A simple definition of budgeting would be: 'The process of estimating the likely costs in the future in order to plan ahead.'

Typically, detailed budgets are prepared for one year ahead, but perhaps within a longer time scale of a corporate development or business plan. The starting point is usually the *sales plan* for the year ahead. The sales plan will be developed by the firm's marketing team. It will take account of such factors as new competition, their view of the state of the economy, which may affect demand for the product, and new or changed products that the firm is launching. This will be dealt with more fully in the Marketing and business performance Unit 7. From the sales plan a *production plan* can be developed and then in turn labour, material, capital and cash budgets. The component elements will of course reflect the individual needs of each firm. The individual budgets are then consolidated into a master budget which allows management to assess the likely profit for the year. (Fig 5.11.)

Using the figures from Bank Top Nurseries shown in Fig 5.12 we can produce a Budgeted Profit and Loss Account for the year ending 31.12.XX assuming that there is a 10 per cent increase in sales and a similar increase in all costs and expenses.

From this budget it is likely that individual departmental budgets will be created, discussed and agreed with the departmental manager. This leads on to the concept of budgetary control where, at the end of specific periods, a depart-

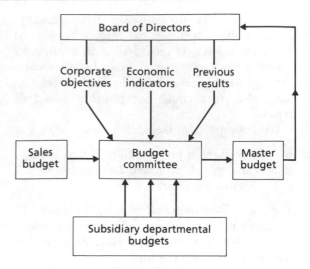

**Fig 5.11 Budget flow chart**

**Bank Top Nurseries**
**Budgeted Profit and Loss Account**
**year ending 31.12.XX**

|  | Current year | Previous year |
|---|---|---|
| **Sales** | 198 000 | 180 000 |
| *Less Costs of Goods Sold* | 82 500 | 75 000 |
| **Gross Profit** | 115 500 | 105 000 |
| *Less Operating Expenses:* |  |  |
| Lighting/Heating | 2 750 | 2 500 |
| Wages | 22 000 | 20 000 |
| Vehicle Expenses | 3 300 | 3 000 |
| General Expenses | 2 750 | 2 500 |
|  | 30 800 | 28 000 |
| **Net Profit** | 84 700 | 77 000 |

**Fig 5.12**

mental and master budgetary report is prepared. This will enable staff to see if they are operating to target and take appropriate remedial action if there is any variance from the planned budget. For example, within building firms one of the main challenges is the fact that most jobs will take a fairly long period of time to complete. Since invoices cannot be submitted until work is completed it can take a very long time to be paid. During this period the building firm will have had to pay for all the materials used as well as wages.

By preparing a budget for the year the firm would be able to see where there is a shortfall in cash and make provision for it, perhaps by negotiating an overdraft. Equally, the budget will enable the builder to see if certain jobs are taking longer than predicted or using more materials. By preparing a budget the builder provides himself with the information that he needs to make decisions.

In the extract below, from a department's monthly budget report (Fig 5.13), we can see that there is a significant overspend on raw materials that requires investigation and solution. This variance from the budget does not necessarily imply that anything is wrong but it does give the management the essential detail that is required to enable them to manage the outcome.

---

## ACTIVITY

Write a brief report for the production manager explaining why the variance in the monthly budget has occurred. You know that your staff have increased efficiency and you have been considering requesting a bonus for them. You are also concerned that more of the material you have to use has to be scrapped and that you want the stores department to tighten up on quality control.

---

## THE BENEFITS OF BUDGETARY CONTROL

As indicated earlier the processes in producing a budget are probably as important as the outcomes and equally this is important in terms of budgetary control. The benefits can be summarised. Budgeting:

● Requires the formulation of policy and definition of objectives in precise terms. This is useful because each department can then see how it fits into the firm as a whole and how it can contribute to the efficiency of the firm.

● Requires the assigning of responsibility to individuals so providing a basis for measuring their efficiency. It thus enables senior management to pass on responsibility whilst still retaining overall control.

● Ensures that notice is taken of cash requirements so that finance is made available when required. For example, a firm in a seasonal business will be able to plan for cash outflows when stock and raw materials are purchased and inflows much later in a season when goods are sold. This is particularly true of farmers who must buy and pay for seed, fertiliser and labour perhaps up to nine months before they harvest and sell the crop.

● Requires co-ordination between the separate budgets of each function of the business.

● Tends to create conditions in which all personnel become more aware of cost and the need for efficient operation of the business. This fits in with latest management practice which gives employees greater involvement in making the firm more efficient, with responsibility for quality and emphasising the individual's role in customer care.

● Enables control to be exercised on an 'exception' basis, that is, management considers only those factors which do not work out to plan, hence the phrase 'Management by Exception'.

● Provides the basis for a 'Management by Objectives' approach to control of the operation of the business. These last two factors will be discussed at length in the People in business and organisations, Unit 2.

| Departmental Monthly Budgetary Report | | | | | | |
|---|---|---|---|---|---|---|
| | Month | | | Cumulative | | |
| Cost | Budget | Actual | Variance | Budget | Actual | Variance |
| Labour | 100 | 77 | −23 | 500 | 430 | −70 |
| Materials | 150 | 165 | +15 | 750 | 765 | +15 |

**Fig 5.13**

## ACTIVITY: BUDGETING: A

In this activity you will research how budgets are allocated. Either for your own area of activity at work or for a department at the college at which you are studying, find out:

- How is the budget allocated?
- How often are budgetary targets checked and is remedial action taken where necessary?

## ACTIVITY: BUDGETING: B

You work in the finance department of your local college and have been asked to draw up a budget for a project in the business studies department that entails them producing some training materials that will be sold to other colleges. The budget is to be prepared for two years on a quarterly basis, showing both quarterly and cumulative figures. Funding for the first year of the project of £50 000 will come from the college and for the second year will be £25 000, at the end of which the project must be self funding. You are given the following supporting information.

Year One:

| | |
|---|---|
| Project manager's salary: | £16 000 |
| Project staffing costs: | £14 000 |
| Administration staff: | £2 000 |
| Print technician: | £3 000 |
| Print materials: | £1 500 |
| Contribution to print equipment: | £3 000 |
| Publicity: | £2 000 |
| Stationery/office costs: | £2 000 |

The remaining funds are to be placed in a contingency fund.

At the end of six months the project manager decides that he should spend more time marketing the product and asks you to allocate £2500 for travel and accommodation for the remainder of the year. In year one there is no other income.

Year Two:

All costs are to remain the same except where indicated; publicity and promotion to be doubled; staffing costs to be halved; 10 per cent to be added to all other costs. Each pack sells for £100 and for the first three quarters of the second year sales are 150, 200 and 250 respectively.

How many must be sold in the fourth quarter to break even and what must be the level of sales in the third year if all college funding is withdrawn?

NB. It may be useful to calculate the answer to the above activity using an appropriate spread sheet package on your computer.

# Sources of finance

In the two previous units we have looked at preparing a Business Plan and producing budgets. These two exercises will in many cases highlight the need for further funding required by the business. A person starting up in business, whether as a sole trader, a partnership or a private limited company will be expected by a potential investor to have a significant financial interest in the business, that is, capital of at least half the initial requirement. If this is not the case a potential investor may rightly ask 'whose business is it?'

## WHAT IS FINANCE NEEDED FOR?

Finance may be required initially to start up the business but future requirements will largely be needed to fund the purchase of fixed assets or to ease cash flow problems and dependent upon this will be the type of funding available.

## PERSONAL FINANCE

Further finance may be injected by the owner introducing more capital or by family, friends or business partners investing in the business. The owner may of course also borrow money privately from the bank to reinvest in the business.

## EXTERNAL FINANCE

Many developments in a business, however, will only be possible with the support of external finance borrowed at commercial rates.

## RAISING FUNDS BY ISSUING SHARES

Both Private and Public Limited Companies are different from sole traders and partnerships in that they are able to raise funds by the issue of shares.

The amount and type of shares that a company can issue will be detailed in its *Memorandum of Association*. This document which must be completed by all companies when they start up in business, details the objectives of the company. A key item to be included in the document is the *authorised share capital*, this being the amount of shares that the company is allowed to *issue*. This may not in all cases be the same as the *issued share capital*, which is the amount of shares that the company has actually *sold*.

The authorised and issued share capital is divided into a number of types of shares, the main ones being ordinary and preference shares.

## Ordinary shares

All companies must issue *ordinary shares*, sometimes referred to as the equity of the company. Owners of ordinary shares take a share of the profits of the company in the form of a dividend. The level of dividend will depend upon the level of profits and thus an investor is undertaking a significant risk. If the company fails to make a profit they will receive no dividend and if the company becomes bankrupt they will be the last to receive any repayment of their investment.

## Preference shares

*Preference shares*, as their name implies, receive preferential treatment in terms of dividend. Preference shares usually carry a fixed rate of dividend, 5 per cent for example, and are paid first out of profits before any dividend is paid to ordinary shareholders. They are, thus, a relatively safe investment and, therefore, receive a lower rate of return. In some cases *cumulative preference shares* may be issued, so that if you do not get a dividend one year the missing dividend may be paid to you the following year if the company makes sufficient profits.

---

### EXAMPLE

---

*In the extract of Cadbury Schweppes plc accounts shown below we can see the normal layout which shows both the authorised and issued share capital of a company in the notes accompanying the accounts. What is also clear*

*is that in this case the cumulative preference shares are of only limited importance to the company and the yield from the company has consistently been much greater than the 3 per cent preference yield.*

| Extract from Cadbury Schweppes final accounts | |
| --- | --- |
| *Authorised share capital:* | *£m* |
| 3% £1 cumulative preference shares | 3.3 |
| Ordinary Shares (806.8 million at 25p) | 201.7 |
| | 205.0 |
| | |
| *Issued share capital:* | |
| 3% £1 cumulative preference shares | 3.3 |
| Ordinary shares (694.3 million at 25p) | 173.6 |
| | 176.9 |

## LOANS AND DEBENTURES

Shareholders are the owners of the company, but a firm may obtain other sources of funding by borrowing as we have seen above. One particular type of loan that applies to a Limited Company is the *debenture*. The term debenture is used when money is received on loan to the company at a fixed rate of interest, often for a fixed period of time, which is detailed in a formal certificate. They are usually used for short periods of time and avoid the expense of selling shares. They are usually purchased by banks and finance companies. Cadbury Schweppes has a range of debenture commitments that pay different rates of interest depending upon when they were issued and the length of the loan.

## BUILDING SOCIETY FUNDING

People normally buy a house with the aid of a mortgage which is simply a long term loan which is paid back with interest over a period of up to 25 years. The loan is secured by the actual property which means that if repayments on the loan are not kept up, the building society may repossess the property. If the owners have owned the property for some time it may be possible to borrow money using the increased value of the property as security against a further loan. This may take the form of a remortgage or a secured loan.

## BANK FUNDING

Finance is available from the banks in one of two forms, either an overdraft or a loan.

An *overdraft* is a facility on a Current Account to go overdrawn up to an amount which is agreed by the bank. An overdraft will usually be used to finance working capital and to ease short-term cash-flow problems.

A *loan* is for a specific sum agreed over a number of years usually to finance specific capital projects.

In both cases some form of security will often be required. This may take the form of a mortgage over such items as insurance policies, houses, industrial plant and equipment or stocks and shares. If the business has a good track record the bank may be willing to accept either personal or directors' guarantees of the loan.

In many cases a firm may want to expand but have no security. It is for this reason that the government has introduced the *loan guarantee scheme*.

## THE GOVERNMENT'S LOAN GUARANTEE SCHEME

This scheme also known as the *Small Firms' Loans Guarantee Scheme* works through the banking system. To take advantage of the scheme a business must prove that it is viable and that all available security has already been mortgaged. The terms of the scheme are that the government will guarantee the bank 70 per cent of the loan. The borrower paying interest at $2\frac{1}{2}$ per cent above base rate and a quarterly premium of $2\frac{1}{2}$ per cent of the loan to cover the cost of the guarantee. This is obviously fairly expensive and there has not been a major take up of this facility.

---

### ACTIVITY

Compare the cost of borrowing £10 000 for one year under the Government's Loan Guarantee Scheme and a bank. For both schemes you will have to find out the bank rate and the bank lending rate.

---

## HIRE PURCHASE

A *hire purchase agreement* enables a business to acquire an asset on the payment of a deposit and pay back the cost plus interest over a period of time. This form of funding is usually more expensive than a loan but the hire purchase company will usually lend a higher percentage cost of the item. This type of business is usually transacted through one of the finance houses such as Bowmaker, Lombard or Mercantile Credit.

## LEASING

A leasing arrangement may also be provided by a finance house. It is mainly used for equipment and vehicles and enables the asset to be rented. There are several types including the *pay back lease* in which the cost of the item plus interest is paid over the period of the lease, at the end of which fresh arrangements will need to be made. With a *lease purchase* there is the option to purchase the asset for a token sum at the end of the lease. Both schemes are more expensive than bank loans but they have the advantage of not tying up capital, and there may also be tax advantages.

## FACTORING

This is another means of raising short term finance. *A factoring company* will pay between 70–80 per cent of the value of invoices and then take on the responsibility of collecting them. This saves having to wait for payment from debtors. Bad debts, which are those that the factoring company have decided are not possible to collect perhaps because the company has gone bankrupt and has no assets or because the owner has disappeared, are normally charged back to the company. Factoring can be expensive but it saves tying up capital and administration costs. Your business would have to have a turnover of at least £50 000 to interest a Factoring Company.

## INSURANCE COMPANIES

Many insurance companies and building societies now offer services similar to those of banks. In particular they will give loans for commercial property purchase. They often give loans at a cheaper rate than the banks and sometimes lend a greater proportion of the purchase price. Insurance companies who operate in this type of market include: Commercial Union: Prudential and Allied Dunbar.

If you are a Limited Company then as well as the opportunity to issue more shares other sources of funding also become available.

## VENTURE CAPITAL COMPANIES

*Venture capitalists* buy shares in limited companies mainly for amounts over £100 000. It is purely 'risk money' that is, money invested in a project or company that has no track record or is launching a new idea or product onto the market. Many of these schemes are supported through the government's 'Business Expansion Scheme' which gives tax incentives to investors who invest in new and growing companies.

Many sources of funding are targeted at particular groups of people or to particular areas of the country.

## BRITISH COAL ENTERPRISES

This lends to viable companies in the old coal mining areas usually at a rate cheaper than the banks. Like many agencies, they are a last resort; that is they will only lend if all other avenues have been exhausted. They will lend up to £5000 for each job created or 25 per cent of the project cost, whichever is the cheaper.

## PRINCE'S YOUTH BUSINESS TRUST

This lends to applicants aged between 18 and 25 inclusive who are registered as unemployed. The scheme provides grants of up to £155 for the disadvantaged and cheap loans up to £5000. But most importantly they offer continuing support and advice.

## ENTERPRISE ALLOWANCE SCHEME

This scheme provides support to people who have been unemployed for at least six weeks. It provides assistance to those who have £1000 of their own money or access to that amount to invest and who have had a business plan approved by a recognised business counsellor. The money is provided from the government through local training and enterprise councils.

## LOCAL ENTERPRISE FUNDS

Each area may have selective funds available provided by local industry and commerce and administered through an enterprise agency. In the Bolton area for example both Shell and the Midland Bank have special local schemes to provide funding for developing businesses.

---

### ACTIVITY

1 You are to explain how you would fund the following developments in your Limited Company. You should research the current rates of interest and the schemes available to support industry in your local area.

(i)   You find that because major companies are delaying paying bills you have cash-flow problems each month and run a permanent overdraft of £15 000.
(ii)  You want to purchase a new fleet of delivery vehicles which would cost in total £100 000 and are loathe to tie up your cash balances by funding a loan.
(iii) All the banks have turned you down in your search for funding for a new venture which will cost £12 500 to set up but giving significant returns if it is successful.

2 You are to produce an article for the business page of your local newspaper which gives details of local financial support for new businesses in your area.

---

## How to make investment decisions

So far we have looked almost exclusively at the internal financial needs of the business. Hopefully in the long term the business will be successful and the business or the owner, rather than wanting to borrow money, will be able to invest it. Savings can be categorised into two areas: (i) savings with banks, building societies, insurance companies, finance houses and the government; and (ii) investment in stocks and shares.

## SAVING WITH BANKS AND SIMILAR ORGANISATIONS

The return on investments with banks are usually easy to calculate once you know the rate of interest and the length of time you wish to invest the money for. By completing the next activity you will acquire a lot of knowledge about the options available.

---

### ACTIVITY

Draw up a chart which shows the return on a series of investments. You should give at least the following information in chart form, but may wish to include more – rate of interest; value of investment at end of 5 years and 10 years; penalties for early withdrawal; whether return is guaranteed; whether you can withdraw on a regular basis. For each investment you should compare at least two alternatives and indicate your 'best buy':

(i)   You want to invest a lump sum of £25 000 for a minimum of 5 years and will not withdraw during that period.
(ii)  You want to invest £50 per month over a minimum of three years but may want to withdraw the interest.
(iii) You want to invest £100 000 as a lump sum for a definite fixed term of ten years and require to make regular drawings.
(iv)  You want to invest £10 000 in a Five Year Government Bond.

---

## INVESTMENT IN STOCKS AND SHARES

Buying stocks and shares means that you are investing in a business and are in fact becoming a part owner of that business. For that reason this type of investment always has a risk element as the business may incur a loss just as it may well make a profit.

If you limit your investment to a limited company it means that your liability as a shareholder is limited to the amount of your original investment or any unpaid element of the shares that you purchased. The different types of shares that companies issue will be dealt with more fully in the Unit 3 Business systems. In most cases you would expect the company to make a profit and if that is the case you will benefit in two ways:

(i)   the company will pay a dividend;
(ii)  the shares should rise in value.

## SHARE DIVIDEND

If the company is profitable and the directors decide to distribute the profit to the shareholders, rather than reinvesting the profit within the company, they will declare a dividend as shown in the example below.

---

### EXAMPLE

*The dividend is a payment per share held which in NORWEB's case is 10.94p per share. (See Fig 5.15.) The dividend is based on the 'nominal value' of the share, that is the price at which it was originally offered and not the current market price.*

*How would you have fared if you had purchased 1000 £1 shares in NORWEB at a price of £3.00 each? You would receive 1000 × 10.94p = £109.40. On an investment of £3000 you have received a return of £109.40 which is equal to 3.6 per cent, not a very good return. You must of course also remember that you may get a larger return when you sell the shares, but that like the profit is not guaranteed.*

---

## SHARE VALUE

When you invested in NORWEB you became a part owner of the company and the value of your share in the company will rise and fall in tune with the company's trading performance. In general, if investors view the long-term prospects of NORWEB as good then the price of the shares will rise. The opposite will of course occur if investors are pessimistic about the future. Though even that does not account for the largely short-term changes in the value of the shares on the stock exchange. These may be affected by such things as:

● investors selling for short term gains;
● investors selling to turn their investment into cash;
● government pronouncements about the state of the economy;

**NORWEB Summary group historical cost profit and loss account** for the year ended 31 March 1991

| | 1991 £m | 1990 £m |
|---|---|---|
| **Turnover** | **1,240.3** | **1,232.1** |
| Operating costs | 1,151.1 | 1,161.2 |
| **Operating profit before exceptional items** | **89.2** | **70.9** |
| Exceptional items (see note below) | (15.0) | – |
| Income from fixed asset investments | 11.4 | – |
| Net interest (payable)/receivable | (15.3) | 4.9 |
| **Profit on ordinary activities before taxation** | **70.3** | **75.8** |
| Tax on profit on ordinary activities | 28.0 | 18.2 |
| **Profit on ordinary activities after taxation** | **42.3** | **57.6** |
| Extraordinary items (see note below) | 6.9 | 4.1 |
| **Profit for the financial year** | **35.4** | **53.5** |
| Ordinary dividend – single proposed 10.94p per share | 18.9 | – |
| **Profit retained** | **16.5** | **53.5** |
| **Earnings per ordinary share** | | |
| After exceptional items | 24.5p | |
| Before exceptional items | 32.5p | |
| Recommended Dividend | 10.94p | |

**NORWEB Summary group historical cost balance sheet** 31 March 1991

| | 1991 £m | 1990 £m |
|---|---|---|
| **Fixed assets** | | |
| Tangible assets | 461.3 | 441.4 |
| Investments | 65.1 | – |
| | **526.4** | **441.4** |
| **Current assets** | 270.7 | 298.4 |
| Creditors – amounts falling due within one year | 177.3 | 222.5 |
| **Net current assets** | **93.4** | **75.9** |
| **Total assets less current liabilities** | **619.8** | **517.3** |
| Creditors – amounts falling due after more than one year | 18.6 | 18.8 |
| Unsecured bonds | 153.0 | – |
| Provisions for liabilities and charges | 29.1 | 6.8 |
| **Net assets** | **419.1** | **491.7** |
| **Capital and reserves** | | |
| Called up share capital | 86.4 | – |
| Profit and loss account | 332.7 | 491.7 |
| **Shareholders' funds** | **419.1** | **491.7** |

The summary financial statement is an extract from the Directors' report and accounts which were approved by the Board of Directors on 26 June 1991.

K G Harvey *Chairman*
B J Wilson *Financial Director*

Fig 5.15

- increased competition from the European Community or opportunities available within it.

Professional investors will, however, look at a range of indicators before deciding whether to buy or sell the shares.

To help us evaluate the effectiveness of our investment there are several analytical techniques we can use which include measuring:

- Earnings Per Share
- Price Earnings Ratio
- Dividend Yield
- Dividend Cover
- Gearing.

## EARNINGS PER SHARE

This is a fairly simple calculation which can be best expressed as the equation:

$$\frac{\text{profit after tax}}{\text{number of shares issued}}$$

Therefore for a company that had made after tax profits of £250 000 and had issued 10 000 shares the earnings per share would be:

$$\frac{250\ 000}{10\ 000} = £25.00$$

Limited Companies are required to show the earnings per share in the accounts and for NORWEB we can see that the figure is 24.5p.

It is important to compare earnings per share over a period of time to see if the figure is going up or down. If it is going down is it because the company is less profitable or has it issued more shares? Like many ratios it should only be used in connection with other analyses.

## PRICE EARNINGS RATIO

For limited companies the *Price Earnings Ratio* is one of the most commonly used tests of a 'good' investment and is usually shown for all companies in the financial pages of newspapers. It shows how many years' earnings per share the share price represents and is expressed by the equation:

$$\frac{\text{share price}}{\text{earnings per share}}$$

For NORWEB this would be:

$$\frac{£2.93}{24.5\text{p}} = 11.9.$$

This figure gives a good clue as to how highly rated NORWEB is by investors. Generally speaking the lower the Price Earnings Ratio the better it is to invest in that particular share. Again it is useful to compare this ratio over a period of time or with companies in the same sector.

## DIVIDEND YIELD

*Dividend yield* is the gross dividend per share expressed as a percentage of the current share price and is expressed in the equation:

$$\frac{\text{Gross Dividend}}{\text{Share Price}} \times 100$$

For NORWEB, therefore, this gives us:

$$\frac{10.94\text{p}}{300\text{p}} \times 100 = 3.6\%$$

Once again, this is not a very healthy return, but it may be offset by long-term growth in the value of the shares.

## DIVIDEND COVER

At the end of a financial year a company may pay out a large dividend, and keep the shareholders happy, or plough the money back into the company. A shareholder would want to know therefore the ratio between profits and dividend. *Dividend cover* shows the number of times the dividend is covered by the profit per share and is expressed in the equation:

$$\frac{\text{earnings per share}}{\text{dividend per share}}$$

For NORWEB this would be:

$$\frac{24.5}{10.94} = 2.2.$$

Thus NORWEB is operating at a relatively low level of Dividend Cover and therefore has not got a lot of slack within the system to work with. NORWEB, therefore, is not ploughing much back into the business, but is paying a high dividend to its shareholders.

---

### ACTIVITY

Explain why the dividend cover for the following companies varies.

| *Dividend Cover of selected companies 1992* | |
| --- | --- |
| POWERGEN | 3.5 |
| Macallan-Glen Distillers | 6.0 |
| ICI | 0.9 |
| Wimpey | 0.8 |
| Owners Abroad | 4.2 |
| Marks & Spencer | 2.2 |

---

## GEARING

A company may look very successful on paper and could from all the analytical techniques used so far be said to be very profitable. In late 1991 the Maxwell business empire, which included the Daily Mirror Group, collapsed largely because it had huge debts. How can you ensure you do not make the same mistake Maxwell investors did and invest in a debt-ridden company? A simple technique is to work out the *gearing* or 'debt/equity' ratio. That is the proportion of the business that is financed by debt. This can be calculated by using the formula:

$$\text{Gearing} = \frac{\text{External Debt}}{\text{Shareholders Funds}} \times \frac{100}{1}$$

For NORWEB this can be calculated thus:

$$\text{Gearing} = \frac{153\ 000\ 000}{419\ 100\ 000} \times \frac{100}{1} = 36.5\%$$

Where a company has a high proportion of its capital in the form of debt in relation to ordinary shares it is said to be *highly geared* and conversely when ordinary shares form the major part of capital the company is said to be *low geared*. In terms of investment opportunity you would be wise to invest in a low geared company as a higher proportion of the profit will be available to shareholders and not just to fund borrowing. To explain this let's look at an example:

| | Company | |
| --- | --- | --- |
| | Low Top Ltd | High Top Ltd |
| Capital: | | |
|   Ordinary shares | £100 000 | £100 000 |
|   10% debentures | £25 000 | £75 000 |
| | £125 000 | £175 000 |
| Gearing | 25 000 | 75 000 |
| | 100 000 | 100 000 |
| | = 25% | = 75% |
| | Low geared | High geared |

Although both companies have the same amount of ordinary shares, because High Top Ltd has £75 000 of debentures it has a high gearing figure of 75 per cent.

What, therefore, will be the effect of the differing gearing levels on shareholders? If we assume that both firms have profits of

£20 000 the effect on the shareholders is shown below:

|  | Company | |
|  | Low Top Ltd | High Top Ltd |
| --- | --- | --- |
| Profit | £20 000 | £20 000 |
| Less debenture interest | £2 500 | £7 500 |
| Amount available to shareholders | £17 500 | £12 500 |
| % Dividend available | $\dfrac{17\,500 \times 100}{100\,000}$ | $\dfrac{12\,500 \times 100}{100\,000}$ |
|  | = 17.5% | = 12.5% |

Because High Top Ltd is a highly geared company we can see that less of the profit is available for distribution to the shareholders.

---

### ACTIVITY

Given the information shown below which company would you choose to invest in? Show your calculations.

**Jones Ltd**
   Capital:  100 000 £1 Ordinary Shares
           25 000 15% Debentures
   Profit:    £25 000

**White Ltd**
   Capital:  150 000 £1 Ordinary Shares
           100 000 20% Debentures
   Profit:    £40 000

---

Most of the information given above can be taken from the financial pages of the daily newspapers. Information varies from one paper to another but is likely to show:

- companies by sector;
- share price and changes;
- buying and selling price;
- yield;
- price/earnings ratio.

An investor who uses all the information available should be able to make a more intelligent assessment of a company's performance and more importantly, whether to invest in that company or not.

---

### ACTIVITY

**1** On p 168 you were asked to collect the final accounts of a range of limited companies. Using all the analytical techniques you have learnt, now produce a report which shows the profitability and potential of two of the companies.

**2** As a group, produce a chart which lists all your companies showing all relevant ratios.

**3** As a group, decide which is the 'most successful' company.

---

## Financial record keeping

In this unit we have so far utilised financial information to enable the business to make decisions. We must now look at the other side of the coin which is the *financial record keeping* or accounting side to the business.

You have both used and produced Trading and Profit and Loss Accounts and Balance Sheets. Where does this information come from? Most of the information will come from the simple records that you must keep to record the daily inputs and outputs of the business. In terms of a small business you could easily list all the sources of information that may be used in buying and selling. (Fig 5.16 opposite). For most businesses we should be able to see that the vast majority of information will come from either invoices or cash and bank receipts. All records fall in fact into seven broad categories:

- sales invoices
- purchase invoices
- bank statements
- receipts
- cheque stubs
- wage sheets
- petty cash book

### SALES

As soon as an invoice is produced then a copy should be put into the *sales invoice file* in numerical and therefore date order so that they can be chased up for payment on a regular and systematic basis. To help in the business it is also

| Information | | Source |
|---|---|---|
| Income | | Till rolls |
| | | Sales invoices |
| | | Bank statements |
| Expenditure: | labour | Wage sheets |
| | expenses | Invoices |
| | | Cheque stubs |
| | materials and | Petty cash vouchers |
| | equipment | Invoices |
| Debtors | | Unpaid invoices |
| Creditors | | Unpaid invoices |
| Bank balance | | Cheque stubs |
| | | Paying in book |
| | | Statements |
| Drawings | | Cheque stubs |
| | | Receipts for stock |

**Fig 5.16 Sources of accounting information**

usual to list all the invoices and show: date; invoice number; invoice total; VAT. The term given to this document is the *sales day book*.

At the same time an entry should be made in the relevant customer's file so that you can see at any one time how much is outstanding, that is, an entry is made in the individual 'debtors' ledger'. When payment is made or goods sent back for whatever reason then entries are once again made in the appropriate debtors' ledger.

## PURCHASES

In similar fashion when we buy goods for resale or materials to be used in production the invoices received are filed in the *purchases invoice file* and summarised in the purchases day book. A record is also made in the individual creditor's file in the creditors' ledger.

## BANK STATEMENTS, CHEQUE STUBS AND RECEIPTS

Information from these sources will enable you to list in your cash file all cash received and paid out, all cheques drawn or paid into your bank account, as well as noting any standing orders or direct debit payments into your account. The file

that this information is recorded in is known as the *Cash Book*.

## PETTY CASH BOOK

In order to save your Cash Book being cluttered up with many small transactions details of small amounts of spending are kept in a *Petty Cash Book* and the Cash Book is updated with details of Net spending at suitable intervals.

## WAGES SHEETS

For many businesses, wages form the major expense and so accurate recording is essential. There are many patent wage recording systems available as well as the simple forms supplied by the Inland Revenue. Net information from the Wages Sheets is transferred to the Wages Account of the business.

In basic terms we have described the essential record keeping system that is required of any business. It should be possible to list any income or expenditure of a business in an account both as a record of the transaction and to enable that information to be used in calculating the financial position of the business at required intervals. In Fig 5.17 you can see where the information comes from to enable the Trial Balance and final accounts to be produced.

Keeping the books then is something that any business person will have to do regularly and accurately from the first week they start trading. Therefore, your bookkeeping method should be one of the first priorities.

In choosing a bookkeeping system there are three questions to ask yourself:

(i) *Will it be adequate for the needs of my business in the long run?*
If your business plan involves fairly rapid growth there is no point in starting off with a simple system which will be inadequate after six months. It would be more sensible to start off with a system that is more complicated than you need at first but which will be adequate for the requirements of your business for some time ahead.

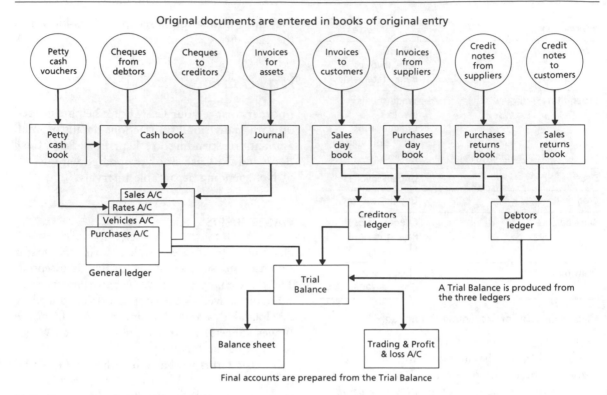

**Fig 5.17 From the accounts to the trial balance**

(ii) *Will it be quick and easy to keep up to date?* Assuming that the system will be adequate to cope with the needs of your business in the foreseeable future, there is no point in having anything more complicated or time consuming than that.

Your system should be as simple as possible. You will have enough demands on your time as a business person without spending any longer than is necessary doing the books – an activity which after all does not make any money for you.

(iii) *Will it cost much?*
This is a very important consideration for any firm and especially for one just starting up.

For the vast majority of new businesses it makes more sense to buy a commercial book-keeping package than attempt to set up your own system. Unless you are a bookkeeping expert you will find the commercial packages much easier to get to grips with.

There are many commercial bookkeeping packages available, one of the simplest being the Simplex system. This package answers some of our original questions in that it is:

● easy to understand;
● not time consuming to complete;
● it provides all the necessary information.

It is unlikely that a new firm or an established small firm would find it beneficial to invest in any of the computerised accounting packages now available.

**COMPUTERISED ACCOUNTING**

In many businesses the volume of transactions will grow to a point where it becomes impossible, time consuming, costly and inefficient to run a manual system. Also in recent years many simple computerised accounting systems have been developed which can be purchased at a relatively low cost. For a sole trader a package including hardware, printer and software can now be purchased for less than £2000. Of course major businesses may require complex accounting systems designed specifically for them that run into many thousands of pounds. The important message though is that computerised accounting systems are now available to all.

---

#### ACTIVITY

Using a suitable spreadsheet package undertake the task shown in the activity on p **190**.

---

## PERSONAL FINANCE

Many of the techniques explained in the previous unit will enable you to manage your personal finances more effectively and some of you will no doubt already have high level financial skills. In this final unit we will examine further techniques that will enable you to plan and control your personal finances.

---

#### ACTIVITY

You are aware that occasionally you are overdrawn at the bank and subsequently have had to pay rather large bank charges. In order to try to improve the situation draw up a Cash Flow Forecast for the year based on the following information:

*Income*:
Net Monthly Income £700
Half-yearly bonuses of 10% of Net Monthly figure paid at end of June and December.

*Expenditure*:
Monthly: mortgage £160; Council Tax £33; car expenses £29; food, household and personal spending £180.
Quarterly: gas £170 (Mar); £120 (Jun); £60 (Sept); £90 (Dec); electricity £80; telephone £48; (both paid Mar, Jun, Sept, and Dec).
Annual: car tax £100 (Jan); car insurance £250 (Feb), household insurance £190 (Mar); holiday £450 (Jul); Christmas shopping £250.

You also have an overdraft of £600 at the start of the year which you intend to pay off at the rate of £50 per month.

Suggest ways in which you could restructure your expenditure and explain how the bank could help you.

---

### HOW CAN THE BANK HELP?

You will probably have a range of suggestions as to how the bank could help you but perhaps priority should be given to opening a budget account.

### Budget planning schemes

Most banks and building societies have budget accounts that allow for the payment of budgeted items throughout the year. The bank asks the customer to record all regular payments such as electricity, telephone, insurance, etc, which are totalled up for an annual figure and divided by twelve to produce a monthly figure which is paid into the budget account. Bills are then paid from this account, often by standing order or direct debit, the bank allowing the account to go overdrawn as the need arises.

---

#### ACTIVITY

Calculate how much money you would need to pay into a budget account to meet the regular bills shown in the previous activity.

---

### OTHER FINANCIAL SERVICES

Financial services for the individual can generally be classified into two: savings and investments and loan facilities.

### SAVING AND INVESTMENT SERVICES

A glance at the advertisements in any newspaper will show the extent of saving and investment opportunities available. The offers available are like any market and you, the consumer, should always be prepared to shop around to obtain the best price and also to obtain the savings package that is right for you. It is beyond the scope of this book to go into detail about individual schemes but saving opportunities can largely be classified as shown in Fig 5.18.

---

#### ACTIVITY

By completing this activity you will develop a thorough knowledge of the range of saving and investment schemes available on offer.

---

| Type of scheme | Short term (less than six months) | Long term |
|---|:---:|:---:|
| Current account | ● | |
| Deposit account | ● | ● |
| Savings account | ● | ● |
| Building society accounts | ● | ● |
| National savings accounts | ● | ● |
| National savings bonds | | ● |
| Stocks and shares | | ● |
| Unit trusts | | ● |
| Endowment insurance policy | | ● |

**Fig 5.18 Saving opportunities**

You are to collect information about the investment schemes detailed in Fig 5.18 and complete the Investment decision tree shown at Fig 5.19. Make a presentation to the rest of your group to justify your recommendations.

### WHAT IS THE RETURN ON YOUR INVESTMENT?

From your earlier research you will see that the rate of interest on investments varies widely. It is fairly easy to calculate the amount you will receive from any investment by using the simple formula:

$$\text{interest earned} = \frac{\text{investment} \times \text{interest rate} \times \text{period in years}}{100}$$

This though is not the real rate of interest because throughout the year inflation will have eroded the purchasing power of your money. For example if you have £1000 at the beginning of the year and the rate of inflation is 10 per cent you would need £1100 at the end of the year in order to maintain your purchasing power.

The real rate of interest, therefore, is much more important than the actual rate and can again be calculated by using the formula:

real rate of interest =
             actual interest rate − inflation rate

ACTIVITY

Find out what the present rate of inflation is and work out the real interest rate on a bank deposit account and a 7.5 per cent National Savings One Year Bond.

## Borrowing money

A new car, a new kitchen, money to get you through college: everyone seems to have an inexhaustible demand for new consumer goods and services and, consequently, often a requirement for money to enable those purchases. In recent years the financial services sector has often been criticised for lending to people who cannot afford to repay and for their lending policies which have helped to fuel inflation. Despite that, the development of new borrowing schemes, designed to tempt you, continues unabated. From time to time you will undoubtedly want to borrow money and in this section we will look at the various alternatives open to you.

### OVERDRAFTS AND CREDIT ZONES

Most banks offer flexible agreed overdraft schemes which are generally the cheapest way to borrow money. To have an overdraft you must first of all have a current account on which the bank will allow you to go overdrawn by a set limit, for example, to an overdraft limit of £500. The advantage of an overdraft is that you only pay interest on the amount owing on a daily basis and this therefore enables you to keep the charges down. In comparing interest rates on borrowing you must also be wary of any arrangement fees that banks may charge which may significantly alter the attractiveness of a particular scheme.

### PERSONAL LOAN

A personal loan is a fixed-term loan for a specific purpose. These are normally more expensive than an overdraft as the interest is calculated on the total amount of the loan for the full period of the loan. As with all borrowing, it is unwise to take on a loan if you are unable to keep up the

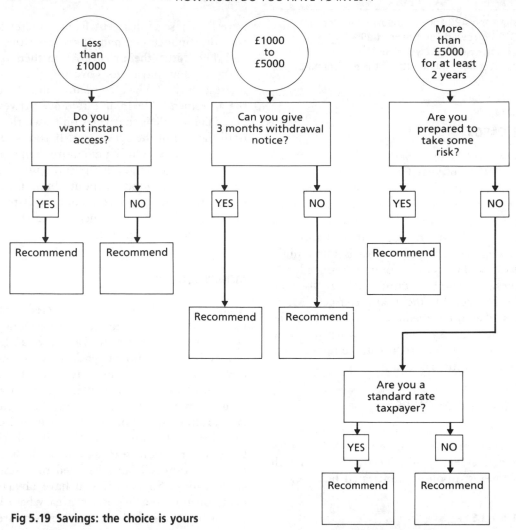

**Fig 5.19 Savings: the choice is yours**

repayments and so the bank will want details of your present and future income to reassure themselves that you are not going to overstretch yourself financially. Many banks also offer repayment protection insurance schemes which will pay your monthly repayments on a loan if you are ill or made redundant.

To enable you to work out which is the best loan for you, finance companies now have to quote the Annual Percentage Rate (APR). Generally speaking the lower the APR the cheaper it is to borrow. The interest rate is charged for the duration of the loan despite the fact that as you repay the loan the amount you owe gradually reduces.

For example, £10 000 borrowed at a fixed rate of 10 per cent will be charged interest as shown:

Interest = amount × rate × years

$$= £10\,000 \times \frac{10}{100} \times 2 = £2000$$

The total amount to be repaid will therefore be the amount borrowed plus the interest which equals £10 000 plus £2 000, £12 000. The APR will be approximately 20 per cent, double the fixed rate of 10 per cent. So if you want a loan remember to check the APR figure.

## CREDIT CARDS

The most widely used bank credit cards in the UK are VISA and ACCESS. These provide a means of payment and allow you to repay the balance on your monthly statement with a set period of about three weeks with no interest charge. If you do not repay the balance the interest charged on credit cards is fairly high. The credit card is therefore only recommended as a means of facilitating purchases that you can pay for before you incur any charges. Many charities also offer credit cards, linked to the Access and Visa system, the charity receiving commission from the credit card company each time you use your card.

## COMPANY CHARGE CARDS

Many large shops such as Debenhams issue their own charge cards for in-store use. Whilst they may be convenient, you will certainly pay a high rate of interest upon any uncleared balance.

## CREDIT SALES

Many large items such as cars, furniture or electrical items can be purchased on credit. With a credit sale you buy the goods and agree to repay a finance company the amount plus interest over a given period. With a credit sale you become the owner of the goods immediately and if you default on your payments the finance company may insist upon full repayment. Credit interest rates are normally very high and are therefore not a good system for borrowing, but from time to time if goods are not selling well businesses may offer cheap or even interest free credit. In all cases, however, credit has to be paid for and it may be worthwhile you negotiating a lower initial price rather than having the cheap credit.

## HIRE PURCHASE

Hire Purchase is different from a credit sale in that the finance company purchases the goods and then 'hires' them to you. You then agree to make regular payments covering the cost plus interest to the finance company until the end of the agreement. The main difference between this and a credit sale is that you don't own the goods until the end of the agreement. If you default on payments and you have paid more than one third of the value of the goods the company is unable to repossess the goods without obtaining a court order. In many cases companies will prefer to negotiate with the customer rather than going through the court system.

## MONEY LENDERS

Many people have such bad credit ratings, because they have defaulted on previous credit agreements, that the only way they can borrow money is from a money lender. Every time you borrow money, use your credit card, pay off your mortgage or pay a weekly sum to a catalogue firm the information may be used by a credit rating firm who, for a fee, will advise firms on whether you are a good credit risk or not. Other information, such as your address or type of occupation will also be used to assess your credit rating. So even if you have always paid debts on time but live in an area where lots of people have defaulted on repayments or are in an occupation that is given a low credit rating then you also could have a low credit rating through no fault of your own. There are many, legal and illegal, money lenders who meet the needs of people who are desperate for credit and because they are taking on a bad risk charge very high rates of interest. They are also rather unscrupulous and will follow up bad debts in intimidating ways and will go to the lengths of bankrupting people.

| Type of loan | Purpose | Maximum and Minimum Amount | Features | Benefits | Disad-vantages | APR |
|---|---|---|---|---|---|---|
| overdraft | | | | | | |
| credit card | | | | | | |
| store card | | | | | | |
| personal loan | | | | | | |
| car loan | | | | | | |
| college loan | | | | | | |
| professional training loan | | | | | | |
| money-lender | | | | | | |

### ACTIVITY

Study the case studies below and make appropriate recommendations on how they should finance their planned expenditure. You should make an oral presentation of your recommendations to the rest of the group.

**1** There is a sale on and John wants to buy a camera that has been reduced in price to £250. He knows that in fifteen days' time when he is paid he will be able to buy it, but the sale ends tomorrow.

**2** Amjad wants to buy a new Citroen BX for £11 500 with a deposit of £2500 and credit from Citroen Finance at an APR of 18% over two years. Alternatively he can obtain a car loan from his bank with an APR of 20%.

**3** Maureen wants to do a Dale Carnegie Management course at a price of £3000. She is prepared to borrow money to pay the fees. What is the best option?

**4** Trevor has a very low credit rating and is unable to obtain a loan or an overdraft from his bank. He has a store card from Debenhams and wants to use it to buy a mountain bike for £450, knowing that he will not be able to pay the bill off for several months. His friend tells him he has seen an advertisement in the local paper offering unsecured loans from a registered moneylender at 20% over one year.

## MORTGAGES

Buying a home is considered to be one of life's most stressful experiences. Working your way through the range of mortgage facilities available is probably equally as stressful.

### Capital and interest repayment mortgages

This is the basic loan for home purchase. A fixed amount is borrowed for a specific period of time and each month you repay a portion of the capital and an interest payment. The interest rate, set by the building society or bank, varies in line with interest rates in the economy. If interest rates rise then your repayments may rise so it is important that you take this possibility into account when negotiating a mortgage.

### Endowment mortgage

An endowment mortgage is a straightforward loan for home purchase which is combined with a life insurance endowment policy. Each month you will pay only interest payments and your life assurance premium, the capital element being paid when the insurance policy matures at the end of the specified period.

There are many schemes linked into endowment mortgages such as *fixed rate mortgages* for people who want to take away the worry of interest rate changes. *Low start mortgages* are for young people who know that their salary will rise in future years but want initial lower repayments.

If you are negotiating a mortgage you must always be aware that the adviser helping you will have a vested interest in that they are in business to make money. One way in which they make money is by earning commission on insurance policies. Is the deal that they are offering best for you or best for them?

In many cases all the first year's insurance premiums on an endowment mortgage may go to the insurance broker in the form of commission. Regulatory bodies such as the Financial Intermediaries, Managers and Brokers Regulatory Association (FIMBRA), set up in 1979, are supposed to control the excesses of financial consultants but each day alarming stories of inappropriate lending are seen in the press. The role of regulatory bodies will be dealt with more fully in Unit 6 Business resources.

## Pension mortgage

A relatively new development, this is an interest-payment only mortgage linked to a pension plan. If you are self employed or are not a member of a company pension plan this offers a relatively tax-efficient way of purchasing your home.

## HOW LARGE A MORTGAGE CAN YOU OBTAIN?

Mortgage companies, such as banks or building societies, generally have two or three formulae that they work to in calculating the maximum amount that can be borrowed, although in most cases there are ways in which you can borrow more money. Normally you will only be allowed to borrow 90 per cent of the lender's valuation of the property. This is largely to protect the lender from a fall in the price of houses and perhaps the enforced sale of a property.

They will generally lend only up to three times the major earner's salary plus the secondary salary. More recently lenders have been using a formula which says that your mortgage repayments plus other long-term commitments must not exceed 35 per cent of your individual or joint salaries.

## TAX RELIEF ON MORTGAGES

To encourage home ownership in the United Kingdom the government grants tax relief on the mortgage interest rate up to a maximum of £30 000. This means that the mortgage repayments will carry a much lower rate in real terms for anyone who is both a taxpayer and a mortgage holder. Most schemes operate through Mortgage Interest Relief at Source (MIRAS) which enables you to pay an interest payment net of tax to the lender. The lender then claims the tax back from the Inland Revenue.

---

### ACTIVITY

Ahmed and Elizabeth Hassan are planning to buy their own home. Elizabeth earns £16 000 per year and Ahmed only £2500 in a part-time job whilst he is studying at college. They also have building society savings of £5000. They have seen a new house which costs £60 000. Based on the formula of lending only 90 per cent of the valuation (the building society valuing the property at £57 000), and lending three times the major income plus the secondary salary what are the prospects for the couple?

---

## Protecting the borrower's interests

Over the last year or so you will undoubtedly have seen in the press reference to such instances as the death of Robert Maxwell and the associated loss of pension funds, the sale of inappropriate insurance policies and the wholesale repossession of mortgaged properties. The government has long been aware that any business attracts its share of unscrupulous people and has now taken action through a series of government acts and the setting up of regulatory bodies to give more protection to the consumer.

### FINANCIAL WATCHDOGS

FIMBRA and LAUTRO are the two most important organisations set up to regulate insurance and investment services.

LAUTRO is at the moment taking action against at least ten companies over their sales methods as it is feared that tens of thousands of people are being sold insurance policies which they either do not need or which are unsuitable for their needs. Many sales people in the insurance business are employed on a commission-only basis and, therefore, must sell in order to receive any income. The policies they have sold have in some cases been more to their benefit than that of the client.

It is always worth remembering that most of the first year's premiums on an insurance policy will go in the form of commission to the sales person and that all businesses, including banks, are only in business to make money.

Although FIMBRA has had some success in ending the worst excesses of investment fraud it is only really with the advent of the Investors Compensation Scheme set up in 1988 that the consumer has had any financial backup in the case of fraud. It is recommended that before you hand your life savings over to a financial adviser you ensure that they are legally authorised to carry on an investment business. You can check with the Central Register run by the watchdog Securities and Investments Board (SIB).

You should also find out what kind of official authorisation the adviser has – some firms may not be allowed to handle your cash – and how the return on any scheme will be achieved. Be wary if you are not asked about your income and outgoings, and if the adviser suggests you cash in other investments to enable new investments to be made.

The Consumer Credit Act of 1974 provides a considerable degree of protection for the individual and it is this act that ensures all credit arrangements show the APR which will enable you to make an accurate comparison. The act regulates all types of consumer credit including hire purchase, personal loans, credit cards, overdrafts, credit sales and budget accounts. The main protection comes from the insistence that all credit providers must be licensed to do so. These licensing arrangements are under the control of the Director-General of Fair Trading but are policed locally by consumer protection departments.

In all cases of borrowing you are reminded of that old legal term 'caveat emptor' – let the buyer beware.

## Personal taxation

In the previous pages we have concentrated on how both individuals and businesses earn money, both from work and from the return on savings and investments. Most of their income, whether it is earned or unearned will be subject to taxation. It is important to understand the basis of taxation as research suggests that at least 20% of the population are paying more tax than they need to.

## INCOME TAX

For most people the most important tax to them is income tax. This is tax paid on all income, both earned and unearned but is subject to certain non-taxable allowances which depend on the individual's personal circumstances.

### Calculating your income tax

Most employed people pay their income tax through the Pay As You Earn (PAYE) scheme which means that your employer will deduct the appropriate amount from your wages and pay it on your behalf to the Inland Revenue.

If you look at your wage slip you will be able to find your tax code. This will give you information about the amount of income you can receive in the year before you start to pay any tax. If your code number is 365L the L means that you are a single person or are claiming the wife's earned income allowance and that your total earnings before you pay tax are £3650. Your tax code is always your allowance minus the last digit. If your code ends with an H this means that it incorporates the married mans' allowance.

There are many other allowances that you can offset against tax such as subscriptions to professional bodies, specialist equipment or clothing you must buy, payments under deeds of covenant and maintenance payments if you are divorced.

Each year the Government updates the allowances, usually in line with inflation, and this with your appropriate code should allow you to calculate the amount of tax you have to pay in the year. By looking at the Tax Allowances shown in Fig 5.20 and the Tax Bands in Fig 5.21 you can make some simple calculations.

| Tax Allowances 1992 | |
|---|---|
| | £ |
| Single person | 3445 |
| Married couple | 1720 |
| Additional personal | 1720 |
| Blind person | 1080 |
| Widow's bereavement | 1720 |

Fig 5.20

| Tax Bands 1992 | |
| --- | --- |
| £ | % |
| 0–2000 | 20 |
| 2001–23 700 | 25 |
| Over 23 700 | 40 |

**Fig 5.21**

If you are a single person earning £12 000 per annum and have no dependants and no other allowances your tax liability can be assessed as shown:

| | |
| --- | --- |
| Income | £12 000 |
| Less personal allowance | £3 445 |
| Taxable income | £8 555 |

Tax due:

| | |
| --- | --- |
| 20% of £2000 | £400 |
| 25% of £6555 | £1 638.75 |
| | £2 038.75 |

### ACTIVITY

Assess the tax liability in the following cases:

(i)   A married man earning £26 000 pa, with professional subscriptions of £90.

(ii)  A married woman, claiming the married couple's allowance and earning £30 000 pa.

(iii) A single person earning £15 000 pa with allowances of £60 professional subscription and £40 for essential clothing.

# 6

# BUSINESS RESOURCES

## Introduction

The aims of this unit are to:

- introduce you to the sorts of physical resources used in business
- look at the different types of physical resources used by different businesses
- consider the physical resources used in a particular job
- show the sorts of decisions firms have to make in acquiring physical resources
- look at the ways that organisations try to make sure they are getting the best out of the resources they have.

## What are physical resources?

What do we mean by physical resources? In any business, as we have already seen, there are all sorts of inputs to the organisation: these will probably include money, the work of the owners and employees, ideas, some sort of raw materials, machines or equipment and somewhere to work. It is these last few which are the physical resources of the business, as opposed to the people who are the human resources of the business and the money which makes up the financial resources of the business. Almost all businesses require a mix of these three (*see* Fig 6.1):

1 physical resources
2 human resources
3 financial resources.

### ACTIVITY

Think of a small business you know, or of a business idea on a small scale and try to list what would be needed to start the business up. When you have listed the different resources you think would be needed, try to categorise them under the headings above. An example relating to a window cleaning business has been started to give you some help.

**Business:**
Sole trader window cleaning business in rural Derbyshire.

**Resources needed:**

| Physical | Financial | Human |
|---|---|---|
| Ladder | Loan to buy car | Owner |
| Car | Overdraft if business | Some part- |
| Soap/cloths | poor | time help |
| Garage to store | | |
| car etc | | |

The above is obviously not a complete list of all the things which would be needed to run the business and not everything will fit so neatly into the categories; for instance if the owner of the business has his car serviced by a friend he needs financial resources to pay for it, he is using the human resource of his friend to do the work and he will have to use some physical resources (oil, filters etc.) in the process. For the business you are working on try to make the list a bit more complete and, where you have trouble deciding where a particular resource should go, make a note of why.

For a larger business the list you would make would be very long indeed, and many large businesses have whole departments devoted to just keeping track of all the physical resources they have and trying to make sure they are used as well as possible.

Making the most of the physical resources is very important as the wrong decision in buying

**Fig 6.1  A business requires a mixture of three resources**

or using them can cost a lot of money just as making the right decision can save a lot of money, as is illustrated below:

---

### EXAMPLE

---

*One large business recently decided to switch to diesel cars for all of its 312 company cars. They had to pay about £400 more per car when they bought them but they saved money on servicing which was cheaper and less frequent, they got better fuel economy and the fuel cost less per gallon, they also can expect to get more for the cars when they sell them. They estimate that they will have saved over £250,000 in three years by doing this as well as helping the environment by burning less fuel and causing less pollution. They will also be able to use the fact that they are environmentally aware as a public relations plus – it won't just save money, it'll also look good and help their public image.*

*Another business (much smaller) recently decided to economise on the ingredients which they used for their ice cream;*

> *'the result tasted awful and we had to scrap a whole batch of production. This cost us money not only because we couldn't sell this particular batch but also because our customers had to wait an extra day for deliveries – causing some bad will and a lot of complaints.'*

*They know they lost about £1300 on the cheaper ingredients and the overtime they had to pay to make up*

production and have no idea what the cost of the damage to their reputation is.

## How to classify the physical resources needed by an organisation

You can classify physical resources in different ways. In this unit you will look at them under a number of headings which are given below and, after you have read these brief definitions we will go on to have a closer look at each of them:

### LAND

This can be a small area for a market stall or thousands of acres for a large farm. Land and the buildings on it will probably be among the most expensive purchases that many businesses have to make, and could make the difference between success and failure; for example a retail business which chooses the wrong location for its shop (factory seconds in a wealthy village perhaps) will soon find that it doesn't have enough customers.

### ACCOMMODATION

This can be a shop, a factory, or an office block, etc. Almost all businesses will need somewhere to work from – at the start of a business, that may be a garage or a room in a house but, as a business becomes established it will probably need to get some sort of premises of its own. These premises will need to be suitable for the business and may be built specially for the organisation, adapted from an existing building or used as they are bought. This will also include temporary accommodation such as Portakabins or a caravan used as a sales office on a building site.

### EQUIPMENT

Also known as 'plant' this ranges from an ocean-going liner to a calculator on someone's desk. Equipment can be a major cost for a business and will often be hired rather than bought. It is possible, for instance, to hire a car as a business user for a reasonable rate and keep the money that would have been needed to buy the car outright to use somewhere else in the business. There are a lot of decisions that a business or organisation needs to make in order to choose the best plant or equipment for its purposes: it will have to look at the quality of what it is buying; the cost; how long it will last; how reliable it will be; and so on. It can be a very hard decision to make but if the business gets it right, it will benefit; get it wrong, however, and the business will suffer like the ice cream firm mentioned above.

## CONSUMABLES

These are also known as raw materials, such as oil for the plastics industry, seed for a farm or clothes for a boutique. This category also includes energy used by the organisation. Raw materials can be a major cost to a business and there are a number of systems of stock control, such as JIT (Just In Time) which tries to reduce the cost of holding stock in a business. Apart from the stock of things to sell or the raw materials to turn into finished products to sell, businesses (and even service businesses which do not actually produce or provide goods), also need items such as paper, batteries, printer ribbons and computer disks to keep them running. All of these count as consumables as well, even though they don't go directly into what the business is providing for its customers.

## THE LEGAL BACKGROUND

All of the physical resources mentioned above are, in legal terms, 'property'. Property is classified in law in this country in different categories, with each category having different rules as to how it has to be bought and sold and what can be done with it. Before we look at each of these categories, it is necessary to have a look at the legal background to owning property so that you appreciate the special rules which apply in different cases. The main categories are set out, with brief examples, in Fig 6.2, which is based on examples taken from a building and housing development firm.

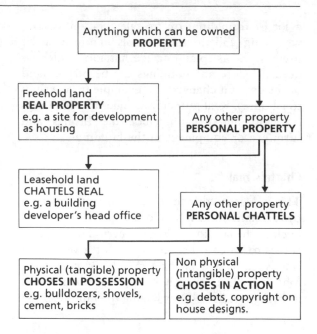

Fig 6.2 The main categories of property

## DEFINITIONS OF THE CATEGORIES USED REGARDING PROPERTY

### Real property

This is freehold land which the owner has to buy using a written contract and which you own directly from the crown. This land is subject to

Fig 6.3

a lot of formalities on its sale (known as conveyancing) and also has controls on how it can be used such as planning permission which is needed before any buildings can be put on land or the use of it changed (for example from a shop to a house). Real property includes any buildings on land but won't include the fittings and furniture or equipment in the buildings.

### Chattels real

This is leasehold land which is rented or leased by a tenant from a landlord and which will go back to the landlord when the period of the lease comes to an end. Leases can be for a very short time such as a week or a month, or may be as long as 999 years; such a long lease is often seen as being just as good as having the land freehold

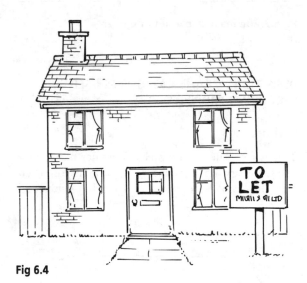

**Fig 6.4**

as the length of the lease is always '999 years unexpired' – that is to say that the lease always has 999 years to run. The main problem with leased land/property for many businesses is that, as they are not the real owners they have to ask permission for any changes they want to make and, if they do something which improves the value of the property they will lose the money invested in it when the land goes back to the owner. For this reason many businesses would rather borrow on a business loan or mortgage to buy property rather than rent it, although renting

usually works out cheaper on a month-by-month or year-by-year basis. Leases have to be in writing and are subject to a number of controls to give tenants some security and rights over the property while they have it.

### Choses in action

This is the legal term for property which cannot be touched. This includes all sorts of property which businesses will make use of such as

**Fig 6.5**

copyrights and patents to protect their ideas from being stolen by competitors, and debts: you cannot touch a debt but the money which it represents can be very important to a business, as pointed out in Unit 5.

### Choses in possession

This is the term for the sort of property which you can actually touch. It will include a lot of the

**Fig 6.6**

fittings of any business and will cover everything from an aircraft to a paperclip. Such property is easier to sell than land and can be sold by a simple oral agreement. The problem with such oral agreements is that people can disagree later over what the terms of the agreement were. For this reason many organisations make sure that they have some written evidence of a contract having been made and the terms on which it was agreed; hence, if there is an argument later they have some proof of what they claim to be the real story.

---

### ACTIVITY

For the window cleaning business mentioned in the Activity on p 201, make a note of what property it will have which falls into each of the categories above. (The owner, Peter, uses a room in his house as an office and rents a garage from a friend on a one year lease):

1 Real property

2 Chattels real

3 Choses in action

4 Choses in possession

---

Having looked briefly at the sorts of property in law we will now have a look at each of the main forms of property in a business in a bit more detail before going on to see how they are chosen, acquired and used in businesses.

## Land

Land is a relatively scarce resource, mainly because there is no real way to manufacture any more of it, although there are ways to get better use out of it. This is why high rise buildings were erected and why modern houses tend to have smaller rooms than older ones – as land becomes more expensive people try to find ways to make it work harder. In some countries in the world the land is very scarce indeed, so costs huge amounts of money; Tokyo in Japan, for instance, is one of the most densely populated cities in the world and its property values are also among the highest in the world. On the other

hand there are places in the world where land is very cheap – such as in deserts and other areas where there is not a lot of demand. In Europe land tends to be quite expensive, especially in big cities, and Britain is one of the more expensive countries in Europe in which to buy land.

---

### ACTIVITY

Using an atlas or a database, look up and compare the population densities in different cities and countries. A list is given below but you can use other figures if these are not easy to obtain.

| Country | Population density | Cities | Population density |
|---|---|---|---|
| Hong Kong | | Tokyo | |
| Canada | | London | |
| France | | Paris | |
| England | | Berlin | |
| etc | | etc | |

Where would you expect land to be the most expensive?

Why are there such differences in the figures? Why don't people spread out into more under-populated areas and reduce the overcrowding in densely populated ones?

---

Even though land is scarce, and is usually also expensive, almost all organisations will need to buy, or lease, some land for the business. Even in the case of a business which is run from someone's home, they are using the land there to help them to run the business. Some businesses will need a lot of land, such as a market garden; whereas others, such as an insurance broker or a jeweller, will need a lot less. The cost of the land that is needed to set up and run a business can be a major obstacle to people going into business. Even where a relatively small amount of land is needed it may be expensive due to its location; a jeweller, for example, will need to be in a town centre – they could get the same size piece of land cheaper in the middle of the countryside but this would be of little use to them. A cheaper alternative to owning land is to pay the owner for the use of it for a fixed time; this system of renting or leasing property is very common in business as it allows organisations to use their money to run the business rather than tying it up in buying land. Land which has been bought outright, is, as mentioned above, known as *freehold land* or *real property*. Land which you rent or lease is known as *leasehold* or *chattels real*. One of the first decisions that a new business often has to make, therefore, is to 'rent or buy?' Once that decision has been made the right property has to be found and the purchase made or the rental agreed. Businesses also need to be aware of the limits as to what they can do on land they have bought or leased. These are the headings we will look at next.

## TO RENT VS TO BUY ...

When a new business is being set up – a pottery for instance – it will need to be located somewhere suitable. The person setting the business up has a number of alternatives:

- to find an existing place, fully equipped
- to find somewhere to convert, maybe an existing shop
- to find a bit of land with no buildings and build a pottery.

Which one they will choose will depend on a number of factors; such as how much money they have, how sure they are that the business will work, and how fast they want to be set up and operating, etc. If, as is usually the case for a new business, they are short of money they may decide that, rather than spending the money necessary to buy a property they should rent: that way, if the business isn't successful they merely hand the property back to the original owner at the end of the lease rather than having to try to find a buyer for it.

## ACTIVITY

1 Complete the table below to describe briefly the advantages and disadvantages of buying and renting property. Some examples have been inserted as a start:

| Advantages | Disadvantages |
| --- | --- |
| **Rent** | |
| Cheaper to get property | Have to pay rent |
| No need to sell | Rent may go up |
| Some maintenance is done for you by owners | May have to ask owner's permission to do anything |
| **Buy** | |

2 Read the following short case study and decide whether the business should rent or buy. Give your reasons in a brief memo.

*Charlotte and Matthew set up in business some two years ago as interior decorators. Charlotte has a flair for colours and design and Matthew is good at the practical side of the business, as well as keeping track of the finances. They have, until now, worked from home but as Charlotte's parents, who they live with, have now decided to move to France they have to find some property that will let them carry on the business and provide accommodation. After a lot of searching they have found a small empty detached shop property they would like to have. It has a flat over the shop and is well located in the centre of town. At the moment their business is doing well and they are sure that having a shop in town would bring in more orders for them. Their only possible problem is that another firm has recently set up and, being a bit bigger, they have been able to cut prices and take some contracts away from Charlotte and Matthew.*

*The couple have £12 000 in a reserve account for the business and estimate that the property would need about £6000 spending on it before it suits them. They also have their own savings of £10 000. The property is priced at £92 000 or can be leased for five years at £12 000 down and a rent of £500 per month (this rent can be reviewed after two years and then again after four). The owner says she has no objection to the shop being converted to be suitable for interior decorators. Matthew has looked at the cost of a mortgage and found that if they put ten per cent of the value of the property down they will have to pay about £800 per month mortgage.*

To help you with this activity you may want to look at the cost of mortgages by collecting information from local banks and building societies. If you have the chance to speak to someone you know in a business you could also ask them about the difference between buying and renting.

All land in this country belongs to the Crown and, when you buy or rent land you take one of two 'estates' in land – freehold or leasehold. In practice there is little chance that the Crown would ever interfere directly in the property you buy unless you break the laws relating to the way people are allowed to use land.

### Freehold land

This is property which is as close to absolute ownership as you can get. Once you have taken a piece of land freehold you have the right to pass the land on by sale (or by will on your death) to anyone who has the capacity to own land. In the case of a limited company, as the company never 'dies', the land would only be passed on by being sold.

Freehold land remains your property for as long as you wish to hold it and can even be leased or rented to someone else without losing the ownership of it. In order to buy land freehold you will need to use the services of a solicitor or a *conveyancer*, and although you can do this job yourself it is safer to employ an expert. They will draw up a written contract known as a *Conveyance* and will make sure that there are not going to be any problems with the property you have bought, as far as they are able. Among the things that they will check for you are:

● easements and rights of way
● property charges
● planning applications

### Leasehold land

This is property of which you have the use for a length of time. The owner of the land is known as the *landlord* and the person leasing or renting it is known as the *tenant*. Most leases will fix a period of time, at the end of which the lease will expire and the land will go back to the original owner. Other leases may be for a shorter period of time with a view to them being renewed regularly; these are known as 'periodic tenancies' (weekly or monthly lets of property are of this sort) and either party can give notice that the lease is to end after a particular period. While a tenant you will have 'exclusive possession' of the property that you are leasing and should be able to treat the property in virtually every respect as if it were your own. The exception to this is that, as the land has eventually to go back to the original owner you must normally check with them to get their permission before doing anything which might affect the value of their property. If you are taking a lease for a longer time than a few weeks or months it is worth having the lease checked out by a solicitor or other adviser before you agree to it – otherwise you may find that you have problems later.

There are some leases, sometimes known as '*virtual freeholds*' which always have 999 years to run. Such leases are really just the same as freehold except that you may have to pay some 'ground rent' to the person who actually owns the land, even though it will never be returned to them, and you may have to get their permission before you can alter the property. If you are considering taking on this sort of lease it is important to make sure you know what you need to get permission for, what it will cost to get it if you need to, and to find out what the ground rent is – it is very often a small sum but could in some cases be quite a lot of money. If you do buy a lease like this you usually have the right to buy the freehold in which case you will have to pay the expenses of both the seller's and your own legal advice, which can be quite costly.

---

### ACTIVITY

Try to find out what the most common obligations of a landlord and a tenant are and enter them into a table like the one overleaf. When you have completed your table compare it with the results other people have in order to get a more complete picture.

| Landlord | Tenant |
|---|---|
| Allow the tenant to have 'quiet enjoyment of the property' | To pay the agreed rent at the agreed times to the landlord. |

## Controls on the use of land

The law controls the use of land very closely: there are many things which you cannot do with land which you own without the consent of a council or a government department. If the land is leasehold you will probably have to ask the permission of the owner – the landlord – before doing anything other than what the land was leased or rented for. The main controls on what you do with land can be put into the following categories:

**1  Planning controls**. You may have to get permission from the local council before altering the use of land, making major changes to buildings on land or building on land.

**2  Pollution controls**. As the environmental problems of businesses become better known there are ever tighter controls on businesses to reduce the amount of pollution they produce.

**3  Law of nuisance**. You cannot use your land in such a way as to be a nuisance to other people and there are legal controls to prevent you from doing so.

**4  Safety rules**. There are laws to ensure that you keep your property safe and that it does not present a risk to people using it.

### ACTIVITY

As a group think of some reasons why there should be controls on the way people use land. Why shouldn't you be free to do exactly what you like with property you have bought or rented?

## PLANNING CONTROLS

Planning controls exist to ensure that land is used in the right way in the right place; this will prevent someone from opening a large and noisy factory in the middle of a quiet residential area or opening a pub/disco next to a retirement home. Planning controls are run by the local authority who will be able to tell you what sort of use a piece of land is currently for and what the chances are of getting permission to do something else with it. So, if someone wants to build a factory they will need to find land which either has or will get, permission for industrial use – they cannot just buy a piece of farmland and expect to be able to do what they like with it.

Broadly speaking, you have to get permission if you want to 'develop' the land which you own. Development includes the three main areas listed below:

**1  Changing the use of a building or a piece of land**; for example from a sweetshop to a restaurant. For businesses there are a set of 'Use classes' which group different types of business together. It is usually possible to change within a Use Class without any real problems but if you want to change from one class of use to another you will have to apply for Planning Permission.

**2  Building on land** – Whether a brand new building or an alteration to an existing building. Some minor changes only require a lower level of approval called Building Regulation Approval. The planning authority may either grant or refuse the plans which you put to them. If they feel that the plans are not completely unacceptable they may approve them, subject to certain conditions being met; for instance you may be asked to build the property in a local material or make the alteration in a style which will fit in with the local area.

**3  Demolishing properties** or parts of properties on the land which you own. Demolition is counted as a development of land and you will need to get permission for it. These rules are especially strict if the building is one which has some architectural or historical interest or is sited in an area like a National Park where there are special rules as to what can and cannot be built, demolished or altered.

Much planning law comes from the Town and Country Planning Acts and you can get detailed guidance on what they say from the local council. The application process is outlined in Fig 6.7.

In many places in the country land has been 'zoned' on a plan of the area for different uses. You can go to the council and look at a plan which shows you that some areas are considered to be for industrial use, others are 'green belt' (i.e. land which is to be kept green by being used for farming or in some other way where it is not built on), and other areas are kept for residential use. If you buy land in an area which is zoned for one use rather than another you will probably find it hard to convince the council to allow you to do what you want with it, if this does not fit in with the zoning. If you do buy land to build a factory on in an area which is zoned for industrial use or a house to convert to a shop in an area designated for retailing you are still not guaranteed to get permission to do what you want with the property. To be sure of being granted the council's permission, you should apply for outline planning permission before you agree to buy (or get the seller to do so); then if this is granted you know that you will be able to do what you intended with the land subject to the council agreeing the fine details when you actually send them your full plans. If you buy property which has already been used for business purposes or which is residential and you would like to convert to a business use (from a house to a shop, for example) you will also have to get permission. In this case there is a number of established 'use classes' for property and, if you come within a particular class you can change to another use in the same class with very little problem, but it will be more difficult to get permission to change to a use in another class. For example, changing the use of a shop from selling clothes to selling shoes will not be a problem as they are in the same use class; but changing the same shop into a fish and chip shop would be harder (although not necessarily impossible) as this is in a different use class and would need permission. In addition to making sure that the planning rules are followed so that businesses and residential property all fit

Intention to develop land in some way for a business or other use

Check with the local authority as to whether permission is required and what sort of application is needed if permission is required.

Apply for the necessary permission from the Local authority. You will need to provide:
● plans
● outline of the development
● fee

A decision will be made on the application. It may be:
● accepted in full
● rejected in full
● accepted subject to certain conditions you will have to meet.
If you are not happy with the decision you can appeal against it.

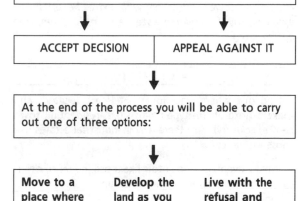

| ACCEPT DECISION | APPEAL AGAINST IT |

At the end of the process you will be able to carry out one of three options:

| Move to a place where you can do what you want | Develop the land as you wanted | Live with the refusal and cope with the situation you already have |

**Fig 6.7 The planning application process**

together within the plan for the town or the area, the local authority will also make sure that any major building work you have done on property, or any property you have built for you on land, comes up to the minimum building standards known as '*building regulations*'. If you are having any work done on property you will need to find out whether you will need building regulations approval, and if you do, the local authority will inspect the work you have done to make sure it is up to standard.

---

## CASE STUDY

*Different countries have different approaches to where they allow businesses to set up and what sort of businesses they mix together. In the UK for instance, there are usually hotels in residential areas and in the centre of towns and cities or near motorways. In France you will also find hotels in these places but in addition will find that, in large towns or in towns on very busy roads, there have recently been a lot of hotels built on industrial estates. These industrial estates are themselves usually located just outside the town on, or very near to, a main road or a ring road around the town. These modern hotels tend to be very cheap and are aimed at people who just want to break a journey, so have very few facilities apart from a clean, modern and well equipped room at a low price. There are now starting to be some similar chains in the UK but they are nowhere near as popular as in France where there are at least ten different chains all competing to offer better rooms, at lower prices or with extra benefits (for example, toys for children, satellite TV in the room, free coffee, etc.).*

---

## ACTIVITY

**1** Find out where your local hotels are located, and make a note of the type of area (i.e. residential, town centre, country). Are there any in industrial estates like those in France?

**2** What advantages do hotels like those in France offer:
(i) to the developers of the hotel; and
(ii) to the guests using them?

**3** What is different about France that might have encouraged the development of these hotels?

**4** What do you think your local council's attitude would be to an application to build a hotel on an industrial estate?

**5** Do you think there would be a market for hotels like this:
(i) in England; and
(ii) in your area?

---

### Penalties for failing to follow the planning rules

If you decide to go ahead and develop property in some way without going through the planning process you will be in breach of the law and the local authority can – and usually will – take action against you as a result of it. The action they take will depend on how badly you have breached the law and what you have actually done on the property. If the alteration or development is one which they would have approved anyway, and they are satisfied that you did not actually intend to evade the planning process but acted as a result of poor advice or in ignorance of the proper procedure, you may be given retrospective approval for the development you have made. If, however, the development is not one which would have been approved you may be taken to court and either fined or ordered to make some alterations to the development, perhaps by facing an extension in a local material, altering the height of a roof or changing an access route. In extreme cases, where people have built entire properties where they should not have done so, and the planning authority would not have approved the development they have been ordered to remove the building and restore the land to the state it was in when they found it.

In all of the above cases, if the planning authority has to take you to court and wins its case you will probably have quite heavy legal costs to bear as well as the fine (if one is imposed) and the cost of complying with what you are told to do. Bear in mind also that you will probably have the costs of the planning authority to meet as well as those of your own. All in all, it will usually be a lot cheaper and easier to check whether you will need planning permission for any changes which you intend to make to property, and then go through the correct procedures to get it if necessary.

### Controls on how the land is actually used

These controls will include those on pollution, on the safety of the property and any nuisance that the land or the use of it causes to other people. Having gained permission to build a factory on a piece of land, you will not then be able to make as much noise, smoke and pollution as you like. Nor will you be able to ignore the safety of people who come onto the property: in fact you have a responsibility to make sure that the property is as safe as it can be for anyone invited onto it and, in some circumstances, for trespassers and people who are not supposed to be on the property.

## Controls on pollution

There are controls to help prevent businesses from causing all sorts of pollution. The most common forms of pollution are noise, smell, smoke/dust/dirt, and chemicals and it is usually the responsibility of the local council to make sure that businesses don't breach these rules. There are specialist government agencies such as Her Majesty's Inspectorate of Pollution and the Health and Safety Inspectorate who will also look at the way businesses are controlling pollution on their land. If a company does breach the rules relating to pollution in any way they may be subject to court action which could result in a fine or an injunction (i.e. an order to stop doing whatever is causing the problem) or both. In addition to any fine imposed, the firm will probably also have fairly heavy legal bills to meet. Among the main Acts of Parliament which give local authorities the power to control pollution in its various forms are the Control of Pollution Act, the Environmental Protection Act and the Clean Air Act. You should also bear in mind that what is acceptable in one place (an industrial estate a long way from any residential property, for instance) will not always still be acceptable somewhere else. Hence, a factory that is permitted to produce a certain amount of smoke or steam in one location may have to comply with very different rules if they move to another area. These controls on pollution have been a cause of some businesses leaving the developed countries of Western Europe and setting up manufacturing plants in countries where the rules are not so strict and which are desperate to attract foreign investment and jobs and have little experience of the problems that can be caused by pollution. Such countries are

becoming fewer but there are still many places in the world where people are exposed to risks which would be unacceptable in Western Europe. There are also many companies who are willing to expose people to pollution and poor working conditions as long as they see a larger profit at the end of the year as a result of not having to pay for expensive treatment or disposal of waste and for not providing the safety precautions required by law in other more developed countries. The UK has improved the control of pollution over the last few years but it was still referred to as the 'dirty man of Europe' at recent environmental conferences, and there are still few beaches in the United Kingdom which come up to the standards set for cleanliness by the European Community.

## The law of nuisance

Another control on the way in which you use your land is the law relating to 'nuisance'. This is part of what is known as the *law of torts* and, although it is often a civil matter (*see* Unit 4 which looked at the difference between Civil and Criminal law) there may be occasions where a local authority or one of the agencies such as the Health and Safety Inspectorate may use the law of nuisance to stop someone using their land in a way which causes problems to other people.

Briefly, the law relating to nuisance is split into three types of nuisance:

**1 Private nuisance** – where someone who has land next to property which is causing a nuisance can claim some compensation for the trouble, damage or cost they have suffered. If, for example, you live near a factory that emits a cloud of smoke which corrodes the new paint you have just finished putting on your house, you may have a claim in private nuisance. This is a civil action and the person affected will have to take court proceedings themselves, although they may be able to get help and advice from a local authority as well as Legal Aid to help them to pay the cost of a claim.

**2 Public nuisance** – where the problem resulting from the way someone is using their land affects a lot of other people. For example, if a factory emitted clouds of smoke which caused a lot of people in a town or village to have to repaint their houses or was so dense that drivers on a nearby main road could not see properly this could possibly amount to public nuisance. This is a criminal action and will normally be brought by the local authority.

**3 Statutory nuisances.** There are a number of Acts of Parliament (statutes) which define certain actions as nuisances. This makes it far easier for a local authority or an individual to bring an action, as there is no uncertainty as to whether the behaviour complained of is a nuisance – all you would have to prove is that the person concerned was actually doing whatever is defined as a nuisance in the various acts.

Quite a lot of the law relating to nuisance, especially private nuisance is 'common law'. This is as a result of the decisions made by judges in cases over the years becoming a set of rules under which people can try to get some help to compensate them for what they see as somebody else's wrongful actions. This means that each case will be decided on its merits, taking into account the rules which have been set in earlier similar cases. The section below goes into a little more detail about the law of nuisance. This is followed by an activity which asks you to consider whether any

action would be possible in a number of cases and if so, whether you think it should be in private or public nuisance (or both) or whether it is a statutory nuisance.

**1 Private nuisance**
Essentially private nuisance relates to interference with another person's enjoyment of their land or property which can be regarded as unlawful: so the fact that your factory has been painted bright purple might annoy someone but it is unlikely to be a nuisance (unless you are in a special area where there are controls on how property should look); on the other hand, however, if your factory is sending out poisonous fumes and causing someone on the next piece of land to be ill this will almost certainly be a nuisance. If you want to bring an action in private nuisance you have to show

(a) that your 'enjoyment of your land' has been interfered with;
(b) that the interference was not direct (direct interference is probably trespass);
(c) that the interference has damaged the property or caused some suffering to you; and
(d) that whatever has caused the problem is unlawful.

(*a*) *Enjoyment of the land has been interfered with.* In order to show this you will have to produce witnesses, statements or photographs or some other proof to show that whatever you are complaining about actually happened. For example, if the paint on your house is ruined don't repaint it without telling anyone and then try to bring a claim of nuisance later: find witnesses, photographs of the damage etc., and keep receipts for the new paint, bills from painters or a record of the time you have had to spend on sorting out the problem. All sorts of things have been found to be nuisances in past cases in the courts, and these include:

● smoke
● tree roots
● clouds of fumes
● noise

Of course this is not a full list; it can always be added to – nor is it a guarantee that in your case you will win just because you have been subject to one of these. Each case is looked at on its own merits and there will be a lot of factors to be taken into account as no two cases are ever exactly the same.

(*b*) *Indirect interference.* If someone comes onto your land and tips paint on to your car so that you have to have it resprayed this would not be a 'nuisance' in the legal sense – this would be a direct interference and there are a number of remedies you could seek. If, however, fumes from a local factory settled on the car and corroded the paintwork this could be seen as a nuisance if you then had to have the car resprayed. The difference is that in the first case there was some direct action by someone to cause you harm; whereas in the second case there was no direct action and the harm was caused by something rather than someone.

(*c*) *Damage has been caused.* This may be damage to the land, to buildings on it or to the comfort of the people on the land. It is not enough to show that there is a lot of noise coming from a factory next to your property at certain times unless you can also show that it has caused some harm: so if you are away all summer and, on returning, are told that the noise coming from a factory next to your house has been terrible this is no basis for an action in nuisance, although it may be if it continues. Factors which have been found to be nuisances in some cases include:

- smoke damaging clothes
- fumes corroding paint
- fumes causing illnesses/discomfort
- excessive noise stopping people enjoying their homes.

As above, these are merely examples, and the decision in each particular case will depend on all of the facts available.

(*d*) *Unlawful interference.* This is the crucial question: was the action lawful or not? People have very different views on what is acceptable and there will always be arguments about what is and is not permissible in different circumstances. It is the job of the court to decide in a given case whether there is a nuisance or not. The fact that someone doesn't like the sound of

a cock crowing in the morning on a farm doesn't necessarily mean that this is a nuisance in the legal sense; indeed, in a recent case the court decided that this was a natural part of life in the country and the people who complained about the noise had no case. In deciding a case the court will look at all the factors in the case, and some of the main ones include:

- Was the person or the property specially sensitive? If you want to set up a business as a recording studio and you buy premises next door to a bus garage in the middle of a busy town, because they are easy to get to, you will have to accept that you will need to soundproof the premises if the recordings are going to be free of traffic noise. You would have no case if you tried to claim against the bus company in nuisance. Similarly the fact that you hate guitar solos doesn't mean you could use the law of nuisance to stop your next-door neighbour playing records of guitar music (although you might be able to do so if they play them very loud or at unusual times, or both).
- What was the reason for them doing what they are doing? In one case a farmer who had a dispute with a neighbour deliberately fired guns near the neighbour's property in order to scare the neighbour's animals. The fact that this was intended to cause harm was enough for the court to decide that this was a nuisance.
- The location of the problem: something that would be perfectly acceptable on an industrial estate would not be acceptable in a residential area. So, if a haulage firm is based in an industrial estate they are probably free to have lorries arriving virtually 24 hours a day. If they are based up a quiet country lane with a lot of residential accommodation they would probably have to make sure that they reduced lorry movements or stopped them completely between certain hours, or risk having a successful action brought against them in nuisance. (Of course, the planning laws would try to make sure that this situation didn't arise in the first place.)
- How long the problem has existed. A one-off act is far less likely to be considered a nuisance

than something that has been continuing for a long time. This doesn't mean that no single action could be considered a nuisance – just that it would need to be more serious for a one-off problem to be considered a nuisance than something that was happening regularly. So, for example someone living next to the TT race track in the Isle of Man would probably not be able to make a claim in nuisance because the event is only once per year, whereas someone living next to a new track which is used five days and six evenings per week may be able to make a claim even though the actual level of noise is lower.

If you have an action in nuisance brought against you, either as a business or as an individual there are some 'defences' you may be able to use:

(i)   The problem was not caused by you as owner of the property but by people outside your control. If, for example trespassers on land next to your shop hold an acid house party without your consent, as the owner, you would not be liable in an action in nuisance by people living nearby.

(ii)  The act is authorised by Act of Parliament (which effectively overrules the common law).

(iii) The person complaining has agreed to the situation. So if the person living next to a new motorcross track has been offered, and accepted, double glazing to reduce the noise in return for not objecting they cannot change their mind later and claim in nuisance.

If you have an action in private nuisance brought against you and you lose, you will have to pay damages to the person affected by the nuisance and will probably also have to meet their legal expenses as well. Depending on the damage caused and how long the case has taken in court to prepare and defend, this could amount to quite a large sum of money.

## 2 Public nuisance

Like private nuisance, public nuisance is concerned with situations in which someone is using their land or property in a way which is causing problems for other people; in this case a lot of people rather than an isolated or small group. In order for there to be a case in public nuisance there has to be:

> *Some action or failure to act which affects the comfort or convenience of a class of Her Majesty's subjects*

'*Some action or failure to act . . .*' If you have a business which produces dense clouds of smoke and you choose to do nothing about it, but allow the smoke to blow across a road (and make it difficult for people using the road to see), this would probably be a public nuisance. This could either be seen as an action (causing the smoke) or a failure to act (not installing filters to reduce or eliminate the smoke).

'*. . . affecting the comfort and convenience . . .*' There are all sorts of actions which have been held to affect the comfort and convenience of people – the example above is one, or selling ice creams out of a shop window so that crowds form and block the pavement is another, and having a golf hole next to a road so that golf balls often hit cars are further examples.

'*. . . of a class of Her Majesty's subjects*'. If you are the only person affected by a nuisance there will be no claim in public nuisance. For an action in public nuisance to succeed there will need to be a substantial number of people affected – in the examples above the 'class of people' affected are those using the road or pavement.

Actions in public nuisance are usually brought by the local authority rather than individuals and they will often be a result of people having complained to the local authority about a problem. Most local authorities would not start an action without having spoken to the owner of the property to try to get the problem sorted out in a friendly way first, unless they felt that the nuisance was so serious that it had to be taken to court. In the event of something causing a danger the local authority may have powers to enter premises and stop the nuisance immediately or may be able to get a court order very quickly (even in the middle of the night in an emergency). The fact that an action has been brought by the local authority in public nuisance will not stop an individual bringing an action in private nuisance as well if they can meet the conditions for it.

In the event that a business is found to be causing a public nuisance they will probably be fined and have an injunction taken out to stop them doing whatever has caused the nuisance. They will probably also have to pay all of the legal expenses involved in the case as well and may attract quite a lot of adverse publicity.

### 3 Statutory nuisance

There are all sorts of statutory nuisances coming under a variety of different Acts of Parliament such as:

- the Sexual Offences Act
- the Highways Act
- the Public Health Act
- the Clean Air Act
- the Control of Pollution Act
- the Noise Abatement Act

Statutory nuisances are controlled by the local authority which, as mentioned above, will usually try to sort things out on an informal basis if they feel there is a problem unless the problem is so serious that they feel it has to be taken before a court. If the local authority cannot sort out a problem on an informal basis they can, after having served a legal notice requesting the owner to sort out the problem, take the person causing the nuisance to court to get an abatement order. If this order is not complied with they can take action to stop the problem themselves and charge the owner or person causing the nuisance for this.

---

### ACTIVITY

Find out from the library, or from the local authority what the main Statutory Nuisances are and the Acts of Parliament which control them. Put the results into a table like the one below:

| Nuisance | Act of Parliament |
|----------|-------------------|
|          |                   |
|          |                   |
|          |                   |

Combine your results with other people to get a full list.

---

## SAFETY RULES

There are many safety controls and laws designed to make sure that the buildings we work in, the transport we use and the environment we live in are safe. Businesses using land are subject to a lot of these rules and this section will look briefly at two of the main ones:

1 Health and Safety at Work Act; and
2 Occupiers Liability Act.

### Health and Safety at Work Act

This Act was passed in order to provide a very full system for making sure that people are safe when they are at work. It was the result of a report from a Royal Commission set up to reform safety laws and replaced a very complex and difficult set of laws which placed different standards on different businesses for safety. The Act places duties on both employers and on employees regarding safety and these are set out very briefly below:

**Employers . . .**
**To ensure as far as is 'practicable' that they provide a safe working environment for their employees to safeguard the health safety and welfare at work of their employees. This will include safe premises, safe systems of work and training for staff.**

**Employees . . .**
**To take care for their own safety and the safety of others who may be affected by their actions. Not to interfere with equipment provided for safety. To work in a safe manner.**

As far as land is concerned, the main requirement of the Act is that employers provide safe premises for their employees, invited visitors and members of the general public who may be affected by their activities. Hence, a shopkeeper has to ensure that the shop is safe for customers in the main areas, that the areas where customers don't go are also safe for the staff who have to work in them and that there is no risk to any passers-by resulting from his actions or inactions. (For example, the failure to look after the fabric of the building could lead to tiles falling off the roof and hitting passers-by – this would be a breach of the Act.) The Act is enforced by the Health and Safety Inspectorate who have, in cases where there is an immediate danger, very wide powers including the closure of a business.

### Occupier's Liability Acts

These Acts place a duty on any occupier of land to make sure that it is reasonably safe for people who come onto it. There are two main categories of people protected by the Acts:

1 People on the land with the consent of the owner/occupier. This includes the customers of a business, any contractors and people delivering goods.
2 People on the land without the consent of the owner/occupier. In some circumstances it is possible for the owner of land to be liable for the injuries received by a trespasser on land.

This will normally only apply if insufficient care has been taken to exclude people from the land or if there is a very significant hazard which is so severe that warning of it is a necessary duty.

---

## Accommodation

---

The accommodation a business uses can be very important to its success and can vary widely: some businesses need huge areas of land and many buildings in order to be able to operate; and others will need a lot less, with perhaps just a garage space, a small stall on a market or a shop or office in a large complex. In order for the accommodation to be right for a business the premises they use will need to meet a number of requirements:

1 **Being in the right place.** If you run a firm which is concerned with selling to holidaymakers you will need premises in popular holiday areas. If you export to France a lot then it would make sense to be located in the south of England.

2 **Being the right size or type.** If you haven't got the space to run your business properly you will not be as efficient as you could be, and if the buildings you are using are old they may cost more to run than newer ones. Also, the property

you use gives an image of the business: no-one would expect to find an upmarket advertising agency occupying a scruffy building in the middle of nowhere, and if they did, they wouldn't feel as confident as if the firm was in glossy offices in the centre of the business district of a city.

3 **Being affordable.** You will pay a great deal for the accommodation in which to run a business and, while there is no point in the premises being too small you don't want to have to pay for space that you can't use. Obviously some types of building are cheaper than others and there are some areas in which the property is cheaper than in others. Bearing in mind the need to have the right sort of accommodation and the need to be in the right place you will probably go for the best value accommodation you can find.

This unit will look at a number of factors relating to the choice of accommodation. The main ones are:

● What to look for in accommodation
● Making the most of premises
● Financing premises

### WHAT TO LOOK FOR IN ACCOMMODATION FOR A BUSINESS

In choosing the land or accommodation for a business it is very important to be aware of what you need and then look specifically for that. The other way of approaching the problem is to look at properties and try to make up your mind whether they are suitable or not. The problem with this second option is that you may get carried away with enthusiasm for some of the good points of a particular office or factory and miss some of the problems. You will also probably be in the position of having someone trying very hard to sell the property to you – and a good salesperson will be very persuasive.

There is a system which you can follow in deciding which property is suitable for you. This is a nine point plan and is shown in Fig 6.8.

1 **Reviewing the business needs.** This is a most important stage in the process of finding a

**1 Review the needs of the business**. What do you need from your property *now*? What will you need in the *future*?

**2** Make a list of the things the property *must* have – **the essential requirements**

**3** List all of the other things that you would *like* the property to have – **the desirable features**

**4 Get details of as many properties** as you can which could be suitable for your needs

**5 Check each one against the essential requirements**. Any that fail to meet the essential requirements you should throw away NOW.

**6 Look at the remaining properties** to see how many of the desirable features they have

**7 Make a shortlist** taking into account all of the factors so far – desirable features, price, location and your 'gut' feeling.

**8 View the properties** and make sure that they are what they claim to be. Explain at this point that you will not decide on a property until you have seen all of the ones on your list.

**9 Go away**. Think. Ask advice. Visit favourite properties again. Check prices, permissions etc. Then **DECIDE**.

**Fig 6.8 Which property to choose?**

property. It is at this stage that you have the chance to consider all of the things that you may need in the business, such as access, floor space, lighting, display areas, and parking. You also have the chance to consider what the business may need in the future: there is no point in buying a property and spending money on it if it isn't going to be suitable for you in a couple of years' time. It may be that the business is intended to expand, or that you want to start selling goods on a retail basis from a factory. Whatever your plans are, you have a chance to take them into account at this stage.

**2 Set essential criteria for the choice of premises.** This stage is where you are trying to decide what the premises **must** have if the business is going to gain from them. Consider very carefully what you need and what you want. If parking is going to make the difference between a busy and a quiet shop you may list it as essential (perhaps you are going to be selling heavy or bulky items). If it isn't too important but could encourage some extra customers it may go onto the desirable list. Once you have made this list and are happy with it, it will become a checklist that you judge potential properties against; and if a property lacks even one of these essential criteria it will not be suitable for you and you shouldn't consider it any further, however good it is in other respects. Key areas to consider will be the ones you have identified in the stage above and you will also need to consider one that you may have missed in the stage above – **price**. Set a budget which you can afford and make sure you stick to it. Put the details of any properties which go above your limit straight in the bin. There is no point in buying the ideal premises for your business if the cost of them bankrupts you.

**3 List the 'desirable' features of the property.** This may be quite a long list. If it is then you will probably need to put things in order of importance to you. So, if a security system and a car park both feature on the list you will be able to rank them and decide which you would place most emphasis on. This list is the one you will use to help you to come up with a shortlist of businesses to look at as all of the businesses you look at will meet the essential criteria for the business. Any of them should be fine for the business; this stage is to consider what will make the best possible property for the business.

**4 Obtain details of suitable properties.** There are a number of different sources of information on properties which are available for businesses; these include:

- Estate agents
- Local papers
- Enterprise agencies
- Business clubs
- Going and looking for 'For Sale' signs
- Trade press
- Specialist business transfer agencies.

Try to get as much information as you can and get as many suitable properties to consider as possible. This will help you to get familiar with the jargon which may be used to describe the properties and will also help you to get a 'feel' for the price of properties and the facilities which may be available on different properties. Remember that you are under no obligation to the people supplying you with details – consider them in your own time and don't be pressured into going to view a property until you have got all of the details you want – and don't be afraid to ask for more information if the details you have are not sufficient.

**5 Test each property against the essential criteria.** This is the stage where you need a bin liner handy. Look at the details you have for properties and sort them into two piles:

(a) **Possible:** properties which meet the essential criteria
(b) **Not suitable:** properties which fail to meet one or more of your essentials. These are the ones that go in the bin liner. Don't waste any more time on them.

**6 Test each property against the desirable criteria.** Put the properties which survived the last stage onto one side and try to sort them into a rank order of the best to the worst. None of them should actually be unsuitable as they will all have met all of the essential criteria, but there may be some more you want to put in the bin at this stage – perhaps because you have two similar properties and one is badly over-priced.

**7 Shortlist.** Choose the properties which you think are the most suitable and make arrangements to go and see them. Try to limit the shortlist to a reasonable number and make sure that you are not trying to see too many places in one day – if you are rushed you may miss something important in one of the properties. For each of the properties you have shortlisted make a list of things you want to ask or to check and put these down on paper so that you don't forget to ask the questions. Make sure that you have clear arrangements as to who you meet, at what time and where. You don't want to waste your time.

**8 View the properties.** Go and see what they are really like. Glossy photos and over-the-top descriptions can make a property sound better than it is and, sometimes, people leave out important disadvantages. If you are being shown round by an estate agent or other salesperson make it clear to them that you have a list of properties to see and that you will have to see all of them before you can decide which to buy. Don't be pressured by lines such as 'If I can show you the ideal property today do you have the authority to buy it today?' Just explain again that you want to be able to make a real choice and have time to reflect on it. Make a point of noting the answers to all of the questions you have to ask about a property and checking that what is claimed to be there really is there: does the 'spacious car park' mean a slot for three cars? Is the factory floor really 1300 square metres? Who does the access road belong to?

**9 Decide.** Having got all of the information go away and think. Look at the options and try to decide which is best. When you have got your ideas sorted out you will be well advised to go and talk to someone else and get another opinion. You will also need to consider at this stage the difference between the price asked for a property and the price you are likely to have to pay. This is probably one of the things you will have tried to find out when viewing the properties but you may have to go back and ask owners or estate agents what their lowest price would be. Don't be embarrassed to make a low offer – they can only say no.

ACTIVITY

---
### ACTIVITY
---

**1** In looking for business premises you may run up against a lot of unfamiliar jargon. This activity is designed to help you get to grips with some of this jargon. In groups of three or four (or individually if that is more convenient) find out what the following terms mean:

- All main services
- Long lease
- No restrictive covenants
- Light industrial use only
- Outline planning permission for conversion to ....

**2** Take a description of a property and go to have a look at the premises from the outside (or actually view it if you can). Having viewed the property rewrite the description of it in two ways:

**(a)** as honestly as you can; and
**(b)** to put the property in the best possible light.

What lessons can you learn from this about reading particulars of properties?

**3** Compile a list of 'What they really mean' for estate agents' descriptions:

| What they say: | What they mean: |
| --- | --- |
| Limited access | Can't get to the place |
| Quiet location | Impossible to find |

**4** For the business outlined below, draw up a list of the essential and desirable criteria that you think the owners would need. They intend to buy suitable premises rather than rent.

*Andrea and Gary have set up a business retailing computers. Initially the business was run from home, but later Gary managed to get space in a local office equipment suppliers at a nominal rent; this gave them access to many facilities and they gained a lot of custom. The business has branched out into doing an increasing amount of work in selling systems to businesses and setting up the software for them. Andrea has also developed the training side of the business to go along-side the physical installation of the machines. They have now grown too big for the space they are using and*

*need premises where they can bring people in to train them on packages. They have much more stock than they used to and are aware of how much money they have tied up in it. Most of their sales tend to come from recommendations by existing customers and through taking space at trade exhibitions. They are now working over quite a wide area but still draw a great deal of business from the three main local towns. At the moment they are in the town centre and some customers have to travel quite a distance if they come to the shop, although Andrea or Gary will often go to them rather than the customers coming to the shop.*

| Essential | Desirable |
| --- | --- |
| Easy to find | Good security system to protect stock |

## MAKING THE MOST OF PREMISES

Unless you have a property actually designed and built for your business the chances are that the property you operate from will not actually be perfect for your business. Even if you do have a property designed and built for you, you may find after a few years that the business has developed and changed and that the property may not suit your needs any longer. Some of the most common problems which businesses have in terms of their premises are illustrated in the activity below:

---
### ACTIVITY
---

Read the information below and answer the questions at the end of the case study.

*General Foods Ltd was set up to supply 'own brand' goods to local shops which are not a part of large chains. The company operates from a base in the northeast of England and has four regional depots. The London depot was the second one the company set up and is the supply centre for the southeast and for Central London. Since the business was set up five years ago trade has grown significantly and there is a far higher volume of traffic using the depot than there used to be. In addition to this a new housing estate has been built on the approach road to the estate where the warehouse is situated and this has resulted in there being a lot more traffic. General Foods are also concerned at the cost of the building in terms of the location: being near Central London, the rent is high and the communications are not as good for the rest of the southeast as they could be.*

*As the volume of trade increases the company has also been aware that they have been short of space at times over the last year, especially in the area of frozen foods where the storage is very costly. The depot is based next to a building which could be converted for similar use and General Foods have been told that they could get this at a reduced rent for a time. There is spare space on the site they are on but the landlord would expect them to bear the cost of any building or conversion. They have a ten-year lease and have to give four months' notice if they intend to leave. Leases are selling quite well in this area and they should be able to sell the remainder of the lease quite easily if they price it realistically.*

**(a)** Do you think General Foods should be considering a move to new premises? If not, what could they do to make better use of their current depot?

**(b)** What recommendations would you make to General Foods about the sort of property they should be looking for if they decide they should move?

**(c)** What factors did you take into account in deciding whether they should move or stay put?

Some of the most common problems that organisations have with their premises are:

● Lack of space
● High running costs
● Poor access
● Market has shifted so that a location is worse than it used to be.

## Lack of space

If the premises are genuinely too small for a business there are two options available:

1 to move; or
2 to extend.

Both of these are expensive and will involve the business in major disruption. The main advantages of moving and the advantages of extending/altering the property the business currently has are set out in the table below.

There are also disadvantages to each of these options, such as having to go through the process of getting planning permission to extend

| Moving | Extending |
|---|---|
| ● Get a new property which suits the needs of the business | ● Keep a known location and premises |
| ● Opportunity to restructure financing | ● Chance to have extra facilities custom built |
| ● Opportunity to improve the location of the business | ● None of the costs or problems of sale and the purchase of a new property |
| ● Allows you to look at other changes or developments | ● Business will probably operate normally throughout the extension/alteration |
| ● May be an opportunity to expand or diversify | ● Can be done at a time to suit you |

premises. You can work these out from the information above and from talking to colleagues and tutors.

There is a third option if the business premises which you have seem too small and that is to make better use of the space you have. There are many ways in which a business can look at improving the use of the space it has available to it, without going to the cost of a full relocation or major alterations to the premises with all of the problems that these entail (cost, dirt, loss of trade, etc.). Some of the most common ones are listed below. There are firms of consultants available to businesses who will look at the use you are making of the premises which you have and suggest ways to make more efficient use of the space:

● by improving the layout of the premises and the flow of work within them;
● by reducing the requirement for storage space by shifting to computer-based rather than paper-based storage; and
● by improving the efficiency of stock delivery and reduce the stock space by moving closer to a JIT stock system.

These measures, and others like them, will help to improve the use that you get out of the premises and may make a move or major alteration to the premises unnecessary.

Another option is to consider moving a part of the operation of the business to another site while leaving the main business where it is. Could the storage be shifted to a warehouse locally? Would the sales department benefit from having a separate set of offices in the town centre? Can the accounts section move to another site?

Relocation of the whole business can be very expensive: a recent survey has estimated that the cost of moving a business lock, stock and barrel is about £14 500 per employee. This obviously amounts to a major cost and will involve much disruption to the business while the relocation is going on. Undertaking major alterations to the business will be almost as traumatic and possibly only a little less expensive.

## High running costs

If a property is expensive to run it will be a drain on the efficiency of the business as a whole and will make the profits smaller. There are a number of reasons why a property may be expensive to run:

*It is old and requires a lot of maintenance.* This is something which affects many businesses. As properties age they start to need minor repairs and then more major ones such as re-roofing or the installation of new heating systems. In some cases there will be the added complication that the building may be what is known as a 'listed' building and this will impose very strict controls on the work that can be done to the building and the materials to be used. There is no real way to reduce the running costs of an older building to the level of a newer one but the best way to reduce the costs is to plan maintenance ahead and work to a programme to keep the property in good repair. It will be much more expensive to repair the damage caused by a leaking roof and re-roof the building at the same time than it will be to inspect the roof, keep it in good condition for as long as possible, and then plan for a convenient time to have the work done when you have had a chance to shop around for the best price for the work. If you wait for problems to occur you may find that the work causes more disruption as you have not planned for it and that you are paying more than you need to for the work. There may also be a penalty in that the disruption to the business could lose you customers.

*It is badly insulated or planned and wastes energy.* There are grants available to businesses to help them to make the most efficient use they can of energy. These grants will help with the cost of a consultant to look at the premises and suggest changes which would make them more energy efficient and will also help with the cost of some of the work that may need to be done as a result of a survey like this. The measures which can be taken will depend on the nature of the business and will range from fitting low energy light bulbs and encouraging staff to switch off unnecessary lights, through to the installation of a new type of furnace in steelworks with lower running costs and maintenance costs than an older model. There are very sophisticated energy management systems available to businesses now and many businesses have saved a lot of money by more careful use of energy.

*The location of the business may be expensive,* either in terms of the cost of the property (for instance, in or near to a major industrial centre), or as a result of the costs of getting materials and products to and from the site. In either of these cases the business will need to look at whether they are sure they are physically located in the right place for the business. It may be that you have little choice about where to locate and, if this is necessarily an expensive area there is little that the business can do about it. It is possible for some businesses, however, to relocate and to move to premises which are cheaper to buy and operate for them. Many areas of the country are trying to attract businesses to do just that at the moment and they offer businesses a range of benefits associated with moving away from the traditional industrial centres. These include lower prices for property, modern buildings designed to be cheaper to operate and maintain, pleasant working environments for staff, the availability of lower cost labour than in some other place and the 'quality of life' which can be offered to staff who choose to move with the business.

*The property is too large for the current needs of the business.* If this is the case there are two main options open to the business: move to a smaller set of premises which will be cheaper to run and may release some capital for use elsewhere in the business; or try to lease a part of the premises to another business. If this second route can be taken it can provide a very good solution as there will be none of the upset and problems associated with moving the business to a new site, and the running costs of the operation will thus be reduced. It may also be that there is an opportunity for the two businesses to share some facilities that both of them want but do not need access to all of the time. This is quite often done in business parks where a number of small to medium-sized businesses will have the use of a central reception, typing service, message taking facility and other business services. None of the businesses would want to bear the cost of such facilities on their own but, by sharing the access to them they provide themselves and their clients with a higher level of service without dramatically increasing their costs.

## Poor access

As areas develop and change and as the needs of businesses develop it is possible that there will be occasions when premises have poor access to them. This may be a result of increased traffic into the business, the development of other properties and housing around the business location or the general increase in traffic on the roads. Some businesses have seen access to the business reduced by the closure of rail lines or ports on which they once depended and this process has been continuing over the last few years. In this case the only real solution for the business is to relocate to an area where the access to the services they require – whether road, rail, air or sea – is better than in their current location. Relocation is an expensive option and not one that any business will undertake lightly. Relocation is looked at in a bit more detail, later in this unit.

## The market for the company's products has shifted so that a location is worse than it used to be

A business will set up where it can best serve the market for its products. As the organisation grows it will develop new markets and may find that the original location – while still convenient for the original market – is now not convenient for other areas of their business needs. If this happens the business will probably have to consider relocation as mentioned above. Other alternatives are to set up other factories or plants in the areas where they now have major markets if this is viable or to try to alter the distribution of products to take account of the location of the business. Any such decision will have to be the result of a very careful cost-benefit study and will require the business to carry out a lot of research. No two cases are ever the same and the solutions to a problem of this sort will be as individual as the businesses concerned.

---

### ACTIVITY

---

Working with colleagues in small groups, prepare three case studies, which each illustrate cases where a business should take some action to make the best use of its premises. For each case study you should also prepare a model answer. When you have done this you should swap with another group and get them to look at your case studies and suggest solutions. Compare your answers with theirs and discuss why there are differences in the answers (if there are). A simple example of a case and answer is given below:

**Case**
*Smith Benson have been concerned to find out that their energy bills have increased 35 per cent over the last two years. 15 per cent of this has been the result of price rises but the rest is increased energy use in the business, especially heating in the winter. The Directors have noticed that some areas of the business are very warm and others are colder. This has meant that the heating has had to be run high to heat the cold areas and has made other areas very warm – indeed staff in these areas have had to have the windows open.*

**Solution**
*The firm is wasting heat. They probably need to insulate better and fit controls which will allow them to control the level of heat in each area. This might mean some*

*fairly cheap and simple additions or it may require a new system. If a new system is required they may want to look at different sources of energy. Whatever they decide to do they will need to carry out some level of cost benefit analysis to see if the savings they can make are higher than the amount of money which they will have to spend.*

## FINANCING PREMISES

If you are looking for business premises to buy, unless you are very fortunate you are unlikely to actually have available all of the money that will be required to purchase the property outright. One option is to rent and we looked at this as an option in some detail in an earlier section of this unit. Apart from renting, there are a number of possibilities open to you as a business purchaser:

- Personal loan
- Business mortgage
- Bank loan.

These have already been examined in Unit 5 Finance and this section is merely a reminder of the advantages and disadvantages of the main forms of financing available to a business looking to acquire property.

### Personal loan

If you have a substantial asset, such as a house, you may be prepared to raise a mortgage on that property (or extend the one you already have) so that you have the money available to buy property for the business. There are a number of advantages and disadvantages to doing this:

| Advantages | Disadvantages |
| --- | --- |
| • Process is quite easy | • Home is at risk |
| • Fairly quick to arrange | • Have to pay arrangement fees |
| • If your mortgage is low it may be beneficial in terms of tax | • May be harder to charge as a business cost |
| • Keeps loans together | • Involves you in putting more money into the business |
| • Repay over a long time | |

### Bank loan

Your bank may be prepared to lend money to you for the purchase of a business property. If they are prepared to do so they will normally require quite a substantial deposit and will want a lot of detail to make sure that you will be able to repay the loan. The banks have been criticised recently for 'irresponsible lending'– i.e. giving money to people who had little chance of paying it back – and, as a result of this they have become a lot more careful about who they lend money to. The loan will probably be over ten to fifteen years although you may be able to negotiate a longer or shorter term if you want it. Again there are a number of advantages and disadvantages:

| Advantages | Disadvantages |
| --- | --- |
| • The bank knows you and knows your business | • Cost can be quite high |
| • You can choose how long a period to make the repayments | • Banks can be very cautious and slow |
| • Keeps loans with one organisation | • Have to find a substantial deposit in most cases |
| | • Puts all your 'eggs in one basket' |

### Business mortgage

Like a domestic mortgage, a business mortgage will normally require at least a ten per cent deposit and some proof of the ability to repay. The mortgage may well be over a longer term than the banks will willingly offer. The process can be quite slow if you have not dealt with the lender before as they will want to find out about you and about the business before they come to a decision. They will also need to value the property to make sure that if it has to be sold there will be enough money available to pay back their loan.

| Advantages | Disadvantages |
|---|---|
| • Longer term may be available | • Another lender to deal with |
| • Interest rates will probably be competitive | • May not be as flexible as the bank |
| • May require a lower deposit than the bank | • Cautious about what they lend, and to whom |

## ACTIVITY

Draw up a chart to compare the cost of borrowing to buy a business property. Assume that the business is looking to buy a property at £125 000. Draw on as many sources of finance as you can find and, for each one, give the information below:

| Deposit (%) | Term in months | Interest rate (%) | Repayment per month | Total repayment | Total cost |
|---|---|---|---|---|---|
| e.g. 10 | 300 | 11% | £1023.60 | £307 080 | £319 580 |

Also make a note of the main points of each of the sources of finance and compile them as a quick reference guide. This could be done on a database or on a card index.

## BUSINESS LOCATION

A lot of what we have looked at above will affect the location of the business. Most businesses start in a fairly haphazard way with the owner of the business setting up in the area which they know well; usually their local one. As the business grows there will be problems such as the ones listed above: of the business becoming too large for the original premises; of high running costs; and other problems. Any of these are likely to cause a business to consider a move. This is also an opportunity for a business to consider its location and try to decide whether it is actually in the best possible place for a business of this type. We have discussed this briefly in the accommodation section and the most obvious examples given are those of businesses such as shops which are very dependent on their location. Some businesses are 'location sensitive'; i.e. the choice of the location of the business is crucial to its success. In the case of a shop, for example, the wrong choice of location will mean that the business does not attract enough customers and this will probably mean it won't survive too long. There are other businesses, however, which are not quite so dependent on the correct location for their survival. Nonetheless, being located in the wrong place is going to have an effect on businesses of this type as they will either make less sales or will have higher costs than they could achieve if they were located more favourably. For such businesses the location means that they will make less profit than they should.

There are many factors which need to be taken into account in the choice of a business location, and these factors are essentially the same for a large organisation as for a small one. The main difference is that a large organisation will have a far wider market and some of these factors will then become more difficult to take into account.

### Location of market

For many businesses, especially direct services such as hotels or restaurants it is necessary to be located where the market is. This is usually a far safer bet than expecting the market to come to you. If you are good enough at what you do this might eventually happen as in the case of certain restaurants. In most cases, however, it is safer to set up where the market is. If you are located in a seaside resort, for example, you will know the local area well and will be able to judge where the largest market for your type of operation will be quite easily. This becomes harder for a business which regards the whole country, or indeed the whole world, as its market. The decision as to where to locate is now far more open and there are many more choices to be made.

### Government influences

The Government, local authorities and the European Community offer incentives to businesses to set up in areas where they feel that there is a strong social need. So, businesses are offered a range of options if they want to set up in particular areas of the country – mainly those where there are few jobs. Such areas will offer a range of incentives to businesses to locate there; these can include:

- assistance with finding sites and building
- grants to help to equip the business
- low interest loans
- rent holidays
- assistance with recruitment
- technical and business advice.

This is not a complete list but it includes some of the main incentives. These incentives can, in the case of some areas of the country be very substantial for a business which is trying to create jobs. So, the ill-fated De Lorean car venture in Northern Ireland gained a lot of government assistance in order to try to help the business to set up in a location which it would not otherwise have considered. This process is not limited to this country. In France for example there has been a lot of Government assistance to the Euro Disney project. The intention is that this will create wealth in the country and that the people of the area will benefit from the jobs and prosperity which such a project brings.

## Costs

Business property is more expensive in some places than in others. If you have the option of setting up anywhere you like and being able to operate the business effectively it will make sense to look for the cheapest location you can find which meets your needs. Often the cost of the property is a reflection of how close it is to the main business areas, so a Central London property will be far more expensive than one on the outskirts of the city.

Traditionally, property has been more expensive in the south of Britain than in the north and this is still true, although the difference is not as marked as it once was.

## Safety

There are some sorts of business which can be considered hazardous. This may be a result of the nature of the work they do or the substances which they handle. Whatever the reason for this, such businesses need to be located in a place which is as safe as possible for the people who may be affected by them. Hence, British Nuclear Fuels would not locate a plant in an area with a history of earthquakes, and an explosives factory or storage facility would not be located in the middle of a town. Such organisations tend to be located well away from any population centres. On a similar premise, a business which receives a high number of deliveries would probably not want to locate in an area reached through a housing estate where there would be many children playing.

## Services

Businesses need access to their essential services. Almost all areas will have access to most of the basic mains services but if there is a need for a special power supply or for access to large quantities of water this will help to determine the best location for them.

## Climate

Many agricultural businesses in particular are sensitive to climate and will try to locate in an area which best suits the products they intend to produce. So, as far as England is concerned, vineyards are found in the south of the country and sheep farms tend to be in the north. Other businesses used to be far more sensitive to climate than they are now with the advent of air conditioning and heating: Lancashire, for example, used to be the centre of the cotton industry because it was damp and this helped with the production of the cotton.

## Labour

Businesses need access to a labour force with the skills they want to use. Some areas may have a shortage of labour, others may not have the skills which a business needs. If a business can find an area with a high level of unemployment and a good level of the skills they need, it will make sense for them to locate in that area if all other criteria are met. This will also probably have the advantage that they will have to pay lower wages than they would have to pay if they were to locate in a place where they would be in competition with other firms for labour.

## Cost of living/quality of life

It will be easier to attract staff to work for a business if the area has a low cost of living. This also applies to the facilities of the area and the 'quality of life'. If a business can offer staff an area where they will be able to live in pleasant surroundings, have a relatively low cost of living and have access to good schools for children and good communications, this will be very attractive to many people living in crowded areas with high cost housing, poor communications and no access to the countryside. Such people will probably be prepared to move to the new area for no more salary on the basis that they will be able to live better in the new location.

---

## Equipment and plant

---

Businesses need equipment of many different types in order to be able to run effectively. The equipment required for a business will vary according to its

- Size
- Aims/goals
- Products/services.

Equipment and plant do not include the types of resources which are actually consumed by the business in the provision of the product/service it provides. So, for example, a car will be part of the *equipment or plant* of the business but the petrol it uses will be a *consumable*. For some items it may be difficult to decide whether they come into the category of consumable or equipment – how would you classify a paperclip for instance?

---

### ACTIVITY

---

For the small window cleaning business we looked at earlier in this unit (see p 201), make a list of the equipment that the business will need to operate and the consumables it will require. If there are any items which you aren't sure of, make a separate note of these. An example is given for you below:

| Equipment | Not sure | Consumables |
|---|---|---|
| Vans | Paperclips | Soap |
| Ladders | | Cloths |
| Computer | | |

Compare your list with the list other people have made. Are there any areas where you all agree? Any major disagreements?

Discuss the areas where you are not sure and try to decide whether the items are consumables or equipment and develop a definition for 'plant/equipment' and for 'consumables'.

---

The equipment you have identified will probably fall roughly into the following main categories:

- *Capital equipment* used directly in production of goods or the provision of services
- *Transport* to bring materials into or take finished products away from the business. In the case of a service provider the transport will take the service to the customers in many cases.
- *Small plant and equipment* used to support the operation of the business.

In acquiring these resources, the business has a number of choices to make about the quality it wants, the amount of money it can afford to pay and whether a particular piece of plant will be worthwhile. There are many cases where the investment is small enough for the business not to be too concerned about the actual purchase – items like staplers and small office equipment for example. It is a waste of valuable time to do a thorough search to find a stapler 50p cheaper if it takes someone three hours to do. The saving is far outweighed by the cost of the time used in the search.

The responsibility for the decision as to what to buy, particularly in the case of major resources for the business, will normally rest with the senior management of the business. In making this decision they will have varying degrees of help. In a large business there will be:

- *Management accountants* who can appraise the value of a project using techniques like the ones examined in Unit 5.

- A *purchasing manager* or section who have professional purchasing skills and can find suppliers, interpret contracts and negotiate a good deal.
- *Technical staff* who can advise on the suitability of particular equipment and can deal with technical sales people from a position of knowledge rather than having to take things on faith.

All of these people will help to contribute to the business making a better decision as to what to buy and will be able to provide the person responsible for the decision with more facts on which to make their decision. In a small business this expertise may not exist and the owners of the business will have to make the decision for themselves. There are a number of risks to this if they are not familiar with, say, computers and are faced with an unscrupulous salesperson who wants to sell an expensive system rather than one that is right for the customer. The process of acquiring resources is set out in Fig 6.9.

## PLANNING WHAT EQUIPMENT IS NEEDED

At this stage the organisation will need to look at the requirements it has for capital equipment of one sort or another. This may be done:

- as a part of annual review of the needs of the business
- on a one-off basis as the need for a piece of equipment becomes apparent
- as part of a rolling programme to replace or update the equipment of the business
- as a result of some sort of emergency.

Much of the acquisition of resources should be as a result of the planning process of the business where the organisation sets targets for the year or for a longer period and predicts the resources required to achieve the plans they have set. Changes in the environment for the business will also contribute to this planning process and the business will predict the level of sales it will have or the demand for the service which it provides in order to be able to predict its requirements for resources to meet the demands placed on it. As noted above there may be situations where there

---

1 **Decide on the plans for the business** as they affect the resources needed. The inputs to this process will include the state of the current equipment, the expected sales and the intentions of the business with regard to expansion.

2 **List the equipment required**. Small purchases will probably be made automatically – this process will normally be confined to larger purchases (what constitutes a larger purchase will depend on the size and nature of the business).

3 **Gather information** as to the various options open to the business in terms of the equipment it needs. It is at this stage that some technical knowledge can be most valuable. It is also at this stage that the viability of projects can be assessed using techniques such as DCF.

4 **Decide whether the business can afford** all of the equipment required. If it can't then there are two options – cut back or look for a cheaper way to achieve the same end.

5 **Decide whether to lease or buy** the equipment (if leasing is an option open to you). There are advantages and disadvantages to each.

6 **Shortlist the equipment** using a process similar to the one we looked at for premises – using essential and desirable criteria.

7 **Make a decision** as to what is the best option for the business. **Do it**.

**Fig 6.9 The process of acquiring resources**

is a need for a piece of equipment on a one-off basis or as the result of some sort of emergency and, while these cannot be planned in the same way as, for example the introduction of a new product line, allowance for them may be made by the provision of some 'slack' in a budget. The advantages of planned-for purchases of equipment are clear:

1 There is time to gather information.
2 There will be no hold up to production as the introduction of new plant can be planned for a convenient time.
3 There will be the opportunity to negotiate the most favourable price for the equipment.
4 The expenditure can be budgeted for and the best way of financing it can be identified and arranged.

## INFORMATION GATHERING

In any purchase there will be a stage where the organisation gathers information about:

1 Its needs: what do we want this equipment to do?
2 The available options: what is available which can (or claims to be able to) do what we want.
3 The costs of the various options or the different prices which can be obtained from different suppliers of the same option and the levels of service which different suppliers offer.

There is a cost to this stage of the process and, as mentioned above, there are purchases for which the information gathering stage will be very short. This is most often because the price of the item is low and the cost of finding out more about the availability of the item and prices from different suppliers will be too high. This process will also be cut short when the equipment is either only available from one source or is so consistently priced that it will be the same price from any supplier.

For larger purchases the information gathering stage will be quite lengthy and the organisation will have to consider the best ways to get the information it needs. In the case of very technical equipment it will need to be gathered by someone who has a technical knowledge of what the organisation requires. This person will probably also feed information back to the purchasing side of the organisation (if there is one) so that they can evaluate the prices and levels of service. This is a prime consideration in many areas of industrial purchasing where the organisation will be very concerned with the level of support and service which they get with a product. Any such purchase has to be considered as a 'package' of which price is only a part, albeit an important one.

In smaller organisations this will have to be done by the owner/manager and this person may not be as well qualified to assess the merits of the various options as would some other people. In this case it makes sense for the business to try to get information from other businesses and to make use of tests of equipment to give them a clearer view of the advantages and disadvantages of the options open to them. The trade press for a particular industry or business will normally be a good source of information of this sort and you may also be able to get advice through a trade association.

If the equipment is not part of a pre-planned purchase (where the viability of the purchase should already have been looked at) the organisation should now try to decide whether this is a useful investment for them to make and there are a number of project appraisal techniques which can be used to do this. You have already looked at DCF which is among the most common of such techniques (*see* p 172–4).

The information gathered, when taken together with the budget for the organisation, should also allow the business to decide whether it can afford the purchase. This is a different question from whether it is a good investment. If the business is unable to raise the money which is required to make the purchase or will have to pay heavily in terms of cutbacks in other areas of the organisation to do so this may be an indicator that the investment should be postponed. There is no point in buying a machine which will pay for itself after three years if the business is likely to have problems finding the money to pay its staff wages at the end of the month.

Another decision to be taken at this stage, as the information about the purchase becomes clear, is whether to lease or to buy. This is a similar decision to the 'rent/buy' decision as far as land is concerned.

(Refer back to the Rent/Buy decision referred to on p 206 for some ideas.)

## ACTIVITY

Complete the table below, having researched into the advantages and disadvantages of leasing or buying equipment. (Refer back to the Rent/Buy decision referred to on p 206 for some ideas.)

|  | Advantages | Disadvantages |
|---|---|---|
| Rent | ▪ ▪ ▪ | ▪ ▪ ▪ |
| Buy | ▪ ▪ ▪ | ▪ ▪ ▪ |

## SHORTLISTING

This process should be fairly similar to the one we have looked at for the purchase of premises, and is shown in Fig 6.10.

## TRANSPORT

Transport is something of a special case in the acquisition of resources. Most businesses will have some need for transport for the staff of the business and for the goods produced by the business or the raw materials it needs.

There has been a major shift to the use of road transport since the early 1980s and many organisations now rely almost entirely on the road system for the distribution of their goods. These organisations have a choice as to whether they should:

● Buy and operate their own vehicles
● Lease vehicles and operate them themselves
● Use commercial carriers to collect and deliver for them
● Sub-contract the distribution of goods to one of the specialist firms who provide a service in this area.

Each of these have advantages and disadvantages for the business and, as with the acquisition of

**1 Review the needs** of the business. What do you need from the equipment?

**2** Make a list of the things the equipment *must* have – **the essential requirements**

**3** List all of the other things that you would *like* it to have – **the desirable features**

**4 Get details** of as many options as you can which could be suitable for your needs

**5 Check each one against** the **essential requirements**. Any that fail to meet the essential requirements you should throw away NOW.

**6 Look at the remaining ones** to see how many of the desirable features they have

**7 Make a shortlist** taking into account all of the factors so far

**8 Review the options** and take any technical advice you need

**9 Decide**

**Fig 6.10 The process of shortlisting premises**

any other resources, the business will have to look at its planning and at the 'package' of services provided to them by the various options they have open to them.

In providing transport for staff many companies offer company cars to staff who need them. Such vehicles may be hired, leased or owned, and the best solution for different businesses will depend on the use they make of the vehicles and the amount of money they are prepared, or not prepared, to tie up in the purchase of vehicles for staff.

## Consumables

Any business will need to make use of some sorts of consumable resources. In most businesses these fall into three main categories:

1 *Raw materials* which are used directly in the production of goods or the provision of a service
2 *Incidental consumables* which are used in the operation of the business but are not directly a part of the products or services of the organisation
3 *Energy used* to operate the business in one area or another – this will include energy which is required to run the production process and the more general uses of energy that are a part of the overall running of the business.

Each of these areas of resources has to be controlled to make the most efficient use possible of them and to ensure that the business is not wasting money by purchasing the wrong items or at the wrong price. In a large organisation it will be the responsibility of the specialist purchasing department or section to buy the goods and services which the business needs and the people in this section should be professionals in this area of work. Smaller organisations will not be able to have a section or a person whose sole responsibility is to buy resources for the organisation and this is likely to be part of the job of someone in the organisation. It may even be the responsibility of many individuals to find sources for the goods and materials which they need and to contract for them directly. If this is what is happening in the business there is likely to be a level of waste as the organisation could probably get better terms and prices if they had a policy on buying and put a lot of business into one firm in order to attract a discount from them.

---

### ACTIVITY

For the window cleaning business we mentioned on p 226 list the consumables which this business will need. Use the definitions of 'equipment' and 'consumables' from the start of the section on equipment and plant (*see* p 201) if you are in any doubt as to whether something comes into the category of a consumable or equipment.

| Energy | Raw materials | Other consumables |
| --- | --- | --- |

---

The two key categories are:

1 Raw materials; and
2 Energy;

and these two are likely to account for the main bulk of the spending by an organisation on consumable resources.

### RAW MATERIALS

The raw materials which a business uses will depend on the nature of the organisation. In some cases the raw materials will be very close to the state in which they were retrieved by the primary sector, in others an organisation will buy in components or resources as raw materials which have already been processed to quite a high level.

---

### ACTIVITY

List the raw materials used by the two businesses below and say how close each of the resources is to the original state in which it was recovered by the primary sector.

1 *Les Massandières is a restaurant operated by Françoise and Mario. The business prides itself on the fresh foods which it uses and on their attractive presentation of these foods. The business has recently added a lunchtime menu which draws heavily on fish for the meals and offers a charcoal grill when the weather is suitable.*

2 *Angela and John operate a business which supplies imitation plants to hotels and other businesses. They buy*

*in component parts (leaves, stems, artificial soil, pots, flowers etc) of plants and assemble them into the sizes and shapes which are needed for a particular area. They can create a display for virtually any area and have a wide range of types of plant to help to create a tropical feel, a village look or any other requirement a client may have. One of their major energy expenses is heating as they use glues which have to be dried at a high temperature to fix the 'plants' together.*

| Raw material | Source/level of manufacture |
| --- | --- |
| | |

The decision for a business as to what to buy will be dictated in part by what it wants to do and in part by the constraints on the organisation. So, a restaurant, for example, has a choice as to how 'raw' it wants its raw materials to be. At one extreme is the restaurant which prides itself on using only the freshest ingredients and has to spend a lot of time and labour in preparing them to serve to their guests. At the other extreme will be the restaurant which buys in 'cook-chill' meals and merely reheats them ready to serve to guests. The meals will be relatively expensive but there will be far lower expenses in terms of the preparation of them for service to the guests. These organisations, although both in the same business, are trying to do very different things and will have to purchase different raw materials in order to meet their goals.

Just as with the choice of equipment, the organisation will have to gather information as to what is available and decide what will best meet its needs. In making this decision they will have to consider the 'package' that a particular supplier will offer them. The service they get from a supplier will be of paramount importance as they will be dealing with the business on a regular basis and will depend on the suppliers they choose: a restaurant which is let down by a supplier and has no vegetables to serve on a particular evening will lose a lot of money and could suffer irreparable harm to its reputation.

The main elements of the package that a business will look for from a supplier are:

1 Good prices (given the service or lack of it)
2 Reliable service
3 Prompt delivery
4 Good quality materials
5 Attention to detail
6 Willingness to deal with special requests.

Different businesses will place emphasis on different areas of the service offered to them. One business may be particularly keen on quality, whereas another may be more interested in price.

Once the materials are purchased they will have to be stored and controlled within the business. Storage is important to ensure that stock stays in good condition and, in the case of perishable goods, that they are used in as good a condition as possible.

## STOCK CONTROL

Stock control is an important part of the operation of most businesses and can save or cost a lot of money.

---

### ACTIVITY

Read the extract below and consider what the problems of the business were in relation to stock control when Steve took it over and what he has done about it.

**Steve:** *'I took over this business, 'The Gadget Shop', about three years ago. It was a mess. Like me, the person who started it was fascinated by gadgets – anything that was a bit different – bright ideas, clever penknives with 101 uses – all that sort of stuff. When I took over I had no real idea of what the stock was. There hadn't been a proper inventory and I was pretty sure just by looking around that I got a good deal. The stock records were nonexistent and I had to spend about four days working out what we had. What I found was that we had lots of some things and not many of others. It seemed that the system, if you could call it that, was to order 50 of anything. For some items that was 49 too many, for others it meant having to reorder all the time and running out of stock a lot. I decided to try to keep track of sales and work out how many items we sold in a month and to order enough stock to last a month. I had to allow a bit extra to cope with delivery times though. We keep the stock records on computer now and I can* *tell exactly what we've sold at the end of the day; so if something is selling fast I'll reorder a bit early. I've switched some suppliers as well, where I've been able to, to firms who can deliver fast. This means I can carry less stock as they'll get things to me in 24 hours, so I can let the stock get low if I want to. Of course with some suppliers when they're the only source you just have to live with what they offer, usually poor service and high prices. I reckon we've got the stock just about sorted now and we can concentrate on finding new lines and testing them to see what goes fast; that's the lifeblood of this business and I can't afford to be stuck with lots of something that doesn't sell so I'll put a small order in first. If it sells we'll order a few more and let it build from there. With what I pay the bank for my overdraft I have an incentive to keep the stock as low as I can – I could easily tie thousands up in stock and that would really cost me at the bank.'*

| Problem | Action |
| --- | --- |
| | |
| | |
| | |

There are all sorts of systems which businesses can operate to control the level of stock and keep their stock records up to date, and many organisations now keep stock records on computer. Whatever system is operated it will try to do a number of things in every case:

1 *Keep accurate track of the level of stock* to ensure that the business does not run out of supplies it needs
2 *Keep the level of stock as low* as is practical and safe so as to reduce the amount of money tied up in stock
3 *Establish the levels at which goods should be reordered* and the quantities in which they should be reordered to meet the two requirements above
4 *Identify any stock losses* and help to identify the reasons for them.

There are a large number of different systems for recording stock and most businesses will have developed a system which works for them. The essential features of the system are the identification of the correct time to reorder, so that the

business doesn't run out of essential stock, and the identification of the quantities to order in. There are costs involved in placing and to receiving an order, and a large order will attract a better price than a small one. For these reasons there will be an *economic order quantity* which represents the best value for the organisation to order. This quantity should be ordered when the organisation reaches the *reorder level* they have identified as being the safe level of stock for them to hold. This should be enough for them to last until the order is delivered to them. This waiting time between placing an order and having it delivered is known as the *lead time* on the order and this will be different for different goods and suppliers. A short lead time is a part of the package which many suppliers try to offer to their customers.

Many large businesses have recently moved onto systems known as *JIT* (*Just In Time*) stock systems. The idea of JIT is that the supplies needed for a business arrive at the very last minute (just in time), before they are to be used. This will reduce the level of stock, reduce the work in storing stock and the space needed for storage and eliminate the costs associated with the storage and control of stock to a large extent. The theory works well and there is a number of organisations which operate this very effectively. Others have found that they are operating systems which are 'just too late' rather than just in time and have returned to the system of keeping a stock against emergencies.

### ACTIVITY

What do you think the problems would be with a JIT system if it went wrong?

What sort of business would best be able to use a system like JIT?

### ENERGY USE IN BUSINESSES

As mentioned in the section on accommodation on p 216, energy is a major cost for a lot of businesses and this is a good reason for them to try to make the best possible use of the energy they buy. In addition to this there is a growing

1 Identify the **current level of energy usage** and the forms of energy used.

2 Carry out an **energy audit** to identify how much energy is used where and the areas where the biggest improvements can be made. This audit should also identify possible improvements.

3 Gather information on the **improvements** which could be made – changing fuels, running publicity campaigns for staff etc.

4 Carry out **cost benefit studies** to decide which improvements are viable and which are the best to do.

5 **Implement the action** – starting with the areas of largest saving first.

**Fig 6.11 Cutting down on energy usage**

consciousness, as a result of environmental awareness, that wasted energy does more than damage the profits of the businesses concerned – it can also damage the environment we live in. To this end many businesses are becoming far more energy conscious. For a business concerned to make the best use of the energy it buys there are a number of stages which they should go through and this is shown in Fig 6.11.

There are many organisations who will carry out energy audits for a business to try to help them to make more efficient use of energy, and there is now a lot of technology which can help in this process. There are also some grants available to help businesses which want to save energy, and these will help to reduce the cost of some of the measures which the business takes.

## The mix of physical resources

Different organisations use these physical resources in different mixes. Just as some businesses are capital-intensive, relying heavily on their physical resources, others are labour-intensive, requiring little in the way of physical resources but needing a lot of labour (as mentioned earlier). A bank, for example, will have relatively little land for the amount of turnover of the business, but it will use a lot of other equipment such as computers, office furniture, paper etc. A farm on the other hand may have relatively large amounts of land for the turnover of the business and relatively little in the way of other equipment.

---

### ACTIVITY

List two examples of businesses which:

**(a)** Need a lot of land but not much equipment or stock; and

**(b)** Need a lot of equipment and stock but not much land.

---

## Limits placed on businesses by physical resources

A business which wants to grow will probably need to acquire further physical resources if it is to do so. The exact mix of these resources and the nature of them will depend on the nature of the business and the way in which it wants to develop. Any plans for the growth of a business will, therefore, include plans for the acquisition of physical resources (as well as human and financial) to allow the business to change in the way it has planned. If a business is unable to acquire the resources it needs to change and develop, it will be unable to respond to the changes in its environment and will eventually be overtaken by more progressive competitors.

---

## Summary

Every business needs a mix of the following different physical resources if it is to survive:

- Land
- Accommodation

- Plant and Equipment
- Consumables
- Energy

All these resources will be combined in different ways in different businesses. This 'mix' of resources will be determined by the nature of the business and the plans which it has for either coping with the present or changing in the future.

*Land* and *accommodation* are among the most expensive resources which the business has and they will need to choose the location of the business very carefully to make sure that the place and the property will suit the needs of the business both at the present time and in the foreseeable future. There are quite a lot of legal controls on the way in which a business uses land and property to make sure that there is no interference with other people in society.

*Equipment and plant* for a business have to be chosen very carefully to make sure that they meet the needs of the business. In choosing the equipment to buy, the business should be working to a plan for the development of the organisation and should be able to gather information about what is available to them to help them to meet the goals of the business. Large items of equipment or plant may be hired rather than bought and this will reduce the amount of money tied up in the business. One of the main areas of advance in equipment and plant for businesses in the recent past has been in the area of new technology.

*Consumable resources* fall into two key areas – raw materials and energy. Like other resources which the business requires, they will need to make a decision as to what they need to operate the business and where to get it from. This decision will not be made solely on price but will take account of a complex of different features offered to the business by different suppliers. Once the resources for the business have been acquired they need to be used efficiently and there are ways in which businesses can maximise the use of the resources they have, such as energy audits and scientific stock control methods.

The efficiency with which the business uses resources will be one of the major determinants

of how successful it is. The business which

1 identifies clearly the resources it needs to meet its aims and goals;
2 finds the best resources in terms of price, quality and fitness for its purposes to help it to achieve those goals;
3 combines and uses the resources efficiently and safely, taking into account the needs of the community, the workforce and the business; and
4 monitors and controls the operation of the business to keep the use of the resources it has at a good level

will have a head start over its competitors when it comes to gaining trade and making profits on the business which it does gain.

## ACTIVITY: PLANNING CASE STUDY

The case study below gives you the chance to consider some of the issues which surround an application to develop a piece of land. Everyone will get the same briefing paper to start with. You will then be split into four groups:

**(1)** The *company*
**(2)** The *opposition* locally
**(3)** The *planners*
**(4)** A group of '*other parties*' interested in the outcome

Each group will have some additional information to help them to plan their case and to give a little more background to the situation.

**Tasks:**

**(a)** Read the briefing material.
**(b)** Carry out the brief for your group.
**(c)** Take part in a role play of a public meeting chaired by the local planning committee members.
**(d)** Consider what options the planners have and recommend the decision you feel they should make in a case like this.

You may, depending on the time available, want to discuss this with friends or colleagues and may be able to get some information from your local council as to their policy on planning applications.

**The office block: background information**
*Eastern Computers plc have recently decided to move their Head Office out of London to the outskirts of Trentgate, a small village with good access to the M4*

corridor. There is a greenfield site at the edge of the village which is currently a small farm let on a one year lease. The site was bought by Eastern at the end of last year and, at the time, they said that they were considering its use as a leisure and residential centre for their staff.

Trentgate is an agricultural community which has seen a large number of jobs go as small farms have been bought up by larger ones and technology has replaced jobs. This has led to quite a high level of unemployment. The village has a small housing area at the back of the village and there are villages in easy reach where there is more housing available. The village has three main shops, a Post Office, a bakery and a general store. None of the shops are doing well but they are all surviving. There is a pub, a small school and a park/play area just off the main road. Recently the village won a 'Blooming Britain Award' and, as a result of this, has seen more visitors; indeed, some people think that this is an area which could be exploited as many visitors remark on how 'peaceful and unspoilt' the village is.

Access to the village is poor but Eastern have said that they are prepared to pay 30 per cent of the costs of upgrading the main access road that they will use. Eastern have also emphasised that quite a lot of their current staff would not move with them and that there would be jobs for local people both in the Head Office and in the construction phase. They have given a guarantee to use as many local firms and as much local labour as possible. Other inducements they have offered include:

- A sports facility on site which could be used by the community at weekends and some other times by arrangement.
- Assistance to train local people to take up the jobs that would be on offer.
- Childcare facilities on site for staff, with priority going to locally recruited staff.

There has been a lot of initial opposition to the scheme. The farmer who sold the property to Eastern now claims that he was misled by them and that if he had known what they intended he would never have sold to them. The local council planners have already said that, while they cannot make a decision until a full application comes in, they can see potential problems in a number of areas:

1 The building may be out of character with the local community;
2 The increase in traffic will put a strain on the road system;
3 The increase in population if a lot of staff move to the area will put a strain on housing and schools etc.;

4 The construction phase would involve a lot of heavy lorries on the main road through the village – near the school and the playground; and
5 The site is very close to a site of 'Special Scientific Interest' which is the home of several rare species of toads – they would not cope well with the noise.

In addition a number of other points have also been raised by local residents:

- The farm is the traditional meeting point for the local hunt
- Eastern have a very poor labour relations record and have been taken to court on a number of occasions for breach of contract
- The community desperately needs the jobs to stop more people leaving
- A lot of people coming into the area will put up the price of housing so that local people cannot afford it.
- The tourist trade could be badly affected by this development.

### (1) The company
You are currently paying a high rent for premises in London and this is a chance to have a purpose-built office at a lower cost. It is also a chance to reduce staff costs as you are sure that you will be able to employ local people for far less than you would have to pay in London.

The opposition to the scheme has not really been a surprise but you feel that the jobs and the money that it will bring in are powerful arguments and that you have made a good offer to the community that they would be stupid not to take. You may be prepared to make a few concessions – but not many.

Your task is to try to sell the advantages of the scheme and explain to the community what they are being offered. You are also aware that the local planners will be listening very carefully to local opinion.

### (2) The opposition group
You represent a group of local people who have lived in the village all of your lives and don't want to see it change. You feel that this would disrupt, and possibly ruin, the village and don't want anything to do with it.

Your task is to try to find as many problems as you can to show why it would be a bad idea and you have a few facts to bring to the meeting:

- 70 per cent of Eastern's staff will drive to work; this will mean an extra 400 cars in the village.
- No-one in the village has any of the high tech skills that Eastern will want and Eastern have already told staff they will recruit 'low level' labour locally – so no good jobs for locals.

- The Managing Director is related to the Chairman of a large construction group based in London which to date has been given all of Eastern's work. They have a poor safety record and pay low wages to imported labour – not many local firms would get much if they were to build the Head Office.

### (3) The planners

Your task is to consider all the issues and try to decide what the advantages are for the scheme and what the problems would be. Do not make a decision at this stage as you will have to listen to what other people have to say and would, in any case, have to wait for a detailed proposal from Eastern before you could really comment in full.

Bear in mind that there will be three possible decisions when the application comes in:

1 Grant it
2 Refuse it
3 Grant it subject to conditions Eastern will have to meet.

For now, list the advantages of the scheme and the disadvantages, and be prepared to run a meeting to discuss it. You will need to introduce the topic, control the meeting and sum up at the end.

### (4) Other interests

You form the audience to the meeting. Each of the organisations listed below will have a view. Your task is to select one organisation, decide what its view is and be ready, individually, to argue the case at the meeting:

- Local building federation
- Trades union regional office
- Playgroup Association
- Road safety campaign
- The local hunt
- JobCentre
- Wildlife Preservation Society
- Society for the Preservation of Rural England.

# 7

# MARKETING

## Introduction

Marketing is essential for businesses to survive. For products to sell, customers' needs have to be met, customers need to be informed about the product and the products need to be suitably priced and distributed to sales outlets. This is the process of marketing. Marketing affects business performance because without it customers' needs may not be satisfied which, in turn, leads to poor business performance. This unit deals with the marketing process and business performance and seeks to look at the following:

- What is marketing and why is it important?
- Who are the customers?
- What are the needs of customers and how do customers buy?
- What are the elements of the marketing mix?
- What are products and services?
- How are products and services priced?
- How is the product distributed?
- How is the product promoted?
- How is Information Technology used in marketing?
- How do companies keep their customers?
- How can the quality of service to customers be improved?
- What is a marketing plan?
- How is marketing research conducted?

## What is marketing and why is it important?

The excerpt below is from an interview with Mr and Mrs Gray who were interviewed to find out why their business has been successful while many of their competitors failed. An analysis of their experience highlights what marketing is and why it is vital for business success.

---

### CASE STUDY

#### We expanded while others went bust ...

*'We bought a small hotel in Blackpool many years ago when Blackpool was booming with long-stay visitors. We provided the basic bed, breakfast and evening meal package like all the other hotels in the area. We took pride in our service and enjoyed the work very much. We found that we had a lot of repeat business year after year and we expanded by selling our hotel and buying a larger one.*

*However, new trends began to develop: more people went abroad on package holidays and experienced higher standards of accommodation than were currently offered by many hotels in Blackpool. Customers became accustomed to expect en-suite bathrooms, a choice of menu, and entertainment, all of which was only provided in the very large hotels in Blackpool. A second trend was the increasing number of day trips and a decline in long-stay holidays as a result of improved motorway networks and increasing car ownership. Finally, there was a period of strikes which hit the pockets of our customers, the worst of them being the miners' strike which seemed to last forever. All this led to increased competition as hoteliers sought to fill their empty bedrooms. Some tried to increase their advertising but their service remained the same and their profits decreased. Many hoteliers experienced a vicious circle because as profits decreased they couldn't afford to advertise. Many hoteliers could not pay the large bank loans they had taken when business was booming, and hence they were forced to close.*

*We had been fortunate because by the time the effect of the trends were being felt, we had secured a hotel in a prime location, which had been large enough to be able to provide a range of facilities which customers now expected, including entertainment. We had never over-priced our service and had become fairly efficient, while giving our customers care and attention. We aimed our service at families and didn't try to be all things to all people. We always mixed with our visitors and asked their suggestions for improving our service, especially over a drink in the bar. We treated our staff well too, paid them sufficiently and trained them well. Visitors continued to recommend us to their friends and we found that our staff started to do this also. We always made sure we had a good supply of business cards and gave them to customers and staff freely to give to their friends. We increased our advertising at off-peak times.*

*We then bought the hotel next door when it came on the market. We expanded while other hotels went bust. The ones which eventually went out of business kept increasing their prices as they had done in previous years when there were high levels of inflation, their service was the same as it was years ago and they made no attempt to improve or update it. They acted as if the holiday makers would continue to pour in as usual, only they didn't ...*

A variety of factors contributed to the success of Mr and Mrs Gray's business. What did they do that could be considered good business practice?

1 They made themselves knowledgeable about their customers' needs.
2 They did not try to be all things to all people and did not try to attract customers whose needs they could not satisfy.
3 They let their customers know they existed through advertising and gave their staff and customers business cards.
4 They treated their customers well and attended to their needs.
5 They priced their service realistically.
6 They monitored and checked quality.
7 They monitored trends.
8 They changed their service to meet the needs and expectations of customers.
9 They never took their staff and customers for granted.
10 They provided their customers with something which their competitors could not provide.

All this adds up to *marketing*. Marketing involves a wide range of activities which focus on identifying and satisfying customer needs. Custom lost to competitors who are better able to meet their needs means loss of profit, loss of staff, and possible closure, since no business will survive without customers. When customer loyalty is lost it is difficult to win it back. Good marketing can lead to increased performance, growth, and new business. As far as the economy as a whole is concerned, loss of business can lead to a downward spiral as people do not buy, others lose jobs, without income they cannot buy, which in turn causes others to lose their jobs etc. and results in a recession.

The marketing process involves identifying who your customers are and what their needs are. These needs are then satisfied through what is known as the *Marketing Mix*, which has traditionally been seen as four elements, known as the four P's for short (*see* Fig 7.1). Suitable *products* and services are designed and produced. The product/service is *priced* at a level which the customer is prepared to pay and which will meet the financial objectives of the organisation. Methods for getting the products to the customer are determined, distribution channels are selected, transport is organised, and the location for outlets chosen. These, taken together, are referred to as *place*. Finally, the product or service needs to be *promoted,* that is, communicated to the customer in a way that attracts them to buy.

Marketing research activities are carried out on a continuous basis to ensure that customers' needs are identified and satisfied. Marketing research provides information at all stages in this process and helps the supplier to have feedback from the customer to determine current and future needs.

```
■ PRODUCT

■ PRICE

■ PLACE

■ PROMOTION
```

**Fig 7.1   The four P's**

It has been suggested that a fifth P standing for *People* be included in the marketing mix. This recognises the importance of people to organisational success, especially with the growth in the service industry. People need to be trained to do their jobs correctly and deal with customers effectively.

## Who are the customers?

Before you can identify and satisfy customer needs you have to know who your customers are. With an established organisation or an established product, identifying who the customers are can be a fairly easy task, for example:

- Staff in retail shops can observe customers, record the numbers of male and female customers and estimate their ages.
- A mail order firm can use information technology to produce a database of customers and be able to produce data relating to where their customers live.
- A local authority can investigate customers visiting a holiday resort through a survey of holidaymakers aimed at identifying where the holidaymakers live, their ages, occupation and their length of stay.

### MARKET SEGMENTATION

The basic idea behind identifying your customers is that the buying public or the mass market is subdivided into sections. This is known as *market segmentation*. The first way in which the market can be segmented (divided) is by:

1 industrial or business market; and
2 consumer market.

### Industrial or business market

The industrial or business market is in itself broad and can be segmented further, for example:

(a) *geographically*

- local
- national
- European
- international; and

(b) *by sector*

- manufacturing
- construction
- service

Another way in which businesses can be classified is by their place in the *chain of supply* or *chain of distribution*; i.e. the chain through which products pass until they reach the final customer. Several chains of distribution can be identified:

**1 manufacturer → wholesaler → retailer → individual**

In this chain wholesalers buy from a variety of manufacturers in order to offer a wide choice for retailers. The wholesalers 'break bulk' by buying from manufacturers in large quantities and selling in smaller quantities to retail firms. The retailers 'break bulk' and sell to individuals who are final customers in smaller quantities. This chain is used by smaller retailers who are not large enough to buy straight from the manufacturer.

**2 manufacturer → retailer → individual**

This chain is used by large retailers who buy straight from the manufacturers in very large quantities and achieve discounts for bulk buying. This allows the larger retailers to sell at lower prices than small retailers like the corner shop.

**3 manufacturer/producer → individual**

Sometimes both the wholesaler and retailer can be missed in the chain and goods can be sold directly to the final customer. Examples of this are farm shops and factory shops where products can be bought at less cost because there are no additional costs taken by a wholesaler and retailer. This chain is also used in service industries where the customer obtains the service directly without the involvement of middlemen, for example, the customer uses a hairdressers or a drycleaners. The products used to carry out the service, however, may have passed through one of the other chains described above.

In some chains of supply importers and exporters are involved when goods are being sold to a different country.

From the chains identified above, it is clear that there are different categories of customers all involved in buying goods

- the manufacturer buys goods in the form of raw materials and turns them into finished products
- the wholesaler buys from different manufacturers, breaks bulk and acts as a warehouse for the retailers
- the retailer buys from different wholesalers or manufacturers, breaks bulk, and acts as a warehouse for the individual customer.

Businesses can also be categorised by the services they provide; for example, solicitors, accountants, schools/colleges; and by size – large, medium or small.

### ACTIVITY

Make a list of manufacturers, wholesalers and retailers in your local area and write them into the chart below.

| Manufacturers | Wholesalers | Retailers |
|---|---|---|
| 1 | | |
| 2 | | |
| 3 | | |
| 4 | | |
| 5 | | |
| 6 | | |
| 7 | | |
| 8 | | |
| 9 | | |
| 10 | | |

| Method of segmenting the market | Examples of segments |
|---|---|
| 1 Consumer Markets | The buying public |
| 2 Age | School leavers, pre-school age, Pensioners, 19–24 age group, over 30s |
| 3 Sex | women, men, girls, boys |
| 4 Religion | Church of England, Roman Catholic, Jewish |
| 5 Geographical area | Global, international, national, local, London, England, European, a village |
| 6 Nationality | British, American, African, Asian |
| 7 Needs | Late night shopping facilities, fast food, microwaves, walking sticks |
| 8 Income | People who earn e.g.<br>£3000–£5999<br>£6000–£9999<br>£10000–£19999<br>£20,000+ |
| 9 Stage in the life cycle | During a person's life certain stages can be identified. It is recognised that at each stage people have different needs.<br>E.g. Single people, married couples, families with young children, families with grown children, middle-aged couples with independent children, aged couples, aged single people. |
| 10 Social class | Segmenting the market by social class involves the division of the population into the Registrar General's five categories based on occupation. These categories are:<br>Class 1  Professional<br>Class 2  Lower Professional<br>Class 3  Skilled Worker<br>Class 4  Semi-skilled Worker<br>Class 5  Unskilled manual worker<br>Although occupation can be said to be the most important single measure of a person's social class, there are other determinants of class such as the way people interact with others, their possessions and values. |
| 11 Interests | People with particular interest, e.g. fishing, sport, photography |
| 12 Lifestyle | Lifestyle is the way people live; how they spend their time and money. There is a link between lifestyle and other factors such as social class, occupation, income.<br>Segmentation by lifestyle is based on the fact that the more information you have about your customer the more you can effectively communicate with them, and develop new products to meet their needs and package the product effectively.<br>E.g. families in which both parents work, people who travel frequently |

---

# STUDENT SURVEY

Q1        In which town do you live?

Q2        Are you a full-time or part-time student?
          If the answer is part-time, answer Q3.

Q3        Are you:
          (a)    in full-time employment?
          (b)    in part-time employment?
          (c)    taking part in a government training scheme?
          (d)    unemployed?

Q4        Identify which age category you fall into:
          A      16-19
          B      20-25
          C      26-35
          D      36-45
          E      46+ years.

---

## Consumer market

The consumer market can also be segmented in many ways. The chart on p 240 gives a brief explanation of these and provides examples of market segments.

Carry out the activity below to develop skills in identifying customers.

---

### COLLEGE/SCHOOL-BASED GROUP ACTIVITY

---

Complete the questionnaire above. Collate the results of the class, and analyse the results to determine the following:

(a) The list of towns in which course members live.
(b) The number of people from each town.
(c) The number of full-time students.
(d) The number of part-time students.

(e) The number of people:
    (i)   in full-time employment;
    (ii)  in part-time employment;
    (iii) taking part in a government training scheme;
    (iv)  unemployed.

(f) The numbers of students in each of the following age categories.
    A. 16–19 years    B. 20–25 years
    C. 26–35 years    D. 36–45 years
    E. 46+ years

You have identified the customers for your BTEC National Award in Business and Finance at your school or college by segmenting the market by age, geographical location, and sex, by part or full-time attendance and by whether students are employed or unemployed.

For marketing to be effective, it is essential for organisations to define their market in as much detail as possible, this is known as identifying the *target market*. To appreciate the need to identify target markets complete the activity below.

A *customer profile* is a way of describing a target market. Below are two customer profiles for people buying brief cases. Compare the profiles and explain the differences in the marketing mix of the products by answering the following questions for each profile:

(a) What material will the product be made of?
(b) What will the product look like?
(c) What price will be charged for each product?
(d) Where will the products be sold?
(e) How will the products be promoted?

| Customer profile | |
| --- | --- |
| Age: | 40–65 years |
| Sex: | Male or female |
| Geographical area: | London |
| Purpose: | Transporting important documents |
| Occupation: | Top management |
| Income: | £30 000+ |

| Customer profile | |
| --- | --- |
| Age: | 5–7 years |
| Sex: | Male |
| Geographical area: | England |
| Purpose: | Transporting school books, lunch box, pencil case. |
| Occupation: | School pupil |
| Income: | Parents' income – below £15 000 |

## What are customer needs?

What and from whom the customer buys, i.e. their buyer behaviour, will be determined from what they want out of the product or service; for example, some factors which encourage people to buy (i.e. the determinants of buyer behaviour) are:

1 *Quality*. The quality of the product or service is normally linked to the price. The right quality to suit the needs of the buyer will be selected.
2 *Value for money*. Individuals and organisations will buy products/services which offer value for money.
3 *Service*. This refers to the service offered both during and after the sale, reliability of delivery etc.
4 *Convenience*. This can refer to the convenience of purchase as well as convenience in the use of the product/service.
5 *Necessity*. Some products/services are necessities rather than luxuries, and the only choice open to the buyer may be which brand to purchase.
6 *Financial*. This is concerned with price and terms of purchase, e.g. 0 per cent finance offered.
7 *Economic*. This is linked to financial but includes bulk buying or something that is cheaper or more economic in the long run.
8 *Social*. Some products are bought for social reasons which may range from loyalty to the seller for social reasons to the purchase of a product/service to be sociable and to gain or maintain friends or because it is expected.
9 *Cultural*. Cultural differences can affect clothes and food purchased and many other products/services which are reflected in one's way of life.
10 *Customer expectations*. Customers buy certain products/services because of their own expectations.

Using the list of 'determinants' of buyer behaviour given above identify products/services which you have bought as a result of each one. For example, what have you bought because it offered value for money? etc.

Customers have different types of needs. For example, customers need:

● products/services

- information
- safety
- security
- quality
- guarantees.

To illustrate this, imagine a couple with two children, one of seven and one of two years old. Their washing machine breaks down and they need to buy a new one. Several needs can be identified in this situation:

1 The need for a product – a new washing machine.
2 The need for a service – delivery service (and finance perhaps!)
3 The need for information – what kinds of machines are available, prices, special deals.
4 The need for safety – for the two year old – possibly a special catch on the door.
5 The need for security – that the make is a good one, that it will not break down, perhaps selection of one recommended or a make which they have had before and were happy with.
6 The need for quality – choosing a good, well known make.
7 The need for a guarantee – one actually with the machine or one purchased separately. This is linked to security needs.

Business organisations have similar needs, as can be shown by the activity below.

## ACTIVITY

Bilbow Ltd produces high quality, realistic, soft toys and buys the material from Fabrics UK. Identify the needs of Bilbow in buying the materials but remember that their needs are dependent on the needs of the final customer.

| Need | Reason |
|------|--------|
|      |        |

A social scientist by the name of Maslow identified a hierarchy of needs which has been described in Unit 2 People in Business. Organisations provide products and services to meet the needs identified by Maslow, and this is illustrated through the following activity.

## ACTIVITY

### Maslow's hierarchy of needs

Give examples of products which fulfil the needs identified by Maslow. Some examples have been given to start you off.

| Need | Examples of products |
|------|----------------------|
| Basic physiological needs | 1 Breakfast cereal<br>2<br>3 |
| Safety and security | 1 Burglar alarms<br>2<br>3 |
| Love and sense of belonging | 1 Deodorant<br>2<br>3 |
| Self-esteem | 1 Clothes<br>2<br>3 |
| Self-actualisation | 1 Fast, powerful, expensive cars<br>2<br>3 |

The need for love and a sense of belonging, and to be accepted by others is strong and gives rise to the concept of reference groups. Customers may be members of many groups, but the people who influence the customer's behaviour are known as reference groups. For example, you may buy the kind of clothes approved of by your friends at work, college or school.

People have needs which are not related to psychological influences but are of a purely practical nature. Examples of these needs are late night shopping because in many families both husband and wife work, convenience foods for the same reason or because some people do not like to, or cannot, cook. These practical reasons for buying are known as '*rational*' reasons.

Businesses buy products and services to meet needs too, and normally the products bought will be components such as raw materials and services. However, the basic need of any business is to fulfil the needs of their customers and, therefore, reliability, low cost and prompt delivery feature as needs of industrial customers.

To highlight the type of factors affecting the buying decision please do the activities below.

---

### WORK PLACE ACTIVITY

At work, interview a member of staff with some responsibility for buying. This person may be in the Purchasing Department. Ask that person if they would:

(a) tell you about a product or service which they have recently purchased
(b) explain why they chose that particular supplier
(c) explain why they chose the particular brand or item
(d) tell you who was involved in the decision of what to buy.

---

### COLLEGE BASED ACTIVITY

#### Choices

Ask your tutor if s/he can tell you who is responsible for buying computers in the department/section/sector. Ask that person if they would:

(a) tell you about the last computer hardware or software bought
(b) explain why the particular purchase was made
(c) explain why the supplier was chosen
(d) tell you who was involved in the decision of what to buy
(e) tell you if they were happy with the supplier
(f) tell you if they were happy with the product

---

### INDIVIDUAL ACTIVITY

#### How did you choose?

Identify a product or service you have bought recently and answer the following:

(a) What need did the product/service fill?
(b) Where did you buy the product or service?
(c) Why did you choose this supplier?
(d) Did you ask opinions of anyone before you bought the item or service?
(e) Were you satisfied with the product or service?
(f) Will you shop there again?

---

The results of the activities you have carried out may illustrate the complexity of some of our buying decisions. There are many factors affecting how we choose between products and brands. Our need for love and a sense of belonging and affiliation means that we often seek the approval of others. Rational factors such as price are often important when we buy. Sometimes we choose to buy the most expensive brand because we think that it must be the best quality, especially when we don't know much about the product, and often it's for snob value. We may have seen adverts for the product or we may just want to be different from others. Sometimes a person can decide to buy on impulse – unplanned and immediately, whereas sometimes they may collect information and spend weeks or months choosing which product to have. In general the period of search is long for expensive items whereas for inexpensive items it tends to be short.

An important task in marketing is to find out how people do choose. There are several types of marketing research methods which try to find out how customers choose; however, one very simple way is for sales staff to act as market researchers. They deal with the customers directly and can observe customers' actions, listen to their comments and ask appropriate questions.

The buying process in industrial markets is considered to be more rational than in consumer markets in that industrial buyers tend not to buy on impulse and the decisions are based on rational factors such as comparing price, quality, reliability and delivery. There also tend to be various people involved in the decision of what to buy in industrial markets. Once an industrial buyer has found a suitable supplier he tends to keep the supplier where possible because there is always a risk involved in changing supplier.

In order to combine your knowledge of market segments and customer needs, carry out the following activities. You can obtain the information by questioning customers, through discussions, observations and through discussions with your supervisors and peers.

---

### WORK PLACE ACTIVITY

#### Your customers and their needs

Complete the table below by identifying, for your organisation,

**(a)** the different market segments (types of customer); and
**(b)** the needs of the different types of customers.

If you are employed by an organisation which has a large number of target markets, identify three only.

| Segments | Customer Needs |
|----------|----------------|
| 1 | |
| 2 | |
| 3 | |

---

### COLLEGE BASED ACTIVITY

#### Holidays

Complete the table below by identifying:

**(a)** three different market segments (types of customer) who take holidays; and
**(b)** the needs of each segment identified.
**(c)** Give examples of the kind of holidays available to meet the needs of each of the three segments.

You may find that looking through some travel brochures will help you to identify market segments and give examples. An example has been given for you.

| Segments | Customer needs | Examples |
|----------|----------------|----------|
| Interest e.g. Ski-ing | Snow Accommodation | Special ski-ing package holidays |
| 1 | | |
| 2 | | |
| 3 | | |

---

### INDIVIDUAL ACTIVITY

Identify the needs of:

**(a)** businesses
**(b)** young people
**(c)** adults
**(d)** elderly
**(e)** disabled.

---

### SUMMARY

1 To market products and services effectively it is essential to establish who your customers are and what their needs are.

2 Market segmentation is dividing up the mass market and grouping buyers according to their similarities.

3 There are many factors which can affect a customer's choice of product/service bought.

4 The type of customer has implications for the elements of the marketing mix.

5 A customer profile is a description of the customers.

---

## Products: what is a product?

There are many items on the market which are practically identical and are differentiated only by the brand name and the advertising message. Yet technically these products would be considered to be different products because the product includes the item itself, its name, the branding, the packaging and everything which makes up the image of the product. It is, therefore, the total package which is sold to customers. Services are also products and many people now use the words 'products' and 'services' interchangeably. Many firms selling products often involve a service element too, such as salespeople, delivery, aftersales service, and demonstrations.

With services, the staff who provide the service can often be seen as part of the service, making them part of the product. This is the main reason for the introduction of the 5th P into the marketing mix.

The *augmented product* is the added value which exceeds the formal offer, e.g. friendly staff in a bar: the formal offer is a drink or purchases at the bar; the added value is friendly staff serving the drink. When families go to McDonald's, the fast food chain, the children are given a balloon – the balloon is added value and is another example of the augmented product.

People buy products because the products have benefits which fulfil the needs of the customer. In this section of the unit we saw that the market can be divided into segments and may have different needs. Products are also differentiated in order to meet the differing needs of people: for example, in the travel and tourism industry, there are products which reflect the differing needs of particular age groups, families, single people, school groups and specialist holidays, such as walking, caravanning and canoeing.

## PRODUCT MIX

Many organisations offer a range of products and services. The complete set of products and services offered by an organisation is called the 'product mix'.

### Product/services to meet customer needs

The marketplace is constantly changing due to changes in the population, changes in customer tastes and needs and competition. There are many products, services, and selling organisations on the market trying to attract a defined population with a limited spending power. The products and services need to meet customer needs or they will not be successful in the marketplace.

Demographic studies reveal that in Britain there is an ageing population. During the period between the early 1960s and the mid 1970s the birth rate fell. This has resulted in there being a significant decrease in the number of school leavers from around 1986. The fact that people are living longer together with the decline of young people has resulted in a larger number of old people than ever before.

The population changes have resulted in changes in goods and services produced. Complete the activity below to consider the implications of demography, that is, the study of the population.

---

### ACTIVITY

#### An older market

Identify the implications the ageing population has for the manufacturers of the following goods and service organisations:

(a) Electrical appliances, such as washing machines, televisions
(b) Tour operators
(c) Night clubs
(d) Hairdressers
(e) Publishers

---

The product should be easy to use, comfortable, designed to specifications, designed for safety – i.e. designed to meet customer needs – and will only be successful if it does meet needs. This is important in both the consumer market and the industrial market. Product reliability is a key factor which industrial buyers take into consideration when choosing suppliers.

### PACKAGING

In consumer markets there are many situations in which packaging is highly important. The product may be bought as a gift and needs to look attractive. The packaging also offers protection during storage and transportation, and if you consider the number of competing brands of particular products the packaging needs to attract attention at the point of sale. In the case of food and other products the packaging gives vital information about the product. Packaging has other functions too; it can act as a container to hold the product while in use and can also be used to dispense the product, e.g. an aerosol can.

Services also have packaging. A customer who goes to a restaurant to eat will be concerned about the atmosphere of the restaurant, its comfort, its decor, the music played and of course the meal being presented in an attractive palatable way. This forms part of the packaging, and part of the service itself.

Attractive packaging has, in the past, been thought to be unimportant in industrial markets because of 'rational' buying behaviour – the packaging simply protected the product. More recently, however, the belief is that it is not unimportant since industrial buyers are people. Like the packaging of consumer products, the packaging of industrial products can tell the industrial customer how to use the product and can also inform them of other products in the range.

### Environmental issues concerning products and packaging

In today's society there is an increasing awareness of environmental considerations when designing products and packaging. There is increasing publicity about environmental issues through the media, and many people will not buy products which are not environmentally friendly, for example those which have been tested on animals, aerosols, and products containing CFC gases. With environmental issues now being included in school education as part of the National Curriculum the future may see a further rise in awareness of these issues which in turn may pressurise organisations into producing environmentally friendly products and packaging.

Environmental issues are not only concerned with the production, testing and packaging of products but also relate to service industries. *The Observer* (21 April 1991) reported of a 'green' initiative launched by McDonald's fast-food chain. The measures taken include requiring suppliers to use 'corrugated boxes containing at least 35 per cent recycled paper'. The article also reports that management and staff in the restaurants are to give waste reduction 'the same considerations they devote to cleanliness, quality, service and speed.'

## THE NEED FOR NEW PRODUCTS

Because of changes in the business environment products do not last for ever. Products are created, introduced into the market, sales grow, reach a peak and then decline. Sales decline because competitors enter the market with competitive products, new products come on to the market, customers' needs change, fashions change. Products are thus said to have a lifecycle (*see* Fig 7.2).

## FINDING NEW PRODUCTS

Since sales of a product eventually decline it is essential to remember that new products need to be found. This is also the case for services. Service organisations are constantly introducing new ideas to meet customer needs, for example, late night shopping, cafés and restaurants in large retail organisations, new credit cards, cash dispensers, new savings accounts, and Switch, etc.

New products are not only products which are completely new to the market, they may be products revamped (new products from old), new ingredients added, new size, new shape, new packaging or a new image.

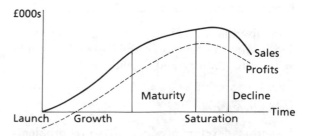

**Fig 7.2 The product life cycle**

Ideas for new products can originate from many sources, for example:

- combining products, e.g. cassette radio, two products in one
- brainstorming
- observing competitors
- monitoring international developments
- using inventors
- marketing research
- Staff
- Customers' suggestions
- Customer complaints
- SWOT Analysis

## Combining products

This is a method whereby successful products are combined to make a new product, e.g. cassette and radio combined to make the radio cassette, the alarm clock and radio combined to give the radio alarm clock.

## Brainstorming

This is a technique which is aimed at generating ideas. Several people take part and each person in turn makes a suggestion. The suggestions are written down without comment. The procedure takes place until all the suggestions have been exhausted.

## Observing competitors

Organisations watch their competitors' products to look for successful innovations and copy them.

## Monitoring international developments

Organisations also monitor international organisations for any new successful ideas which could sell in this country and copy them.

## Using inventors

Inventors develop products to solve problems and sell their idea to industry.

## Customer complaints

Many ideas for new products can originate from customer complaints. Customer complaints can tell you what the customer does not like about the product or service, and monitoring them can, therefore, provide valuable suggestions for a new improved product or service.

## Marketing research

Marketing research helps you to investigate the needs of customers, and their opinions and attitudes to your products and services. This can give you vital information for product development. Market research can also identify needs which are not being satisfied and hence identifies gaps in the market for new products to fill.

## Staff

Many ideas for new products can be from staff who work in the organisation. Many of the staff will have direct contact with the customers and will know many of their requirements, areas of discontent etc.

## Customers

Ideas can come from the customers themselves especially in the case of industrial customers who may know what products and services they require and can approach a supplier directly to discuss their requirements.

## SWOT Analysis

SWOT Analysis which is undertaken to identify the Strengths, Weaknesses, Opportunities and Threats facing your organisation. Through this procedure ideas for new products can be identified.

---

### ACTIVITY

Carry out a SWOT analysis of an organisation with which you are familiar, for example, your place of work or college. Complete the SWOT table below.

Having carried out the SWOT analysis, suggest ideas for new products/services the organisation could offer.

| Strengths | Weaknesses |
|---|---|
| Opportunities | Threats |

## Price: how do we price products and services?

When identifying and satisfying customer needs, price is an important consideration; if it is set too high customers will not be attracted to buy because their needs concerning price will not be met. If it is set too low, however, your organisation will not make enough profit to survive and will not be able to produce and, again, will be unable to meet customer needs.

Generally, the price set should:

1 Cover costs.
2 Make sufficient profit.
3 Reinforce the image of the company and the image of the product itself.
4 Enable the product to compete with other similar products/services.

Sometimes an organisation may decide to set a price which does not cover costs to gain market share, to squeeze a competitor out of the market, or to make use of resources lying idle.

There are several strategies or policies which can be used when setting price. Examples of the main strategies are explained in the Table 7.1 below.

**Table 7.1 The strategies involved in setting price**

| | |
|---|---|
| 1 Skimming policy | This is used when a product is new and is an innovation. The price is set high, normally to try and recoup high development costs by making high profits before other competitors bring out a copy of their own variation of the product. Normally if a high price is set sales volume tends to be lower |
| 2 Penetration pricing policy | This is the setting of a low price in order to achieve as large a share of the market as possible. Price is low, and sales volume is high. |
| 3 Target pricing | The organisation calculates what price to set in order to achieve a certain level of profit. This involves estimating sales and calculating the 'what ifs'. |
| 4 Price discrimination | The same product is priced differently in different markets. Unless there are actual reasons for this, such as distribution costs, customers will resent it if they find out. |
| 5 Cost plus pricing | The cost of producing the product is totalled and a certain percentage is added on. For example, cost of production is £3.00, mark up is 50%, selling price is therefore £3.00 + (£3.00 × 50%) = £4.50. |
| 6 Contribution pricing | A price is set which covers variable costs but contributes to the coverage of fixed costs. The full cost of the product is, therefore, not recouped. Contribution pricing is used when plant, machinery and labour would otherwise be unused; for example: <br><br>Variable Costs (VC) = 22 <br>Selling Price (SP) = 30 <br>Contribution = 30 − 22 = 8 <br><br>Each unit contributes 8 to fixed costs but does not cover them completely. |
| 7 Negotiation | Sometimes in industrial markets there is no set price for products or services and price is negotiated depending on the needs of the buying organisation. |

Although there are many different policies and many factors affecting the price of a product one important consideration is setting a price that the market or customer is *prepared to pay*. Why charge less? You certainly can't charge more. The price the customer will be prepared to pay depends on a variety of factors, some examples of which include:

- The market price for the product or service
- Price elasticity of demand for the product
- Psychological factors.

## THE MARKET PRICE

Market forces, also referred to as '*supply and demand*' is an important factor when setting price. The *supply* refers to the availability of the product and competing firms selling a similar product, and *demand* refers to the number of products people will purchase. Supply and demand is an economic theory which works on certain assumptions: the theory says that in general if the price rises demand falls and if the price falls demand increases. But this does not happen all the time and this is why certain assumptions are attached to the theory; these are:

1 There are many buyers and sellers
2 Buyers and sellers are free to enter or leave the market
3 Tastes, incomes and the prices of other products don't change
4 Buyers and sellers have perfect knowledge about all of the products in the marketplace
5 The products are the same (homogeneous).

These assumptions together form what is called the conditions of *perfect competition*.

The theory of supply and demand can determine the market price, i.e. the price the market will bear. It works like this:

1 A demand schedule is estimated for different levels of prices.
2 A supply line (known as a supply curve) and a demand line (known as a demand curve) are plotted on a graph.
3 The point where the supply curve and demand curve cross (known as the equilibrium point)

identifies the market price for the product (known as the equilibrium price) and the number of products bought and sold (known as the equilibrium quantity).

The example below shows how this happens and the Activity following gives you the chance to work through an example for yourself.

### Supply and demand example

The table below gives you the quantity of the product supplied and demanded for different prices. So if the price was 10 then 15 would be demanded and 10 would be supplied, if the price was 14 then 9 would be demanded and 16 would be supplied.

| Price | Quantity demanded | Quantity supplied |
| --- | --- | --- |
| 10 | 15 | 10 |
| 11 | 14 | 12 |
| 12 | 13 | 13 |
| 13 | 11 | 14 |
| 14 | 9 | 16 |

You can now draw two lines on a graph. Taking the price and the quantity demanded you can draw a demand curve with the above co-ordinates. Now taking the price and the quantity supplied column you can draw a supply curve with the above supply co-ordinates.

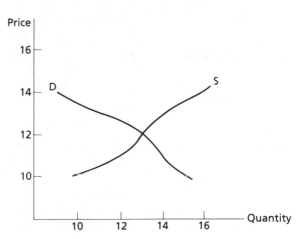

You will see from the graph that the equilibrium point is when the price is 12 and the quantity bought and sold is 13, i.e. where the supply and demand curves cross. If you look at a price which is higher than the equilibrium price you will see that there are more goods supplied than customers want to buy. Similarly if you look at a price which is lower than the equilibrium price you will see that demand exceeds supply.

---

### ACTIVITY

#### (What is the market price?)

Using the information below:

(a) Draw a graph to show the supply and demand curves; and
(b) Identify the equilibrium point.
(c) What is the equilibrium price and quantity?

| Price | Quantity demanded | Quantity supplied |
|---|---|---|
| 150 | 14 000 | 10 000 |
| 160 | 13 000 | 10 500 |
| 170 | 11 000 | 11 500 |
| 180 | 9 000 | 12 700 |
| 190 | 6 000 | 13 900 |
| 200 | 3 000 | 15 000 |

---

The theory of supply and demand is useful because it forces your organisation to think about your competitors. If you charge more than your competitors for the same products, customers will buy from your competitors unless they have a good reason for buying your product, such as better service or better availability. You must remember that the theory has limitations due to the assumptions of perfect competition. In practice there is not always free entry and exit in the marketplace, for example, patents restrict entry. In some markets there are not many buyers and sellers, there may be a *monopoly* situation where there is only one supplier in the market, or a *duopoly* with only two suppliers, or an *oligopoly* with few suppliers. In the case of a monopoly where the product or service is vital to customers a rise in price may not mean a drop in demand. In duopolies and oligopolies one firm can affect the market price of the product. Read the example below to illustrate this.

---

### EXAMPLE

#### Petrol price war

*In a medium-sized town there are two petrol stations which are located fairly close to each other. You could say, therefore, that in that town a duopoly existed for petrol. One firm was larger than the other. The larger firm, wanting to put the other out of business, reduced its petrol prices so the smaller firm followed suit. The price war continued until the larger firm substantially reduced the prices and customers queued for hours to get cheap petrol.*

---

In this case one firm was able to affect the market price for the petrol in that town. The assumption of perfect knowledge means that everyone knows what price is being charged elsewhere. This assumption helps to achieve an equilibrium because customers would know if there was a cheaper supplier. Other firms would have this knowledge too and, therefore, reduce their prices to attract custom. Under perfect competition the products are homogeneous, that is identical, and are not differentiated in any way. In reality, however, this is not the case. Products are usually not identical and are differentiated by advertising, brand names and packaging for example. In many industrial markets there may be only a few buyers; indeed there may even be one buyer, and the buyer in these situations exercises a certain control over the price. It should be mentioned, however, that in cases where there are only a few buyers and sellers it is important to get the price right for both the buyer and seller because many buyers want to have a long-term relationship with their suppliers and vice versa and, therefore, both parties seek to negotiate suitable prices which allows the supplier adequate profit for survival and growth and allows the buyer to keep costs low too. Finally, perfect competition does not take account of psychological factors affecting price.

### PRICE ELASTICITY OF DEMAND

Elasticity of demand measures the way in which demand for a product or service responds to change in price. What will happen, for example, to the demand if the price of the products rises by a particular amount? Under normal circumstances if the price rises the demand falls and, therefore, the figure obtained for the price elasticity is invariably negative. Price elasticity of demand (PED) is calculated by the following formula:

$$\frac{\% \text{ change in quantity demanded}}{\% \text{ change in price}}$$

## Calculating price elasticity of demand

In order to calculate the PED you need to determine the quantity of the product demanded at different price levels. This can be done by monitoring sales of a product before and after price changes. You can then use the formula presented above to calculate the PED. For example, assume that the product is priced at £5 and 1500 units are sold. If the price rises to £5.50 and the quantity demanded drops to 1000 units, you can calculate the PED like this:

**% change in quantity demanded =**

$$\frac{\text{change in quantity}}{\text{old quantity}} \times 100 =$$

$$\frac{1500 - 1000}{1500} \times 100 = 33.33\%$$

**% change in price =**

$$\frac{\text{change in price}}{\text{old price}} \times 100 =$$

$$\frac{5.50 - 5.00}{5.00} \times 100 = 10\%$$

**Price elasticity of demand =**

$$\frac{\% \text{ change in quantity demanded}}{\% \text{ change in price}} =$$

$$\frac{33.33}{10} = 3.33$$

PED = 3.33

## Interpreting the results

The value of elasticity obtained can range from

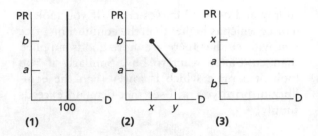

(1)   (2)   (3)

zero to infinity. Zero elasticity occurs when a change in price does not affect the quantity demanded at all. An elasticity of infinity occurs when a change in price results in an infinite change in demand.

There are three theoretical situations to demonstrate elasticity. Look at the three diagrams above.

In diagram (1) you will see that if price increases from point *a* to *b* there is no change in demand. In this case demand is known as *'perfectly inelastic'* – a change in price will produce no change in demand.

Diagram (2) shows the situation where a change in price from *a* to *b* produces an equal change in demand from *x* to *y*. In this case the demand curve is said to be one of *'unit elasticity'*.

Diagram (3) shows that a change in price results in a theoretical infinite change in demand. If price is changed from *a* to *b* demand is reduced to zero. Where price changes to *x* there will be an infinite demand. This situation is known as *'perfect elasticity'*.

In reality there would be very few, if any, demand curves like the ones shown in diagrams (1) or (3). Nor is it likely that any curve would have the same elasticity over any part as in diagram (2). However, the theories are useful because they allow you to assess the effect of a change in price on total revenue because it is not necessarily the case that if you reduce price you will have an increase in total revenue due to an increase in demand. By calculating the PED you can predict the change in revenue resulting from a price change, by following the steps listed below:

1 Calculate the PED using the method above.

2 Establish whether demand is elastic, inelastic or unitary.

If PED is *greater* than one, demand is *elastic*

If PED is *less* than one, demand is *inelastic*

If PED is *equal* to one demand is *unitary*.

3 Determine the effect of a change in price on total revenue.

*If PED is elastic:*

● a decrease in price will lead to an increase in total revenue

● an increase in price will lead to a decrease in total revenue

*If PED is inelastic:*

● a decrease in price will lead to a decrease in total revenue

● an increase in price will lead to an increase in total revenue

*If PED is unitary:*

● a price increase or decrease will not lead to a change in total revenue.

Now try the activity below to practise calculating and interpreting PED.

---

### ACTIVITY

**What will happen to total revenue if ...?**

For the following price situations, calculate the PED and explain what effect the price change would have on total revenue.

**(a)** The price rises from 4–49 to 4–99. As a result, demand falls from 10 000 to 8000 units.

**(b)** The price falls from 50p to 30p as result demand increases from 1000 to 2500 units.

**(c)** The PED of a product is −0.3; will a rise in price produce an increase or decrease in total revenue?

---

The PED of a product is affected by several factors. One important factor is whether or not the product has any close substitutes. A product with extremely close substitutes will be likely to have a highly elastic demand and if price increases there will be a fall in demand because people will buy the product which is a close substitute, provided the price of the substitute does not rise also. The situation is different for products with few, if any, close substitutes. A rise in price may cause a small fall in the quantity demanded. Some products have a highly elastic demand because they can be easily dispensed with, for example, some products and services we consider as luxuries. Generally, if the price of a luxury item rises, there is a relatively large drop in quantity demanded. Some commodities have almost perfectly inelastic demand curves because their purchase is vital; these are called *necessities*. When the price of these goods rise there may only be a small drop in demand because customers still buy them.

## PSYCHOLOGICAL FACTORS AFFECTING PRICE

There are many psychological factors affecting price, for example, often a low price is associated with 'cheap and nasty' goods and some people like to boast about how much or how little the product or service cost. Examples from research which illustrate the existence of psychological factors affecting price are:

1 A price ending in 99p was found to be perceived as substantially less than a price rounded up to the nearest pound. You will have noticed that many items are priced accordingly, for example, £1.99, £6.99. Arguably, many people are now aware of this and the technique doesn't work with those people. One firm actually states in their catalogue that it does not use the 99p price ending because they will not insult the intelligence of their customers. Noticeably, however, their target market is such that it would probably be familiar with the psychology of pricing.

2 Research found that an item with the price ending with 97p sold better than when the price ended with 93p.

3 Research revealed that customers chose to buy a face cream which was more expensive than another because they said the expensive cream was better quality. The face cream was identical.

4 Some people buy expensive products for snob appeal.

## Place: How shall we distribute the product?

When products or services have been created, priced and promoted the customer hopefully will want to buy them. Therefore, they have to be available. Place refers to the place where the customer can buy the product and the method by which the product gets to the customer. This involves decisions such as:

- Who will stock the product
- Method of distribution
- Availability of product or service.

### WHO WILL STOCK THE PRODUCT?

One problem which manufacturers face is to get retailers to stock their product. If the product is a completely new product it will have no sales history and it may be difficult to persuade retailers to stock it. The image of the outlet is important too, and must be compatible with the image of your product. Try the Activity below and see what image you think various retailers have.

---

### ACTIVITY

#### What's the image?

Below you will see a table containing the names of well known retail outlets and following that a list of words. Choose the words which in your opinion best describes the image of each of the outlets. Then compare your list with other students and discuss the similarities and differences.

| Outlet | Image |
| --- | --- |
| Marks and Spencer | |
| Tesco | |
| British Homes Stores | |
| Next | |
| Thomas Cook Travel | |
| Midland Bank | |
| Trustees Savings Bank | |

Image descriptions:

- upmarket
- cheap
- downmarket
- clean
- tidy
- modern
- reasonable prices
- old fashioned
- expensive
- poor service
- dirty
- good service
- bad service
- untidy
- poor service

---

### METHOD OF DISTRIBUTION

Products have to get from the manufacturer to the customers and there are various channels by which this can be done. Products can be sold straight from the factory in a factory shop, or can be sold to wholesalers, known as *middlemen,* or *intermediaries* who then distribute the goods to retailers who in turn distribute them to the customers. The middleman needs to anticipate demand for the product, buy in advance, and then store the products until they are needed by retailers. Large retailers, however, do not use middlemen. They buy direct from manufacturers in order to gain purchasing economies by buying in bulk and so reduce costs. They are then able to pass these savings onto the customer, be more competitive, or increase their profits.

The channel of distribution chosen and methods of transportation affects packaging design and also the price at which the product is eventually sold. In recent years there has been an increase in what is known as *third party distribution* where firms use the services of a third party to transport their products rather than have their own transport fleet. There are many reasons for doing this but mainly it is due to the expertise of the third party and reduction in costs by not having to maintain their own fleet.

In business-to-business marketing, a reliable delivery service is a key factor in determining a supplier, since late deliveries can mean loss of orders, getting behind on schedules and loss of reputation for the buying firm as they fail to meet their orders.

Either for the firm in which you work, or for your work experience placement, investigate the channel of distribution used for a selection of products.

| Product | Channel used |
| --- | --- |
| | |

## AVAILABILITY OF PRODUCTS OR SERVICES

The location of the outlet and opening times are necessary considerations since customers need to be able to buy the product or service offered. Over the last decade there has been a growth in out-of-town, one stop shopping facilities and late night opening. This is not just in retailing but in other services such as hairdressing. There has also been an increase in telephone and computerised shopping facilities and firms selling by mail order.

## Promotion: How is the product promoted?

Promotion is communicating information to your customers. You may wish to tell the customer that your organisation exists, give details of the service you provide, or that your product is better than all the others. Whatever the message is you are communicating it to the customers. An organisation may promote one product, a complete product range, its services, or its corporate image.

In the marketing of products and services, promotion is vital but whereas a product can be stored, a service can't so it is vital to be able to market your service in times of low demand to attract more custom.

### THE BUYING PROCESS

Products and services are created to fill needs but often there are several competing brands or designs from which customers can choose. For example, baked beans are a product, but there are many different brands of baked beans, including 'own' brands. How do we choose among alternatives? We may choose a particular brand or make because we recognise it, or because it's 'what we always buy', because it has no additives or colouring, because we like the taste, because it's the cheapest or dearest, because we are attracted to the packaging, or because there is a special offer.

The model of consumer decision making shown in Fig 7.3 below identifies five stages which we go through when we buy products.

The decision making process, or buying process, is started by the customer *recognising that a problem or a need exists*. This may be triggered off by any of the five senses, for example, the sight of a product or hearing about a product, or its smell or taste. It could be as simple as, for example, the rumbling of the stomach or it may be the result of advertising telling us we have a need, or having been given a free sample of the product to taste. When we believe that the need is strong enough the *search* begins for a product or service to satisfy the need. The search may be short and simple like scanning the eyes across a counter to choose a chocolate bar, or it may take a long period of time and be very involved where we seek, collect and analyse information about the alternatives, seek advice and read consumer magazines, such as *Which?*

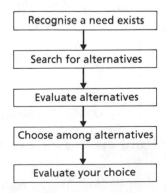

Fig 7.3 **The model of consumer decision making**

and specialist journals. We then *evaluate alternatives*, and *choose* whichever product best fills our needs. The process, however, does not end at the purchase of the product. *We evaluate our choice* and store our thoughts away for future reference. We may eat the chocolate bar and enjoy it and buy it again, or we may decide it wasn't to our taste. Many people think that advertising will sell people products they don't want, but the post-purchase stage would dispute this because, although advertising may encourage us to buy the product once, if we don't have satisfaction from it we won't buy it again nor will we recommend it to others.

There are many promotional methods available, but the best kind of promotion is a *satisfied customer* who will advertise and promote your product by *word of mouth*. When customers buy products and services there is usually a certain amount of risk involved and so personal recommendation by a friend helps to reduce the risk.

Some examples of other ways products are promoted to the consumer market are given below:

● free samples, trial size products, money-off coupons
● window displays, merchandising and salesforce
● advertising
● brochures, business cards, logos and letterheads
● sales literature
● leaflets and circulars
● free gifts
● public relations

Advertising is known as *above the line* promotions and all the other methods are known as *below the line*. Promotional methods have different strengths and weaknesses. Some examples are given below.

## PROMOTING TO THE CONSUMER MARKET

### Free samples, trial size products, and money-off coupons

Customers often become *brand loyal* to a particular brand and buy it all the time. Brand loyalty can be strong and customers may need an incentive to try a new brand. Free samples encourage customers to taste or sample the product in the hope that they may like it and switch brands. Often free samples are coupled with a special offer to encourage the customer to buy the product immediately after trying it. Products are often produced in a mini size, known as a *trial size*, to allow the customer to try the brand at little cost. Trial size products allow the customer to try the product with the hope that they will like it enough to switch from their current brand to the new brand.

### Window display, merchandising and salesforce

Known as *silent salespeople*, merchandising and display can promote sales effectively. Attractive window displays attract customers into the shop and once inside attractive presentation of merchandise can tempt the customer to buy. Point of sale material at checkouts and cash points can draw the customers' attention to special promotions. The salesforce is a vital part of promotion especially when in the service sector where the salesperson and the service is almost indistinguishable. Good training in customer care, selling techniques and product knowledge is essential.

The design of shops is now a very sophisticated business and there are some 'rules' to follow in the layout of stores. For example:

● Most new supermarkets have their *entrances on the left* of the store because people find it easier to turn a trolley to the right.
● Products placed on the *end of an aisle* will sell faster than those placed in the middle.
● Many supermarkets will place *fruit and vegetables at the entrance* to give an image of health and goodness.
● People don't like to spoil a perfect display, so many organisations will deliberately leave a hole, known as a '*starter gap*'.
● Products placed at eye level sell better than those placed higher or lower, in fact there is a well known display maxim '*eye level is buy level*'.

## Advertising

Advertising can attract the customers' attention and give the customer vital information about the products. Advertising on television can allow an image to be put across very forcefully. Unfortunately for companies promoting the product, many people choose the interval between programmes to make the tea and they may miss the adverts completely – nevertheless, television advertising is a very powerful tool. Advertising in newspapers (local and national) gives the opportunity of your advert being seen by a wide audience; and specialist magazines and journals can allow you to reach your target market easily. Firms can also advertise in cinemas, on billboards, buses, the firm's own vehicles, and posters. Posters can be colourful, attractive and eye catching. They can be displayed relatively cheaply in places frequented by the target market: for example, posters for nappies can be displayed in baby clinics; posters for toothpaste and toothbrushes in dentists' waiting rooms; and health care products or health care services in hospitals and in doctors' waiting rooms.

## Brochures, business cards, logos and letterheads

Well designed and attractive brochures and business cards will be kept by customers and can enhance the corporate image of the organisation. Logos of certain companies are instantly recognisable through advertising.

## Sales literature

Sales literature giving specifications, advantages and benefits of the product can be useful for customers, especially when the customer is searching for expensive items.

## Leaflets and circulars

Leaflets and circulars can be put through doors and sent through the post. If they look a little different they can attract the customer's eye and can give a lot of information quite cheaply. But many leaflets go straight in the waste bin without being read because they fail to attract enough interest in the customer. This is often sent out by post as *direct mail*.

## Free gifts

Some organisations give free products such as balloons to children, lipstick with a girls' magazines and small gifts in boxes of cereals. Collecting tokens for a free gift, or collecting sets of an item encourages multiple sales and can encourage the customer to switch brands permanently.

## Public relations

Public relations, known as PR for short, is the way the public, your customers and clients and your staff and even shareholders see the firm. Public relations activities include:

- house magazines distributed to employees to keep them informed of what is happening in the company
- sending out press releases to newspapers, magazines and journals
- giving free samples, holding competitions and sponsoring activities
- giving talks to different sectors in the local community.

Good public relations is important to ensure that the public have a good impression of the organisation since this helps to recruit good quality staff and can increase custom.

## PROMOTING INDUSTRIAL PRODUCTS AND SERVICES

Industrial products and services can be promoted through specialist trade journals which enable the supplier to reach the target market directly. Direct mail, exhibitions and public relations activities are used too. Free gifts such as calendars, diaries and pens, usually displaying the company logo, are used often because they will be around the house or the office for a long time – especially the calender which will be displayed on the wall and diaries which will be looked at and used many times throughout the year, possibly every day. All the time the promotional gifts are being used the company's name is in the customer's eye. Promotional gifts need to be chosen carefully to give the right image of the organisation.

In business-to-business marketing there is usually a large service element, since many products are technical and technical advice from representatives is essential. The salesforce is, therefore, a vital part of promotion, as is good after-sales service.

---

## ACTIVITY

Select four promotional methods which you are most familiar with and identify the advantages and disadvantages of each one.

| Method | Advantages | Problems |
|---|---|---|
| 1 | | |
| 2 | | |
| 3 | | |
| 4 | | |

---

## HOW DOES ADVERTISING AND PROMOTION WORK?

Advertising and promotions work through the senses by triggering off a need in the customer. TV advertising uses sight and sound; newspapers and journals use sight. Free samples of food use touch, smell, taste, sight; and touch is often used in retail outlets where customers are encouraged to feel the material, or the texture of a product. Radio, of course uses sound only. The use of smell can be used to promote food sales.

Read the reports below which demonstrate the power of the senses.

### A canteen manageress

*'In the morning we do bacon butties but we don't put the fan on straight away. We open the doors and let the smell of the bacon waft across the canteen and down the corridors. We sell more that way.'*

### A café owner

*'We used to display the cakes and gateaux at the counter at the far end of the shop where we served from. But we have recently moved the cake display to the window so that people passing by will be tempted in at the sight of the cakes. It certainly works.'*

### The supervisor in a small food retailers

*'Before we open the shop we grind fresh coffee and let the smell of it go through the shop. This has increased our sales of fresh coffee tremendously.'*

---

## ACTIVITY

Investigate how five firms of your choice use the senses to sell.

| Firm | Sense appealed to | Method |
|---|---|---|
| 1 | | |
| 2 | | |
| 3 | | |
| 4 | | |
| 5 | | |

---

## DESIGNING WRITTEN MATERIAL FOR PROMOTIONAL ACTIVITIES

In many, often larger, organisations specialist staff are employed to prepare and organise promotions. Even where specialist staff are involved, outside agencies are often employed. However, many smaller firms do not employ specialist staff or use consultants to prepare and design promotional activities. You may, therefore, find yourself having to select promotional methods, write a press release, or design a business card, letterheads and other business stationery, brochures, leaflets, posters or adverts. You may need to choose where to advertise.

This section is designed to help you develop some of the practical skills involved in doing tasks of this nature by concentrating on designing written material. There are many desk top publishing packages on the market which, when used with the right system, can enable you to create written material which looks very professional.

### Identify the market segment as clearly as possible

Before you can design any type of promotional material you need to define your target audience as clearly as possible. You will need to know:

1 their needs
2 their language
3 the kind of people they are
4 where they are located
5 what newspapers and magazines they read

and any other information which will help you to visualise the customer. Being aware of their needs will help you to advertise the products because you will be able to sell them the benefits of the product that will cater for their needs. Knowing their language is vital because you need to be able to communicate to your customer in terms they will understand. Knowledge of their geographical location will help you decide on where to advertise or distribute circulars etc. Likewise, knowing what newspapers and magazines they read will help you with decisions as to where to advertise.

You will be able to collect information about your target market through marketing research activities and from experience of dealing with them, but if you know the type of magazines and newspapers they read you can get additional information from this source by reading some of the articles and advertisements in the newspaper, the correspondence columns and job advertisements. This will tell you about the language they use and the sort of jobs they may do.

### Finding the costs involved

Costs of advertising vary depending on the magazine or newspaper in which the advert is appearing. They also depend on the size of the advert. If you are designing brochures, circulars, leaflets or business stationery there are different costs involved depending on the quantity involved, the type and quality of paper and whether or not you are using colour which can be quite expensive. You obviously cannot spend more money than you can afford but good promotional material is an investment because it portrays an image about your organisation and your product and services.

### Be clear about the size

The amount of space you have available to communicate your message is an important consideration. You need to ensure that you do not squeeze too much information into too small a space. So don't prepare your message and then try to fit it into the space available. Determine your space first.

If you are planning an advert, what is the size of the advert? Don't forget to find out the costs involved – the larger the size the higher the cost. If you are producing a leaflet or brochure you need to know the space available. How many pages will the brochure have and what size are the pages and can you write on both sides?

When you have decided on the space available map out the actual size on paper to give you a clear picture of the amount of space you have to work with (*see* Fig 7.4).

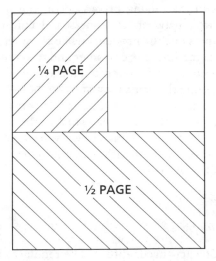

**Fig 7.4 The sizes of an advert**

## THE MESSAGE

### Know your product/service

You need to know the product or service you are selling in as much detail as you can. What does it do? How is it made? What makes it different from its competitors, that is, its *unique selling position*? Some products have no unique selling position, they are almost indistinguishable from other similar products. If this is the case with your product try to find a feature of the product which competitors are not using to sell the product. It can become your product's *unique selling feature*.

### Select the information

It is vital that you tell the customer something new about the product, something he doesn't know already. It may not be possible to tell the customer everything that you would like to say about the product due to lack of space so you need to be selective and pick out the most important information. To do this you will find it useful to list the information you would like to say in order of priority. Space is at a premium and everything you say should be of value so never use two words when one will do.

There may be different messages for different parties in the buying process. You can make a distinction between customers and consumers. Customers buy the products while consumers use them. Sometimes the customer and the consumer are the same person but often this is not the case. To illustrate this, let's look at baked beans again: children like baked beans; parents buy the baked beans; and the retailer stocks them. The manufacturer of the baked beans needs to cater for three parties with different requirements from the baked beans:

1 The *retailer*
2 *Parents*
3 *Children*

How do their needs differ? The retailer is interested in the profit the beans make; the parents in

price and nutrition; and children in taste, colour and image – often picked up from adverts.

To illustrate further, read the explanation given by a journalist of how she presents information about computer software to different parties.

*'If I am communicating information about a new accounting package to two markets: computer firms and accountancy firms, I would tell them different information. I would present technical information to the computing firms because they are specialists and would understand the language. To the accountancy firms I would sell the benefits of the product; i.e. how the package will make their jobs easier, faster or cheaper; after all they want to know how the package will help them.'*

### Your language

Make your message simple and clear, don't make too many points or the reader will be confused and will not remember any at all.

Above all, speak in language that your customer will understand – the importance of this point is explained in the following extract:

*'Research suggests that only 40% of people in Britain understand what "vulnerable" means, only 17% know what a "decade" is, and if you use "empirical" over 95% won't know what on earth you are talking about.'*
*(Stuart Turner 1987)*

If you are communicating with the trade they are likely to understand the technical language and want to know the technical details in order to make comparisons.

### Attracting attention

When people are browsing through magazines and newspapers there are lots of advertisements hoping to catch the reader's eye. The reader spends about 1.5 seconds on an advert. Your advert needs to catch the customer's eye, and keep attention. Research has shown that the following aspects of an advert are important in attracting and keeping attention. It applies not only to adverts but also to brochures and leaflets too.

- illustrations, pictures and photographs
- a main headline
- the bottom right-hand corner
- captions and subheadings
- the main story
- themes
- colour
- layout
- typeface.

**1 Illustrations, pictures and photographs.** Illustrations are good for attracting attention initially by having a main illustration, picture or photograph. Smaller illustrations, charts and diagrams can hold the reader's attention and direct them into the main body of the material. If you use graphs and charts you should keep them simple.

You can use the following aids to help hold the reader's attention:

- Clip art (*see* Fig 7.5)
- Computer art which is relatively inexpensive if you have the hardware and software available (*see* Fig 7.6)
- Human art which can bring originality

Clip art is copyright-free illustrations which can be found in both computer form and paper form. The paper form of clip art is normally bought in books (clip art books) from art shops. You can scan paper clip art into a computer package using a scanner. Illustrations can be enlarged or reduced to fit using the photocopier or by scanning.

When you need to give your customer an accurate picture of the product or aspects of a service, as for example, is the case with conference centres and hotels, you can use photographs. Although it costs more money, it is worthwhile having the photographs taken by a professional photographer; but be careful, the impression they give should be realistic otherwise the customer may be disappointed with the reality if it doesn't match up. Done professionally, squared up photographs can look very attractive.

Computer graphics can be effective but you need to be careful that they fit in with your

**Fig 7.5 Clip art**

image. They are sometimes considered to be too modern for a traditional market.

Much publicity material is sent by facsimile and, if the material contains photographs and illustrations, they can look unrecognisable if they are not faxed carefully. It is better to take a photocopy of the material and use the photocopy for the fax rather than the actual material. If you make sure you have a clear photocopy the fax will be clear too.

**2 The headline.** The headline is often said to be the most important aspect in attracting attention. The picture and the headline need to work together to tell a story: the headline tells one part of the story while the picture tells another. A headline should not simply describe the picture and the picture should not simply illustrate the headline, rather it should tell the reader something new. When writing a headline you should:

1 Keep the headline short
2 Avoid using 'ing' in the headline if possible
3 Write the headline in the present tense.

Starting a headline with 'How' and 'Why' can attract interest. Buzz words can be used in headlines to attract attention, for example: free, magic, money off, bargain, unique, offer, now.

**3 The bottom right-hand corner of an advert.** Research into how people read adverts revealed that after they have looked at the main picture,

**Fig 7.6 Computer art**

if there is one, and the headline, they then look at the bottom right-hand corner of the advert. You should, therefore, make full use of the bottom right-hand corner to encourage the reader to continue reading. For example it could be used for:

- the company logo
- a sales slogan
- a coupon to send for more information
- a coupon to send for the product or a free trial

**4 Captions and subheadings.** If possible put the name of the product or service into the caption and use the caption to direct the reader to the text. The use of buzz words in subheadings, like those mentioned above, can attract attention.

**5 The main story.** You can make the main story interesting by:

- Not beginning the main body of the material by repeating anything already said.
- Going straight into the story rather than opening with the name of the product.
- Talking about the reader and their hopes and desires rather than the company itself.
- Presenting facts clearly and logically.

- Talking to the reader by using the word 'you'.
- Using questions to attract attention.
- Numbering points if you have several points to make.
- Not cramming the promotion too full of information because it can be confusing to the customer.
- Making good use of space.
- Using well known characters
- Quoting experts and independent testers and testimonials.

The use of testimonials are especially useful when promoting a service where there is no tangible outcome from using the service.

**6 Themes.** There are many themes which can be used to attract attention. Some examples are given opposite.

**7 Colour.** Colour is useful to:

- convey images (such as 'modern' or 'up-market'),
- create impressions
- attract attention
- create interest
- give information

| Theme | Description |
|---|---|
| Time | The setting can be in the future or in the past rather than in the present. |
| Before and after | The message is that before the product or service was used things were bad but now having used the product things are so much better. |
| Invented place | Rather than a real place in geographical terms, an imaginary place is invented. Normally it is connected to the product and the name of the product could form part of the name of the invented place. |
| Invented character | A special character is invented. It may have nothing at all to do with the product. |
| Comparisons | Comparisons are made with other products. |
| Give the customer a challenge | Challenge the customer, for example, to find a better product or a cheaper product or to eat a certain quantity. |
| Animal imagery | Animals are used to attract attention even when they have no actual connection with the product. |
| Amusement | Amuse the reader to attract and keep attention. |

- add reality
- help people to remember.

However, although there are many advantages of using colour it costs money which is one reason why it can give an upmarket image, and can look more expensive. Using one colour on coloured paper can look effective and is cheaper than full colour.

It should be remembered that grey and red will not fax and should be avoided if you are planning to use a fax machine. One firm revealed that one of their clients has grey and red stationery, and when a letter is faxed through they can only tell who it is from by the fax number.

**8 Layout.** Information can be laid out in a symmetrical, asymmetrical or in an irregular way. It is not advisable to mix symmetrical and asymmetrical layouts because this does not look effective. The use of white space can be used to create interest and attract attention.

Titles, subheadings and text can be centred. Left-hand margins can be straight (justified) which gives a more formal layout but this can cause problems with spacing. Alternatively, the left-hand margin can be 'ranged left' where the right-hand margin is not straight. This can look ragged if long words are sticking out at the end of the sentence but you can use hyphenation to help overcome this.

You can indent paragraphs and blocks of text and use tabs for tables.

Lines, called 'rules', can be used for separating text. They can have different thicknesses and tones but mixing different thicknesses and tones does not look effective. Boxes can be used to highlight points or for effect but like rules should not be overused. Boxes and text can be shaded or reversed, like a negative, to make them stand out.

---

### ACTIVITY

#### Finding effective layouts

Look through brochures, magazines, journals and newspapers and find examples of layouts which look effective. If possible keep them in a file for reference or sketch the layout and keep the sketch. If you are sketching, identify where the print is, where margins are, where illustrations are and where there is white space. Make a note of what appeals to you at first and what else you notice when you look at the material in more detail:

| Item | First appeal | Detail |
|---|---|---|
| | | |

---

**9 The typeface.** Your choice of typeface is important because it can give an image and

**(a)    Times New Roman (serif)**

Select your typeface according to how traditional or modern you want your document to look.

**(b)    Univers (sans serif)**

Select your typeface according to how traditional or modern you want your document to look.

**(d) Courier**

```
Select your typeface according to how traditional
or modern you want your document to look.
```

**Fig 7.7 Selection of fonts (a) Times New Roman (b) Univers (c) Courier**

impression like colour can. A typeface is called a *font* and the variations of a typeface by sizes of print and by weight is called a *type family*. The different sizes are known as 'point sizes'. Different point sizes are used for headings, subheadings, and the main text. The larger point size is used for headings so that they are distinguished from the main text. The point sizes chosen should take account of where the material is going to be read, and the characteristics of the market segment itself (age). If the point size is too small the material will not be read.

The upright version of a typeface is called *regular*, *book* or *roman*. If it slopes to the left it is called *classic* and if it slopes to the right it is called *italic*. Italic can be used to highlight certain words, phrases, quotes or technical terms.

The normal weight for text is *medium* or *regular*. However you can use *bold* or *extra bold*, *light* or *extra light* for effect. Like italic, bold can be used for emphasis. It is important to choose a suitable contrast between background and weight of print. The eye finds too much contrast disturbing but too little contrast is not very effective.

When selecting your typeface use *serif* faces for a traditional look and *sans serif*, for example, Univers or Helvetica, for a more modern look (*see* Fig 7.7). A serif is a short extra line on the arms of letters, whereas sans serif does not have this. When words are close together the serif helps the eye to read the text. If, however, the words are a long way off as they are on a bill board or at exhibitions serifs can make the words difficult to read because they tend to blur the shape.

We read words by their shapes and it is easier for the eye to recognise the shape of words with upper- and lower-case than those with only uppercase. It is, therefore, not advisable to use full words and sentences in capitals in the main body of the text; but oversized capitals can be used for effect to begin paragraphs.

The experts say that it is not advisable to use more than one or two type families in the same document because it does not look effective.

### Proofreading

Proofread your material carefully to check for spelling errors, punctuation, hanging hyphens, 'widows' and 'orphans' (first or last line of the paragraph separated from the rest of the paragraph by a page break) and check page layouts.

## Retaining customers

Today's marketplace is highly competitive, not just for private sector businesses but for charities and public sector services. The Thatcher Government based its economic policies on 'market forces' and privatised numerous public sector organisations through selling shares, putting services out to tender and creating civil service agencies. If an organisation is to survive in today's competitive environment it is essential that all departments and personnel within the organisation make the identification and satisfaction of customer needs the prime goal. To fail to identify customer needs means that they will only be satisfied by chance, if at all. If you do not satisfy customers you may have no customers unless your organisation holds monopoly power and the customer has no choice of supplier.

Producing satisfied customers takes more than having a marketing department, or carrying out some research, or advertising. It is a whole organisation's approach involving all staff in presenting a positive image. Organisations which take this wide view of marketing are more successful because they provide a better service to their customers and clients. There are many factors which contribute to giving a positive image of an organisation, for example:

1 Doing jobs well
2 Good customer relations
3 Good employer-employee relations
4 Dressing appropriately for work
5 Ensuring that everything sent out of the organisation, such as letters, brochures, business cards and leaflets is well presented
6 Good training in telephone techniques and customer service.

No amount of money spent on advertising and public relations activities can create a good image if the product or service provided to customers is not up to standard.

---

**COLLEGE/SCHOOL BASED ACTIVITY**

**(Who markets?)**

For each of the staff below describe how they might help towards enhancing the image of your college or school.

(a) Receptionist
(b) Switchboard operator
(c) Secretary
(d) Lecturer or teacher
(e) Typist
(f) You

---

**WORK-BASED ACTIVITY**

**(Who markets?)**

For each of the staff below describe how they might help towards enhancing the image of your workplace.

(a) Receptionist or Customer Service staff
(b) Typist
(c) Switchboard Operator
(d) Staff with whom you work
(e) You

---

## Quality of service

Quality of service can be improved through:

- incentives which are based on quality
- good job design
- making the person doing the work visible to the customer
- team building and team work
- creating a pride in the job attitude
- motivation

**1 Incentives.** 'Employee of the month' awards are an example of an incentive as used today by many large stores such as Asda and McDonald's.

**2 Job design.** Jobs are interesting and people can have a sense of pride in the job, i.e. it is worth doing. The job is designed that is possible instead of the employee being unable to do the job properly because there is too much of it to do in too short a time period.

**3 Visibility.** Examples of making the person doing the work more visible to the customer includes introducing the staff to the customer; for example, this sometimes happens in private hospitals where the doctor or surgeon visits the patient, or in car repairs where the mechanic speaks with the customer. In some restaurants the chef is visible to the customer.

**4 Teambuilding**. Teamwork can foster co-operation and an unwillingness to let the team down. Peer group control can be an effective factor in the achievement of quality.

**5 Pride in the job**. Selection of good staff coupled with effective training programmes can ensure that staff are good at their jobs and can take a pride in doing the job well.

**6 Motivation**. Highly motivated staff will provide a good quality service provided they are properly trained to do the job.

**7 Knowing the customer**. A close relationship with the customer is essential for the achievement of quality in the service sector. Quality is satisfying needs and customer needs will only be met through knowing the customer.

Unlike a product, a service cannot be stopped, examined and reworked or recycled. Quality in the service industry emphasises *people* as the fifth P of the marketing mix. Because a service cannot be returned if it is faulty there will have to be other measures taken to monitor the quality of the service provided. These will include questionnaires, as used by many hotels, to try to get the views of customers on the quality of service they received and ways in which it could be improved.

## QUALITY ASSURANCE SYSTEMS

Quality is a key to customer satisfaction. Lack of quality leads to lack of customer satisfaction which can lead to loss of custom and damage the performance of the business.

Among the key components of quality assurance systems are:

**1 Prevention** – trying to ensure that faults do not occur; this attitude of quality assurance rather than quality control should help to reduce the costs of inspection and reworking of goods. An example of this is the process of ensuring that

the design is right before the products are made; this should reduce the problems and errors.

**2 Detection** – picking up faults at the earliest possible stage and making sure that the necessary action is taken to correct the problem, preferably so that it does not recur rather than just remedying an isolated fault.

**3 Correction** – Corrective action needs to be taken quickly. The cause of poor products needs to be established and put right after the shortest possible time. To make this happen everyone has to be alert to the key quality issues.

**4 Inspection** – incoming goods are inspected to ensure they conform with the requirements and the company's own products are inspected to ensure they conform to the specification required.

As a part of their drive towards quality many organisations are now trying to gain BS5750 (the British National Standard for quality systems) or the International Standard ISO 9000, which are quality assurance standards. The BS5750 gives the requirements for procedures and criteria for a quality-orientated system to ensure that the products leaving the factory meet customer requirements. Its aim is to get the quality right first time through a quality system. The systems have to be operated by the business and there will be audits to make sure that the procedures the business has claimed to follow are in fact being implemented. The adoption of a system like this should help to focus attention on quality and provide 'fail-safes' for quality checks.

Operating to these standards should give an organisation certain benefits:

- Cost saving due to more efficient procedures
- Satisfied customers, because quality is built in at every stage
- Reduction of waste
- Reduction of re-working of designs and procedures.

Other reasons for firms wanting to gain BS5750 standards are because they want to:

1 retain customers who are looking for their suppliers to meet this standard as a part of their own quality systems

2 have the Kitemark symbol on their products
3 have the reference to the Standard on company headed notepaper. This should be of significance to other quality orientated firms with which they are dealing. It is a guarantee that they will operate to set quality systems and that the systems have been independently assessed as effective and audited to make sure they are complied with.
4 discipline employees – to force managers and employees to work to a quality system which is comprehensive and which is inspected for compliance.

Quality assurance results in quality systems being implemented in all the activities and functions concerned with attaining quality – from design through manufacture to service. The effective implementation of such a system controls costs, prevents defects and leads to customer satisfaction. It is the 'attitude of mind' that quality is vital and that it is the responsibility of all of the people in the organisation.

### Service businesses and quality

Service organisations are generally perceived as harder to ensure quality in than manufacturing type businesses. This is partly because until a service is delivered there is nothing to see and, once it has been delivered there may be no tangible evidence of the standard of it. However there are some guidelines to ensuring quality in service organisations and there are quality standards which apply to them.

## The marketing plan

In any organisation it is essential to have effective planning. In the area of marketing there will be various inputs to the development of the marketing plan for the organisation or a section of its operations:

1 **Marketing research** activities enable an organisation to identify customers' requirements. Customer requirements can only be satisfied if they are known.

2 **Sales forecasting** enables organisations to anticipate a demand for products and services and is an essential activity because it ensures that customers' requirements can be sufficiently met.

3 **Product planning and development** ensures that the products and services are produced to the specifications and quality desired by customers.

4 **Efficient methods of distribution** enable products and services to be available when they are required by customers.

5 **Promotional planning** ensures communication with the customer is provided in order to inform the customers of the existence and nature of the product or service. Promotional planning activities include advertising, and other methods of sales promotion, and media selection and planning.

6 **Profitability.** Many organisations which are non-profit making need to market their products and services effectively if they are to survive. Even if they are not motivated by profit they are still concerned with:

(a) Identifying customers'
(b) Identifying customer needs
(c) Providing products which meet customers' needs
(d) Telling customers about the product
(e) Persuading customers to buy
(f) Encouraging the customer to use the product/service more
(g) Getting products to customers when they are needed
(h) Researching
(i) Finding new products and new markets.

7 **Analysing the environment** within which the business operates. Any organisation has to be concerned with ensuring that it is aware of what is happening around it in the environment and this is a vital part of planning. This area has already been looked at to an extent in Unit 4. Unit 8 Business innovation is also concerned with the analysis of the business

environment under the headings given in the box below:

> ● Social environment
>
> ● Legal environment
>
> ● Technical environment
>
> ● Physical environment
>
> ● Political environment
>
> ● Economic environment

Taken together these activities together can be described as *marketing* and they form the key inputs to the marketing plan for the business.

As with most areas of business planning there will be a number of levels to the marketing plan:

**1 Review of organisational goals.** In order to develop a marketing plan the business will have to review the overall aims within which it aims to operate as this will provide the framework in which the marketing plan has to operate.

**2 Setting marketing strategies.** Just as the business as a whole will have longer term objectives and aims so will the marketing plan. So, a business may have decided to cultivate an upmarket image or to pursue a new market. These are not short-term objectives but do need to be planned for in good time.

**3 Setting operational targets.** The shorter term planning to meet the immediate objectives of the organisation. This will be the main bulk of the plan and will contain the detailed aims for the operating period (normally a year). This should set clear targets against which the effectiveness of the methods and strategies chosen can be assessed.

## Marketing research

### HOW DO FIRMS FIND OUT ABOUT THEIR MARKET?

Organisations identify customer needs and opinions through marketing research activities.

Marketing research is vital for all organisations, whether large or small, because it is their source of information about their customers. Without market research money can be wasted, opportunities missed and customer needs not met. Successful firms are consumer-orientated and carry out marketing research regularly. You can research the market and every element of the marketing mix. The list below gives examples of the type of questions you may use research to answer.

### What to research

Your customers

● Who are your customers?
● Where do your customers come from?
● What is the size of the potential market?
● What does the average person spend on item X?
● What are your customer needs and opinions?
● What is the lifestyle of your customers?

**Competitors**
● Who are they?
● What is their pricing policy?
● Are their products' prices lower/higher than yours?
● What level of service do they give?
● What image do they give customers?

**Product**
● What type of products do people want?
● What features in the product do people like and dislike?
● Is the product easy to use?
● What do people think of the material, the colour, size etc?

**Price**
● What price would customers expect to pay for the product or service?
● What is the highest and lowest price the customer is prepared to pay?
● How important is price to them?

**Promotion**
● What is the image of the product or company?
● What do people think of the advertising?

- What image is given by different colours, lettering?
- Can customers open the packaging easily?
- Does the packaging attract attention?
- Do people remember the adverts?
- Has the message got across?

## HOW TO RESEARCH

The marketing research process involves various stages and these are shown in Fig 7.8.

### Defining the problem and setting aims

Marketing research data costs money to collect. There are labour costs and costs of materials and printing. Often this money can be money well spent because market research can help you to make decisions and reduce the risk of costly errors. To get the most out of your research activities you need to make sure that you have established what the purpose of your research is. Is there a problem that research can help solve? Do you need information to help you to make a particular decision?

### 2 Selecting/designing suitable research techniques

Marketing research techniques range from very simple to very complex. Some very simple techniques include:

- analysing sales to find out what the customer is buying so that you can restock

- keeping a customer-wants book and noting if a customer asks for a product which you don't stock. You may find that many customers may ask for a particular product or service which, if you provided it, would increase your sales.
- observing customers' reactions to products and services, listening to their comments and simply asking their opinions.

There are other recognised techniques which are commonly used and it is to these that we now turn.

### CLASSIFICATION OF RESEARCH TECHNIQUES

Marketing research techniques can be classified into types. The first classification which can be made is the division of research into *primary research* and *secondary research*. Primary research is collecting data or information first hand, and secondary research is collecting and using data which has been collected for some other purpose and is therefore already available. This is often referred to as *desk research*. Some sources of primary data which can be useful for businesses are:

- Monthly digest of statistics gives details of consumer expenditure in different categories.
- Social Trends (HMSO)
- Family Expenditure Survey (HMSO)
- Census Data (HMSO)
- Trade press
- Mintel or other reports

Primary research can be divided into two categories: *quantitative research* and *qualitative research*. There is a fundamental difference between the purposes of these two types of research which determine the research methods used. Quantitative research aims to find out **how many** people act in certain ways whereas qualitative research aims to find out **why** people act in certain ways. Often a mixture of qualitative and quantitative research needs to be used to find out the required information.

### QUANTITATIVE TECHNIQUES

Quantitative techniques are aimed at finding out

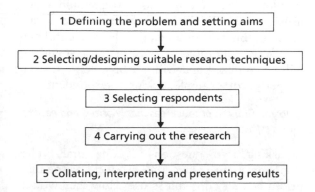

**Fig 7.8 The marketing research process**

how many people buy a certain brand or shop at a particular place, or have seen a certain advert. *Direct observation* and the *questionnaire* are the main methods used. Questionnaires can be sent through the post, conducted by telephone or face to face, and can include rating scales for measuring attitude. Questionnaires are useful because you can obtain a lot of information through them, but can be difficult to design.

## Direct observation

Simply observing and counting how many is a useful method but takes quite a lot of time. An example of direct observation is a customer count – how many buy, where they pass, how many look in a particular shop window, how many pick up a product, how many people pass a particular spot.

## Questionnaires

1 **Face-to-face.** Because the research is done face to face you can get more information from the respondent; but it is easy for a respondent to refuse and give an excuse. It is worth remembering that some people do not have time to stop and answer questions, and others may not wish to. This should be respected.

2 **Postal.** Questionnaires can be sent through the post. Mailing lists giving names and addresses of potential customers can be purchased. The response rate of postal questionnaires is poor, although reminders can be sent to increase the response rate. It can be helpful to phone and check that your questionnaire has been received as a memory jogger. Research shows that if you enclose a stamp and an addressed envelope rather than an SAE, the response rate is increased substantially; the reason given is that the respondent has to stick the stamp on themselves and then feels guilty if they do not return the questionnaire because the stamp can be used for something else. Increasingly, companies are using the Business Reply Service which obviates the need for stamps.

3 **Telephone.** Questionnaires conducted by telephone can be relatively cheap provided the calls are local calls and not long distance. The respondent however can easily put the phone down. Bias can occur because not everyone has a telephone and some numbers are ex-directory.

When *designing* a questionnaire, it is important to be very clear about what information you want to collect, and what it will be used for. When you have established this, write it down in a list to refer back to. Then prepare your questions to collect the desired information.

The number of questions should be kept to a minimum because if there are too many questions your respondent (i.e. the interviewee) will not spare the time to take part in the survey. The number of questions will obviously depend on the information you want to collect, this is why you need to set out the information before you even start to write the questions and consider how you will use the information. If you collect information which is of no use you have less space and time to collect the information which you can make use of. You should avoid asking questions which require the respondent to remember facts which happened a long time ago, because the memory can fade and you may be given inaccurate responses.

Your questions should be:

- as *short* as possible
- *clearly worded*
- *simple* to understand.

You should not ask long questions or by the time your respondent has heard the ending they will have forgotten the beginning. The wording should be clear and, therefore, you should avoid using words which are ambiguous and mean different things to different people. Be careful not to ask two questions at once or the respondent will be confused and will not be able to answer properly, for example, asking a respondent:

*Do you find the product reasonably priced and easy to use? Yes/No*

is asking two questions at one time. The respondent may find the product reasonably priced but very difficult to use. How then would they reply?

Questions asked can by categorised as:

- open or closed
- leading questions
- probe questions
- direct and indirect

## Open and closed questions

Often you will need to find out the language and opinion of customers without putting words into their mouths. *Open questions* are used for this purpose. You do not give the respondent categories of responses but let them answer the question posed in their own words and then write down the answer in the words the respondent has used. For example:

*Why do you go to the Palace nightclub?*

*Closed questions* occur when you provide a number of possible answers to the question. The respondent then chooses his answer from among the alternatives you have given, for example:

*How often do you borrow books from the library?*

*(a) weekly*
*(b) fortnightly*
*(c) monthly*
*(d) other (please specify)*

Closed questions can be easy to analyse because you can easily calculate how many people borrow books from the library weekly, monthly and so on. But difficulties can arise because you may miss out some of the categories which may be important, for example, in the above case many people may borrow books approximately every three weeks or every two months or three months. It is usual to include an 'other' category to take account of possibilities you may have missed but if you have too many categories the respondent in a face-to-face interview will forget them. You can carry out preliminary research to find out the type of responses you are likely to get before you decide on your categories by using open questions e.g. you may ask people:

*How often do you borrow books from the library?*

If many people respond by saying 'once a year' then you could add this in as a category.

## Leading questions

You need to avoid using leading questions at all costs, not just in questionnaires but in other research methods. Leading questions occur when the question is presented in such a way that the expected answer is indicated. For example:

*You enjoyed your meal, didn't you?*

This is a leading question because it is phrased in such a way as to tell the respondent that the interviewer wants him to answer 'Yes'. Quite often in marketing research the respondent will tell the researcher what he thinks the researcher wants to hear and asking leading questions will encourage respondents to do just that.

## Probe questions

You may wish to take the respondent's answer a stage further and probe questions enable you to find out more by going deeper. For example:

*Can you tell me why this happens?*

## Direct and indirect questions

A direct question is straightforward with no ulterior motive, e.g.

*Do you drink instant coffee? Yes/No*

Sometimes, however, respondents may not be willing to tell you the answer to your question because they may feel embarrassed or emotional. In these circumstances indirect questions can be asked to alleviate the problem and allow the respondent to safely answer the question. Indirect questions are based on projective techniques, such as the third party tests described below. For example:

*What reasons may people have for not buying instant coffee?*

The question is not about the respondent but about some other third party.

Carry out the activity below in order to see the problems which badly written questionnaires can cause and to learn how to design good questionnaires by putting some of the advice given above into practice.

---

# QUESTIONNAIRE

Dear Client

In order to improve the service we provide for you we would greatly appreciate it
if you would kindly complete this short questionnaire and give it to the receptionist
as you leave the restaurant.

1  Did you feel the service and food met your expectations?
     YES            NO

2  Would you say the meal was value for money?
     YES            NO

3  How often have you visited the restaurant?

4  Why did you first visit the restaurant?

5  Would you recommend the restaurant to your friends?

6  Do you regularly have meals in restaurants?

Thank you for your help.

---

**Fig 7.9 An example of a badly worded questionnaire**

---

## ACTIVITY

**(a)** Read the questionnaire shown in Fig 7.9 and note any problems which respondents may have when answering.
**(b)** Redesign it to improve it by using the guidelines and information given above.

## Rating scales

Businesses need to keep in touch with their customers' attitudes towards their products and services, and there are various ways in which this can be done. They could use a projective technique, like the ones described above, or they can use rating scales which can be used on their own or incorporated into a questionnaire. Two types of rating scales which are of particular use are:

1  *Likert scale*
2  *Semantic differential scale.*

The Likert scale provides a series of statements and respondents are asked to what extent they agree with the statement. For example:

| Statement | Strongly Agree | Agree | Disagree | Strongly Disagree |
|---|---|---|---|---|
| 1 The meals served in the restaurant offer value for money. | | | | |
| 2 The service provided was excellent | | | | |

A semantic differential scale gives the respondent a set of terms and the respondent is asked to rate where their opinion lies on the scale, as shown below:

> Please indicate your attitude to your visit to Wheelsmiths Ltd by putting an 'x' in the appropriate place on the scale below.
>
> Very enjoyable __ Very boring __
>
> Very education __ Not very educational __
>
> Very worthwhile __ Not very worthwhile __

These rating scales are used to measure attitudes and can be analysed simply by calculating how many people responded in different ways.

## Qualitative research techniques

Qualitative techniques can help to find out **why** customers like or dislike your products. They allow you to find out their language so that you can make use of it to promote your product. They help you to find out information about your target market which you could not obtain from using quantitative techniques. Many of the techniques used have been derived from clinical psychology. Some of the more common ones are:

- sentence completion
- word association
- in depth discussions
- third party.

Each of these techniques are explained below.

**1 Sentence completion.** The respondents are given the beginning of a sentence and are asked to complete it. For example:

*'I think ice-cream Mars Bars are..........'*

*'I like shopping at Tesco's because..........'*

*'Bounty Bars taste special because .........'*

Respondents will complete the sentence in their own words, allowing the researcher to gain information which could not be gained through using quantitative techniques. The researcher can also find out the language used by respondents which can help with designing questionnaires or creating adverts. The researcher can find selling points for products, what attracts the customer to buy the product or their attitude to the product. You often find sentence completion coupled with a competition.

**2 Word association.** This can work in several ways. For example: the respondent can be asked to say the first word which comes to mind in response to a particular word said by the researcher; or, the researcher could ask respondents to say the first word that they think of when he says 'Sainsbury's' and the respondents would answer in turn. Respondents may give a range of answers, including 'food, food store, good value, queues, speed, good quality'.

The theory is that the respondents, saying the first word to mind, will give the salient points; i.e. what they actually feel about Sainsbury's based on their opinions. If, for example, many respondents simply said food, it could indicate that Sainsbury's was mainly thought of as a store in which to buy food rather than the many other products it sells. It could indicate that advertising may be necessary to stress the many types of products sold by Sainsbury's.

Word association can work in another way. Respondents can be given a set of cards, with each card containing a different word, and asked to look through the cards and select the terms which they feel best describe the product or service. So a researcher researching people's image of Sainsbury's could prepare a set of cards with a variety of words, e.g. upmarket, down market, value, quality, expensive and so on, and would ask the respondent to look through the cards and select the ones which they think best describe Sainsbury's. The researcher then notes the answers. This can be taken a stage further to enable comparison of perceived image by asking the respondents to select words which best describe a competitor, e.g. Tesco.

**3 In-depth discussions.** These can be carried out either on an individual basis or on a group basis.

On an individual basis they are like personal interviews where the researcher asks the respondent questions and discusses points in some detail to find out the required information. Group discussions, also called focus groups, have advantages over the individual discussion in that a group can obtain more ideas and there is a snowball effect in that one person's response can spark off ideas in other participants. In-depth discussions can elicit useful information but take a skilled researcher. They normally take place in an environment like the sitting room in someone's home so that the respondents feel comfortable and at their ease.

**4 Third party.** There are several variations of this technique but they are all based on the same philosophy. It is difficult to get people to talk about some subjects and give their true opinions. The third-party techniques are designed to overcome these problems by introducing a third party and focusing the research on them. For example, a very famous piece of research was carried out many years ago which helped to establish third party as a qualitative research technique:

---

### CASE STUDY

#### The situation

*When instant coffee was first introduced into the market it did not sell. When asked why they did not buy it, respondents said they did not like the taste but this information clashed with research carried out during the test market stage.*

#### The research technique

*A special technique was devised, known as the **shopping list** technique, to try to uncover the real reason why the instant coffee did not sell. The technique was very simple. Two shopping lists were drawn up, identical in every way except that one shopping list itemised instant coffee and the other fresh ground coffee. One hundred respondents were divided into two groups of fifty and one group was given the shopping list itemising the instant coffee, whilst the other was given the list itemising the fresh ground coffee. The respondents were asked to describe the person who wrote the shopping list.*

#### Results

*The results obtained were that the respondents who had the shopping list itemising the fresh ground coffee described the person as caring, hard working and family orientated; while the respondents who had the lists itemising the instant coffee described the shopper as uncaring and lazy.*

When people were asked why they did not buy the instant coffee they were not willing to say 'I wouldn't like people to think I'm lazy' or 'because it would make me feel lazy' so they simply said 'I don't like the taste'. The research technique required the respondents to describe the kind of person who bought instant coffee – it didn't ask them about themselves at all. The introduction of this third party allowed the respondents to give honest answers.

Other third-party techniques include:

- telling a story, where respondents are given a picture and asked to describe what is happening to the person in the picture.
- cartoons, where situations or cartoons are presented and respondents are asked to fill in the bubble.

There are, however, many more techniques – they are really only limited to the researcher's imagination.

## SELECTING RESPONDENTS

Who will you involve in your survey? Sometimes the target market is too large to include everyone in your survey and therefore a sample of people are included. If the target market is small you could use the whole population. Selecting your sample is very important because your research needs to have validity. You need to be able to take the results and say that they are representative of the whole population and that you can, therefore, draw valid conclusions. The smaller the sample the quicker the data is to collect – and the cheaper. The total population is called the *sampling frame*. There are several types of sampling but the choice depends on the type and reason for the research and the aims of the research.

One method of sampling is a *random sample*, where each person has an equal chance of being included in the survey. If you had a big hat, and the names of all the people, you could put all the names in the hat and pick them out at random; thus each person would have an equal chance of being chosen. Since, in many cases, it is impossible to know the names of the people *random number tables* are used, which are found in statistical tables. To read the tables you can begin anywhere on the table and go up, down or across to get the number. Random numbers can be generated by computers.

It is possible that some people will refuse to take part in the survey and you would need to ask the next person. This will reduce the validity.

### Systematic sampling

You decide to take a sample of 500 out of a population of 20 000 which is a ratio of 1 to 40. Choose the first sample member at random and then every 40th until you total 500. So, if you were conducting your research into a mini business to set up in college using this method you would stand in a suitable location and choose a college user to question at random, and then stop the 40th person passing by and question them, and then the next 40th and so on until you have asked 500 people. The problem of people refusing to answer is the same as that with the random sample but is treated in the same way. If someone refuses to participate just ask the next available person.

### Stratified random sampling

The population is divided into strata; for example different ages, income, social class, geographical location and then a random sample is taken from each strata.

### Cluster sampling

This is normally restricted to particular geographical areas and then a random sample is taken. The results will be valid for the areas sampled but great care should be taken if reading more into these results – you cannot make predictions about the whole country based on samples in specific areas.

### Judgement sampling

With this method you decide on your sample in the way you think fit. You may choose certain people because they are available. This is only used when a more structured sample is not available for some reason, such as lack of time.

### Quota sampling

You obtain a breakdown of the total population by categories, e.g. age, sex, income and then make your sample have the same proportion of people in each category as is found in the total sample. You, therefore, have a quota or number of people to include in the survey in different categories, for example *x* number of females, aged between 18–24, in a certain income bracket.

## CARRYING OUT THE RESEARCH

The research should be carried out by trained researchers who are well briefed on the techniques to be used, sample required etc. In-depth interviews take very skilled researchers but even researchers carrying out face-to-face interviews require training. The researcher needs to take care not to imply the answers he/she expects the respondent to say.

## COLLATING, INTERPRETING AND PRESENTING RESULTS

### Collating results

You can use tally sheets to collate data. For example if you wished to record the number of people using a service between the following hours:

(a) 9.00–9.59
(b) 10.00–10.59
(c) 11.00–11.59
(d) 12–1 pm

Your tally chart would look like that shown in Fig 7.10.

| Time | Number of people |
|------|------------------|
| (a) 9.00–9.59 | ⊞ ⊞ |
| (b) 10.00–10.59 | ⊞ ⊞ ⊞ ⊞ ⊞ |
| (c) 11.00–11.59 | ⊞ ⊞ ⊞ |
| (d) 12–1 pm | ⊞ ⊞ ⊞ |

**Fig 7.10  A tally chart**

The fifth tally is used to cross out the previous four – this makes it easy to add up the totals.

You can use computer programs to help you with the collation.

## Analysing results

Once results have been obtained and aggregated in some way they need to be interpreted. In some cases the results are self-evident: if 79 per cent of your respondents have told you that the reason they did not rebuy a particular brand of cat food was because it made their cats ill you can draw fairly obvious conclusions from this. In other cases the results will not be as clear cut as this and there are a wide range of very sophisticated statistical techniques which can be called into play to decide what is and what is not significant in particular results. These packages are often computer based and allow for the quick analysis of information and the presentation of the findings in a convenient and professional form.

## Presenting findings

It is usual to present your findings in report format with graphs and charts shown in the appendices. You could use a computer to help with the presentation of the report by word processing written work and using a suitable package to produce charts and graphs contained in the appendices.

---

### ACTIVITY
#### (Research methods)

As part of BTEC National courses in Business and Finance, many centres ask full-time students to set up mini businesses or run young enterprise activities. Some decisions, which conducting marketing research can help to make, are:

1 Who will our customers be?
2 What kind of products will we sell?
3 Will we offer a service? If so, what kind?
4 What will the opening times be?
5 Where will the business be located?
6 Where will we get stock from?
7 How much will we charge?
8 What will we call the business?
9 How do we promote the business?

What kind of research methods would you use to collect this information?

| Information | Method | Reason for choice |
|-------------|--------|-------------------|
|             |        |                   |

---

## Marketing consultants

So far in this unit we have assumed that you will be undertaking marketing activities yourself. This is often not the case and there are a wide range of businesses concerned with providing marketing services and information to businesses of all types. Some of the services which they offer and the advantages of using them are discussed in this section.

Many organisations engage consultancy firms and specialist organisations to carry out marketing activities. The services of these consultancy firms are offered to all kinds of organisations – small local organisations, large multinational companies, public and local authorities. Ex-Prime Minister, Mrs Thatcher, hired the services of an advertising agency to help her project the required image.

There are specialist firms offering consultancy in and the provisions of:

● Marketing research
● Advertising and promotions

- Public relations
- Training in telephone skills.

Among the advantages of hiring outside help is that you are hiring specialist expertise with knowledge of the market. Below are some examples of the type of services offered.

---

### EXAMPLE 1

---

**John Arden Research Associates,** *a partnership offering marketing research services, list the following features about their service.*

- *We have a great deal of experience in many different consumer and business markets, products and services, foods and non-foods, from sweets to new houses!*
- *We are professional members of the Market Research Society, with commitment to the highest quality standards.*
- *The research methods we use are all tailormade to each particular situation. They range from short street interviews to in-depth consumer and group interviewing. They also include desk and library research from existing published sources and telephone market research.*
- *We have our own internal IBM/Tandon Marquis specialist survey analysis computer facilities which are being consistently upgraded and improved.*

The advantages of using a marketing research consultancy offering services, like the one described above, are that the staff are professionally qualified in marketing research, have lots of experience, know the markets, and have appropriate computer facilities.

---

### EXAMPLE 2

---

*British Telecom offers several marketing services to business, one of which is a special consultancy service called **PhonePower**, which helps businesses to improve telephone communications. The consultants at PhonePower can work with firms to help them to use the telephone for:*

- *Advertising and promotions*
- *Marketing research*
- *Improved customer service*
- *Selling*
- *Dealing with complaints*

*In addition to the consultancy services PhonePower offers a Training Service.*
*British Telecom provides a marketing service, **British Telecom Telephone Marketing Services**, which is one of the largest marketing agencies in the country and a telephone research agency, **The Research Shop**.*

### Example 3
*Prontaprint offers printing, copying, art and design which can help businesses. They can produce all kinds of promotional material – business cards, leaflets, multicoloured brochures, forms and posters and computer stationery, for example they use the latest computerised techniques, including desktop publishing, to ensure professional results.*

---

## Advertising agencies

There are numerous advertising agencies whose services are employed by many types of organisation to help with PR activities and advertising campaigns. Advertising agencies can employ a range of staff who play various roles in putting the advert together. There are many different roles, and all of them important but some of the roles below will give you an idea of the type of specialist staff employed by advertising agencies. Obviously in a small agency more than one role will be carried out by a member of staff.

1 An *Account Team*, which collects information about your firm, the product, the market segment and your competitors.
2 A *Creative and Media Department*, which works with the Account Team to decide on the details of the campaign.
3 A *Creative Team* consists of a Copywriter and Art Director. The copywriter is responsible for deciding on the slogans and headlines and the art director sketches the way the advert will look.
4 An *Illustrator*, who prepares a finished rough to show the client (the firm hiring the services of the advertising agency) for their approval.
5 A *Typographer*, who selects the typefaces to be used and orders the typesetting.

6 An *Art buyer,* who commissions professional photographers and graphic artists.

7 *Media planners,* who prepares schedules for newspaper advertisements and television commercials.

There are also firms specialising in **pubic relations**. They make sure that your company's name gets in the public eye and organise promotional activities including exhibitions, advertising and press coverage.

A full range of **freelance services**, such as artwork and design, photography, copywriting etc. are offered by individuals on a local basis.

---

## ACTIVITY

### Help from outside

(a) Look in the *Yellow Pages* to find the names and addresses of firms offering consultancy and marketing services.

(b) Write or telephone for information about their services.*

(c) Make a list of the full services on offer.

(d) How can organisations benefit from using these services?

*If you are using this information for discussion in class, only one person in the group need send for the information.

# 8

# BUSINESS INNOVATION

The aims of this unit are to:

- understand the forces which make organisations change.
- predict the changes which a given organisation will need to make if it is to prosper, or indeed survive.
- research, using available sources of information, the trends affecting organisations at the moment.
- outline the problems of managing change and techniques to make this easier in organisations.
- look at the process of innovation and the problems firms have in getting hold of and making the best use of new products/ideas.
- consider the effect that change in a business has on the people who work in the business and the community it is a part of.

## Introduction: what is business innovation?

This unit is concerned with innovation and change. Innovation is the process whereby something genuinely new is taken from the stage of being just an idea to actually working as a fully fledged (and probably profitable) product. This could be a new product, a new way of doing things or a new idea, and many organisations spend a lot of their time and money on the research and development of new products/services/systems so that they can keep ahead of the competition. A good idea has to be tested to make sure that it is workable; it has to be tried out on potential buyers to make sure they want it and it has to be put into a form where it can be handled easily and, in the case of a product,

produced easily and as quickly and cheaply as possible. And, once something has been taken through this process and is a success, you then have to start looking for the next product, or new idea in order to keep ahead.

Change is the process of adapting the organisation to what is going on around it. All organisations have to face change for much of the time. The changes they have to face come from all sorts of pressures and areas and mean they have to keep track of what they need to do, plan for it, make sure that it goes according to plan and ensure that it has worked properly. The main pressures on businesses to change can be sorted into six categories:

**1 Social**: i.e. What is going on in society. If there is a high proportion of older people in a country (as is happening in many countries in Europe at the moment) then a business may have an opportunity to sell specifically to them – holidays perhaps, or a magazine about retirement.

**2 Legal**: new laws imposing new duties or opening up new opportunities – new laws recently passed have meant that anyone who cares for children as a business have to meet a lot of very strict rules under the Children Act – childminders for instance have had to buy fire equipment and first aid kits which is a cost to them but an opportunity for manufacturers of these things.

**3 Physical**: i.e. change in the physical environment in which a business works; a factory may now be too small for a growing business or a new road may mean that what was a good site for passing trade is now too quiet.

**4 Technical**. Changes in technology mean that

there are always new and better ways to do some jobs; so a firm using a computer for desktop publishing may want to get a new and faster computer, a more sophisticated piece of software or a colour printer in order to keep up to date or get ahead of the competition.

**5 Economic**: i.e. what is happening in the economy. If there is a recession this makes things hard for many businesses and they may see sales fall; this may mean that they have to lose staff, cut costs or sell assets to make ends meet.

**6 Political**. Political decisions often cause change for businesses – for instance the decision to become a part of Europe and join the EC has had a lot of effect on many UK businesses and will continue to do so in the future.

These pressures for change will mean that organisations have to adapt and cope with what is thrown at them. Some of the changes they will be able to see coming and will be able to plan for, but others will arrive suddenly and the organisation will have to cope with them as best as they can in the time available. Many of the larger organisations in both business and government spend much time and money to try to find out what is going on in the world around them so they have time to plan for change – this helps them to have as many facts as possible to work with and also helps them to make the best decisions they can in the circumstances.

Once an organisation has decided what they need to do to cope with change they will have to decide how best to go about making the changes which they need to make. This process can be very difficult as most people don't like change and would often prefer to keep things as they are rather than try something new which they feel may not work – as the saying goes 'If it ain't broke; don't fix it.' In order to bring in the desired changes, an organisation will have to work out the best way to do so which will help people to adjust. This process, which is often referred to as *Managing Change*, is very important, and organisations which do it well have a big advantage over those who don't.

Innovation and change go together as topics very naturally – any new idea or product that an organisation takes up will mean that there has to be change; from the retooling of a production line to the purchase of a different computer system. This will have an effect on the people in the organisation, and the change will have to be managed effectively. Equally, change in the world outside the organisation may provide the basis for innovation in the business, so the invention of the microprocessor and the opportunities presented by computers have been the basis for many good ideas and products. The stricter environmental controls recently brought in have pressed businesses to find ways of saving energy and recycling waste. Innovation means that there has to be change and change provides the opportunity for innovation. One thing is certain, any organisation which doesn't change to meet the world around it and which ignores innovations will not survive. Those who plan ahead, who manage change well and who innovate carefully – choosing the best to use and develop – will not only succeed, they will flourish.

This unit will now look at the forces which may influence an organisation to change, the information available to businesses to find out what is happening and the process of managing change. It will also look at the process of innovation and the way organisations go about getting hold of new ideas and the process of taking a good idea to the stage of being something the organisation can really use. It will draw heavily on the other areas of the book and you will have already learnt quite a lot about some of the topics covered in this unit.

## Pressures for change

All organisations constantly face change. There are some minor changes such as new forms to be completed or a new security system to be used; and there are major changes such as the relocation of a business to a new base. Some changes seem minor to people at one level of the organisation but more important to others: the directors may not be as concerned about the rise in price of food in the canteen as the rest of the workforce, and some changes, such as people leaving and new ones arriving, will only affect a relatively small number of people. This unit is mainly concerned with the changes which are forced on the business from outside and the way in which the business plans to cope with them so as to make the best they can from the situation.

As outlined above, any organisation has a number of different factors affecting it and, for convenience, this text has used the headings:

1 Social
2 Legal
3 Physical
4 Economic
5 Technical
6 Political

All of these have been discussed in other units and so this section does not attempt to deal with every detail about all of these areas, but rather, to look at the key factors in each of them which will cause a business or organisation to change.

At the end of this section of the unit there is an activity which asks you to analyse the environment for a particular business and make predictions about how this particular business/industry is going to develop and change in the future. Having completed this you may then be able to make some constructive suggestions as to how particular businesses within this industry should develop if they want to survive and be successful.

## SOCIAL PRESSURES

In any society there is constant change and businesses need to adapt to this if they are going to survive. Some of the changes in our society are fairly easy to see, they are common knowledge and people tend to take them for granted; some are very sudden and have to be adapted to very quickly; yet others are slow changes which can easily be missed if you are not paying a lot of attention to the environment around your business/organisation. There are a number of key areas which you need to look at to identify the changes in society which may affect a particular business.

- *Demographic* change: the structure of the population and the way that it is divided up
- Changes in *tastes and fashions*

- Changes in the *patterns of work*. There has been a move towards more flexible working hours and times, and this has meant that many people have free time when they would not have done and have ceased to have free time at the 'traditional' times of the week.
- Change in the way that *people spend their time*: as a society we are far more leisure conscious than we used to be and spend more money on leisure pursuits.

One example of an industry that has had to deal with a lot of social change is the football industry – below is a table listing some of the changes that have taken place in society and the effect these have had on the football industry over the years.

**Changes in the football industry**

| Change | Effect |
|---|---|
| Increasing population | Potentially more spectators to come to games – and potentially more money |
| People moving to live away from town centres | People are not so close to the grounds and drive in for matches. This causes parking and traffic problems. |
| Increased TV ownership | People can watch matches on the TV and may, if the weather is poor or tickets costly, think this is a better alternative to going to the ground |
| Flexible working hours | Many people are working at the times games are played |
| Change in women's role in society | Women are less likely to automatically accept the absence of their husbands/boyfriends for the duration of the match |
| People are more health conscious | They may, therefore, be more likely to play sports than watch them |
| More leisure pursuits available | So people have a choice of things to do and, with increasing car ownership, can get to many different places |
| Fear of violence and hooliganism | Many people have an image of football matches as dangerous for families and so will not want to take children to some games. |

## ACTIVITY

**1** Look at the local community and the businesses working in it. Can you find ones that reflect the changes which have been listed in the table below as occurring in our society. One example has been completed to give you a start:

| Change | Business example |
| --- | --- |
| People working different hours | Supermarkets open late and on Sundays. |
| Ageing population | |
| More interest in sport | |
| Fashion changing fast | |
| More car ownership | |

Can you list any other changes with business examples of how firms have responded to the change; or can you find other examples as well as the ones you have listed above?

**2** For an industry of your choice construct a table like the one for football above. In constructing the table try to talk to people who work in the industry to get their views.

## LEGAL PRESSURES

There are many areas where the law of the country will have an effect on businesses and force them to take certain actions. There are a number of possible reasons for this:

- *Health and safety* – where the activities of the business could damage people or the environment. The Health and Safety at Work Act is an example of this sort of control on businesses.
- *Financial* – to ensure that the business contributes to the running of the state. Tax statutes to make companies pay tax on their profits are of this type.
- *Social good* – to make sure that businesses operate in a way which makes for a fairer or better society. Equal opportunities rules are an example of this sort of law.
- *Consumer protection* – there is a large body of law which is aimed at the protection of

consumers of goods and services, both in terms of making sure that the goods and services provided are safe and that the consumers are not being disadvantaged by the organisation's treatment of them – the Sale of Goods Act and the Consumer Credit Act are examples of this sort of legal pressure on business.

The legal pressure on businesses is constantly changing and the law has to adapt to make sure that the legal control of businesses has kept pace with social change and other pressures for change. Legal pressures are very often the result of other pressures as illustrated in the example below:

## EXAMPLE

*'After the Bradford fire (in 1986) there was a lot of concern in the football world about the issue of safety. Politicians on all sides said that it was something that needed to be sorted – and quickly. There was a high level of social concern with many parents refusing to allow children to go to matches in case the same thing happened in another stadium. The effect of this was to create a political pressure for some sort of control on the construction of the stadia and to ensure that there were precautions to try to prevent the same sort of tragedy recurring. The result of this political pressure was direct legislation which forced the clubs to take all sorts of extra precautions.'*

This can be summarised, as shown in Fig 8.1.

The law is always changing and developing to make sure that businesses are regulated. Current concerns are many and there are always new laws which businesses have to respond to. Key areas of concern recently have been:

- Control of pollution
- Consumer safety
- Frauds involving limited companies
- Regulation of the banking/financial services sector

and there has been specific action in all of these areas over the last few years. There are also gradual changes to the law all the time in order to keep it up to date with new developments in the way that businesses operate. Where there is

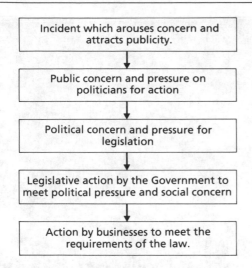

Fig 8.1 An example of legal pressure on business

a key development in technology there will also probably be some control of it at some point; for example, the practice of holding data on people on computer has been regulated by the Data Protection Act. One major influence on the law in the United Kingdom at the moment which results in businesses having to adapt to meet changes in the law results from our membership of the European Community.

When we joined the European Community we committed ourselves to having laws which are similar in many areas to those in other European countries – some of the Equal Opportunities laws we have are, for example, a direct result of our being a part of the European Community. There have been many other changes which have been made in order to bring the law in this country into line with the law in other European countries so that our businesses can trade more easily with Europe. The main areas where this has taken place include:

1 **Control of the standards** businesses operate to in making goods. It used to be the case that every country in Europe had a different set of rules for how goods had to be made. Children's toys for instance were subject to different safety rules in almost all countries. This meant that manufacturers had to produce lots of different versions of toys; one to be sold in each country. With the 'harmonisation' of the law there is now an EC standard for the production of toys and a toy made to this standard can be sold in any EC country without any modification. This has made it easier for companies to trade in all areas of the EC and has allowed firms to compete in markets they hadn't bothered with before because of the cost of meeting the regulations.

2 **Controls on the way companies run** have also been subject to the process of harmonisation to make sure that companies and businesses have to be run to similar standards in each country of the EC. The intention of this is to simplify the process of setting up businesses in other countries and to make sure that something which is legal in one country in the way a business runs is not illegal in another.

3 There have also been **controls on the way in which businesses treat employees** – many of our laws on Equal Opportunities are a result of this area of EC harmonisation and we have, for example, recently signed an agreement which will take maternity benefits in this country closer to those available in other countries. In this area many of the rules were set to a minimum standard and countries are free to go beyond the minimum if they want to. This way there is a basic level which people can rely on in all countries, but they may get even better treatment or rights in some.

4 **Controls on the way businesses operate**. Such controls include the Data Protection Act – which is designed to prevent businesses abusing the power and access to information which computers and databases give them. There have also been measures to protect consumers by increasing the rules on safety of products and services.

There is a section which gives an introduction to the way English law works in Unit 4 if you need to revise this (*see* pp 155–65).

Businesses claim that there are a number of problems which they face with legal changes:

● The changes required are very often so expensive as to make firms borrow more, or, in extreme cases, go out of business.

**The European Parliament, Strasbourg**

- The changes may be made at short notice and businesses may not be able to adapt to them in time.
- The businesses may not be aware of small changes to the law and will be in the position of breaking the law as a result of ignorance. Unfortunately a court does not necessarily accept this as an excuse – the old maxim which states that 'Ignorance of the law is no excuse' still holds good today in our courts.
- Businesses claim that the changes forced on them by the law are very often not necessary for the vast majority of businesses and that honest businesses are being penalised as a result of the actions of a few dishonest or careless businesses. While this may be true in many cases there does not seem to be any other way to control businesses.
- There are also complaints that every change in the law makes life more complex for businesses and that the law should stay out of business as much as possible. One cabinet minister in the Conservative government once said 'The business of government is not the government of business', and this has been a reflection of the way many businesses see things as well.

ACTIVITY

**1** Look in your local papers and a national paper over a period of a week. Can you find any examples of businesses which have had to adapt to new legal requirements in any way?

**2** In your workplace or in a business with which you are familiar, try to find out what sorts of legal changes have affected the business over the last few years. Put the changes into the form of a table like the one below which has a couple of examples from the football industry filled in:

| Change | Effect |
| --- | --- |
| Legal requirement for all-seater stadia as a result of the Hillsborough disaster | Very high conversion costs for a lot of clubs which they have had to pass on to supporters in the form of ticket prices. Capacity of ground reduced so gate income falls. |
| Laws requiring increased levels of fire safety and general safety in grounds as a result of the Bradford disaster. | Costly changes to ground and, for some clubs a loss of income as the alterations were made and the stadia were out of use. Again, the cost of the changes has had to be passed on to supporters in the form of higher ticket prices. |

## PHYSICAL PRESSURES

Many industries are located in specific places as a result of the physical properties of the area.

- Historically Lancashire became the centre of the cotton industry because it was damp and this helped with the spinning of the cotton
- Manufacturing businesses sprang up near seaports so that goods could be transported easily
- Vineyards are located in the south of the country where the climate is better for this crop
- Coal pits are located where there is coal at a level and in a place where it can easily be extracted.

These physical pressures on a business as to where it should locate are still important today. Many of the pressures on businesses as to where they locate have been dealt with in Unit 6 Physical Resources and it would be easy to assume that, once the correct location for a business has been found that is the end of the matter. In fact, the physical environment for businesses and the appropriateness of a particular location will also vary over time. The pressures may not be as obvious as legal controls on business or changes in taste and fashion but they are still important as the example below shows:

### EXAMPLE

*'We set up in the old factory about twenty years ago – it was a good location at the time, close to the town and it allowed us to get lorries in easily. Over time the area became more built up and there was a lot of housing put up in the vicinity. This meant that there was more traffic and we had to control the times lorries could arrive and leave because of complaints from people living locally. The final straw was when they tried to limit lorry movements even further because of the danger to children playing on the roads and got a lot of publicity in the local press. This did us no good at all and was really unfair; we had limited movements voluntarily and had made all drivers aware of the problem. Besides, we were here first! We moved to this new factory about 18 months ago. It's a really good site now although we would never have looked at it before they put the new motorway in. With the motorway there have been a lot*
*of people moving out here and there is quite a good local market. We have no problem with access now and can save time as we're well out of town and the lorries don't have to deal with town traffic.'*

This is an example of change in the physical environment for the business. Better communications, a change in the location of the market and difficulty in gaining access to the old site have all meant that there is now a good site in what was previously a poor location. These sorts of decisions are often also made on the grounds of cost and it is one of the benefits of new towns and out of town industrial sites that they are cheaper than premises in town centres or near to main population centres.

### ACTIVITY

What has changed in the physical environment for business in your local area? Compile the results onto a table and state what sorts of businesses will have benefited from the change and which will have suffered as a result. You may want to talk to local businesses, employers or local authority personnel to get some ideas from them. (Many local authorities produce material which sells the benefits of the area and lists some of the innovations and changes in it – this can be a good source of ideas.) An example has been started to give you the idea:

| Change | Effect | Business example |
| --- | --- | --- |
| Pedestrianised town centre | More shoppers using the centre during the day. Attracts people from out of town. | Town centre shops have gained. Outlying shops have lost out as have some other Towns' shops. |
| New motorway past the town. | Faster to get to places. More businesses moving in. More people commuting from here to jobs in other towns. | Local firms have seen rents rise. Has attracted new businesses to set up here and employ local people because of cheaper rents than in existing areas. |

## ECONOMIC PRESSURES

The economy affects the way businesses operate. As discussed in Unit 4, the economy tends to be cyclical and there are times of boom followed by times of slump. The times when these will occur are hard to predict and many businesses find that they are not well prepared to cope with either of them. There is a number of key areas of the economy which businesses need to look at if they are to try to cope with the pressures for change which the economy faces them with.

1 Exchange rates
2 Inflation
3 Unemployment
4 Recession/boom

### Exchange rates

These are very important to any business which either imports or exports goods or services. They are only marginally less important to businesses which don't directly export or import as changes in the prices of goods they buy here will also be determined partly by exchange rates. When the exchange rate for the pound drops against other currencies this will have three main effects:

1 It will make it more expensive for a UK firm to buy goods from abroad; this in turn will mean that there are higher costs to be passed onto customers, so a fall in exchange rates will mean an increase in prices here.
2 It will make UK goods more attractive to foreign buyers (in the short term at least) and there will be the chance to sell more to the export market as the prices of our goods fall relative to the prices of the goods sold by competition in countries with stronger currencies.
3 It will reduce the profit margins for the companies involved in the goods which they sell in the UK market – or mean that they have to increase their prices in order to maintain their profit margins.

Obviously, if exchange rates move the other way this will mean that the effects above are reversed: it will make components cheaper and help profit margins but will make it harder to sell to the export market.

One possible development which would reduce this pressure on firms is the advent of a single European currency. If this happens there will be far fewer currency transactions and, as much of our trade is with other EC countries for many transactions, the exchange risk will be removed. At the moment this seems to be quite a long way off but there is a great deal of pressure on the government from many areas of business and the community in this country and within the EC in general for there to be moves to a common currency.

If a business is to cope with the effects of a move in the exchange rate it needs to be able to predict how long the move will last. If there is a long-term change in the value of the pound the business will have to decide where it would like to concentrate its sales and how to adjust its prices. If there is a short-term move, however, the company may decide to 'wait and see' before making any decision. One problem with this is that it is difficult to determine whether any move in currency is a short-term one or is likely to be permanent.

### Inflation

The current government has put much time, effort and money into the reduction of inflation to a level similar to that of our major industrial competitors. The advantages of a low level of inflation are

● Certainty in prices for businesses
● Usually, a low level of interest rates
● Control of costs as price and wage rises are low.

Conversely, a business can have a number of quite severe problems in a time of high inflation:

● Wage costs are difficult to predict as salary and wage claims try to keep pace with the cost of living; this makes it hard for a business to be able to quote prices for any real length of time into the future.
● Increases in the costs of components and raw materials are frequent and unpredictable (they

are coping with inflation as well). This again makes it hard to know what the costs of the business are and what they will be in a few months' time. This in turn makes it even harder to be able to quote a firm price and be confident you can make a profit at that price

● Much management time is wasted in making sure that the business negotiates the best prices and that the wage and salary increases are negotiated. Time will have to be spent as well in trying to set prices.

● When coupled with the uncertainty of exchange rates there are all sorts of problems in providing prices for export markets.

A business which is trying to cope with a high level of inflation will find that a lot of the control which it would like to have over costs and prices is taken away from it by the process of inflation. Dealing with the effects of inflation on the business will take up valuable time and there will be an inevitable effect on orders as the business is unable to quote firm prices or has to pass cost increases on to customers – never a popular move.

There are countries in the world where inflation has reached such a serious level – known as '*hyper inflation*' – that there are constant price rises and businesses and individuals find it extremely hard to cope with the effect of this. The final effect of such a situation can be the total collapse of the economy, as happened in Germany before the Second World War when the currency inflated to the point where the economy reverted to barter and no-one had any faith in the money at all.

## Unemployment

Some level of unemployment is inevitable in any society with a market economy. In planned economies it is possible for there to be 100 per cent employment but in a market economy, such as that of the United Kingdom there will always be a level of unemployment for a number of reasons:

**1 Frictional unemployment** – people leaving one job and moving to another are unemployed during the time between leaving a first job and moving to another.

**2 Cyclical unemployment** – there are seasonal industries where there is a demand for workers at one point in the year and less of a demand later in the year. In theory someone who works in a bar job in a seaside resort in the summer could go and get a job in a ski resort in the winter. However, there are disadvantages to doing this, such as finding accommodation, and there will always be people who work for a part of the year but not for all of it.

**3 Structural unemployment** – there may be a demand for certain skills from businesses and relatively few people with those skills. There will then be a time lag while people are trained to do the jobs and, during this time there will be people without the skills to match the jobs which are on offer from businesses. Eventually there will be enough people trained to do the jobs and businesses will be able to attract people with the skills they need to work for them. The computer industry was an example of this. When computers first became a major part of business there was a very high demand for people with computer skills and relatively few people with the skills needed. Colleges and universities put on courses and people trained in these areas until there were enough people to do the jobs which businesses had on offer. In fact there were eventually more people with skills in these areas than there were jobs to go round.

In most of the industrialised economies of the world, including the UK's, there will always be a level of unemployment above the basic minimum. This is, in part, a result of the fact that there have been many moves to make businesses more efficient and to automate production. Unemployment is also a function of the economic policies of the government in power: if the government places a lot of emphasis, as the current government does, on the reduction of inflation this has the effect of slowing down the economy and reducing the amount of spending. This in turn has the effect of making businesses less busy and reducing the number of jobs available. Most economists would now agree that there is a direct link between keeping inflation low and a higher level of unemployment.

For a business there are advantages and disadvantages to both high and low levels of unemployment in the economy as shown below:

**Low levels of unemployment**

| Advantages | Disadvantages |
| --- | --- |
| A busy economy with people in work means more demand for goods | May find it hard to get staff to work for you if there are a lot of jobs |
| People will be concerned to get on in their jobs and work hard for promotions | May have to pay higher wages to attract people and keep them |
| Taxes may fall as there will be less of a call for public services and benefits | Poor employers will find it harder to retain staff who will go elsewhere for jobs. |

---

### ACTIVITY

Complete a similar table for high levels of unemployment. An example has been filled in as a start:

**High levels of unemployment:**

| Advantages | Disadvantages |
| --- | --- |
| Many people will apply for any job – no trouble getting staff | People may not feel it worthwhile to train and get qualifications if they fear there won't be any jobs to go to |

---

*Note*: you may need to have more space in the table you fill in, than shown in the table above.

---

A business will look at the levels of unemployment in the economy and this will be an influence on how they decide to recruit, train and retain staff. If they think that they will have no trouble attracting staff to work for them, and that this is likely to continue for the foreseeable future, this will probably have an effect on their policies in all sorts of areas of employment:

● Wage levels

● Benefits
● Training
● Length of contracts offered to staff.

If, on the other hand, they can see a time coming when there will not be enough people to go around the jobs they will have to offer – maybe because they are working in an area where there is a shortage of skilled people – they may choose to deal differently with staff in an attempt to try to keep them with the business as long as possible and to attract other people to want to work for the business as well. This is, in fact, a very good policy as, even in times when there are high levels of unemployment and it is easy to find people who want jobs, a good company which treats people well will have the pick of the very best staff and this will help to make the business more competitive and successful.

There are a lot of statistics available in the local area and nationally as to the state of the labour market: this information is often referred to as 'Labour Market Intelligence', or LMI for short. Good sources of information are the *Employment Gazette* and the local JobCentre. There are also computerised information services which your college or school may subscribe to and which will give you information on the labour market.

---

### ACTIVITY

Answer the following questions, with reference to your local area.

(a) What is the percentage of people unemployed in the region?

(b) What are the current areas of skill shortage (i.e. where there is a demand for people to do jobs and not enough people with the skills required to do them)?

(c) Are wage levels higher or lower than the National Average?

Try to find out the same information for a very different area and compare the two. So, if you live in a seaside resort in the South, try to compare with an industrial area in the North.

What differences can you see in the pictures you have formed of the two areas?

What effect would these differences have on employers in the two areas?

## Recession/boom

Any economy has times when the economy is doing well and times when things are harder. These times of boom and recession are a major determinant of the way in which businesses behave and they have very different effects on businesses.

*Boom times* are when the economy is doing well and there is a high level of demand. At times like this businesses are concerned with

- expansion
- with making enough products or providing enough services to satisfy demand
- finding new and innovative products as profit margins tend to be high.

Many businesses in a boom have the problem that they are not able to grow fast enough to meet the demand that they have available for their products. While boom times may also mean that there is a lot of competition and that good staff are hard to find and retain, most businesses would prefer this to the effects of a recession.

*Recessions* are times when the economy is not doing well. There will tend to be a high level of inflation and low demand for goods and services with money being scarce. At times like this businesses have a different set of problems:

- consumers will tend to be very careful with their money and will only buy what seems to be good value
- people are worried about losing their jobs and will have to be careful with purchases, so impulse buys are reduced and mainly necessities are purchased
- with low levels of demand comes the problem of having too many staff or too many premises – this may lead to the business having to reduce staff, cut costs and close offices/premises if they are to survive the reduced levels of demand for their goods.
- if a business is having real problems they may have to sell goods off cheap in order to get some money in. This will reduce their profits and mean they will find it hard to invest in growth if the business does pick up
- many businesses will cut costs in a recession by reducing expenses in areas where there is

little in the way of an immediate impact on the business – research and development, training, and public relations for example. The problem with doing this is that if business does pick up the firm will be badly placed to take advantage of it with poor publicity, a lack of trained staff and no new products to develop. So, a company may find that it survives a recession only to be wiped out by competitors who have kept these parts of their business going when things improve.

During all of the economic pressures, a business has to try to look ahead to predict what is going to happen in the economy so that they are best placed to take advantage of conditions which can help them and they are best prepared to cope with times which are likely to give them problems. The businesses which do this effectively will make the economic environment an input to their planning and they will try to turn potential problems to advantage: so, a luxury food retailer seeing a recession coming may make the decision to open a subsidiary of the company dealing with lower priced products which can be seen as better value. A company which expects unemployment to fall in the future so that staff are hard to find may want to take action now to be seen as a good employer with many benefits for staff so that they have an advantage in competing with other firms when staff are hard to find.

### ACTIVITY

Look at the national press over the period of a week and keep track of the information which suggests whether the economy is in a recession or in a boom and what the future might hold for it. When you have all of the information together write this up in the form of a report on the week and give your predictions for the economy based on what you have read and what the predictions in the papers have been.

You will find that the economics and finance pages of the papers have a lot of information and may also find magazines such as the *Economist* useful. There will also probably be some news in the more general sections of the paper.

If you can you should then compare your report with one produced by someone else.

**(a)** Did you find similar information?

**(b)** Have you made similar predictions for the economy over the next few months/years?

## TECHNICAL PRESSURES

Technology is one of the fastest changing areas in business at the moment and there are many examples of the way that technology has changed business.

---

### ACTIVITY

Read the case study below and identify the uses of technology which would not have been possible ten years ago.

'Vikki is the Marketing Manager for a national company specialising in selling office equipment and furniture. She was promoted to her present job where she is in charge of sales and marketing for the entire country two years ago and says she has never worked as hard in her life. On a typical day she will leave home at about 7.15 in the morning after checking the answerphone in the office (from her telephone) for any messages that have been left overnight from overseas customers. Her day will have been organised some time in advance but there are always problems to attend to at the last minute and she has recently had a portable phone installed in the car which she can take with her when she leaves the car so she can be contacted on the way to her first appointment. Her office (if she is actually going in to the company that day), is based in the company Head Office about 25 miles from where she lives and she can always contact her secretary, Pat, to see if anything urgent has come up. Any urgent documents can be faxed to her at home or at a client's number if she knows the client well enough and Pat knows when she will be there. She has recently started to use an electronic organiser when she is out of the office so that she can make use of the time in-between appointments to write up reports and check her schedule. It contains a great deal of information but she is not fully sure of everything it can do yet and hasn't really had the time to get to grips with it. One advantage of the organiser is that she can type reports and memos straight into it and either load them into her computer at home or send them down a phone link to the office with instructions to Pat on what she is to do with the information. She will usually try to spend at least half of the week out of the office seeing major customers and sorting out problems; this might be few full days or a half day every day of the week depending on where she is going.

One of the main problems she has had to deal with over the last week has been a fault in a batch of equipment delivered to a major customer. The company has recently invested in a computerised accounts system and the printers which were supplied to them will not work properly with the computers. Vikki has had the technical staff in over the weekend and is going to see the company herself this morning to make sure that everything is working properly. After this first visit she will drive up to see one of the company's suppliers who have recently installed a lot of computer controlled machinery on their production side. They claim it will allow them to custom make orders more easily and Vikki is interested in seeing the facility as it may be something she can promote to her clients. She will stay in a local hotel that night and use her portable computer to look over some reports on the performance of the company over the last year, as she has a report to finish for a board meeting the next week. Any documents which are not on disk can be faxed to her at the hotel or sent direct to her over a phone link to her computer. She has also got to look at the draft of some publicity material and send in any amendments so that the printers can change the specification if they need to; she already knows that she wants some of the background colours changing on some of the illustrations and has been told that this will not be a problem – it can be done quite quickly and easily on a colour laser copier.'

You should be able to identify many uses of technology here; a couple have been listed below to get you started:

- Portable phone communications
- Colour laser copiers
- 
- 

---

Changes in technology have given organisations all sorts of advances in a number of areas:

**1 Communications have been improved** and made more portable – it is now quite easy to be in touch with a business wherever you are. This includes portable phones, pagers and fax technology as well as modem (phone) links for computers.

**2 Production has been automated** and can be faster and more accurate in many areas than was possible when working manually. Computer-controlled machines are also more flexible and allow businesses to run small, specialist orders more efficiently.

**3 Administration of businesses has been aided by computers** and the use of them has allowed businesses to be more flexible in the way they operate

**4 Locations are no longer as important** to many businesses and there are businesses where people work from home and send information from computer to computer by phone links

**5 Businesses have access to a lot of information on computer databases** and computers give them the power to control and process the information very fast – this leads to fewer errors in the running of the business and increases the accuracy of the administration of the business. This area has now been controlled by the Data Protection Act to make sure businesses don't abuse this access to information.

**6** New materials have meant that **new products can be developed** and old ones can be made more efficiently and easily than they used to be. So, we now have cars being made from plastic, engines being made partly from ceramics and plastics used for all sorts of products which they could not have been used for before.

All of these changes represent both a threat and an opportunity to businesses, as shown in Table 8.1.

**Table 8.1 Threats and opportunities represented by technological change**

| Threats | Opportunities |
| --- | --- |
| 1 If the business doesn't take advantage of the opportunity of technology, competitors will gain an advantage. | 1 If you can get a new product working and selling well before anyone else you may be able to make large profits. |
| 2 Technology costs money. | |
| 3 There is always a risk that a new process or product won't work well. | 2 Technology offers you a way to cut costs in both staffing and production. |
| 4 Customers may not like the changes you make. | 3 You may be able to make people's jobs more pleasant by removing boring or dangerous jobs. |
| 5 Staff may not either – and retraining costs money. | 4 More efficient running of the business is good for the business and for the customers. |

Any business, in deciding whether to invest in new technology has to look very carefully at the pros and cons of the purchase before deciding what to do. There are advantages and risks both to being the first in the field and the first to buy in new machines or try new systems. The cost and scope of the technology are also factors in deciding whether or not to go ahead – you may take the decision to try a new paperless stapler in the general office quite easily; whereas you would probably take rather longer to decide to convert all of the paperwork for the business onto a brand new computerised system which has just come on to the market and which promises to cut your administrative costs to 10 per cent of their current level.

## ACTIVITY

Read the case study below and write a short memo to the managers of the business concerned to advise them of the possible advantages and disadvantages of the purchase. Produce a second memo which assumes they have decided to go ahead and advise them of what to check and what to try to find out before they actually part with any money.

'Christopher and Dominique Bray have run their own wine importing business and retail operation for the last ten years. The firm is successful and they have a reputation for finding wines which are of good quality but are not generally available in this country. They buy in reasonable bulk and have storage both at their shop and their offices at home. They sell a lot by mail order and have built up quite a large list of customers. It is now becoming very time consuming for them to keep track of mail order customers and to decide which offers they should send to which customers (as some people are not interested in certain areas, types of wine or prices it is not sensible to send every offer to every person). At a recent trade show Dominique was shown a new computer mailing system which promised to be able to form a 'profile of every customer' and match offers to the customers. The sellers claim that it will produce letters and envelopes automatically with the current offers on, will keep track of the responses and will recommend customers to drop from the lists or only to mailshot at certain times of the year (such as Christmas). The system is also able to be used as a desktop publisher and word processor. Dominique has had a demonstration of the system which involved an imaginary business and seemed to work well. The system is expensive but, *if it works it will save a lot of time and will allow them to target their marketing very effectively.'*

## POLITICAL PRESSURES

There are several areas where political pressures affect business:

- Through their making laws which compel businesses to take certain actions
- Through their control of the economy and the effect they have on the economic welfare of the country and of individual firms
- Through their control over the physical environment – decisions on where to put roads, whether to allow a New Town to be built and the incentives given to businesses to set up in certain places
- Through their decisions on taxes and duties payable on goods. If the government wished to stop people smoking they have the ability to put up the price of tobacco to the point where people have no chance to buy it in any quantity.

All of these controls are exercised by the government in power, and less effect is exercised by the Opposition party, although their support for certain measures is essential if the government is to have any hope of governing by consent.

While there are direct political controls on the way in which businesses operate there are also indirect influences which politicians can exercise. During their term in office since 1979, there has been a general attitude in the Conservative Party that the government should

1 Stay out of business where possible
2 Return businesses such as the public utilities to the private sector
3 Encourage the formation of small firms
4 Try to make the public sector more responsive to the needs of the public whom it serves.

Also, while there has been legislation to enable these things to be done there has also been a more subtle shift in that there is now a change in the way in which people see the role of the public and private sector and the attitude which they have to business in general.

One of the key functions of political pressure is to get action quickly in areas where there are specific problems – so the example we looked at earlier in this unit of the swift political reaction to the Hillsborough disaster and the Bradford fire are relevant here as well (*see* Fig 8.1 on p 283).

---

### ACTIVITY

Can you think of any other actions taken by government as a result of social concern on a political issue? Make a note of any you can think of in the form of a table like the one below and combine your list with others to get a picture of the effects of political pressures on businesses:

| Concern | Action |
|---|---|
| Pollution damaging the environment | Clean Air Act<br>Control of Pollution Act<br>Environmental Protection Act |

---

## Pressures for change working together

A business will have to try to make sense of the environment in which it operates if it is to be able to plan for the future with any certainty. A failure to monitor what is going on around the business will mean that the business is not able to adapt to cope with changes and has to try to cope with emergencies it has not foreseen. No business, even those with large research teams, will be able to foresee everything that is going to happen to it but they will at least see more than the business which doesn't look ahead. Some of the businesses which are most prone to not planning ahead are small owner-operated businesses where the owners of the business are too busy operating the business and coping with the problems which occur on a day-to-day basis to be able to do anything about looking forward and deciding what to do about the future.

The process a business should go through to monitor the changes about it are set out in Fig 8.2; not every business will be able to go through all of these stages all of the time but they should at least be aware of them.

Gather information on what is happening around the business and in the business environment in general.

Analyse what is going on under the headings listed above: Social, Legal, Physical, Technical, Political, Economic.

Look at the Strengths and Weaknesses of the business in each area.
Look at the Opportunities for the business and the Threats in each area.
(This is known as a SWOT analysis)

List the alternative actions the business could take in each area and as a whole to cope with the changes which are occurring.

Get as much information as you can on each area and on each of the alternative courses of action before you decide what to do.

**Fig 8.2 The process of monitoring change**

---

### ACTIVITY

Read the passage below and try to go through the process outlined above for the business. Present your conclusions in the form of a brief report to the owners of the business.

*Many small businesses of the 'corner shop' type in the centre of towns are finding it increasingly hard to cope with the competition from the large supermarkets. At one time they were the 'forget shop' where people could go to pick up impulse buys and to fill in gaps in the weekly shopping. Now it is more likely that the weekly, or monthly, shopping will have filled the freezers of their customers with convenience foods to be picked out*

*at leisure. If one item has been forgotten another is always to hand. They used to have a role as a social centre for the area as well; when everyone knew one another. Now, as more and more people move to live out of town there is less in the way of a community and, therefore, less of a need for a community shop. The owner/managers of these businesses used to have the advantage that they were open when the main shopping areas weren't but that has gone too. Many of the large supermarkets have opening hours which rival the corner shop and far lower prices as a result of their ability to buy in bulk. The recession has made people more conscious of getting value for money and the big chains emphasise this in their marketing; 'value' is a watchword for them and they have attractive offers to tempt customers in to buy their goods.*

*Many owners of such small businesses also feel that they are drowning in a sea of red tape. Recent changes to the laws in the areas of Health and Safety, food handling and data protection have given them more rules to follow and more inspectors to make sure that they do. To these people the government's claim that they support small business and have done more to help it than any other previous government rings very false indeed.*

*Hard times in the economy have led to suppliers squeezing the small business to pay up more and faster where they don't have the option of squeezing the big players in the food retailing market. So, small firms are getting 15 days' trade credit while the large firms are paying out at their leisure.*

*All of the new technology which allows the big firms to become more efficient is expensive. Small retailers find it hard enough to fund the cost of a decent till and stock control system; the thousands required for a full bar coding and scanning system are right out of reach and even the more sophisticated electronic tills which would do away with the requirement for labour intensive stock checking are complex and expensive for a small business to take on.*

*The move away from the urban housing areas to suburbs has reduced the market for such shops as has the change in working patterns which means that the supermarkets can now be open at the times when most people want to shop. When taken with the controls on parking in many urban areas, and the creation of bypass road systems which take people round the areas where such shops are located rather than into them, this spells a major problem for a retail institution in this country.*

Fill in the influences given in the passage (and any others you can think of) on a table like the one below:

| Social |
|---|
| Legal |
| Political |
| Economic |
| Technical |
| Physical |

From the information you have can you carry out a SWOT analysis for businesses of this type?

| Strengths | Weaknesses |
|---|---|
| | |
| Opportunities | Threats |
| | |

## Sources of information on trends and changes?

There are a number of ways of gathering information which will help you to understand the environment the business is operating in. Not all of these will be available to every business but there are some which are widely available and there are a lot of agencies which have been set up to help small businesses in particular which will try to help you to carry out research into the business environment. If you have the resources, there are also a lot of consultancy firms who are willing to make recommendations, at a price, as to what your business should do. The main sources of information include:

1 **Market research**. This is covered in Unit 7 (*see* p 248) and there is a lot of detail in that part of the book. Market research can be expensive if it is carried out as a large scale exercise but even small businesses can ask customers what they think of the business and can look out for information as to what the market is doing. Being aware that this is useful and keeping alert is the first stage in finding out what is happening around you.

**2 Desk research.** This is the term given to research which is carried out by checking reference materials. There are many statistics published by the Government and by other people which are of use to businesses in finding out what is going on. If you want to know the structure of the population in ten years' time the Census data will give it to you. If you want to know what the average family spent on leisure activities the Family Income and Expenditure Survey will provide it. If you are interested in the number of households with a video or satellite receiver the Social Trends research can tell you. There are statistics available in the average college or lending library which can help almost any business to see a little way into the future at least. There are also good articles in trade journals, the national press and magazines which bring together a lot of research and try to make sense of what is happening to business in general or to one special area. In addition to these publicly available sources of information, there are commercial services which specialise in trying to predict the future of a given industry or section of an industry. Perhaps the best known of these is Mintel, whose reports are usually available in large college and university libraries.

**3 Gathering information in the business.** Your own customers can tell you a lot about what is happening and what they expect from you as a business. If you listen to them and encourage them to give you their views there may be a lot of valuable information to be gained. Employees in a business also gather a lot of information and many businesses make little effort to gather that information to a central point and make use of it. This is a valuable source of market data which the business should make full use of where it can.

**4 Business clubs/societies/trade bodies.** All these bodies have a vested interest in helping a business to get the best information as to what the future holds for them. They will run conferences, organise advice and often produce a publication which is aimed specifically at people in this area of business. Such publications will help to update you on the latest technology and trends in the business as well as providing a pointer to the problems people have had and how they have coped with them. Attending the functions and conferences organised by such organisations is a good chance to talk to people who may have encountered some of the problems you have as a business and to get new ideas.

---

### ACTIVITY

Look in the library at your school or college. Make a list of the information there which could help a business to predict the environment it will have to face in a few years' time and complete a table like the one below. An example has been filled in as a start.

| Source | Information |
| --- | --- |
| Family Expenditure Survey | Gives data as to the way families spend their incomes and the way this has changed over the years. Useful for seeing downward or upward trends in spending and thus finding areas to get out of (or into). |

---

## The effects of change

As businesses change to cope with the world around them this will have an effect on the way they work on the people who work in the businesses, on the communities they are a part of and on the clients of the business. The challenge for businesses is to make the process of change one that gives benefits to as many as possible and which is achieved with as little upset as possible. The actual process of managing change in a business is examined later in this unit. This section will look briefly at the effect that change on a business can have on the groups mentioned above.

### THE EFFECTS OF CHANGE ON WORK

As organisations change this will have an effect on the work that is actually done in the businesses and firms affected. Over the years there are few areas of business or the public sector which have not seen a lot of change in one form or another. Many of the changes which have affected businesses have already been looked at earlier in the text and in this unit. Among the main effects of change on the work people have to do are:

1 Automation and the introduction of technology
2 Increased control over the operations of a business
3 More flexibility in the way businesses can respond to the needs of their clients and their staff
4 Removing some of the more unpleasant and boring jobs which people have had to do
5 Introducing new patterns of work.

### Automation

The advent of automation has meant that businesses are able to use machines to replace the labour supplied by people. In developed economies there will normally be a high level of automation as a result of the fact that the cost of labour is high. This provides an incentive for businesses and other organisations to automate and remove labour costs. Automation has advantages where the work is predictable and there are fairly standard requirements. It has fewer benefits if the system has to cope with a lot of variety as people tend to be more adaptable than most machines. The advantages of machines in businesses are often summed up as:

- Machines don't take breaks
- Machines are never ill or call in sick with a hangover
- Machines don't get tired
- Machines work at a steady rate and don't vary
- Machines don't need canteens, toilets or welfare officers
- Machines don't get sick pay if they're not working

---

### ACTIVITY

Find a number of similar statements to sum up the disadvantages of machines. The list has been started for you:

---

1 Machines have no initiative
_____
2
_____
3
_____
4
_____
5
_____
6
_____

The effect of automation where it is appropriate for the business is to reduce the costs which the business has to face and allow them to produce more efficiently. The effect on the jobs which are left in the business will depend on how the automation or technology is used. In some cases technology applied in this way has meant that the jobs which are left become more routine and leave little room for initiative on the part of the employees who are reduced to the status of machine minders. This was a common complaint about many of the uses of computers in business; that they removed the interesting work and created data input jobs which were boring and required fewer skills than the jobs which were replaced.

The other side of the coin is that the use of technology can remove boring routine jobs and leave people free to concentrate on the more creative tasks which people do best.

---

### ACTIVITY

Read the passage below and compare it with the one about Vikki on p 290.

**Roger**
*'I've been working here for about three years. I hate it but it's a job I suppose and it's quite well paid. My job is to input the reports we get from our researchers onto the computer system so that they can be analysed. We all have to be absolutely accurate and there is a check made by having two people input the same data. They're compared by the main machine and if they aren't identical the supervisor has to check to see which is correct. Get too many of those and you're going to lose a lot of bonus pay as that depends on two things – speed and accuracy. Speed is easy to see: one press of a function key and the machine will give you a score for the day, the job you're working on, the month and your*

*average since you started here. These are checked every week and you have to make sure you get up to the target or you'll go onto the basic pay; and that's lousy money. What I really hate is the way that we all seem to be running around doing what the machine tells us. I think that's wrong. We should be able to have a terminal at home and work there at our own speed if we want to – if they give you a quota of work and you do it by the deadline what does it matter if you manage 30 keystrokes a minute or 3000? That way we would be able to relax when we want to and they wouldn't have to have such a big office. I put that into a suggestion box once and got a letter back saying that the management "thought this was not a viable proposition in the current industrial climate" – whatever that means.'*

Both Vikki and Roger use technology in their work. One has found that it has made life less pleasant, whereas the other has used it to make life easier and more flexible. What are the differences in the ways that technology has been used in these two cases?

## Increased control over the operations of a business

As computers provide managers with more data on which to base decisions, as new materials provide businesses with cheaper, easier and faster operations than they have had before, as computer controlled machines make manufacturing flexibility possible and as automation of some jobs cuts costs, there is a lot more control for managers over the way in which the businesses they run operate. Better information and the ability to adapt rapidly to the forces in the environment around the business make the business more competitive and give managers and the workforce of a business the scope to make decisions quickly.

## More flexibility in the way businesses can respond to the needs of their clients and their staff

Businesses have taken advantage of the opportunities presented to them to alter the way in which they work and there are working patterns now which would have seemed very strange even 20 years ago. Systems such as flexitime provide a high level of flexibility for the staff of a business and allow the business to still get the work and commitment it wants from the staff who work for it. There are also schemes for career breaks for parents who want to take extended leave to look after their children, workplace child care to allow fathers or mothers to bring children to work with them and be confident that the children are being well cared for and, in some businesses, many services which are available to staff at their place of work. In the case of one national retail chain the services available to staff at work include medical care, chiropody and hairdressing. All of this flexibility should have the effect of allowing people who work in such businesses to be able to fit their life more easily around their work. The benefits for the organisation which can do this are clear:

● A *motivated workforce*
● *Lower staff turnover*
● A *good reputation*
● The *ability to attract good staff* and hold on to them.

There are also gains for the clients of the organisation if the organisation is able to be more flexible in the way in which it responds to their needs. A customer whose wishes are met is more likely to place repeat orders and will also feel that the business is capable and efficient. This will have the effect of helping to ensure customer loyalty and satisfaction. There have been a number of initiatives aimed at helping businesses to meet the customers' needs more flexibly and efficiently:

1 **Customer first/customer care policies.** It is often quoted that for every complaint you receive about the service your organisation provides, there are 10 dissatisfied customers and that, on average every dissatisfied customer will tell 17 people about how they feel. This means that for every customer who complains there are 169 other people who have had bad reports about your organisation. Taking this as a premise, customer care policies encourage people to try to treat customers well, to take care of their needs and to 'get it right first time, every time'. This is obviously a very high standard but it is a good ideal to aim for and, if it can be achieved, will have many positive benefits for the organisation.

**2 Total quality programmes.** These aim to improve the quality of everything which the organisation does and make sure that the organisation meets the needs of the customer exactly. TQM, as it is known, has to be seen as the responsibility of everyone in the organisation if it is to work effectively and, for this reason, it is a long-term change to an organisation which will require a lot of time and resources if it is to work effectively. The aim of the process is to produce an organisation with '*nil defects*. It is recognised that this is an impossibly high standard but it is seen as a goal for the organisation to try to reach. In any organisation which is trying to achieve total quality there will be a need for a policy to try to encourage the development of the necessary culture and the organisation will have to go through a process like the one outlined in Fig 8.3.

These stages on their own will not provide TQM but they are necessary for any business which is aiming for this sort of programme. Perhaps the most important thing is the change in the culture of a firm which is required to make this work. It has to affect everyone if it is to be effective. One major multinational company has an 'open door' policy within its TQM programme for dealing with complaints which staff have. Any member of staff with a complaint can take it to the person they feel is the best one to sort it out; their line manager, the plant manager or the chief executive of the company. This has the effect of making everyone accountable and making it plain that the organisation is serious about quality. TQM means a very different way of working for a lot of people who have been used to quality control where there are inspectors whose job it is to find problems. Under a TQM system the responsibility for faults lies with the individual and they cannot dismiss errors as 'someone else's problem'. At the moment in some organisations there is a feeling that quality is the responsibility of a few people in the organisation. In a TQM organisation everyone recognises that it is the key to the survival of the business and the future of all of the people in it.

Make a public commitment to improving the quality of everything the organisation does – both internally and externally.

Provide a way of making sure that the needs of customers are accurately and quickly determined – if you don't know what the customers want you have little chance of providing it for them.

Look at the quality of the work currently done in house with a view to improving it to meet the demands of the customers and reducing the amount of waste and the money spent on inspection and reworking.

Look at the quality of the work done by contractors and the goods bought in from other firms. If they are not up to standard the whole business will suffer – remember the GIGO law: '*Garbage in; garbage out*'.

Encourage all of the staff in the business to be quality conscious and to take responsibility for the quality of the work they do – this will further reduce the waste, reworking and inspection costs the business has to face.

Review the processes and systems continually to see if they can be improved

Monitor the satisfaction of customers and get any problems brought to you – far better that customers tell you of their problems than other people. There is a lot of good sense in the notices you see in some businesses: '*If you were pleased with our service; tell your friends. If not, tell us.*'

**Fig 8.3 The process involved in trying to reach total quality**

## Removing some of the more unpleasant and boring jobs which people have had to do

Technology and automation between them have had the effect of reducing the number of routine jobs which people have to do. They have also created some new ones as the case study above about Roger shows. Apart from removing routine jobs, changes in the way in which businesses operate has meant that there are also fewer dangerous jobs as machines can be used to do jobs like this without such risk to life or limb. Such advances include the handling of dangerous materials such as radioactive waste and chemicals and the heavy industry jobs like steel production where machines can now do many of the more dangerous jobs instead of people. This is a result of the availability of better technology and changes in social attitudes as well. There are still countries in the world, however, where there are few controls on Health and Safety and where the levels of wages are low enough that it is cheaper for businesses to use people for dangerous or hazardous jobs than it is for them to use machines.

Unfortunately there are also businesses which are quite happy to work in these countries as they have less controls on the way they operate and can make higher profits.

### ACTIVITY

For a business with which you are familiar make a list of the main changes to the work that the business does that have taken place over the last few years. You may need to talk to people who work in the business to get ideas from them. Put the results in the form of a table like the one below:

| Change | Reason |
| --- | --- |
| Tills are easier to use and faster to put goods through. | Laser scanning tills make fewer errors and allow goods to pass through fast. They also make stock control and staff planning more efficient |

## THE EFFECTS OF CHANGE ON WORKERS

People tend not to cope particularly well with change, and the problems associated with actually managing change in an organisation are dealt with later in this unit under the section on 'Managing Change'. When a business changes the people within the business will also have to change and this will have a number of possible effects. In most cases there are two possible outcomes from changes in a business and most people fear the worst. An old saying goes 'Expect the worst, hope for the best' and this is how many people view change in a business. If the business has planned the changes well and has been able to manage the changes they have made rather than having something thrust on them by an emergency they should be able to get the most benefit out of the changes. Some of the most common fears people have about changes and the effects that they will have on them are listed below:

- That they will lose the skills they have and be *replaced by a machine*. This is a standard fear and many people have had experience either directly or through a friend (or a friend of a friend) of this happening. They may know that they are not going to lose their job but fear being reduced to the status of a machine minder rather than using the skills they have taken a long time to acquire.
- That the business will exercise more control and allow them *less flexibility* in the way they do their job. The case study above about Roger illustrates this sort of fear and it is one which can sometimes be well founded if the changes allow performance to be monitored more easily by the organisation. Another part of this fear is the worry that new systems or new machines will take away any scope for making decisions and leave the person with less power than they used to have.
- That the business will move on to *new styles of working* which are harder for the person to cope with. So, a person in a factory which is moving to a continuous production running 24 hours a day may fear being made to work shifts if this is something which will cause them problems in their family or social life.

- That their health and *wellbeing will suffer* as a result of being asked to cope with change for which they are not prepared, as a result of having to work harder, at different times or in a different way. There are very high levels of stress associated with any changes in a business and especially with the uncertainty about what is happening during major changes in an organisation. Many people start to fear the worst and there are usually rumours in any organisation as to what is happening and what will be the result of changes; these rumours may be based on hearsay, fiction, or the experience of what has happened in other businesses.
- That they will make a lot of errors during the settling-in time which will follow any change and that they may be seen as not being competent enough to cope with what has gone on. This can lead people to worry about losing their job.

---

### ACTIVITY

1 For each of the fears and problems listed above try to look at the opposite side of the coin and write a short paragraph explaining this. For example:

**Fear of losing their skills**
Another way of looking at this is as an opportunity to gain new skills and to use the skills they have in a different way. So, someone who has spent a lot of time and effort in acquiring skills is a valuable asset to a business and they will want to make the best use they can of the experience the person has built up over the years.

2 How would you suggest that a business tries to 'sell' the benefits of change to its employees?

---

## THE EFFECTS OF CHANGE ON CLIENTS

The expectations which clients have are among the major forces which persuade a business to change. In changing to meet the needs and expectations of their clients a business will seek to improve the service which it offers to its customers and clients. Among the most common ways that a business will seek to improve its service to customers and clients are:

1 *Better service*/products

2 *Fewer errors*/problems
3 *Gain customers* as a result of good reports
4 *Reduce costs* so as to make prices more competitive

## Better service/products

Any business has to update the products and services which it offers if it is to survive. You have looked at this process in Unit 7 Marketing and Business Performance and there is a section later in this unit on the process of innovation in businesses. Most businesses will look at the service they provide to their customers on a regular basis with a view to trying to make it better. Large organisations will gather information on what their customers think about their products and services from systematic market research and may employ an agency to do this for them. Smaller organisations should look at the service they provide critically and talk to their customers in order to try to find out what they are doing right and where they could improve the service they offer to their customers.

## Fewer errors/problems

Total quality management (TQM), customer care programmes and staff training are all changes which will affect the quality which clients get from the business. There are also other ways of improving the quality of the services or products which are provided and these will include altering the design of products to make them more reliable, changing the manufacturing process to make the goods cheaper, taking advantage of advances in technology to make goods to better tolerances. If a business can reduce errors to an absolute minimum they will have the opportunity to reduce their costs in the scrap and wastage of products, in the inspection and quality control (everyone is their own inspector) and in the reworking of products which fail to meet standards. Such reductions in costs will allow a business to either make higher profits or quote lower prices and gain more business. In either case they are gaining a competitive edge from using change to benefit their clients and customers.

### Gain customers as a result of good reports

An efficient business offering a good range of high quality products will generate more and more business for itself. The effect of this is to boost profits and, if the firm reinvests these profits this should allow them to further increase the quality of what they offer and the range of goods and services they provide. Success breeds success, after all.

### Reduce costs so as to make prices more competitive

Many of the areas we have looked at above will have the effect of reducing prices and this may also be the aim of changes which the organisation makes. The advantage to be gained from lower costs is that the organisation can either maintain its current prices and make higher profits or may be able to reduce prices slightly and gain more business. In either case it allows the organisation more adaptability and the chance to make higher profits from existing customers or from gaining an increase in trade.

There is, of course, a risk that a change an organisation makes with a view to gaining some or all of the benefits mentioned above does not work and they provide a lower level of service or find that they have increased their costs to the point where they are less profitable than they were. It is for this reason that it is necessary to consider the introduction of changes very carefully, weigh up the advantages and disadvantages and plan carefully as to how to introduce the change so that the organisation and those connected with it will benefit from the change rather than suffering as a result of it.

### THE EFFECTS OF CHANGE ON THE COMMUNITY

As organisations change, for whatever reason, they will have an effect on the communities of which they are a part. In the case of a single large employer, the effect of a major change will be very marked and make a large difference to the economy and nature of the area. In the case of smaller organisations the changes may not be so obvious but it is often the case that, when they are all put together, the effect of the small organisation in an area is as large as that of the big employers. It is also a fact that the economies in an area are interdependent. So, a large firm will provide wages to its employees who will spend these earnings in local businesses, and they will have contracts with local firms for services and for the supply of goods. The most severe change which can affect a community in the short term is the closure of a business with the attendant loss of jobs, and possibly bad debts, which go with it. Other changes will have just as large an effect over time but they tend to be less dramatic than the closure of an employer organisation, especially a large one.

---

### ACTIVITY

---

Consider the business outlined below and state what you think the effect on the local community will be if it is closed.

*Losweigh is a small town in the northeast of the UK. The town is fairly isolated and has benefitted from the decision, ten years ago, of the government to move a major base for the provision of supplies to the area. Part of the reason for the decision was the isolated nature of the area as, among the supplies which are kept at Losweigh, are a number of items which could be dangerous. It is not a 'secret' base but the security is good. The base employs 3500 local people and there are about 1000 Army staff stationed there as well. Most of the Army personnel live in accommodation on the base but there are about 190 houses which have been bought, over the years, by the Army and which are used as accommodation for married officers and their families. A lot of local firms are very dependent on the base for the contracts which it has with them and there are many areas where the base has provided help to the community in the form of assistance with community projects or by making base facilities available to the community. It has just been announced that the base is to close as a result of the cutbacks in the armed forces – the so-called 'peace dividend'. Armed forces personnel are to be moved to other bases and the Army has said that the closure of the base will be complete within six months. They have offered some help to local employees to retrain for other jobs and have also said that there will be about 180 jobs in another base where some of the work from Losweigh is being transferred – this base is in Kent.*

What do you think the effects on the local community will be?

Produce a brief outline of what you think might happen to the town of Losweigh as the base closes.

In your answer to the activity above you will probably have identified, among other things, the effects outlined below.

- job losses
- loss of trade to local firms
- people moving away
- housing prices falling
- closure of local businesses dependent on the base
- Less income for the Local Authority.

These effects are common ones as businesses change and we will look at some of them in a little more detail:

## Structural change

When a business changes it is likely that there will be some change in the number of employees which it uses. In many cases change is seen as being the automation of a plant, or the closure of a factory to transfer work to another plant and, in these cases it is job losses which we are concerned with. There are, however, many cases where businesses expand and take the chance to take on extra workers in order to meet demand. These cases don't make the news as often as dramatic job losses. There are a number of effects for a community if there is a loss of jobs from an employer. The effects are the same, irrespective of the size of the job loss; they are just easier to see if there is a massive change in the number of people employed in a particular area:

1 The people concerned will suffer *a loss in income.* This will mean they have less to spend with other local businesses.
2 There may start to be more of a *demand on the state for income support,* housing benefit and other assistance.
3 There will be *more competition* for any jobs which are available.
4 *People may move away from the area* to places where they are more likely to be able to find another job.

5 There may be an *increase in social problems* such as homelessness if the situation is more than short term.
6 The area will be seen either as one where *businesses don't succeed* or, if presented correctly may be able to attract businesses to move in by the promise of a large pool of skilled labour and (probably) low wage rates.

### ACTIVITY

What do you think will happen if there is a large increase in the number of jobs available in an area?

## Multiplier effect

Economists talk about the multiplier effect of spending. To take a quick example.

*Sturzaker, Tattersall and Waterworth are a firm of solicitors based in a prosperous southeast market town. They have recently moved into the estate agency business and are doing very well in this area. They have decided to build new offices in the town as a combined 'one stop' legal and house/business purchase centre. They have bought a site with a small property on it and this is to be demolished by the local builders over the next few weeks. After that, work will start on building the new offices from scratch. They have been inundated with calls since the plans became public from all sorts of firms offering them products they will need for the new offices. They are also going to need more staff and have asked the local JobCentre to help them to find people with the skills they need.*

In this situation there is a lot of money going into the local economy. The builders who are going to construct the building, for example, will probably need to hire more labour to help with the project; they will spend money with builders' merchants on the materials they need. The builders merchants will, in turn have to place orders with other firms for the goods which they supply. All of the firms who will provide decor, furniture and equipment will make slightly higher profits as a result of the extra work. The new employees will have wages which they will spend in local firms. So, the money that is actually being invested will be multiplied as different firms all become more prosperous as a result of the initial investment.

There can also be, however, the opposite situation where there is a 'reverse multiplier'. This occurs when money is taken out of the local economy as with the example of the base at Losweigh which you looked at earlier. In this situation there is a knock-on effect which multiples the damage, as shown in Fig 8.4.

---

### ACTIVITY

What could be done to reduce the effect of this reverse multiplier in a community where there have been high levels of job losses?

Can you think of any examples of actions the government or local authorities have taken to try to prevent this downward spiral from continuing? How successful have they been?

---

### Skill shortage

If an organisation expands they will need staff with the necessary skills to help to run the organisation. This may not be a problem in a lot of areas but there are certain skills which tend to be in short supply. These are known as 'areas of skill shortage'. Such areas will be filled eventually as people realise that there are jobs in particular fields of work and retrain in order to be able to get the jobs which are available. This can, however, take a long time if the skills are complex and require a high level of training for people to be able to cope well at work. Skills shortages may be the result of expansion of a business or they may be the result of working practices changing. So, for example, the shift to using word processors rather than typewriters in many businesses meant that there were not enough word processor operators at one point. This shortage has been remedied by the provision of training and there have been a lot of courses provided by firms and by schools and colleges to help to fill the gaps.

---

### ACTIVITY

Try to find out by using the *Employment Gazette* or by using a database to which you have access if there are any areas of skill shortage in this country at the moment. When you have found out what the areas are try to decide why this might be the case and enter the results in a table like the one below. This can be compared with the results which other people have to try to get a complete picture.

| Shortage | Reason |
|---|---|
| Staff who can speak Modern European languages. | Because there is an increasing amount of trade with Europe and firms are having to deal with other firms in different countries. |

What do you think can be done to try to remedy the skills shortages you have identified?

If you get the chance you may be able to ask local employers or the local JobCentre or Economic Development Unit about skill shortages in your own area. Do they seem to be the same as the ones which you found for the country as a whole? If not, what makes your area different?

---

### Mobility of labour

This may also be an effect of changes in businesses as people who lose jobs are unable to find jobs in the local area and move away to places where they are more likely to be able to find work. This also acts in reverse – a decision to build a factory in a particular area will attract

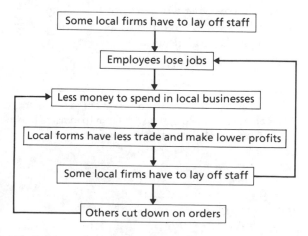

**Fig 8.4**

people to move to the area as they know that they are more likely to be able to get jobs there.

## How do organisations manage change?

Most people do not like change. Whether we are talking about our personal lives or our work most of us are comfortable with what we know and are not happy if something or someone tries to make us change; you will hear all sorts of sayings which express this in one way or another:

*The old ways are always the best*
*Stick to what you know*

However, one thing is clear from what we have already looked at in this unit and in the rest of the text – organisations and people have to change if they are to survive. The pressures which make them change differ over time and across different organisations, the speed of change is different, the changes which need to be made are different in different organisations – but they all have to change to cope with all of the things we have looked at in the environment and because of competition from other businesses.

In the activities in this unit so far you have looked at the pressures on businesses to change and some of the ways that they have had to react to these pressures. This section of the unit is concerned with trying to show how organisations can make change as easy and as simple as possible. If you can change easily when you need to, you have an advantage as a business because you can react to changes in the environment or threats from competitors far more easily and quickly than other organisations. This will help you to be more successful and will help to protect the future of the organisation and the people who work in it. This section will look at:

1 *Obstacles to Change*
2 *Attitude Barriers*
3 *The Importance of People*
4 *Helping People to Change*

### OBSTACLES TO CHANGE

All of us cope with all sorts of changes all the time, both at work and in our own personal and social lives, so we should be fairly good at it. Unfortunately that isn't the case. Most people don't like having to change and they find it a very stressful experience. There are a number of reasons why change at work can be seen as particularly stressful. They have already been mentioned on p 299, but to briefly recap:

- People are afraid that change will mean there are fewer jobs. This is especially the case if the change is forced on the business or organisation by hard times or if the change involves automation (bringing in machines to do the jobs that people do at the moment).
- There is a fear that change will make life harder or that you will not be able to do the new job that you are given. If this is the case you may then be afraid that you will eventually lose your job in favour of the machine which has been brought in, or another employee who is better able to cope with the new way things are being done.
- There is very often a real concern that the change is not really necessary – as mentioned earlier you will hear people saying 'If it ain't broke, don't fix it' implying that you should only change things when they are not working for some reason.
- There is a fear of the unknown. You don't know what the job, or the firm will be like after a major change and you may be afraid of having to move to a new site, a new office or a new job. You may be losing the company of people you have worked with for a long time and be worried about fitting in with a new part of the organisation

---

### ACTIVITY

Interview at least five people and ask them to rate themselves on the scale below; then ask them to indicate how good 'most people' are at coping with change:

| GOOD | | | | | POOR |
|---|---|---|---|---|---|
| | 5 | 4 | 3 | 2 | 1 |
| Me | | | | | |
| Others | | | | | |

Compare your results with the rest of the group: most people will probably have rated themselves as 3/4/5 and other people as 2/3. This suggests that everybody thinks that it is other people who can't cope with change. As they can't all be right can you suggest any reasons for this result?

After they have done this ask them to rate, in order, what they see as the five most important problems people have with change at work and if there are any other fears/concerns which have been missed off the list:

- Fear of losing your job
- Worry about not being able to cope
- Fear that it will make life harder
- Worry about not fitting in after changes
- Resentment of management interfering
- Concern about all the extra work involved in making the change
- Worry about the effect on friends
- Fear that the business is doing the wrong thing
- Worry that it will lead to your being paid less
- Not knowing what is going on

In doing the above activity you will need to copy the two scales out onto paper or card (or they could be desktop published).

After you have done this compare your results with others in the group and come up with a rank order of the main fears people have about change.

---

## ATTITUDE BARRIERS

Attitude barriers are the fears people have and the attitudes which they have to changes in the way they work or in their lives in general. Attitude barriers come from three main sources:

1 *Preconceptions*: the experience people have had of change before and the responses they have learned to it. This tends to be the result of their practical experience at work and will be the result of the way that they have been treated in the past or the way they have seen others treated.
2 *Prejudice*: the person's own views, often reinforced by the family group. This tends to be the result of both the experiences of the family and the 'inherited wisdom' from older generations of the family.
3 *Myths*: the things that 'everyone knows' and which come from the social group. They are part of the accepted wisdom of the group to which the person belongs and are taken as common sense. Unfortunately, as Mark Twain said, 'Sense is anything but common'.

Taken together there are a lot of attitudes here which, if they are opposed to what is going on can make someone uncooperative and mean that they are not at all committed to the changes which the organisation is trying to achieve. One of the main tasks in challenging these attitude barriers is the requirement to make people recognise that there is a need to change and that it is in their interests to help the process as much as they can. This process can be a difficult one and the organisation will need to communicate very effectively with staff if they are to overcome the barriers to change which are formed by the attitudes of those affected.

## IMPORTANCE OF PEOPLE

No change in an organisation will work without the cooperation and commitment of all those affected by it. It is necessary for everyone to be seen to be committed to what is going on. This will include the senior management of the organisation who will need to be seen to:

- direct what is going on and encourage people
- set an example by their own behaviour
- hold the organisation to what it is trying to do.

Anyone who is trying to introduce a major change in an organisation will have to try to develop an atmosphere where the people are going to be committed to what is going on. In order to do this they will need to:

- sell the benefits of the decisions that are taken
- present the ideas as to what is going on and be prepared to answer questions about it
- state clearly what is happening and why
- actively look for suggestions, help and cooperation
- be honest about potential problems and encourage people to find solutions to them.

## HELPING PEOPLE TO CHANGE

In order to help people to change and to cope

with change there are a number of practical steps that can be taken to try to make the process easier for all concerned:

1 *Communicate clearly* with people about the background to the proposals which are being made and the process of decision making to get to the point the business is at at the current time

2 *Involve them in two-way communication* – get their ideas and the involvement of all of those who are going to be affected. Take notice of what they say and deal seriously with fears and problems

3 *Keep people up to date* and give them reports on what is happening. Start training and preparation early

4 *Recruit new staff early* and try to make any transfers before the last moment.

5 *Avoid busy times to make major changes* and consider the easiest way to do things. Make sure that the systems have been tested to minimise the problems.

6 *Consider the people in the process* and make sure they have the chance to voice fears and concerns and to make suggestions. Treat them seriously.

7 If there are *unpleasant decisions to be taken they should be faced early* and the people affected should be given the best possible deal. Not to do so will cause resentment and fear among those left.

## How do organisations attempt to innovate?

Businesses need new products to survive. These products may be genuinely new or just redevelopments of older or existing products. There are three standard categories of new products which are recognised in most markets:

1 Products which are really new and are based on an original idea or invention. This may be something that is brought to the organisation or may have been developed by them 'in-house' as a part of their Research and Development effort.

2 Products which are a relaunch or repackaging of an existing product. The 'new improved' sort of product which may look a little different but is not genuinely original.

3 Products which imitate successful products which have been introduced by the competitors. Such products will probably try to imitate the original fairly closely at first.

Innovation is mainly concerned with the first of these categories – the genuinely new idea. If a business is to bring a product like this onto the market there are a number of stages it will need to go through before the idea has been transformed into a commercially viable product. How long this takes and how the process is managed is different for almost all businesses but many of the steps are the same.

1 **Getting ideas in to the business**. Large organisations have their own research departments whose job it is to come up with new ideas and they will be the source of many ideas. Individuals in a business will have ideas for new products and these should also be collected and examined as should the suggestions made by customers who may suggest either genuinely new ideas or ways to improve existing products. Businesses will probably also get approaches from 'inventors' who have also had product ideas. There are people who make a good living from doing this but there are also people whose ideas are not viable or, worse, are copies of a competitor's products.

2 **Sorting out the good ideas from the bad**. At this stage the organisation is looking for ideas which will suit it. The fact that an idea is rejected at this stage may be a result of it not fitting in with the image of the business, being too resource intensive to produce, not having enough difference from existing products or being too awkward to manufacture. In this stage it is sensible to involve people from all areas of the business so that problems with marketing or production or purchasing can be spotted before money is put into a potential product on a large scale. Only a few product ideas should make it through this process. The rest may be discarded, held for later use or the organisation may decide to try to sell some of them on to other businesses

who are more likely to be interested in them, as long as they don't compete directly with the original organisation's business.

**3 Finding out through market research whether there is a genuine need for the product.** This market research will be more extensive as the potential cost of developing the product increases. So, the market research done to find out whether the public will buy a new car will be very thorough. The market research done by a local shop to see if a new type of sandwich will sell will be far less as there is much less money at stake in the second case.

**4 Deciding whether the business has the resources it will need to take the product from being a good idea to being a viable product** ready to be manufactured and sold and then to promote it ready for sale. If the company doesn't have the resources itself it may choose to take on a joint venture partner to put more money in or may try to sell the idea to a larger organisation. The organisation will have to take account of all of the costs involved in developing the product to the point where it can be manufactured in bulk, the costs of setting up a production facility and equipping it and the costs of marketing the product so that people will buy it when it is introduced.

**5 The product will have to be developed.** Prototypes will need to be made and tested to see whether they work and the market research process will continue at this stage to make sure that the product meets the needs of the public who are expected to buy it. Production techniques will have to be decided on and tested and decisions made as to the materials to be used in manufacture and the suppliers who will have to be used. The production process will have to be designed and the planning started for the purchase of equipment and the training of staff. This process is time-consuming and costly but should finish with a product which is reliable, easy to manufacture and which meets the needs of the customers of the business.

**6 Test marketing** is the final stage where the product is still not in full manufacture. The final product, or as near to it as possible, will be marketed in a small area to gauge the reactions of the public. If this is favourable the product will then be fully 'commercialised'.

**7 The final stage is to make the arrangements to produce the product and to market it.** This will involve acquiring the necessary resources and making decisions as to the pricing of the product and the concrete details of where and how it will be launched. Staff will need to be trained and a distribution system set up to make sure that the product can be distributed effectively when it is launched.

### The product life cycle

Once a product has been introduced onto the market it starts to go through a process known as the product life cycle. The life cycle is quite simple as a concept:

- *Products are introduced* into the market and start to grow as they are accepted. Many products don't make it past this stage and the product will probably be a loss maker for the company which has invested to get it to this point. It will take a long time for the product to move into a profit as it will have all of the development costs to cover before it does so.
- Products which are successfully introduced will then *grow and develop*. Sales will rise and the product will attract competition from competitors and imitators. Hopefully the product may start to make a profit at some point in this stage.
- Products will then become *established in the market* and will sell at a reasonably high volume. More competitors will appear and it may be necessary to cut prices to keep the share of the market gained by being the first in the field. Eventually there will be a shake out of the market and some of the weaker competitors will disappear or be bought out.
- Eventually *the product will start to fall away* in terms of sales and profits as competitors introduce new or better products and the appeal of this product falls.

These four stages – **introduction** (or **launch**); **growth**; **maturity** and **decline** can be seen on the graph in Fig 7.2 on p 247.

The rate at which a product will go through the product life cycle will vary with the product. Some basic goods such as soap will have a very long life cycle, other areas such as fashion clothing, have very short life cycles. If a business is to have a set of sound and good products which sell well all the time the process of developing new products and introducing them needs to be fairly constant to try to make sure that, as one product declines, a new product is rising to take its place. If this is done correctly there will be a series of overlapping product life cycles over time as new products come in to replace old ones. This is illustrated in Fig 8.5.

To avoid the very high cost of starting a product from scratch companies will also look at ways of extending the product life cycle and keeping an old product going longer. Relaunches of old products are an example of this. There are a number of ways that a company can try to extend the life of a product:

**1 Modification of an existing product** to have a new appeal and the use of its brand name to promote similar products. Car manufacturers do this with cars with minor improvements to the vehicle and some cosmetic changes which keep a model alive in the marketplace for far less money than would be required to develop a new model. Most car manufacturers look at keeping basic models going for at least ten years and will probably update every two to three years during this time to keep the product alive and competing.

**2 Good promotion** can keep demand for a product high and the public may be loathe to see the product go. The outcry about the Citroen 2CV and the VW Beetle going out of production are an illustration of this and the continued production and sale of the Mini (after many relaunches and modifications) is proof of the appeal of some products when marketed well.

3 A product may be **positioned to appeal to a different sector of the market.** So, Range Rover introduced the very high specification Vogue model to help to boost the model and keep its appeal.

A topical idea at the moment is the compression of development times of products so that they can be developed and brought to the market far faster than has been the case before. This is partly necessary as it appears to be the case that the length of the product life cycle is getting shorter for many products and the public expect to see new products on the market very regularly.

---

### ACTIVITY

#### Organisation survey and report

This assignment requires you to visit two organisations and to look at the changes they have had to face recently and those they will need to cope with in the future. After the visit you will have to choose one of the organisations to concentrate on and write a report explaining how they have had to change recently and what you (and they) feel are the main changes they will have to face in the near future. In this report you will need to compare the main organisation with the other one you visited. The situation and tasks will give you more detail.

**Sources of information:**
Briefing sheet for this assignment
Texts in library and class texts
Class lessons and handouts
Organisation visits
Knowledge of other Core areas

**Skills used:**
In this assignment you will have the opportunity to use many of the common skills, in particular:

- *Communicating*: producing a written report
- *Problem solving*: finding out what you need to know and deciding what the organisation will need to do
- *Managing self*: planning the tasks and the work to meet the deadline
- *Applying technology*: you may choose to use word processing, and other IT applications to improve the presentation of this assignment.

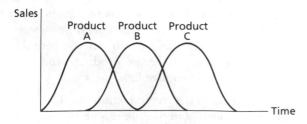

**Fig 8.5 Overlapping product life cycles**

## Situation

As a newly appointed management trainee in the organisation you have chosen you have been asked by your manager to produce a report explaining the way you see the company having changed in the recent past and the things you expect to affect it and make it change in the near future. She has explained that she wants a fresh view and hopes to get some ideas which may have slipped past some of the people who have been with the organisation for a long time and who have got used to thinking of changes, and looking at the company, in a fairly similar way. You are aware that this is also a bit of a test – you are young to be in your job and a lot of people felt that the organisation would have been better promoting from within rather than getting you in from outside. Do it well and it will look good on you, do it badly and it may take a long time before you are really trusted.

## Tasks

**1** Visit two local organisations (having consulted with your tutor over the arrangements) and try to find out what changes they have had to cope with and what they see as the main pressures for change at the moment. Try to find out a little about each organisation before you go so that you can get the most out of the visits.

**2** Research in a bit more detail the pressures for change you have identified from your visit and the earlier research you did on the organisations. Try to make sure you have got as much information as you can from the organisations and from reading. At this stage you can choose one of the organisations to concentrate on, but don't ignore the other.

**3** Prepare a report in correct report format on **one** of the organisations. This report should provide a brief background on the organisation, explain the changes it has recently faced and then, for the largest part of the report, explain what it will have to face in the future and why. A conclusion should summarise your findings, and recommendations should provide some clear idea on what the organisation should do next in order to be prepared to cope with the changes you feel it faces.

Use the second organisation as a contrast and to illustrate your points but do not go into detail on this organisation.

The report should be a maximum of 2500 words and should include a bibliography listing any references you used in your report and the sources of information for your research.

**4** Hand in

**(a)** The report
**(b)** A clear account of the visits you made and what you found out
**(c)** A diary explaining what you did when and the information sources you consulted.
**(d)** The self-assessment sheet provided if you have completed it.

# APPENDIX 1
# SAMPLE ASSIGNMENTS

▪

The following assignments are intended to give you some practice in the sort of tasks which you may have to carry out as a part of your programme of study. The format of the assignments will vary from centre to centre and will also contain some relevant administrative information. Such details have been omitted from these assignments as every centre will have its own system. What you do have on each of these assignments is:

- an indication of which areas of the programme content it draws upon;
- some idea of the sources of information (if applicable);
- an outline situation and tasks.

Some of these activities are quite lengthy and will draw on a number of areas of the programme, others are very short and are quite specific to one unit or one area of content. All of them represent the sorts of activities you could be asked to carry out as a part of the programme and will be useful for you to look at and to work through.

The format of each of the assignments is as set out below:

**1 Title of assignment**: The name of the assignment. This may also include a reference number so that it can be easily identified.

**2 Areas of content**: The main units on which the assignment draws and the areas of content you will need to use in completing it.

**3 Sources of information**: An outline of the main sources of information for the assignment. These may include visits, class notes, activities and library resources amongst others.

**4 Background information**: A clear idea of the background to the assignment and the nature of the situation you are faced with. This may be in the form of a short case study or a set of specific instructions regarding the role you are to take.

**5 Tasks**: The detail of what you have to do to complete the assignment and how it should be completed.

---

## Assignment 1: Bass and Whitbread – a financial comparison

*Areas of content*:
   Finance

*Sources of information*:
   Company reports
   Library resources
   Financial press

*Background information*:
Throughout Unit 5 you have used a series of analytical techniques. You are now to use these techniques to compare two of the United Kingdom's major brewers: Bass plc and Whitbread plc.

**TASKS**

1 Analyse the data available for each company in order to get as much information as you can about their relative success.

2 Show your analysis of the two companies in tabular form and at the end of your analysis you are to justify your choice of one of the companies as a 'best' investment.

You may have to refer to the financial pages of the press to allow you to obtain some of the data that will be required for the analysis.

## Assignment 2: Profit margin analysis

*Areas of content*:
Finance

*Sources of information*:
Local press

*Background information*:
A client of the accountants where you work has asked for advice on whether to buy a jewellers shop 'as they seem to have quite a high profit on everything'. You have been asked to explain to the client why Gross Profit Percentages are different for different businesses.

### TASK

In your local newspaper you will be able to find details of local businesses for sale. Make a comparison of the Gross Profit Percentages for the following range of businesses, present your information in tabular form and explain any differences in the Gross Profit Percentages.

*Types of business*:
- men's hairdresser
- women's hairdresser
- car breakers
- video rental shop
- butchers
- men's clothing shop
- launderette
- shoe shop
- joiners
- builders
- cafe
- health food shop
- grocers.

If you are not able to find figures for these businesses use alternative businesses that are for sale.

Present the information in a format suitable for the client.

## Assignment 3: Integration

*Areas of content:*
Finance
Business organisations

*Sources of information:*
Company data
Library

*Background Information*:
Bass is a UK-based company with businesses involved in the production and distribution of drinks, primarily beer and soft drinks; the ownership, management and franchising of pubs, hotels and restaurants; the manufacture of amusement machines; and the operation of betting shops and leisure facilities, including bingo clubs and entertainment centres. Much of the Bass empire has been created by a series of mergers and takeovers.

As a newly appointed assistant manager in one of the company's operations you have decided to explain to your staff some of the background to the company.

### TASKS

**1** From the information given below draw up a diagram that shows the integrated structure of the company. You will need to include such relationships as vertical and horizontal integration and so on.

**Component parts of Bass plc**

- Bass Brewers
- Bass Distribution
- Bass Inns and Taverns
- Britvic Soft Drinks
- Coral Racing (Betting Shops)
- Bass Leisure Machine Services (Supplier and operator of amusement and gaming machines)
- Coral Social Clubs (Bingo)
- Coral Snooker Clubs
- Coral Entertainment Centres
- Satellite Information Services (Televised racing and information services)
- Holiday Inn International
- Toby Restaurants.

**2** Prepare this information in a form ready to present to staff in the Holiday Inn part of the business so that they can see the scale of the operations of the company as a whole.

## Assignment 4: Jones Builders

*Areas of content*:
  Business resources
  Finance
  Marketing

*Sources of information*:
  This text
  Library resources

*Background information*:
The solicitor's office in which you work has been approached for advice by the daughter of a client who died recently. She has inherited the family business on the unexpected death of her mother, who was the managing director, and she knows little about it. What she does know is that Jones Builders Ltd have a development in the process of construction.
  In a six month period Jones Builders expect to build ten houses and to incur the following costs in building them:

bricks £180 000
sand £40 000
cement £50 000
insurance £1000

vehicle expenses £10 000
wood and joinery products £200 000
sub-contractors £100 000
labour £150 000
office expenses £2000.

She expects to sell each house for £100 000. Unfortunately the housing market is badly hit by the recession.

### TASKS

**1** Given the above information, calculate the profit and the unit costs. Show the direct costs and overhead costs.

**2** She has sold all the houses except one for which she is offered £72 200. Should she accept the offer or not?

**3** What are your reasons?

**4** Present the information in the form of a short report to the client. You should use suitable computer packages to enhance the presentation of the report where they are available.

## Assignment 5: Rocking Horse

*Areas of content*:
  Financial resources

*Sources of information*:
  Supplied

*Background information*:
You are asked by a friend to work out the minimum quantity of output that he requires each week to enable his business to break even. He makes rocking horses and supplies you with the following information:

  retail price £80

raw materials per horse £16
labour per horse £20
weekly expenses/workshop rent £400
fuel and power £80
other costs £116.

### TASK

Find the weekly break-even point by the graphical method and check your answer by calculation.

## Assignment 6: Craft Products Ltd

*Areas of content*:
  Finance
  Business innovation
  Business organisations

*Sources of information*:
  Supplied

*Background information*:
Your company, Craft Products make clocks out of old 78 rpm records and so far have seen extraordinary growth in profits. This, however, has only been achieved by paying low wages to the workforce. You have recently had a visit from the local low pay unit and have agreed

to increase wages by 10 per cent, largely because you don't want to risk bad publicity creating a poor image for your company if you don't. Because of the effect this cost increase will have on your business you decide to draw up a budget projection for the year.

You have budgeted for 180 000 clocks at a selling price of £20 each and budgeted production costs are: materials per clock £5; labour £2.75 (before the pay rise); variable overheads £1 per clock; fixed overheads £500 per year.

**TASK**

After preparing your new budget, what changes in your business would you want to see? Prepare the information in a clear form ready to explain to the other managers of the business at a special meeting.

## Assignment 7: Financing the organisation

*Areas of content*:
  Finance
  Business organisations

*Sources of information*:
  Banks
  Library texts

*Background information*:
All organisations require finance, but differing types of organisations will meet their needs in differing ways. As an assistant to a business adviser in a business enterprise agency your job involves preparing information to back up the adviser's work.

**TASK**

Draw up a table that shows the type of expenditure for which an organisation might require finance and for each of the following show the most suitable source for that finance:

● a sole trader
● a limited company
● a nationalised industry.

## Assignment 8: Financing capital projects

*Areas of content*:
  Finance
  Business resources

  *Sources of information*:
  Library texts
  Class texts
  Financial press

*Background information*:
Bass plc wants to invest in a new brew house that will cost £20 million. As an assistant to a member of the financial review team in the company you have

been asked to prepare your views on the following questions.

**TASK**

What are the advantages and disadvantages of the following methods of financing such a development?

● issue of shares
● issue of debentures.

This information should be presented in the form of a memorandum to your superior.

## Assignment 9: Calculating the national income

*Areas of content*:
  Business innovation

Business organisations
Finance

*Sources of information*:
  Financial press
  HMSO statistics

*Background Information*:
As the newly-appointed assistant to the schools' liaison officer of a large bank you have been asked to help to prepare some information for a presentation on the economy for a local school.

## TASK

**1** From the following table calculate the:

- gross domestic product at market prices;
- gross national product at factor cost;
- national income.

| National Accounts | |
|---|---:|
| | £ million |
| Consumer expenditure | 90 |
| Government expenditure | 50 |
| Gross domestic fixed capital | |
| Formation | 20 |
| Exports | 23 |
| Imports | 25 |
| Taxes on expenditure | 16 |
| Subsidies | 8 |
| Net property income from abroad | 5 |
| Capital consumption | 10 |

**2** Present the information, and the calculations, in a way that would be easily understood by Year II pupils in a school.

---

# Assignment 10: Colleges take control

*Areas of content*:
  Business organisations
  Business innovation
  Business systems

*Sources of Information*:
  Library texts
  This text

*Background information*:
In the 1990s many government functions have been taken out of the control of local authorities by central government. Schools can opt out of local authority control completely. Those that don't will still have significant control over their own finances. Colleges of further education will be centrally funded from April 1993.

You work for a local councillor who has been asked to speak at a debate on the future of education. In order to bring some attention to this the councillor has agreed to provide a 'for and against' article for the local paper.

## TASK

Research the topic and draft two articles for insertion in the 'education page' of your local newspaper. In one article you are to put forward views *for* these changes and in the other views *against* the changes. Where you have access to the relevant packages this should be produced using a Desktop publishing package.

---

# Assignment 11: European Community

*Areas of content*:
  Business organisations
  Innovation and change

*Sources of information*:
  This text
  EC information from the Department of Trade and Industry
  Library texts

EC databases e.g. 'Europe in the round'

*Background information*:
The EC and its institutions are increasingly important to business in the UK. The local chamber of commerce has decided to hold a 'European awareness day' for local small businesses to find out more about Europe and have invited your centre to provide speakers and presentations on a number of topics.

## TASK

In groups of three, research the following institutions and make a presentation to the rest of the group as a practice run for the presentation to the chamber of commerce:

- the European Parliament;

- the European Commission;
- the European Court of Justice.

Make sure that you have supporting handout material and that the presentation makes use of appropriate audio visual aids.

---

## Assignment 12: The Council Tax

*Areas of content*:
  Business organisations
  Innovation and change

*Sources of information*:
  Local authority publications
  Local press
  This text
  Library texts and resources
  Colleagues, parents, friends

*Background information*:
You have been appointed to a special NALGO sub-committee. Its brief is to consider the pros and cons of the introduction of the new Council Tax in April 1993. The sub-committee is to present its findings to the next NALGO branch meeting.

### TASKS

1 Produce a discussion document for the sub-committee including:

- a detailed explanation of the current method of funding local authorities, including a break down of the major areas of income and expenditure.
- a detailed explanation of the 'poll tax' and the new council tax.
- a detailed discussion of the major arguments for and against both systems.
- a sub-committee recommendation to approve or disapprove the new tax.

2 Give an oral presentation of your findings to the sub-committee.

---

## Assignment 13: A local organisation

*Areas of content*:
  Business organisations

*Sources of information*:
  Local press
  Local libraries
  Local organisations/contacts

*Background information*:
In order to help you to understand the ways in which the local economy operates it is important to consider the types of organisation operating within it. This assignment gives you the opportunity to collect evidence relating to the operation of a given local business and to share this with the rest of the group.

### TASKS

1 In groups of two, research a major local organisation.

2 Make a presentation to the rest of the group that should last for no longer than 15 minutes, in which you should cover the following points:

- the organisation's name;
- a summary of its activities;
- a compound history;
- its major sources of finance;
- the type of organisation;
- its size in terms of turnover, etc;
- the number and composition of its workforce;
- any other areas agreed with your tutor.

## Assignment 14: The Budget

*Areas of content*:
Business organisations
Business innovation
Finance

*Sources of information*:

National press
Library texts and resources
Television broadcasts

*Background information*:
Each year major tax changes are usually announced in the budget. This has in the past been held in March but in future years will take place in the autumn.
Read the following scenarios and complete the tasks below.

*Jennifer Jones* is a single parent. She has a part-time job for 16 hours per week and earns a wage of only £2.50 per hour. She has two children aged 8 and 10 years.

*Michael Williams* is married with three children all under 10 years of age. He works for a small firm and earns £4 per hour for a 40 hour week.

*Frank Hankinson* worked for three years with a building company but has been unemployed for six months. He has now started on a full-time degree course at his local university.

*Jane Lewis* runs her own building company and earns £50 000 per year.

### TASKS

**1** Analyse the financial position of each person before and after the budget and the relevance of benefit changes. Make any assumptions you consider necessary.

**2** Write a report outlining the effects of the budget on yourself as an individual.

## Assignment 15: The legal system

*Areas of Content*:
Business organisations

*Sources of Information*:
European information from the DTI
Library texts and resources

*Background information*:
You work for Business Education Productions Ltd, and you have been asked to produce a radio programme on the effects of current and future legislation on retail businesses. The programme is aimed at business studies students and should make some mention of the impact of the Single European Market. The programme should also focus on legislation applying to:

- buying and selling;
- faulty products;
- safety;
- pricing.

### TASKS

The programme should last for approximately 10 minutes.

**1** Individually, make notes on the main Acts which affect firms that sell to the public.

**2** In groups of three, discuss how the material you have compiled could best be presented on radio.

**3** In the same groups, produce the necessary material for the programme: scripts, sound backgrounds and so on. Rehearse the programme as necessary.

**4** In groups, produce a tape of the radio programme.

**5** Review your team's work and identify and explain the good points of your work and how you would improve it if you were to do the programme again.

## Assignment 16: Business expansion

*Areas of content*:
Business organisations
Finance
Business innovation

*Sources of information*:
This text
Library and learning resources

*Background information*:

QSNAX Ltd is a company that has been specially formed to produce a snack food product. This will be aimed at the health food market and will contain only natural products such as organic wholemeal flour and QUORN™. After launching the initial product the company intends to increase its product range as quickly as possible. Your mother is the creator of this new brand of food and is the person behind the product. The company has decided to locate in your town to produce the product.

A venture capital organisation is interested in making a contribution to the start-up and initial running costs of the company. Your mother also has £50 000 to invest in the new business, but other sources of capital funding may have to be explored.

The venture capital group has asked that a company portfolio be produced. It should contain the following information:

*The factory*: Its location; necessary infrastructure; factory layout; costs; planning procedures.

*The product*: The name of the snack; why it will sell; the retail price; how it can be promoted; who will buy it; where it will be sold; what point-of-sale material will be required; how it will be packaged etc.

*The workforce*: Who you plan to recruit and how; the skills, jobs, working methods you will use; how you plan to maintain staff loyalty.

*The future*: Is a single product a viable proposition? How will you develop new ones? Could you expand into Europe?

## TASK

This is to assemble the portfolio for presentation to the venture capital company. It must contain material that would convince the company that you have a viable business proposition. Facts, figures, diagrams and supporting material are to be included.

---

## Assignment 17: Tourism costs!

*Areas of content*:
  Business organisations
  Business innovation
  Business resources

*Sources of information*:
  Tourist information centres
  Library and learning resources
  Tourism staff in the centre

*Background information*:

Many countries are now developing major tourist industries. Whilst these developments undoubtedly bring benefits they also bring disadvantages and costs. The table opposite shows just some of the benefits and disadvantages that tourism has brought to Egypt.

As a publicity assistant with the local travel advisory bureau you have been asked by a local club who use you for bookings to provide some information on the problems tourism has brought to major tourist destinations and the benefits that have been gained from it.

## TASK

In groups of two, produce a chart that indicates the benefits as well as the disadvantages and costs of the development of tourism in Spain or another mainland European country. This will involve considerable research and where possible you should use specific examples to illustrate your case. You are to make an oral presentation to the rest of the group.

### TOURISM IN EGYPT – SOME OF THE COSTS AND BENEFITS

*Benefits*

- jobs are created in construction, hotels, transport, retail etc;
- local agricultural products have a greater market;
- it allows the economy to diversify;
- tourist development may mean a better infrastructure for the local population such as improvements in sewage disposal, water supply, transport etc;
- income enables the country to preserve the Egyptian heritage, the pyramids for example.

*Disadvantages and costs*

- the economy may become overdependent on tourism;
- tourism introduces western culture which may threaten the survival of local traditions;
- tourism attracts investment from foreign businesses; as a result much of the income generated goes back overseas, as much as 80 per cent in many cases;
- natural landscape may be ruined;
- the influx of tourists may encourage crime, racketeering and those wanting to capitalise by making a quick profit;
- it increases income differentials within the country.

# Assignment 18: The law

*Areas of content*:
  Business organisations

*Sources of information*:
  This text
  Library texts and resources
  CAB publications
  Trading standards

*Background information*:
In this assignment you have a series of short tasks to undertake which will enable you to develop your knowledge of the law.

As a newly appointed volunteer worker in the Citizens' Advice Bureau you have been asked to prepare some material to be given to people worried about the legal process in bringing cases to court.

## TASKS

1 Draw up a chart to illustrate the differences in the cases dealt with in criminal and civil law. It should indicate the courts that are used by each and the appeals procedures in each. You should also clearly indicate how an offence may be both a criminal and civil offence.

2 Conduct a media search. Collect cuttings about cases in the courts from a number of local and national sources. Indicate which cases are civil and which are criminal and in each case justify your decision.

3 Produce an information booklet that is a guide to the different courts in your area. What types are there, where are they located, when do they sit and what sort of cases do they hear? You should also include a section on court procedures.

4 Find out about the small claims procedure in the county court. Prepare an information sheet to help people who may wish to use the procedure.

All of the above information should be in as plain language as possible. Presentation would be enhanced by the use of word processing or desktop publishing.

# Assignment 19: Government

*Areas of content*:
  Business systems
  Business organisations
  Business innovation

*Sources of information*:
  Local authority
  This text
  Local press
  Library and learning resources

*Background information*:
You work for the planning and economic development department of your local authority as an assistant economic development officer.

The department produces a monthly news sheet called *We mean business* which contains items of interest to local business. Part of your job is to contribute towards the production of the monthly news sheet.

## TASKS

1 Produce a four page A3 'paste up' of the next edition of *We mean business*. This can include any item you wish but *must* include:

- an article that highlights the differences between the main political parties with regard to how their policies affect local business. This must include information that has been obtained from an interview or speech involving a local politician or business person.
- the rest of the 'paste up' should be made up of articles that have previously been published in other business publications or in the media. These must have relevance to business and to your area.
- articles produced for tasks 2 and 3 below.

2 Arrange a visit to a council or a council committee meeting. Make sure you know what is on the agenda before attending. From observations and notes taken at this meeting produce a report for *We mean business*. It should mention the business that is discussed, the standard of debate and have an eye catching headline.

3 *We mean business* is to start a young persons' column. You are to outline to a young readership what impact local issues are having on them. You should select your topic from the following list:

- employment;
- training;

- environmental issues;
- the European Community and your town;
- housing.

Remember it is aimed at a young age group, so keep it simple and entertaining.

---

## Assignment 20: Town twinning

*Areas of content*:
  Business systems
  Business innovation

*Sources of information*:
  Library and learning resources
  Town hall
  Information technology staff

*Background information*:
Each town in the United Kingdom will almost certainly have a twin town somewhere in Europe and your college may already have established links with a European college.

Negotiate with your college staff to establish an electronic mail link with a college in Europe.

**TASK**

Your task is to:

- exchange information about your Central Government structures;
- prepare a chart that shows the structure of central government and name the ministers responsible for government departments;
- transmit this to your 'link' college and ask for similar information on that European country's government structure.
- What differences are there between the two governmental structures?

---

## Assignment 21: Voting

*Areas of content*:
  Business organisations
  People in Business

*Sources of information*:
  Library and learning resources

*Background information*:
Many people at your college will be voting for the first time at the next elections. As a group you have been approached by the students' union to produce a *Rough Guide to Voting* based on the format of the well known travel guides and TV programmes.

**TASK**

The guide should give young people information on the following topics which is not exhaustive:

- why they should vote;
- what they are voting for;
- who is allowed to vote;
- where they vote;
- how they vote;
- how to register for the vote.

---

## Assignment 22: Competitive Contract Tendering (CCT)

*Areas of content*:
  Business organisations
  Business innovation
  Finance

*Sources of information*:
  Library and learning resources

  Local authority

*Background information*:
You work for a firm of contract cleaners and have been asked to prepare a business development plan that will enable you to expand to bid for local authority cleaning work.

## TASKS

**1** Obtain details of a service competitive tender from your local authority.

**2** Analyse the tender in terms of what resources the firm will need to enable it to fulfil the tender specification.

(Make any assumptions you feel are necessary.)

**3** Prepare a one year business development plan that should include: outline of growth proposals; personnel requirements; physical resource requirements; financial requirements.

---

# Assignment 23: The Channel Tunnel

*Areas of content*:
  Business organisations
  Business innovation
  Marketing

*Sources of information*:
  Company data for Eurotunnel
  Publicity material from TML
  Press or periodical articles

*Background information*:
The Channel Tunnel will, if work goes to schedule, open in late 1993. The tunnel will bring many benefits to the linked countries, but there will also be major costs, both financial and social.

In this assignment you are asked to look at some of the implications of the tunnel's opening. Bon chance!

## TASKS

**1** Analyse the market for cross-Channel travel and prepare a report for the marketing manager of P & O Ferries explaining what circumstances need to be present for the company to benefit by:

● raising prices;
● cutting prices.

**2** Prepare a 250 word article for your local newspaper on the potential benefits that the tunnel will bring to your town.

**3** Price is only one criteria in deciding what is the 'best' service. Provide a comparison of three ferry services and assess which is the 'best'. You should show what criteria you have used and devise a numerical weighting system for the criteria and in calculating your 'best' service. Your comparison should be in the form of a visual presentation on one side of A3 paper.

**4** Produce a report for the marketing manager of P & O Ferries entitled 'A marketing strategy for competing with the Channel Tunnel'.

---

# Assignment 24: Northern Concrete Conglomerate goes under!

*Areas of content*:
  Finance
  Business organisations
  Business innovation

*Sources of information*:
  Library and learning resources
  This text

*Background information*:
*Yesterday the Stock Market suspended dealing in the shares of the Northern Concrete Conglomerate. This had followed several weeks of speculation about the financial position of the firm. Like many development companies it had seen its star rise in the 1980s only to fall in the 1990s. The growth of the company began in the early 1970s when Jim Dark started Bolton Builders which concentrated on speculative building in the north west.*

*In 1980 the firm became a partnership and in 1985 on the back of the housing boom became a public limited company. By that time the firm had taken over Lancashire Homes and a quarry.*

*Trouble really started for Northern in 1988 when the company took over a midlands firm, Homestead, which concentrated on building sheltered housing for the retirement market. Associated with this takeover was the move of company headquarters to Coventry which was built at a cost of £10 million. The major slump in the housing market, which left many old people unable to release the equity locked in their homes, left Northern with many unsold homes and an HQ now valued at only £6 million.*

*Northern's problems were caused because they had borrowed heavily to finance takeovers and city analysts had been forecasting for some time that Northern would* have great difficulty in meeting demands for interest repayments. The bad news, therefore, was not a shock for the city, only the poorly informed private share-holder suffering.

## TASKS

**1** Which sector of the economy does Northern belong to?

**2** Which sector does the quarry belong to?

**3** What type of integration is Northern's takeover of the quarry and of Homestead?

**4** What does the term 'equity' mean in the above context?

**5** Northern grew from a small sole trader to a plc in just over 10 years. What disadvantages are there from such growth?

**6** List three economies of scale that Northern might benefit from.

**7** What problems did Northern store up for future years by relying heavily on borrowing?

**8** What effect would the downward revaluation of the company's HQ have on the company's balance sheet?

**9** What two major advantages would the firm secure in organising as a partnership rather than a sole trader?

**10** What survival strategy would you recommend for Northern?

**11** Jim Dark is still convinced that the market for retire-ment homes will pick up before the turn of the century. He asks you to prepare a presentation for the next board meeting of the company that will:

- show the growth in the number of retired people over the next 10 years;
- present a strategy for helping these people sell their existing homes and buy a retirement property;
- give ideas for the development of a questionnaire that could be used to check on what the housing needs of retired people are likely to be.

# Assignment 25: Counselling

*Areas of content*:
  People in business
  Finance

*Sources of information*:
  Library and learning resources
  This text
  Trading standards
  Financial institutions

*Background information*:
You work in the personnel department of Electro Ltd, a large organisation which manufactures electrical components. Your company employs many young people, some of whom have problems which they find difficult to cope with, especially in the areas of financial management.

## TASKS

**1** You have been approached by Rita who has recently moved into a flat of her own. After several weeks of running her own flat she is finding that she is running into financial difficulties. You have asked her about her income and expenditure, the details of which are shown below:

| Earnings | £120 | per week |
|---|---|---|
| *Expenditure*: | | |
| Rent | £40 | per week |
| Food | £35 | per week |
| Going out | £30 | per week |
| Clothes | £20 | per week |
| Bus fares | £5 | per week |
| Other expenses | £10 | per week |
| *Money owing*: | | |
| Credit cards | £1000 | |
| Mail order | £500 | |
| Parents | £20 | |

Identify any unnecessary expenses and suggest how Rita could improve her financial management skills.

Recost Rita's income and expenditure and produce a spreadsheet showing your suggested revised income and expenditure for the next six months.

Write a memo to Rita explaining this and also give her the good news that she is to have a pay rise of £20 per week in two months' time (which you should take account of in the spreadsheet).

**2** Jim Jones works for you and has asked for your advice in deciding how to fund the purchase of a car. Jim, after all other outgoings saves approximately £20 per month and already has savings of £500. He has seen a Citroen BX advertised for £6000 and wants your help in deciding how to buy it. Some of the alternatives he has looked at include a bank loan, arranging an HP agreement with the garage, saving up the money or obtaining money from a firm that advertises cheap loans in his local newspaper.

You are to advise Jim on the alternative sources of finance available and especially help him to work out the true cost of buying the car.

Write Jim a memo giving the required information.

**3** You find that many of your young employees wish to purchase their own homes and often approach you to ask advice about the following:

- how to find a house;
- how to go about purchasing a house;
- what the various types of mortgages are;
- what difference it would make buying from a housing association.

You have decided that it would save a lot of your time if you produced some information which would be available for employees who are interested in buying a house for the first time. You should prepare a booklet containing the information detailed above.

**4** Some of your staff have recently invested in life assurance policies as a way of saving and are now regretting the decision. Produce a simple guide for your staff that explains the benefits of life assurance policies but also points out the disadvantages of using them as a means of saving.

## Assignment 26: Our town

*Areas of Content*:
Business organisations
Marketing
Business innovation

*Sources of information*:
Local authority
Tourist information centre
This text
Library and learning resources

*Background information*:
As a recently appointed assistant in the economic development unit of the town council you have been asked to assist in the production of a video to promote the town to businesses.

**TASKS**

In groups of five, produce a video that shows the benefits to companies of locating a new factory in your town. The video should include among other things:

- transport links;
- sites available;
- employees available;
- mention of other aspects of the local infrastructure that you think are important.

## Assignment 27: Net Present Value

*Areas of Content*:
Finance
Business resources

*Sources of information*:
Library and learning resources
This text

*Background Information*:
As a financial adviser with the Enterprise Trust you have been asked to advise on the following cases:

**Case 1**. Capital outlay is £50 000, net cash receipts in

years 1–5 inclusive = £16 000 pa, discount rate = 14%.

**Case 2**. Capital outlay = £20 000, net cash receipts in years 1–6 inclusive = £2296, discount rate = 10%.

**TASKS**

**1** Calculate the Net Present Values of the projects and state whether you would go ahead with the projects or not.

**2** Your firm produces plastic toys and is considering

buying an injection moulding machine for £50 000. It is expected that you will produce 20 000 toys per year and sell them at £5 each. The variable cost of producing each toy is £2. The machine is expected to last for five years.

You propose to finance the project by borrowing at an interest rate of 12 per cent. You are to produce a short report for the production manager which assesses the financial viability of the project.

## Assignment 28: Off the rails

*Areas of content*:
  Business organisations
  Finance

*Sources of information*:
  Library and learning resources
  This text
  Press and periodical articles

*Background information*:
The article provided relates to the Conservative Government's rail privatisation policy. Having read the article there are a number of tasks for you to complete.

### OFF THE RAILS

It is still unclear how Ministers will fix charges for operators to run on old BR track, and whether private sector companies will be prepared to contribute to the massive capital spending programme.

BR says that the track operation represents around 50 per cent of its costs and the private sector must be prepared to pay its fair share. But without the present system of cross-subsidy between services – which enables BR to prop up loss-making services – it is estimated that the taxpayers'

bill for supporting the railways could soar from £1 billion to at least £2 billion a year. This, in turn, would hardly justify the whole privatisation exercise in the first place.

MacGregor has asked accountant Coopers & Lybrand to come up with the best method of charging for use of the tracks, and their report, which is due shortly, may help him solve the biggest immediate obstacle.

But MacGregor ran into his own equivalent of leaves on the

line when a short Parliamentary Bill, designed to pave the way for privatisation, became embroiled in the coal mines fiasco. The Bill was twinned with a similar measure to prepare the sale of British Coal, but both had to be shelved following the row over the mines shutdowns.

At present, there is no immediate date for its reintroduction and insiders see little prospect of the paving Bill reappearing before the New Year.

(Source: *The Observer*, 22 November 1992)

## TASKS

**1** Explain the following terms:

- Privatisation;
- Cross-subsidy;
- Paving bill;
- Capital spending.

**2** In an earlier assignment you were asked to set up an 'electronic mail' link with another college.

Use the link to compare the service offered by British Rail with that offered by the rail network in another mainland European country. You should agree the

criteria which you are to judge them by and students at each college are to research their own system.

Exchange the information and produce a chart which clearly shows the differences in the two countries.

**3** What effect do you think the ending of cross-subsidies will have?

**4** British Rail is considering splitting up its operation into a track authority and a passenger authority. In groups select from other utilities such as water and make a presentation to the rest of the group showing how this practice could be applied to your utility.

---

## Assignment 29: The perfume scandal

*Areas of content*:
  Business organisations
  Finance

*Sources of Information*:
  Library and learning resources
  This text

*Background Information*:
The article provided refers to recent criticisms of the pricing policies of the major perfume companies. Having read the article there are a number of tasks for you to complete.

---

### MMC on scent of perfume cartel

Is it illegal for prices to be fixed? Leading fragrance firms, such as Chanel and Yves St Laurent, fix prices. But last week's decision by the Monopolies and Mergers Commission to investigate the supply of perfume to discount High Street outlets is not an open-and-shut case, **writes Lindsay Vincent**.

The MMC probe, foreshadowed in *The Observer* last month, follows complaints by Superdrug, part of the Kingfisher retail combine, that the major perfume houses were refusing to supply the company, which was cutting as much as 30 per cent off normal retail prices.

Evidence from Superdrug is likely to be supported by submissions from Asda and Littlewoods, which also offer expensive fragrances at prices below those suggested by the leading manufacturers. Director-General of Fair Trading Sir Bryan Carsberg, who has been investigating the retailers' complaints for a year, is anxious to determine whether the stance of the fragrance houses is anti-competitive.

A European Commission ruling has exempted the manufacturers from its competition rules regarding distribution. But the OFT believes that such exemptions could violate the Treaty of Rome.

Leading manufacturers last week declined to comment on the MMC referral. But Superdrug marketing director Geoff Brady described it as 'a victory for consumers'.

(Source: *The Observer*, 22 November 1992)

---

### TASKS

**1** Explain the following points:

- Is it illegal for prices to be fixed?
- What is the other main role of the Monopolies and Mergers Commission?
- What is the OFT?
- What are the major functions of the OFT? Find details of a recent case it has been involved in. How did it justify the decision it made?

**2** In your local area make an analysis of price differentiation in local shops of any two well known perfumes. Show if there are any price differences and what justification there is for any difference.

**3** How do the perfume companies justify keeping prices high?

**4** Research any recent case that has been referred to the Monopolies and Mergers Commission. Produce a short report that covers the following points:

- why was the case referred to the MMC;
- what was the outcome of the case;
- what justification did the MMC make for its decision?

Do you think that the MMC acted in the consumers' interest in your particular case?

---

## Assignment 30: Perks

*of content*:
  *s* organisations
  *business*

*Sources of Information*:
  Library and learning resources
  This text
  Friends/colleagues/parents

*Background Information*:
Read the article shown below, and answer the Tasks following it.

---

### Perks under threat in tax case

Valuable perks enjoyed by millions of employees could be jeopardised by a judgment in a tax case due on Thursday.

At issue in the case, which is being decided by the House of Lords, is the amount of tax that a group of teachers should pay on being allowed reduced school fees for their sons.

If the Inland Revenue wins, accountants believe that many other benefits, like free or cheap travel for airline staff, could be heavily taxed.

Schoolmaster John Hart and his Malvern College colleagues paid one-fifth of the normal fees for their boys' education. This reflected the cost of educating an extra pupil.

The perk was originally not taxable. But an Inspector of Taxes ruled that the teachers should pay tax not on the extra or 'marginal' cost, but on the much higher average cost of educating a child. This would be calculated by dividing expenditure by the number of pupils. The result was an estimated £40,000 tax bill for

Mr Hart. The teachers appealed after losing in the High Court and the Court of Appeal.

Currently airlines can say that the marginal cost of allowing employees to take up spare seats on a close-to-empty plane is very little.

But, if the teachers lose, airline staff could be liable to tax on the total cost of the flight divided by the number of passengers — possibly a four figure sum.

---

(Source: *The Mail on Sunday*, 22 November 1992)

**TASKS**

**1** Which court would this case have been originally heard in?

**2** How would you calculate the 'marginal cost' of taking one extra passenger on an aircraft?

**3** How would you calculate the average cost of educating a child?

**4** Is the marginal or average cost likely to be higher?

**5** You are employed as a salesperson and use a company car travelling some 20 000 miles a year on business. You

only pay the standard rate of tax and earn about £20 000. You are allowed to use the car for private purposes. How much tax will you have to pay for this perk?

**6** It has been argued that all perks from jobs should be ended. Some people, however, argue that for many well paid people a perk is a sign of 'BEING AT THE TOP' and that they prefer a perk rather than more pay. Produce a short report that lists the advantages and disadvantages of having perks. You should also decide which side of the argument you support and justify your decision.

---

## Assignment 31: The Road Lobby

*Areas of content*:
   Business innovation
   Business resources
   Business organisations

*Sources of information*:
   Library and learning resources
   This text

   Local firms
   Road transport periodicals

*Background information*:
Read the article overleaf, then undertake the tasks following it.

# Time to drive a harder bargain with road lobby

In the 1960s Professor Reuben Smeed, a noted transport economist, wrote a paper in which he set out a detailed case for charging motorists according to the costs they cause in congestion. Only in this way, he argued, could unlimited demand for urban road space be brought sensibly into line with restricted supply.

It has taken three decades, 15 Transport Ministers and the threat of gridlock before the force of his argument has been publicly accepted. But, miracle of miracles, the current Secretary of State for Transport, John MacGregor, finally came out in the open last week with a speech accepting that road-pricing could provide the only long-term solution to the inexorable growth of urban traffic.

To be fair to his predecessors, Mrs Thatcher banned any mention of road-pricing during her long reign. When Cecil Parkinson rashly proposed putting forward a paper to Cabinet on the subject in 1988, she flew into a tantrum. Nothing, she cried, must be allowed to obstruct the forward march of 'the great car economy'.

Mr MacGregor deserves thanks for at last opening the debate. But, having poked his nose over the traffic parapet, the Transport Secretary must not stop there. The lengthy research project which he has commissioned into the feasibility of introducing road-pricing in London will not report for three years. When it does, it will no doubt provide some useful theoretical insights. But more valuable, both in proving that road-pricing works and in convincing other members of the Cabinet that it can be made politically acceptable, would be to demonstrate it on the ground.

If Mr MacGregor were to pledge his support and funding for the road-pricing studies under way in Cambridge, Edinburgh and Bristol, there would be no reason why a full-scale trial could not take place within the lifetime of this Parliament.

The case for a coherent transport policy could hardly have been made more starkly than by last week's announcement that British Rail is running out of money to maintain its track, and is having to get rid of another 5,000 workers. As long as the financing bias which encourages the over-use of roads and the under-use of rail continues, British Rail, whether in public or private ownership, will be hopelessly uncompetitive.

Take, for example, the absurd subsidy of more than £10 million a year which the police spend on escorting abnormal loads around Britain's roads. The transporters of these juggernauts should have to pay not only for the police escorts, but also all the other costs involved including compensation for lengthy delays to other motorists and damage to roads.

It is often argued by motoring organisations that cars and lorries pay more in tax than they receive in benefits. But these claims do not stand up to serious examination.

Revenues from fuel and vehicle excise tax amount to nearly £14 billion, which is admittedly far more than direct road costs of £6bn. But when you add other costs, such as congestion, accidents and pollution, it is clear that cars impose far larger burdens on the community than the tax their drivers pay. That is particularly true of heavy goods traffic. A recent study by the University of Leeds found that lorries are undertaxed by as much as 55 per cent. The CBI has estimated the cost of congestion alone at £15bn a year.

It is essential these issues are now faced up to squarely, for there is no way that future transport policy can be planned on a sensible basis until they are.

Why should rail users, for example, be obliged to pay track costs in full, whereas road users pay only a fraction of the true costs of using roads? It is sometimes claimed that it is impossible to quantify environmental benefits. Not so. Take two identical houses, one in a traffic-free street, the other on a heavily congested main road. The huge difference in the selling price makes the point.

Mr MacGregor has promised that he will publish a Green Paper early in the New Year which will address these questions. But it is important that this be seen to be both independent and authoritative. The Department of Transport has been the mouthpiece of the road lobby for far too long.

(Source: *The Observer*, 22 November 1992)

## TASKS

**1** As a group list all the costs that the motorist pays for and then list all the possible costs that the motorist doesn't pay for. How could this imbalance be corrected?

**2** Undertake research to find out why people use their cars in preference to other forms of transport. Choose five typical journeys that people from your area might make and produce a questionnaire to find out what type of transport people use for those journeys and why? You should also try to find out what changes people would require before they changed the type of transport they used.

**3** In attempting to move to a less car-orientated system, the government will come up against a major pro-car lobby. Identify all these 'pressure groups' and find out what their policies are.

**4** Try to arrange a speaker from Friends of the Earth to talk to you about the problems of road transport or obtain information from them and produce a short report entitled *Transport – an environmentally friendly solution*.

**5** What are the benefits of charging motorists for the congestion they cause? What benefits and disadvantages would this type of system have for your area?

## Assignment 32: Europe

*Areas of content*:
  Business organisations
  Finance

*Sources of information*:
  Travel staff
  Financial press
  Travel agencies
  Library and learning resources

*Background Information*:
As part of your course you are to exchange with a college in France.

**TASKS**

**1** Form into groups of three or four students and prepare estimated costs for your one-week visit, comparing alternative means of transport.

**2** Provide a cost summary of your suggestions which should include the following:

● means of transport
● insurance
● means of taking money (travellers' cheques etc.)
● spending money
● sundries.

You have completed your costings and then hear that the government has devalued the pound by 15%. Recalculate the costs of your visit.

## Assignment 33: My town's economy

*Areas of content*:
  Business organisations
  Finance
  Business innovation

*Sources of information*:
  Library and learning resources
  Local authority
  Tourist Information Centre

*Background Information*:
As a part of the attempt by your town to attract business you have been asked to undertake a survey of some aspects of the local economy.

**TASK**

Carry out a survey of industry in your area. You will need to make wide use of a range of local and national statistical information.

Your survey should cover at least the following areas:

● changes in unemployment rates over the last 10 years
● how do your unemployment rates compare with the national and regional rates?
● what changes have taken place in employment in the various sectors? Why have these changes taken place?
● who are the five main employers in your area? What has happened to employment in those firms over the last 10 years?
● list five new firms that have moved into your area over the last ten years. How many people do they employ?
● Provide a summary of your research findings.

## Assignment 34: Who blames Colombia?

*Areas of Content*:
  Business organisations
  Finance

*Sources of Information*:
  Library and learning resources
  This text

*Background Information*:
The El Cerrejon open cast coal mine in Northern Colombia is one of the largest coal mines in the world. By the turn of the century Colombia is expected to be the second largest exporter of coal in the world. It is also helping Colombia to diversify away from its dependence on coffee and cocaine production. The questions based on the article shown overleaf will allow you to look at the implications of such a development for the United Kingdom and for Colombia itself.

## WHO BLAMES COLUMBIA?

LOW WORLD prices have led to a cost-cutting programme at El Cerrejón with the loss of 2,000 jobs — or almost 20 per cent of the total workforce — in the past three years. From a peak of 5,200 in 1989, the company's permanent workforce has shrunk to 4,700, with 100 workers being laid off, under various pretexts, this year. The cuts in contract workers, engaged in cleaning, security and other ancillary tasks have been even greater: their numbers have fallen from 5,500 in 1990 to 3,900, and another 200 may go next year, according to a senior executive of Carbocol, Colombia's state-owned coal development company.

Even so, coal exports brought Colombia $630 million in export income last year, up from $10 million a decade ago. No wonder Colombians have been baffled by reports of their country's role in Britain's political debate in the past month. For Colombia, coal forms part of a successful drive to move exports away from the traditional mainstays of coffee, and more recently, cocaine.

For a country whose 34 million people have a per capita income of around $1,200, this export boom is opening up the tempting prospect of rapid and sustained economic growth. In the long run, that may offer the only means of breaking out of the violence — involving drug traffickers, right-wing para-militaries, left-wing guerrillas and the country's army — that has engulfed Columbia for decades.

El Cerrejón is operated and half-owned by the Exxon Corporation of the United States, through International Colombia Resources Corporation (Intercor), a wholly-owned subsidiary set up for the purpose. Its critics in Colombia accuse Intercor of running a multinational "enclave" that is leaving little behind in the Guajira peninsula except a moving hole in the ground. Others point to the sacking of 17 of El Cerrejón's trade union leaders since full-scale mining began in 1985, and accuse it of exploiting cheap labour. Still others, like Remedios Fajardo, a leader of the local Wayuu Indians, say the mine should be closed down unless it stops polluting the area with coal dust.

(Source: *The Guardian*, 21 November 1992)

## TASK

Answer the following questions:

(a) The per capita income in Colombia is $1200. Where does this place it in World rankings?

(b) If Columbia's per capita income was the same as that in the United Kingdom would you be able to say that the standard of living in the two countries was the same? Explain your answer.

(c) What is a 'multinational'?

(d) What is the Exxon Corporation more famous (or infamous) for?

(e) The Exxon Corporation is the third largest company in the world. How may its involvement in the Colombian coal industry benefit the country and how might its efforts hinder Colombia's development?

(f) The miners at El Cerrejon are paid high wages compared to the national average. Why do you think that British miners accuse the Colombian mineowners of exploiting cheap labour?

(g) If Colombia can produce cheaper coal than the United Kingdom what should happen to the UK mines and the miners employed in them?

(h) What are the arguments for and against subsidising British mines to enable them to compete with the likes of El Cerrejon?

(i) What are the negative effects of such a major development on the economic and social structure of Colombia?

---

## Assignment 35: Industrial research project

*Areas of content*:
  Business organisations
  Business innovation

*Sources of Information*:
  Library and learning resources
  This text

Local authority

*Background information*:
In order to examine the effect of changes in the structure of the economy take one major traditional industry which has been subject to decline and has a close link with the area in which you live.

**TASK**

Chart the decline of the industry you have chosen and analyse the effects its decline has had on both the United Kingdom and on your local area. You should also identify which countries now produce those goods and explain why the comparative advantage in their production has moved away from the United Kingdom.

How could the United Kingdom get back into that market and would there be any sound economic justification for doing so?

---

## Assignment 36: Business opportunities in the locality

*Areas of content*:
  Business organisations
  Marketing

*Sources of information*:
  The following units of this book
  • Unit 1 Business Organisations
  • Unit 7 Marketing
  • Unit 8 Business innovation
  Survey of people and competitors

*Background information*:
Business opportunities can be identified by existing businesses and by people wishing to start a new business venture. Assume you work for a business consultancy firm which has been asked by a client organisation to identify business opportunities in your locality.

**TASKS**

1 Devise suitable marketing research tools to survey the local area and identify business opportunities.

2 Carry out the survey and make a list of the business opportunities identified by the research.

3 Categorise the opportunities into opportunities for new products to be sold in the locality and new services to be introduced.

4 For a small sample of the business opportunities determine:

(a) whether it would be capital or labour intensive;
(b) the resources needed for the venture;
(c) the potential market for the product/service;
(d) the possible income from sales.

---

## Assignment 37: Starting your own business

*Areas of content*:
  Business organisations
  Marketing

*Sources of Information*:
  The following units of this book
  Unit 1 Business Organisations
  Unit 2 People in Business
  Unit 5 Financial Systems
  Unit 6 Business Resources
  Unit 7 Marketing
  Unit 8 Business innovation
  Survey of people and competitors
  Banks
  Small Firms Service
  ACAS

*Background information*:
Assume you wish to start your own small business in the area in which you live. You have available to you £5,000 from your own savings and you have a house worth £60 000. You currently have a mortgage of £40 000 on the house. You have a car.

**TASKS**

1 Identify business opportunities in your local area which would be feasible for you to consider as a business venture.

2 Explain why the business opportunities identified would be feasible and realistic for you to consider as a business venture.

3 Identify any constraints in setting up and running a business of this nature. (For example, consider any skills required which you do not have, lack of contacts or resources, lack of suitable premises in the local area, lack of time.)

4 Produce a business plan for the venture which could be presented to a bank manager when seeking finance.

## Assignment 38: Setting up a business in college/school

*Areas of content*:
Business organisations
Marketing

*Sources of information*:
The following Units of this book
● Unit 1 Business Organisations
● Unit 2 People in Business
● Unit 5 Financial Systems
● Unit 6 Business Resources
● Unit 7 Marketing
● Unit 8 Business innovation
Survey of people and competitors
Banks
Small Firms Service
ACAS
College/school tutors and management

*Background information*:
Many colleges and schools allow groups of students to set up and run a small business in order to gain experience of making decisions, working as a team and many other areas of business. This assignment involves doing the groundwork to prepare for setting up a mini business in College/School.

### TASKS

**1** Join with a small group of students and make a list of the skills and interests of each person.

**2** Make a list of the needs of students in the college/school and identify those already met by college services.

**3** Identify some possible business ideas which could be operated in the college or school.

**4** Conduct some marketing research to find out the actual needs of students and to identify whether there is a likely market for the ideas you have already suggested.

**5** Select a business idea which is feasible to operate in college/school and obtain the agreement of your tutors.

**6** Produce a business plan covering the following areas:

**(a)** the project description
**(b)** the market
**(c)** human resources
**(d)** financial resources
**(e)** physical resources
**(f)** time schedule for setting up the business.

**7** Produce evidence that in producing your business plan as a team you have:

**(a)** discussed and agreed the aims and objectives of the business
**(b)** negotiated and agreed targets for setting up the business as shown by the time schedule in Task **6** part (f)
**(c)** you have agreed the structure and format the business plan should take.

Evidence for this task can be in a variety of forms, for example, observation records by tutors, student reporting and summaries, tapes of discussions, minutes of meetings.

**8** Present your business plan to your tutors and be prepared to answer questions they may ask.

## Assignment 39: Working in business

*Areas of content*:
Business organisations

*Sources of information*:
The following units of this book
● Unit 1 Business Organisations
● Unit 2 People in Business and Organisations
College/school tutors and management
Organisational literature
Staff in the workplace/team members

*Background information*:
This assignment can be carried out by any student involved in running a small business in college/school, or at work or during work experience. It involves you in examining the contribution of team members to the goals of the business.

### TASKS

**1** Select a business and identify its nature.

**2** Identify the members of the team in which you work.

**3** Identify and describe the role of each person in the team and their contribution to:

**(a)** technical aspects involved in running the business;
**(b)** administrative tasks;
**(c)** team work;
**(d)** managing the business.

**4** How do the roles of the various team members complement each other?

**5** A business will have goals concerned with:

**(a)** production
**(b)** sales and marketing
**(c)** distribution
**(d)** customer service
**(e)** public/community relations

Identify the goals of the business in relation to the above.

**6** Which business goals:

**(a)** do you contribute to?
**(b)** does your team contribute to?

**7** Give examples of any other teams within the business. What are the roles of those teams and which business objectives do they contribute to?

## Assignment 40: Business in the local area

*Areas of content*:
   Business organisations

*Sources of information*:
   The following units of this book
   ● Unit 1 Business Organisations
   ● Unit 4 The Business Environment
   College/school tutors and management
   Organisational literature
   Directories

*Background information*:
This assignment requires you to carry out a survey to find out what businesses are in your area. The assignment can be carried out by groups or individually.

**TASKS**

**1** Survey your local area and identify business organisations which fall into each of the following categories:

**(a)** local organisations
**(b)** national organisations
**(c)** multinational
**(d)** public limited companies
**(e)** franchise
**(f)** independents

**2** Identify businesses which are in the town and those out of town. Explain the types of business activity taking place in the town and out of town locations. Map major employers or groups of businesses on a map to illustrate.

**3** Choose two businesses from different categories identified in Task 1 and for each business identify:

**(a)** the name of the business and its nature
**(b)** its purposes, aims and objectives
**(c)** external factors which affect the business

**4** Analyse differences between the two organisations and how this might affect employment within them or the service provided to customers.

## Assignment 41: Meetings

*Areas of content*:
   People in business

*Sources of information*:
   Unit 2 People in Business

*Background information*:
Meetings are held when groups of people wish to meet face-to-face in order to discuss issues, report information, make decisions, and plan. In order to get the most out of meetings the following should happen:

*(a)* the purpose should be clearly defined
*(b)* research and preparation for the meeting should be carried out effectively

(c) an agenda should be agreed and presented to all people who are being invited to the meeting

(d) the following roles are carried out – Chair, Secretary, Minutes Secretary and Treasurer (if necessary)

(e) it is clear what is required by each of the people in the roles.

During your GNVQ Business programme you will have the opportunity to conduct and participate in meetings. For example, your team or class may have meetings to:

- plan assignments
- organise open evenings for your college/school
- plan visits
- devise a business plan
- design questionnaires
- plan surveys
- set up a business
- determine staff requirements

This assignment will require you to analyse and contribute to the administration of business meetings.

### TASKS

1 Attend a meeting and demonstrate that you have carried out research and other preparatory work for the meeting. Some ways in which you may demonstrate this is through your contribution during the meeting, the provision of any documents you needed to supply for the meeting, and notes made in preparation for the meeting.

2 Organise a meeting and demonstrate that you can:

(a) clearly define the purpose of the meeting;

(b) research and prepare for the meeting;

(c) agree an agenda and present it to all participants;

(d) ensure you have people to play any roles required such as a chairperson, secretary, minutes secretary and treasurer (if required).

Some ways in which you can demonstrate these tasks are:

(i) You can demonstrate that you can clearly define the purpose of the meeting through providing an agenda and by restating the purpose of the meeting when the meeting begins.

(ii) You can demonstrate that you can research and prepare for the meeting by, for example:
  - keeping a diary or log to show preparations
  - keeping memos sent to confirm room bookings
  - keeping copies of notices of meetings sent out
  - by smooth running of the meeting.

(iii) You can demonstrate you have agreed an agenda and presented it to all participants by:
  - keeping records of conversations re the agenda
  - sending the agenda to all participants with a memo asking for any suggested changes to the agenda to be reported to you

(iv) You can demonstrate you have people to play any roles required such as a chairperson, secretary, minutes secretary and treasurer (if required) by the roleholders being introduced at the meeting and the roles being carried out.

## Assignment 42: Competences for employment in business

*Areas of content*:
  People in business

*Sources of information*:
  Unit 2 People in Business

*Background information*:
To function effectively business organisations have people carrying out different roles or jobs within the organisation; these include:

- Chief Executive
- Director
- Manager
- Employee/trades union representative
- Specialist
- Professional
- Senior management

- Supervisor
- Assistant

To fulfil roles effectively the roleholder requires training, experience and sometimes particular qualifications are necessary. This assignment requires you to visit an organisation, and interview people to find out information about some of the people who carry out the roles identified above.

### TASKS

1 Arrange to visit a large organisation.

2 Interview appropriate personnel to find out:

(a) examples of people carrying out the roles identified above

**(b)** their job titles and description of their duties and occupational area in which they work

**(c)** training, qualifications and experience necessary for the jobs

**3** Present the information in the form of a document for new staff. The document should be entitled 'Introducing Staff'.

---

## Assignment 43: Recruitment

*Areas of content*:
  People in business

*Sources of information*:
  Unit 2 People in Business

*Background information*:
You are owner/manager of a small video hire business. Since setting up the business you have worked long hours to enable you to make a good start financially. Now, you are more financially secure and have built up a good trade, you would like to employ a full-time member of staff to help you in the business. You would like the person you employ to be able to serve customers, look after the stock, and keep the shop clean and tidy. You can pay £100 per week for 38 hours.

**TASKS**

**1** Describe the kind of person you are looking to employ: what skills, qualifications and personal qualities should they have?

**2** How would you attract candidates to apply for the job?

**3** Identify and describe the selection methods available for you to use to identify the right candidate for the job.

**4** Select the most suitable method(s) for selecting the right candidate and justify your choice.

**5** When determining the recruitment criteria, advertising for staff and selecting staff what legal requirements should you consider?

---

## Assignment 44: Communication systems

*Area of content*:
  Business systems

*Sources of information*:
  Unit 3 Business Systems
  Workplace or college/school
  Staff and supervisors in the workplace,
    school/college

*Background information*:
This assignment is concerned with the communication systems used in a business and an evaluation of those systems. If you are employed on a full or part-time basis you could base the assignment on your workplace. If you are not employed you could use either your work-experience placement or your school or college. The information you require can be obtained through observation and talking to staff.

**TASKS**

**1** Select an organisation and describe its size and function.

**2** Identify the communication systems used in the business, for example:

- internal
- external
- face-to-face
- telecommunications
- electronics
- documentation

**3** Explain the reasons for using each of the communications systems identified.

**4** Explain the strengths and weaknesses of the communication systems used.

**5** Recommend suggestions to improve the communication systems used.

## Assignment 45: Introducing computers

*Areas of content*:
  Business systems

*Sources of information*:
  The following units of this book
  Unit 3 Business Systems
  Experience
  Sales literature

*Background information*:
Your friend owns a hairdressing salon which has manual systems for bookings, ordering, payments, and accounting. Whenever you telephone your friend to ask if he would like to go out he complains that he is 'doing the books'. He sometimes gets so mixed up that you go and help him to sort out the records. You ask him if he has considered getting a computer to make the adminis-

tration easier. He replies that it had crossed his mind but he would not know where to start and he isn't sure that it will be beneficial anyway and that it would probably be costly.

### TASKS

**1** What could a computer be used for in the salon?

**2** What advice would you give your friend as to the reasons for using computerised systems over manual systems.

**3** What costs would be involved in using computerised systems for the salon?

**4** Are there any weaknesses with computerised systems?

## Unit 46: Systems for improving business performance

*Areas of content*:
  Business systems

*Sources of information*:
  Unit 3 Business Systems
  Workplace
  College

*Background information*:
Organisations can have a variety of systems which help them to monitor and improve business performance. If business performance is not measured there will be no clear idea as to how the business is progressing or how individuals are performing. Performance needs to be constantly improving to cope with increasing customer

expectations and demands and competition.

### TASKS

**1** Select a business organisation to study and find out what systems it has to measure performance in relation to:

**(a)** Productivity
**(b)** Efficiency
**(c)** Customer service

**2** What systems does the organisation have for improving business performance?

## Assignment 47: Customers and their needs

*Areas of content*:
  Business performance

*Sources of information*:
  Unit 7 Marketing

*Background information*:
You work in the training department of LBB Ltd, a large wholesale organisation buying and selling fashion footwear. Some of your stock is imported from Italy.
  Your job involves providing and organising training for all levels of staff, and designing training materials.

The organisation has just employed eight new sales staff and you have been asked to deliver part of the induction which is outlined below. It is policy that all new staff receive an induction programme and people recruited straight from school receive information about business in general.

### TASKS

Prepare a talk as part of the induction programme to explain the following information to the new staff:

(a) Identify the various organisations involved in the chain of distribution: manufacturer, wholesaler, retailer, exporter, importer, final customer.
(b) Give examples of organisations falling into each of the above categories to help the new staff understand.
(c) Explain the role of customers in the chain of distribution.

(d) Explain why your organisation must provide the following to your customers:
  (i) goods of high quality;
  (ii) value for money;
  (iii) a good level of service;
  (iv) meet customer expectations.
(e) Explain the consequences of loss of customers to the business.

## Assignment 48: Quality assurance

*Areas of content*:
  Business performance

*Sources of information*:
  The following units of this book
  Unit 3 Business Systems
  Unit 7 Marketing

*Background information*:
Quality assurance procedures are introduced into organisations to try to improve the level of service given to customers. The level of service can distinguish one firm from another and affect whether customers buy from your firm or another one.

This assignment requires you to find out about and compare two approaches to quality assurance.

**TASKS**

**1** Visit two organisations, one in the private sector and one in the public sector.

**2** For each organisation find out:

(a) how errors are prevented, detected and corrected.
(b) the inspection procedures
(c) if a quality audit is carried out, how often and by whom
(d) if there are any relevant standards or legislation regarding quality which the organisation needs to provide for
(e) how the quality assurance procedures and systems improve service to customers

**3** Compare the quality assurance systems which you have found out about and identify what you consider to be best practice.

**4** Identify any weak areas in the quality assurance systems and suggest improvements.

## Assignment 49: Which organisations meet needs?

*Areas of content*:
  Business performance

*Sources of information*:
  Unit 7 Marketing

*Background information*:
You work for the Tourist Information Centre. You have been asked by your manager to carry out a survey of leisure, tourist, cafés, restaurants and retail organisations in your area in order to find out about facilities. Your manager will compile this information into a booklet for people new to the area.

**TASKS**

**1** As a group brainstorm the facilities needed by the following types of customers:

(a) young adults
(b) elderly people
(c) disabled
(d) families with small children

**2** Carry out your survey to find if the organisation is responsive to the needs you have identified by observing facilities.

**3** Record your answers on a questionnaire. This information will be used to compile the booklet.

## Assignment 50: The importance of marketing

*Areas of content*:
  Marketing
  Business performance

*Sources of information*:
  Unit 7 Marketing

*Background information*:
You work in the Marketing Department of Childsplay Ltd, an organisation which manufactures children's toys. You have been asked by your manager to give a talk to pupils of a local sixth form college about the importance of marketing. This assignment requires you to prepare notes for the talk.

TASK

Prepare notes for the talk answering the following questions:

(a) what is marketing?
(b) Why is it important to satisfy customer needs?
(c) What marketing techniques can help an organisation to improve sales?
(d) How does an organisation obtain feedback from customers?

## Assignment 51: Marketing activities

*Areas of content*:
  Business marketing

*Sources of information*:
  Unit 7 Marketing and Business Performance

*Background information*:
This assignment can be carried out by students in college or school who are involved in running a mini business. The assignment will take place over a fairly long time and it will involve you in collecting and analysing sales data, researching needs, and taking action to improve sales whenever necessary. The assignment tasks are not in any specific order as they should all be carried out on a regular basis.

TASKS

1 Analyse sales records and monitor trends in order to establish when sales are declining.

2 Carry out original marketing research activities in order to find up-to-date information about your customers and competitors. Analyse results, draw conclusions and present the research findings accurately.

3 Carry out promotions to increase sales. Monitor the effect of the promotions on sales.

4 From research activities, identify ideas for new products/services to be introduced into the range offered.

5 Identify customer perceptions of the service offered and suggest improvements.

6 Devise a policy statement for customer service.

## Assignment 52: Planning for growth

*Areas of content*:
  Physical resources
  Financial resources
  Business systems
  People in business and organisations

*Sources of information*:
  This book
  Library and learning resources

Banks and financial institutions
Local press
Estate agents

*Background information*:
'The Gadget Shop' is a business based on selling interesting and innovative products by Mail Order. The owner, Steve, has recently come into some money on the Pools and wants to use this to expand the business. He

has decided that a second branch would do well and is looking for suitable premises in a large town where products could be sold on a retail basis. Most of the current trade is mail order with only a few retail customers.

## TASKS

**1** Outline for Steve the likely resources needed to achieve this business aim. You will need to look at:

- Physical resources required and costs
- Financial resources required
- Human resources.

**2** Assuming that he has some £75 000 to invest in the new branch and that he will be able to carry the extra stock on trade credit, outline the total cost of setting up the new branch. You will need to make some assumptions about the cost of property and will be able to select a suitable property from local sources on which to base your estimates.

**3** Outline the timescale over which the project would take place and the lead times needed for the acquisition of the various resources for the new branch. Chart these in an easily understandable form.

**4** Outline the process which he should go through when choosing premises and explain the reasons for this.

**5** Explain the process of recruiting staff and note for Steve the potential problems in employing unsuitable staff.

---

## Assignment 53: Right place, wrong time

*Areas of content*:
  Business resources
  Business innovation

*Sources of information*:
  Library and learning resources
  This text
  Local press
  Estate agencies

*Background information*:
As a business adviser in the local Enterprise Trust you have been approached by the owners of a local small manufacturing business. The business was started some three years ago by the owners as a small joinery business and they have now started to concentrate on specialist staircases for old premises and for prestige properties.

They have gained a great deal of work and are finding their current premises too small for them.

The business employs six people and needs workshop space of about 1600 square feet. In addition to this they need to have material storage and will also require good access for vehicles.

Most of the firm's trade is done by recommendation and they have no need for showrooms as they tend to go to clients to measure jobs and have a portfolio of work they have done to show clients, including videos of special jobs.

They are interested to find out what sort of premises you would recommend for them and what is available in the local area.

## TASKS

**1** Research the needs of a small manufacturing business of this type and try to come up with a list of essential and desirable criteria for their premises. Bear in mind that they intend the business to grow.

| Desirable | Essential |
| --- | --- |
|  |  |
|  |  |

**2** Research the premises available in the local area and match them against the criteria you have identified for the business.

**3** Choose premises which you think would be suitable for them and produce a short report to explain the reasons for your choice. This should show how you have taken account of the:

(i)   Objectives of the business;
(ii)  Local area;
(iii) Grants and incentives;

and should list what you see as the main factors affecting the choice of location for this business.

**4** Outline the process of relocation and the problems the business would be likely to face. This should be done in the form of a chart indicating what would need to be done when and an accompanying set of notes to explain the problems and how you have tried to reduce or eliminate them.

**5** Estimate the cost of the move and present this in the form of a memorandum to the owners of the business.

## Assignment 54: Making it work

*Areas of content*:
 Business resources
 Finance

*Sources of information*:
 This text
 Library and learning resources
 Local businesses
 Local business agencies

*Background information*:
In order to examine the way in which businesses try to make the most efficient use of the resources available to them you will need to contact, arrange to visit, or work with, a local business. This could be arranged through the college, through personal contacts or through direct contact by yourself. There are a number of areas of the way in which the business operates which you will need to examine and these are set out below. In the case of a large business you should not try to examine the whole business but one part of its operations.

**TASKS**

**1** You should arrange to interview a manager in the business concerned to identify:

**(i)** The physical resources used by the business;
**(ii)** The items which are consumables and those which support the operation of the business rather than being used directly;

**(iii)** The plant/machinery used; and
**(iv)** The mix of resources.

The results of this interview and any further investigations you make should be compiled in the form of a report.

**2** Identify the level of use of different physical resources. What are the main costs in terms of physical resources which the business has to bear?

**3** Choose two different areas where the business spends a lot of money on physical resources and explain in detail how these resources are:

**(i)** used in the business;
**(ii)** chosen and bought; and
**(iii)** monitored and controlled in the business.

**4** Explain for each of the two resources identified above how the business tries to make efficient use of the resources and reduce waste.

**5** Produce the information from Tasks 3 and 4 in the form of a chart with accompanying notes.

**6** Make any suggestions you feel would improve the efficiency of the way in which the business uses physical resources. This should be presented in the form of a report which also identifies the benefits of efficient resource use for the business and those concerned with it. Try to quantify any saving you feel the business could make.

## Assignment 55: Recycling

*Areas of content*:
 Business resources
 Business innovation
 Finance

*Sources of information*:
 This text
 Library and learning resources
 Local authority

Pressure groups

*Background information*:
The efficient use of resources is important to businesses and they have also recently come under increasing pressure to be 'environmentally friendly' and adopt recycling and other green policies. This assignment is intended to give you the opportunity to have a look at the policies and practices of a business and to make

suggestions as to how these policies could be changed to take more account of the requirements of both the efficient use of resources and the needs of the environment.

## TASKS

**1** For a business to which you have access, or the centre in which your course is based, try to arrange to speak to the person responsible for the environmental policies of the business. There may not actually be anyone with a specific job of this sort so you may have to speak to a number of people.

With their cooperation try to identify for the business:

(i)   The opportunities which they have taken for the introduction of environmentally friendly policies in different areas of the organisation;
(ii)  Any action they have taken to try to reduce pollution and help the conservation of energy in the business;
(iii) Any policy statements for the business with regard to the environment and to conservation.

**2** If the organisation does not have a policy statement on environmental issues you should draft one for discussion. This should take account of:

(i)   The objectives of the business;
(ii)  The advantages to be gained from such a policy;
(iii) The potential costs of any such policies.

This statement should be drafted in a form in which it could be circulated to employees of the business and to customers/ suppliers to make the policy of the business clear.

**3** Identify areas where the business could take action to conserve energy, reduce pollution or be more environmentally friendly. For three of these opportunities produce brief summaries of the action the business could take, the potential costs of doing so and any savings which could be made. Any other potential benefits should also be stated.

---

## Assignment 56: Communications on the move

*Areas of content*:
  Business resources
  Business innovation
  Finance

*Sources of information*:
  This text
  Library and learning resources
  Communications sales businesses
  Vodafone/Cellnet
  Office supplies businesses

*Background information*:
As a member of the local chamber of trade you have been asked to prepare a report for the members of the chamber on modern communications.

The report has been asked for as there are a lot of members of the chamber of trade who are aware of the new methods of communication in business but aren't sure about what they will do exactly and what the costs of them are.

It has been suggested that the best thing to do would be to prepare a series of short case studies and to have some backup material for members to read. You have also volunteered to be available if anyone wants to phone you to get some specific advice on their needs.

Most of the members of the chambers are small to medium-sized businesses.

## TASKS

**1** Survey the modern methods of business communication available to supplement the basic methods used by most businesses.

**2** Produce a fact card for each one outlining:

(i)   costs;
(ii)  advantages;
(iii) Disadvantages;
(iv)  benefits to a business; and
(v)   suppliers.

**3** Produce a short case study for each one to show the benefits of its use in a given business. This should be no more than one A5 side and should provide a clear example of the use of a particular development.

**4** Be prepared to answer a series of specific questions to be directed to you.

# Assignment 57: Computers for all

*Areas of content*:
  Business resources
  Business innovation

*Sources of information*:
  This text
  Library and learning resources
  Computer sales businesses
  Computer magazines

*Background information*:
Computers are an integral part of many businesses in today's business world. As they become more powerful and more portable they are also falling in price. This has meant that many businesses now have access to computing power.

This assignment is intended to provide you with the opportunity to examine the uses of one form of computing power and the potential advantages to a business of your choice.

**TASKS**

**1** Research the market for notebook computers to the following specification:

  386 Processor
  60 Mb Hard Drive
  2 Mb RAM
  LCD/Gas Plasma screen

This is a minimum – you may find better machines. Find out what sort of cost there would be attached to a machine of this specification and the limits to the time it can be used and the software it can run.

**2** List the advantages and disadvantages of a machine such as this.

**3** For a business of your choice, outline the benefits of a machine such as this and explain whether you feel the business could justify such a purchase.

# Assignment 58: Industrial visit

*Areas of content*:
  Business resources
  Business innovation

*Sources of information*:
  This text
  Library and learning resources
  Industrial visit

*Background information*:
As a part of the programme you will be able to visit different businesses and see some aspects of the way in which they operate. This assignment is intended to provide a structure for you to examine the applications of technology during a visit to a manufacturing organisation.

**TASKS**

**1** For a business visit which has been organised for you try to identify in advance of the visit the forms of new technology used by the business. The categories to be used may be different for different businesses but there are likely to be applications of new technology in the following areas:

● production
● administration
● communication.

**2** While visiting the organisation, make a note of the changes in the way the business has operated over the last few years as a result of the introduction of new technology.

In order to do this you will probably need to ask questions of the people in the business and it may be useful to try to provide them with a list of the questions before you visit.

**3** List the impact that the new technology has had on the business. This may include having fewer people in the business, better quality or more orders.

| Technology | Impact |
| --- | --- |
| | |

**4** Find out what problems the changes have brought. Did the problems arise as a result of the changes or as a result of the way the changes were made?

## Assignment 59: Fax facts

*Areas of content*:
  Business resources
  Business innovation
  Business systems

*Sources of information*:
  Library and learning resources
  This text

*Background information*:
You work for a business which has recently been considering the purchase of a facsimile machine for the main office as a number of customers have asked for the company's fax number.

Before buying the machine the manager wants to know what use it will be, how much it will cost to run and what the best machine to buy will be. She is also concerned to find out how much it will cost to install and whether there are any servicing costs.

The business is a medium-sized courier service in a city centre and they operate a set of van deliveries in the immediate area on a same day basis and an overnight service for other destinations.

**TASKS**

1 Research the market for fax machines and report on the options available. Recommend a 'best buy' for a medium-sized business and give your reasons for this.

2 Assuming that the machine is used fairly regularly, what are the costs associated with

- buying
- installing
- servicing
- running

the machine?

3 Explain what advantages the business could gain from the machine and what problems there could be.

4 Outline the process of actually introducing the machine into the business. Would any training be needed? Would any jobs have to be done in a different way?

## Assignment 60: Change and the individual

*Areas of content*:
  People in business
  Business innovation

*Sources of information*:
  Library and learning resources
  This text
  Medical advice centres

*Background information*:
Change in a business can cause stress on individuals in the business as they have to cope with new ways of working and different circumstances and surroundings in the business. If change is well managed it will reduce the level of stress that people suffer as a result of it.

This assignment is intended to give you an opportunity to identify the effects of change on individuals and the problems it can cause.

**TASKS**

1 Design a questionnaire to find out what people see as being stressful about changes at work. Administer the questionnaire and analyse your results.

2 Research the topic of stress and draw up a list of the common symptoms of stress.

3 Interview friends/parents/colleagues who are willing to work with you and feel they have suffered stress as a result of pressure at work.

Find out how closely they felt to the 'textbook list' of symptoms you have. What do they see as the main causes of this stress?

Are these causes the same as those you identified in the questionnaire?

4 Draft a set of guidelines for a business to explain:

(i)   the causes of stress in employees
(ii)  the symptoms of stress
(iii) the costs to the business
(iv)  the effects on the individual
(v)   The best way(s) to reduce stress at work, especially as a result of change in the business.

# APPENDIX 2
# SOURCES OF INFORMATION

■

This section of the book provides the addresses of some national organisations who may be able to help you with information for your course. If you do contact them you should write, giving a clear outline of the information you require and enclosing a stamped addressed envelope. Make sure you allow enough time if you send off for information; the organisation has to deal with the request, the information has to reach you and then be used as a part of the assignment or task you are doing.

ACAS
Advisory, Conciliation and Arbitration Service
Cleland House
Page Street
London SW1P 4ND

Association of British Chambers of Commerce
Sovereign House
212A Shaftesbury Avenue
London WC2H 8EW

Bank of England
Threadneedle Street
London EC2

British Overseas Trade Board
1 Victoria Street
London SW1H 0ET

British Tourist Authority
Queens House
64 St James Street
London SW1

BTEC
Central House
Uppe Woburn Place
London WC1H 6HH

Confederation of British Industry
Centre Point
103 New Oxford Street
London WC1

Conservative Party
Smith Square
London SW1P 3JA

Department of Employment
Caxton House
Tothill Street
London SW1P 9NF

Department of the Environment
2 Masham Street
London SW1

Department of Trade and Industry
1 Victoria Street
London SW1

Equal Opportunities Commission
Overseas House
Quay Street
Manchester M3 3HN

The European Commission
Rue de la Loi 200
1049 Bruxelles
Belgium

European Community Information Office
8 Storeys Gate
London SW1P 3AT

Green Party
Freepost
London SW12 9YY

Institute of Exports
World Trade Centre
London E1 9AA

Labour Party
150 Walworth Road
London SE17 1JT

Liberal Democrat Party
4 Cowley Street
London SW1P 3NB

National Consumer Council
18 Queen Annes Gate
London SW1

NEDO
National Economic Development Office
Millbank Tower
Millbank
London SW1P 4QX

Small Firms Information Service
Freephone 2444

Trades Union Congress
Great Russell Street
London WC1B 3LS

Training Agency
Moorfoot
Sheffield S1 4BR

# INDEX

·